"They Made Us Many Promises"

D1103990

They made us many promises,
more than I can remember, but they never kept but one.
They promised to take our land, and they took it.
                                        —Red Cloud, Oglala Sioux

"They Made Us Many Promises"
The American Indian Experience 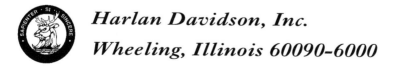 1524 to the Present

Edited by Philip Weeks

Harlan Davidson, Inc.
Wheeling, Illinois 60090-6000

Library of Congress Cataloging in Publication Data
"They made us many promises": the American Indian experience, 1524 to the
present / edited by Philip Weeks.
    p. cm.
  Rev. ed. of: The American Indian Experience. c1988.
  Includes bibliographical references and index.
  ISBN 0-88295-965-4 (alk. paper)
  1. Indians of North America—History. 2. Indians of North America—Govern-
ment relations. 3. Indians, Treatment of—United States—History. I. Weeks,
Philip. II. American Indian experience.

E77.2.T44 2002
973'.0497—dc21

                               2001051867

Cover photo: Crow Indian chiefs, Fort Snelling, Minnesota, 1887. Courtesy of the
National Archives.
Cover design: DePinto Graphic Design

Manufactured in the United States of America
02 01 1 2 MG

Dedicated to the Next Generation

Michael
Sarah, Tim, Halle
Paul, Tom, Dan, Charlie
Weeks
Ps. 139:13–16

Contents 〜

Foreword 🐌

*A*s Americans have become less ethnocentric and increasingly pluralistic, they have been more willing to accept and understand other cultures. The increase in scholarly investigation during the past few decades of racial, ethnic, and minority diversity within American society suggests a growing desire for a more inclusive, deeper, and, ones hopes, richer understanding of the national heritage.

A fundamental dimension of this heritage is that of the American Indians, whose story has been described as "among the most intriguing in history, [one that has] captivated scholars for centuries."[1] Once the indigenous peoples' world became enmeshed in the politics and economics of Europe and later the United States, it was often one of friction and conflict with Europeans and Americans, as well as between and within tribes. The post-Columbian American Indian experience, "from the point of view of the Indians themselves," asserts one historian, "meant the harassing, the overwhelming, and the extinction of a set of ancient, multiform cultures by a monolithic invasion from far away."[2]

They Made Us Many Promises is an introductory work, presenting a profile of the relationship between American Indians and Europeans, and later Americans, from the early sixteenth century onward. Its intent is to provide college students and general readers a clear overview of significant aspects of the American Indian experience with those people who asserted their control over the continent. That story is generally told in this volume within the framework of white history—first because Indian policy was formulated from the white perspective rather than from that of the First Nations, and secondly because whites so influentially affected the American Indians—their lives, culture, and history.

They Made Us Many Promises is a descendent of, but not a "second edition with a new cover recapitulation" of, *The American Indian Experience* (Forum Press / Harlan Davidson, 1988). While retaining about half of that volume's chapters, which have been carefully reviewed and reworked by their respective authors, *They Made Us Many Promises* offers readers six new chapters on important

---

1 Arrell Morgan Gibson, *The American Indians: Prehistory to the Present* (Lexington, Mass., 1980): 2.
2 William T. Hagan, *American Indians* (Chicago, 1979): ix.

topics: the emotional Repatriation issue, American Indian women, Native sovereignty, U.S. Indian policy since the Nixon Administration, Indian affairs during the American Civil War, and Indian–white relations in the Greater Southwest as the eighteenth century waned and the nineteenth century began. This book highlights the expertise of sixteen specialists, each of whom presents an engaging, accessible synthesis of the most recent scholarship in their own area of competence. In addition, each chapter concludes with a short bibliographical essay, an aid to those readers who wish to expand their knowledge of a particular part of the American Indian experience.

This volume follows a time line that extends from 1524 to the present, but it was not always possible to place each topic in a strict chronological order. Similarly, some material in one chapter might overlap some in another. While this was conscientiously kept to a minimum, the drama that unfolds in this volume is not easily compartmentalized, especially the closer one draws to the present. A case in point is Chapters Eleven and Thirteen, which have in common different aspects of some similar topics. The first probes one of the pivotal federal policies in the twentieth century, the policy of termination and relocation. The second investigates one important facet of the contemporary experience for an increasing number of Indians—life in urban America, a reality shaped in no small measure by the policy of termination and relocation. An effort also was made to maintain a rough equality in the average length of chapters, though, admittedly, a few are longer than the average. Nevertheless, this book has been carefully designed for ease of use as a core text in both one- and two-semester courses in American Indian history or as a supplement to any standard U.S. history survey. In either case, *They Made Us Many Promises* undoubtedly will challenge readers' assumptions about the past and current role of Indians in American history.

I would like to express gratitude to the authors for agreeing to participate in this venture and for their dedicated and first-rate work. I also wish to thank Andrew Davidson for shepherding this book to publication and for being such an amicable and superb professional.

Philip Weeks

The Authors ❧

David Wallace Adams, Cleveland State University, is the author of *Education for Extinction: American Indians and the Boarding School Experience, 1873–1928* (1995); "More than a Game: The Carlisle Indians Take to the Gridiron, 1893–1917," *Western Historical Quarterly* (2001); "Fundamental Considerations: The Deep Meaning of Native American Schooling, 1880–1900" *Harvard Educational Review* (1988); and "Schooling the Hopi: Federal Indian Policy Writ Small, 1887–1917," *Pacific Historical Review* (1979).

Donald J. Berthrong (Emeritus) Purdue University, is the author of *The Southern Cheyennes* (1963) and *The Cheyenne and Arapaho Ordeal: Reservation and Agency Life in the Indian Territory, 1875–1907* (1976), as well as several edited works.

Blue Clark, Oklahoma City University, has published in many scholarly journals on the subjects of ethnic studies and American Indian history.

Thomas W. Dunlay, University of Nebraska, is the author of *Wolves for the Blue Soldiers: Indian Scouts and Auxiliaries with the U.S. Army, 1860–90* (1982) and *Kit Carson and the Indians* (2000).

Donald L. Fixico, Bowlus Distinguished Professor of American Indian History and Director of Indigenous Nations Studies, University of Kansas, has published *Termination and Relocation: Federal Indian Policy, 1945–1960* (1986), *Urban Indians* (1991), *The Invasion of Indian Country: American Capitalism and Tribal Natural Resources* (1998), *Rethinking American Indian History* (1997), and *The Urban Indian Experience in America* (2000).

William T. Hagan, (Emeritus) State University of New York College at Fredonia and the University of Oklahoma, is the author of *American Indians* (1961, 1979), *Indian Police and Judges* (1966), *United States-Comanche Relations* (1976), *The Indian Rights Association* (1985), *Quanah Parker, Comanche Chief* (1995), and *Theodore Roosevelt and Six Friends of Indians* (1997).

Laurence M. Hauptman, State University of New York, New Paltz. Among his publications are *Conspiracy of Interests: Iroquois Dispossession and the Rise of New York State* (1999), *Tribes and Tribulations: Misconceptions About American*

Indians and Their Histories (1995), *Between Two Fires: American Indians in the Civil War* (1996), *Formulating American Indian Policy in New York State, 1970–1986* (1988), and *The Iroquois and the New Deal* (1988).

Päivi Hoikkala teaches in the History Department at California State Polytechnic University, Pomona, where she also works in faculty development. Her research interests focus on Native American women in urban areas as well comparative studies with indigenous peoples in Australia and Scandinavia. Her recent publications include "Feminists or Reformers? American Indian Women and Community in Phoenix, 1965–1980," in *American Indians and the Urban Experience* (2001) edited by Susan Lobo and Kurt Peters and "The Hearts of Nations: American Indian Women in the Twentieth Century," in *Indians in American History: An Introduction*, 2nd Ed. (1998), edited by Frederick E. Hoxie and Peter Iverson.

David La Vere, the University of North Carolina at Wilmington, is the author of *Contrary Neighbors: Southern Plains and Removed Indians in Indian Territory* (2000, 2001), *The Caddo Chiefdoms: Caddo Economics and Politics, 700–1835* (1998), and *Life Among the Texas Indians: The WPA Narratives* (1998).

Theda Perdue, University of North Carolina at Chapel Hill. Her publications include *Slavery and the Evolution of Cherokee Society, 1540–1865* (1979), *Nations Remembered: An Oral History of the Five Civilized Tribes* (1980), *Cherokee Editor (1983)*, *Native Carolinians* (1985), *The Cherokee* (1988), *Southern Women: Histories and Identities* (1992), *Hidden Histories of Women of the New South* (1994), *The Cherokee Removal* (1995), *Cherokee Women: Gender and Culture Change, 1700–1835* (1998), and *Sifters: The Lives of Native American Women* (2001).

James Riding In, Arizona State University, is a citizen of the Pawnee Nation of Oklahoma and is currently working on a book about the Pawnee people and their relationships with colonialism. His research focuses on repatriation and historical and contemporary Indian issues. He has assisted various American Indian nations, including the Pawnee, in their efforts to reclaim human remains and funerary objects ancestral to them for reburial.

James P. Ronda, University of Tulsa, is the author of nine books, including *Lewis and Clark among the Indians* (1984), *Astoria and Empire* (1990), *Revealing America* (1997), and *Finding America* (1999).

Dwight L. Smith, (Emeritus) Miami University, is the author of *From Greene Ville to Fallen Timbers* (1952), *Indians of the United States and Canada* (2 volumes, 1974, 1983), *The War of 1812* (1985), *Survival on a Westward Trek* (1989), and is coauthor (with Ray Swick) of *A Journey through the West from Delaware to the Mississippi Territory* (1997).

Graham D. Taylor, Trent University, is the author of *The New Deal and American Indian Tribalism* (1980), co-author (with Patricia Sudnik) of *Du Pont and the International Chemical Industry* (1984); and co-author (with Peter Baskerville) of *A Concise History of Business in Canada* (1994).

Clifford E. Trafzer, Native American Nations Research Center, the University of California, Riverside, is best known for *Renegade Tribe: The Palouse Indians and the Invasion of the Inland Pacific Northwest, Death Stalks the Yakama: Epidemiological Transitions and Mortality on the Yakama Indian Reservation, 1888–1964, Chemehuevi People of the Coachella Valley,* and *Exterminate Them!: Murder, Rape, and Slavery during the Gold Rush.* He recently published *As Long As the Grass Shall Grow and Rivers Flow: A History of Native Americans.*

Philip Weeks, Kent State University, Stark campus. His publications include *Subjugation and Dishonor* (1981), *Land of Liberty: A United States History* (1985), *Farewell, My Nation: The American Indian and the United States in the Nineteenth Century,* 2nd Ed. (2001), and *Buckeye Presidents: Ohioans in the White House* (2002).

Part I ❧
A World Turned Upside Down

They are . . . generous with that they have, to such a degree as no one would believe but him who had seen it. Of anything they have, if it be asked for, they never say no, but do rather invite the person to accept it, and show as much lovingness as though they would give their hearts
— Christopher Columbus's description of indigenous Americans

I heard that long ago there was a time when there were no people in this country except Indians. After that the people began to hear of men that had white skins; they had been seen far to the east. Before I was born they came out to our country and visited us. The man who came was from the Government. He wanted to make a treaty with us, and to give us presents. . . . [Our chief] said, "You see, my brother, that the Ruler has given us all that we need for killing meat, or cultivating the ground. Now go back to the country from whence you came. We do not want your presents, and do not want you to come into our country."
— Curly Chief, Pawnee

Chapter 1 ❧
Black Gowns and Massachusetts Men

Indian-White Relations in New France and New England to 1701

James P. Ronda

Sometime toward the end of the fifteenth century, two worlds virtually unknown to one another drifted into a common orbit. That common orbit would eventually become a collision course, producing changes with unimagined consequences. On the eastern side of the Atlantic were a multitude of peoples, cultures, and languages loosely united by growing acquisitive capitalism, mounting national rivalries, a militant Christian ideology, and an occasional spark of Renaissance curiosity. These were the tribes of western Europe. On the western shore of the great ocean were other peoples busy wresting a living from the land, rivers, and lakes of the coastal woodlands. In hunting camps, fishing stations, and palisaded villages these men and women shaped their days to a rhythm of weather and land. These were the tribes of northeastern North America. Soon Micmac merchants, Huron diplomats, and Mohawk warriors would face French traders, Jesuit missionaries, and English farmers, encounters that would forever change tribes on both sides of the vast sea.

The long and often complex tale of relations between Europeans and Native peoples in the land stretching from the Gulf of St. Lawrence to southern New England and west from the Atlantic coast to the eastern Great Lakes has neither a clear beginning nor a tidy cast of characters. One among many possible "beginnings" may have been the first contact between coastal Natives and nameless and unlettered European cod fishers who ventured toward Newfoundland and the Grand Banks in the years before Columbus's famous voyage. For the French, relative latecomers to the race for American empire, a beginning came in 1524 when the Florentine navigator Giovanni da Verrazzano, under the employ of King Francis I and a syndicate of French merchants to find the ever-elusive Northwest Passage. From his ship, the *Dauphine*, Verrazzano explored the American coast from present-day South Carolina north to Maine. With a keen eye for land, natural resources, and people, Verrazzano produced the first European survey of the eastern edge of what was to become the United States. His experiences with Native people from New York harbor to Narragansett Bay and the Maine coast are especially important for what they reveal about future relations between Europeans and coastal Algonquians.

After a brief mid-April visit to New York Bay and Delaware bands in the region, Verrazzano sailed north to Narragansett Bay. There, in present-day Rhode Island, he and his crew spent nearly two weeks exploring the coast and enjoying the company of friendly Narragansett Indians. While the Narragansetts and their Pokanoket neighbors were perhaps seeing Europeans for the first time, they already had some European trade items among them. The "sheets of worked copper" that some Narrangansetts wore as prized ornaments were probably pounded out pots originally obtained in the codfish and fur trade farther north. Always the careful observer, Verrazzano noted Narragansett techniques of house construction, canoe building, and land management. While the explorer tended to see all Indians through the haze of a classical golden age, what he reported about Native ways was remarkably accurate. As for the Narrangansetts, European weapons, ironware, textiles, and mirrors fascinated them. But the Indians showed no special interest in exchanging Native implements for those of the tribe from across the sea. Confident of their own place on the bay, the Narrangansetts felt neither threatened nor cowed by the crew of the *Dauphine.*

What Verrazzano portrayed as an almost Edenic environment of prosperity and harmony ceased to be the case after the explorers headed northward along the coast of Maine. While changes in the physical landscape were obvious, Verrazzano was not immediately aware that he had passed from a zone of initial contact between Europeans and Indians to one of previous and sometimes violent encounter. That became painfully evident when the *Dauphine* entered Casco Bay and the territory of the Abenakis. It was not the first time people of that bay had seen the tall ships with their outlandish strangers. Abenakis had already engaged in a fur trade with cod fishers. More important, the Abenakis had three years earlier suffered unrecorded troubles at the hands of the Portuguese adventurer Joao Alvarez Fagundes. Abenakis might still desire the metal goods offered by the cod fishers, but they had learned the hard way not to trust white people implicitly, having been victims of sudden acts of violence, kidnappings, and sexual assaults at the hands of European fur traders long before Verrazzano dropped anchor in Casco Bay. In a telling passage in his report to King Francis I, the explorer described the manner in which the Indians demanded that trade be conducted and remarked how canny the Abenakis were in the art of barter.

> If we wanted to trade with them for some of their things, they would come to the seashore on some rocks where the breakers were most violent, while we remained in the little boat, and they sent us what they wanted to give on a rope, continually shouting to us not to approach the land; they gave us the barter quickly, and would take in exchange only knives, hooks for fishing, and sharp metal.

Verrazzano's comments suggest some important conclusions about Indian-European contact before formal French and English ventures pushed inland from the Atlantic. Among the Delawares and Narragansetts, Verrazzano found people confident enough to offer him a warm welcome. There was interest in European goods but no special desire to possess them. So long as Verrazzano's actions were peaceful, these coastal Algonquians regarded him as a wondrous curiosity cast up by the sea. On the other hand, the Abenakis already had learned the bitter lesson that these strangers were to be approached with caution. If the cod fishers wanted furs, they would be exchanged only on Abenaki terms: the Indians would determine the trading site, the goods bartered, and the rate of exchange. Moreover, on no account would the unpredictable Europeans be allowed to occupy the land. The people of Casco Bay were not yet caught up in market forces beyond their control, nor were they dependent on outsiders for the tools of life and the weapons of war. With political power still in Native hands, it was still possible to be selective in accepting pots and other goods without trading away sovereignty and identity. At this point, how long Native people in the northeastern woodlands could remain as masters of their own fate in the face of invaders, both seen and unseen, remained an open question. At the beachhead on Casco Bay, at least, the relationship was being conducted on Native terms.

Jacques Cartier, in 1534, extended French efforts begun by unknown Breton fishermen and continued by Verrazzano. A master mariner from St.-Malo, on the west coast of France, Cartier had already made voyages to Newfoundland and Brazil. More important, the Breton crews of his two ships were experienced in the cod fisheries of Newfoundland. Cartier's first journey to what would become the heart of New France was intended to locate a passage to Asian markets; notions of establishing a lucrative fur trade with Native people and a semipermanent French base were not part of the original plans.

Early in the summer of 1534, Cartier poked and probed his way through the Strait of Belle Isle between Newfoundland and Labrador and then turned south to sail along the western coast of Newfoundland. Disappointed in his quest to find the fabled Northwest Passage, the French explorer then headed southwest toward present-day Edward Island. In July, Cartier reached Chaleur Bay, where he had extended contact with a large number of Micmac Indians. Like the Abenakis, Micmacs had traded with Europeans before Cartier, and they assumed that the French adventurer was yet another stranger in search of furs. With pelts fixed on sticks, the Micmacs avidly pursued Cartier to such an extent that at first the explorer believed he was under attack. Once it was plain that Indian intentions were commercial and not military, a trade in knives, hatchets, and beads flourished. Although some three hundred Micmacs crowded to see the French, Micmac women cautiously remained at a distance. When Cartier later moved to Gaspe Bay and met some St. Lawrence Iroquois, the same pattern of trade and caution was repeated. European traders had often kidnapped coastal Indians, and Cartier seems to have followed the same path. His party took Domagaya and

Taiognoagny, two sons of a St. Lawrence Iroquois headman named Donnacona. Cartier may have planned to use these two young men as guides for future expeditions. And Donnacona himself may have accepted the taking of his two sons as a means to establish proper relations with the Europeans. While the Native people who met Cartier perhaps viewed him as another cod fisher turned trader, Cartier was not interested in gathering furs or even in encouraging such an enterprise. Still determined to find the Northwest Passage, he probed the waters around Anticosti Island and became convinced that the St. Lawrence River was indeed the entrance to the famed passage to the Far East. Pleased with what seemed a successful reconnaissance, Cartier returned to France in early September to seek support for a second, and better outfitted, voyage.

Cartier's second voyage to the Gulf of St. Lawrence (1535–1536) was the most important French undertaking of the period and one that had lasting consequences for Indian-French relations. From his two Iroquois informants, Cartier learned about the size of the river and Gulf of St. Lawrence and of the fabled presence of a "kingdom of Saguenay," which the Indians led him to believe possessed great wealth. Prospects for the river being an eastern passage coupled with immediate rewards from Saguenay were enough to give Cartier financial backing from Philippe de Chabot, admiral of Brittany. Guided by Domagaya and Taiognoagny, Cartier took his three ships into the Gulf of St. Lawrence in mid-August 1535. By September, the French expedition had entered what the two Indians called Canada, the territory of the St. Lawrence Iroquois living at Stadacona. Cartier's progress up the river had not gone unnoticed, and, on September 8, the Stadacona headman, Donnacona, came to greet the French and his long-absent sons. After Donnacona made an especially animated speech of welcome, the whole body of Indians and French moved to Stadacona. While there was no question that Cartier and his crew were welcome visitors at Stadacona, tensions were mounting, probably because Cartier kept insisting on traveling to the rich and powerful village of Hochelaga. And Donnacona surely did not want to see Cartier move on to hand out gifts and dispense what seemed to the Indians as a unique European power to resist and cure disease to another group.

In an especially powerful episode, Donnacona, Taiognoagny, and some village elders disguised three men in costumes of horn and feathers to represent messengers from the god Cudouagny. Taiognoagny breathlessly reported to Cartier that the god had prophesied a death in ice and snow for the French if they ventured to the Iroquois town of Hochelaga. But the effort to deter Cartier failed, and on September 19 the French pushed upriver toward Hochelaga.

As Cartier and his party progressed they met increasing numbers of Indians. When the explorers encountered a welcoming party of some 1,000 Hochelagans, it seemed a sure sign that the voyage was on the brink of success. On October 3, the French tramped from the river to the main Hochelaga village. What they saw was a typical fortified Iroquoian town. A triple palisade some thirty feet high surrounded the village. Inside the palisade were walkways from which

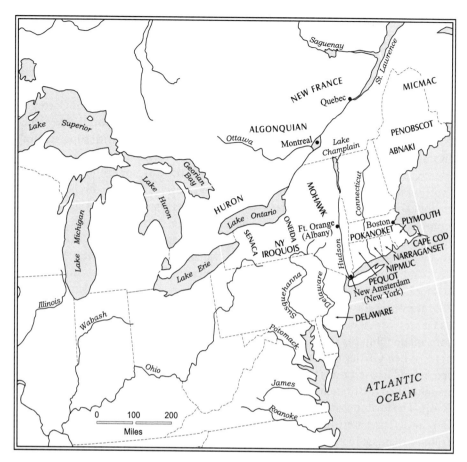

Major Northeastern Tribes in the Seventeenth Century

village defenders could rain stones and arrows down on would-be invaders. Once inside Hochelaga, Cartier found a busy, crowded community of some fifty longhouses. Laurentian Iroquois longhouses were typically 100 feet long and roughly 30 to 40 feet wide. Cartier estimated that at least 1,000 people lived in Hochelaga, making it the most substantial Native settlement yet seen by the French.

If the size and strength of Hochelaga impressed Cartier, the villagers were equally taken with the strangers from the river. The French explorers became an instant attraction, as Indians crowded around to see and touch Cartier and his men. At this point, the Hochelaga chief, an elderly and partially paralyzed man, was brought to Cartier. The chief's long speech seemed part welcome and part fascination with whatever powers the strangers might possess. Even more revealing of Hochelagan feelings were the efforts many Indians made to touch and stroke French bodies. As Cartier explained it, "the girls and women of the village, some of whom had children in their arms, crowded about us, rubbing our faces, and other parts of the upper portions of our bodies which they could touch." Indians who assiduously plucked facial hair always found hairy Europeans a source of amazement. But there was more here than cosmetic curiosity. The village chief, or *Agouhanna*, made it clear what all the touching was about when he made signs for Cartier to touch him "as if he thereby expected to be cured and healed." The Hochelagans did not see Cartier as the Aztecs had viewed the Spaniard Cortés— a returning god ready to wreak vengeance on the unbelieving and disobedient. Rather, the Hochelagans saw the French as mysterious beings with supernatural healing powers.

Cartier's mission at Hochelaga was neither therapy nor ethnography. The Northwest Passage and an empire of trade continued to hold the French imagination. Despite a considerable language barrier, Cartier did obtain valuable geographical information from his Hochelaga voyage. Most important, there he learned information about the alleged kingdom of Saguenay and the Ottawa River that would prove crucial for future French-Indian trade and diplomacy. Although Cartier did not fully understand what he was hearing, his Indian informants were telling him about the Hurons [Iroquois] and other northern peoples and their role in a vast trade network that extended throughout the Great Lakes, stretching as far west as Lake Superior. Cartier was in no position to take advantage of this information, but his successors would make exceptionally good use of it.

When Cartier returned to Stadacona he learned that those French he had left behind had felt threatened by the Stadaconas. Such threats, real or imaginary, had impelled the French to build a substantial fort at the banks of the St. Charles River. The fort's palisades, ditches, and cannons might have kept out the Indians, but the defenses were useless against malnutrition and scurvy. For five months— from November 1535 to April 1536—Cartier and his men were prisoners of the Canadian winter. With dozens of his men dead or dying of scurvy, survival finally depended on Domagaya, who brought Cartier a vitamin-rich potion to defeat the disease.

Before he left for St.-Malo in the spring of 1536, Cartier engaged in one last piece of confused Indian diplomacy. Still fascinated by Donnacona's tales of rich and powerful empires deep in the interior, Cartier decided to kidnap the chief and make him a prize exhibit in France. In collusion with a rival Stadacona headman, Cartier lured Donnacona and his sons to the St. Charles fort. Once inside, the Indians were held under close arrest. None saw his home again.

Back in France, Cartier's second voyage did not generate the same level of interest and enthusiasm as had his first. This time the explorer's reports were less promising, and the presence of North American Natives in French courts and salons was no longer a startling event. Domestic religious and political troubles and the lack of any quick profit delayed official action until 1538. With a temporary lull in internal difficulties, Francis I could again imagine a growing French presence in America. The plans this time called for a permanent settlement on the St. Lawrence River that would serve as a base from which to invade and conquer the kingdom of Saguenay. And beyond that distant kingdom, Asia still beckoned. To meet these goals a substantial expedition of ten ships and large numbers of men and women were assembled. When the recruiting slowed, planners turned to the local jails for potential settlers. Command of the expedition was given to Jean-François de la Rocque, sieur de Roberval. Roberval was an experienced soldier who seemed to have all the qualifications and sufficient energy for such an undertaking. Bypassed for command, Cartier was appointed master navigator. Despite what seemed careful planning, the Roberval-Cartier expedition of 1541–1543 failed. Defeated by scurvy, poor timing, bad luck, and the disillusionment of kingdoms just beyond reach, both Cartier and Roberval retreated from what must have seemed an intractable continent.

The failure of the Cartier-Roberval venture did not spell the end of French-Indian contacts in the Gulf of St. Lawrence. Quite the contrary. While official France was caught up in the bloody Wars of Religion, Breton and Basque fishermen continued to expand their commercial activities off Newfoundland and in the Gulf of St. Lawrence. Evidence is sketchy, but it is plain that by the end of the century at least 500 ships were summering in the region, fishing for cod and whales. At Tadoussac, where the Saguenay River joins the Gulf of St. Lawrence, Basques established an important whaling station.

What developed from these maritime enterprises was a very active but disorganized trade in furs. In the period after Cartier, fur became the principal focus for relations between the French and Native peoples. The exchange of furs for metal and textile items had many attractions for both trading partners. Indians found the products of European industry useful both as luxury goods and utensils for daily life. At this point at least, the trade did not seem to threaten either Indian political independence or economic self-sufficiency. Trading furs with French sailors seemed just one more extension of Native exchange networks that had long been a part of Indian life. For the French, furs seemed an ideal substitute for illusory gold and diamonds. Although the broad-brimmed beaver felt hat had not yet become the rage of European fashion, there was a rapidly expanding market for furs. By the end of the century, an economic partnership between French traders and Indian pelt hunters and processors were firmly in place. At summer fairs, first around Tadoussac and later farther upriver, French merchants and Indian suppliers haggled over price and supply. Indians quickly became skilled bargainers, pitting one French trader against another and never taking the first offer. Both partners enjoyed initial success—success made even more certain when European fashion eventually decreed that every gentleman wear a beaver hat. But by the beginning of the seventeenth century, it already was plain to many French in the maritime fur trade that wide-open competition would eventually destroy all hope of profit. A monopoly grant for the trade seemed a logical solution, at least in the eyes of the French traders. Monopolies were cheap for the crown to grant but virtually impossible to enforce. Nevertheless, grants were indeed issued for posts at Île de Sable (1598) and Tadoussac (1600), both of which amounted to dismal failures. But those failures did not daunt French entrepreneurs, who continued to see the trade as a guarantee of quick profit.

Pierre du Guast, sieur de Monts, was one such venturesome aristocrat who imagined a controlled partnership with Indians as the easy path to riches. In 1603 de Monts obtained a ten-year trade monopoly from the crown. The grant required that he establish a permanent settlement with at least sixty residents. Taking a page from Cartier's bitter winter experiences, de Monts intended to construct his base south of the Gulf of St. Lawrence, at Port Royal in Acadia. While the de Monts venture eventually collapsed, the entrepreneur's cartographer, Samuel de Champlain, made quite a name for himself as an explorer and trader. In addition, and more to the point, Champlain had a broad vision of his own destiny and that of France in America. In the first years of the seventeenth century, Indian-French relations, both on the St. Lawrence River and along the Atlantic coast, would be closely tied to Champlain's initiatives.

Beginning in 1604, Champlain undertook a series of successful explorations along the New England coast, along which he gained valuable Algonquian trading partners among the Penobscots, Abenakis, and Micmacs. Because of eventual English penetration in the region, the French were ultimately less successful in New England than at the other focal point for trade selected by Champlain. In July 1608, he established a modest trading post on the St. Lawrence River at the present-day site of Quebec. Champlain had selected that strategic site because he believed that Indian trade canoes heading for Tadoussac would find Quebec a more convenient market.

Beyond questions of survival, the most pressing issue facing Champlain was finding Native trading partners. The St. Lawrence Iroquois of Stadacona and Hochelaga were gone, and many of the Montagnais Indians and Algonquian tribes continued to frequent Tadoussac. Champlain's quest for trade partners began in the summer of 1609, when sixty Algonquian and Huron warriors appeared at Quebec asking for support in a raid against their traditional enemies, the New York-based League of the Iroquois (Mohawk, Oneida, Onondaga, Cayuga, and Seneca), which was also known as the Five Nations. Without fully understanding the consequences of his decision, Champlain agreed, for unless he made commercial arrangements with Hurons and Algonquians, the entire Quebec project would collapse. Selecting two men to accompany him, Champlain followed the war party up the Richelieu River and into what is now Lake Champlain. Once there, the warriors came upon some two hundred Mohawks. In the fray that followed, Champlain's guns provided the decisive edge—more for their psychological effect than any immediate physical results.

It has become a historical commonplace to claim that Champlain's participation in this raid and in a subsequent one in 1615 produced the coming decades of violence between the French and the imperial Iroquois League. Champlain's actions certainly did nothing to lessen already mounting tensions between northern peoples and the Iroquois. And his growing commercial ties with Hurons and

Algonquians did worry and anger the Iroquois. However, the troubles and suspicions predated Champlain. The French had been trading with and arming Indians the Iroquois saw as rivals and enemies long before Champlain. As Canadian historian W. J. Eccles has written, "Champlain was merely an agent of existing forces; he did not create them."

Champlain's participation in raids against the Iroquois increased his stature among the Hurons and Algonquians, but fur trade profits at Quebec remained unacceptably low. In 1612 a desperate Champlain undertook a bold and innovative strategy. He sent young Étienne Brulé to live with the Hurons. Because Huron trade routes were a family privilege, Brulé's connection to a Huron family became a crucial link for the French. Additionally Brulé set a pattern for other Frenchmen, who also forged personal connections in Native groups. While Champlain's fur trade steadily increased after 1613, those advances brought unexpected problems for the French. If anyone was the junior and dependent partner in the trade at Quebec, it was Champlain. Hurons and Algonquians quickly realized the power they held and began to pressure Champlain for more active support against their common enemy, the Iroquois. Such a demand—one that the French trader could not ignore—was filled with danger for partner and adversary alike.

By 1615 eastern North America had become an intricate and potentially dangerous web of alliances and trade networks. There were now two rival trade centers. Dutch merchants on the Hudson River at Fort Orange (present-day Albany) had made firm commercial agreements with the Iroquois. The Dutch-Iroquois trade was of major economic and strategic importance, since it provided Iroquois warriors with the firearms necessary to wage war against those Indians armed by the French. Even more important, the Fort Orange trade made the Iroquois dependent on European weapons technology and would eventually force Natives to expand their trapping enterprise once regional supplies of fur were trapped out. The French were now established at Quebec and had made at least marginally successful agreements with the Hurons and Algonquians. Tensions between Native groups were nothing new in the woodlands, but the dangers and the rewards had been changed with the arrival of the Europeans, their guns, iron pots, and diseases.

Between 1615 and 1629, relations between the French and their Native partners grew closer. In 1615 Champlain had felt compelled to make a journey to the Huron country to reassure his edgy partners. That trip brought unexpected results when the Hurons forced him to join them on a raid against the Iroquois at Lake Ontario. In a sharp engagement on October 10, 1615, Champlain was wounded. Because Huron and Algonquian warriors did not press the advantage to "defeat" the Iroquois, Champlain believed that battle a loss. But Hurons and Algonquians had achieved more than Champlain realized. There was a temporary halt to destructive Iroquois raids. For the Iroquois, 1615 was a genuine turning point. Survival required access to furs, and, with local supplies dwindling, the

Iroquois now felt compelled to look north to richer grounds. But so long as northern Indians boasted French guns and French allies, the conflict would be one for survival itself.

In the face of all this uncertainty, the fur trade at Quebec continued to grow. But French backers of the venture such as Cardinal Richelieu had expected more out of the American enterprise than an isolated cluster of trade houses huddled along the St. Lawrence River. The absence of a permanent settlement with a stable agricultural base worried the cardinal. It seemed unthinkable that French power could ever be built on anything as insubstantial as trade in fur. To strengthen and diversify the French presence, in 1627 Richelieu created the Company of New France. The company was intended to make Quebec a genuine settlement colony. With substantial funds and the support of influential governmental officials, the company seemed a certain success. But in the following year, England and France once again were at war, and Quebec was an early victim in the conflict. In 1629 English privateers led by the Kirke brothers laid siege to and finally captured Quebec. With the St. Lawrence lost, Champlain was forced to return to France, and, when the nation itself plunged into a long war, all seemed lost for New France.

But by the time Champlain reached France, the international situation had changed dramatically. France and England had signed the Treaty of St.-Germain-en-Laye, which gave back to the French their North American claims. The revitalized Company of New France was swiftly reorganized with new capital, and Champlain was commissioned lieutenant of New France. At the end of May 1633, Champlain and three ships loaded with supplies, a few soldiers, and even some women and children, arrived at Quebec. When a great fleet of Huron canoes loaded with pelts came at the end of July, French profits and survival seemed assured.

The same ships that brought Champlain and the trade goods also carried unique groups of Frenchmen whose lives would become bound up with the Indians' future. Father Paul Le Jeune and other Roman Catholic Jesuits were the first missionaries of that order in New France. In the years to come, the Jesuits would prove to be the single most important force for change—albeit often unwelcome and unpredictable change—in the lives of Native people. Jesuits like Le Jeune arrived in New France with a long tradition of missionary work among non-European peoples, an approach that insisted that each culture did have some incidental values and customs that might be preserved in the conversion to the new religious order. However, throughout the early years of New France, the Jesuits pursued a cultural revolution that called upon potential converts to abandon traditional ways, to become European in lifestyle and Roman Catholic in belief. There were few mission groups better equipped to tackle what amounted to the creation of an Indian new world. Jesuits were personally committed to the course, often to the extent of openly courting martyrdom for the faith. Superb Jesuit education in learning new languages prepared prospective missionaries to deal directly with

Indians without relying on interpreters. The Jesuits also understood the role of ceremony and imagery in Native religious practice. All told, the Jesuits were the most potent force for change to appear in the Northeast. What they were to demand of the Native peoples went far beyond the requirements of the fur traders or the price extracted by disease.

Perhaps the most revealing episode in Indian-mission relations in New France focused on the Jesuits in Huronia [the Hurons' homeland] in the years between 1634 and the late 1640s. In 1634 Father Jean de Brébeuf led Jesuits to work in the Huron villages of Canada. During the first year among the Hurons, the "black gowns," as the Indians referred to these Catholic priests, remained something of a curiosity, even a tourist attraction. Objects the missionaries carried with them, including magnets, clocks, hand tools, and meal grinders, sparked curiosity. Hurons were even more fascinated with writing as a form of nearly magical communication. But for all this interest the Jesuits gained no converts. Hurons tolerated what they judged as Jesuit strange ways and social blunders because they continued to view the French missionaries as honored guests: to anger the guests might endanger the valuable trade with Quebec.

By 1637–1638, however, Huron hospitality began to wear thin. Two powerful forces underlay this shift in attitude. First, a growing number of Hurons began to resent Jesuit mission practices. Although the Jesuits could record Native cultural patterns in the annual *Jesuit Relations* with admirable clarity and objectivity, daily mission techniques were not so nearly dispassionate. The Jesuits hurled ridicule and verbal abuse upon Hurons for practicing traditional rituals and dances. These ceremonies, what the Hurons called *onderha*, the foundation on which life itself rested. To impede the performance of the onderha or to slander those who danced in the traditional way seemed to court disaster. But Huron anger at Jesuit assaults on Native ways was overshadowed by a second, and far more immediate, concern. The arrival of the Jesuits in Huronia had coincided with a devastating series of epidemics. To Huron eyes the Jesuits seemed mysteriously immune from the diseases; the pestilence even appeared to follow the black gowns wherever they went. By 1638–1639 large numbers of Hurons were convinced that the missionaries were dangerous sorcerers intent on wreaking havoc on their people with terrifying diseases. While some village councils debated whether to kill the Jesuits as an act of patriotic self-protection, at least one village gathered up all its European trade goods and cast them into a nearby river in an act of purification. Because Jesuits routinely baptized only those on the edge of death, the belief that the black gowns spread illness gained wide credence.

Stunned by their sudden rejection, Jesuits in Huronia became even more strident in their denunciation of Native traditional practices. The missionaries were critical of Huron sexual mores, child-rearing practices, and the whole round of dances and festivals that gave shape to the traditional calendar of events. If the Jesuits found much to dislike in Huron life, the Hurons were equally forceful in their criticisms of European faith and practice. Hurons argued that Catholicism overemphasized death at the expense of enjoying life. Indians found the prohibition against labor on Sunday to be poor economics. And the European moral precepts, especially those concerning divorce and premarital sexual relations, made little sense. Finally, Hurons pointedly noticed that most French persons they knew paid little or no attention to the rules so earnestly propounded by the Catholic priests in black gowns.

By 1639 there were precious few Hurons willing to listen to the Jesuits, much less let them into villages and longhouses. But the same time the number of listeners was decreasing, the band of missionaries and lay workers was increasing. There were now some twenty-seven Jesuit priests and brothers in Huronia. In order to give some focus to mission work there, a central post named Ste. Marie des Hurons was constructed.

To the casual observer of Huronia in 1640, little had changed in the years of French contact. General good health and a productive harvest marked that year. But a closer look would have revealed a Huron people facing serious internal problems. Those troubles were not the immediate result of the epidemics of the late 1630s. They had struck with awesome severity, killing nearly one-half of the Huron population. But the true measure of the devastation lay not only in numbers dead, there was a steep social cost as well. Among the disease victims were chiefs, clan leaders, wise elders, and skilled craftspeople. Now, at a crucial time in Huron history, with increased troubles with the Five Nations, the Hurons were without many important leaders. Meanwhile, the Iroquois had nearly exhausted their local supplies of beaver. And if the Iroquois could not find and control new sources of supply, their vital connection to European traders on the Hudson would vanish. Fueled by economic pressures, tensions between Iroquois and Hurons began to grow in intensity and violence.

Bruce Trigger, the most prominent student of Huron life and culture, has characterized the years between 1640 and 1647 as "the storm within." Indeed, the Hurons were buffeted by winds both outside and inside their villages. Faced with a mounting Iroquois threat and a loss of leadership, the Hurons became increasingly dependent on the French for security and guidance. That dependence certainly benefited French merchants, who were able to exploit the trade as never before, but it was most evident in the Jesuit mission. As the disruption aided the traders, so it suddenly brought the mission a flood of new converts. These newly minted Huron Catholics accepted the gospel for a number of complex reasons. It is important to understand those reasons since they illuminate not only the Huron situation but also the larger arena of Indian–white relations. There is no doubt that some of the converts made the decision for purely secular reasons. Catholic Indians obtained preferential treatment in the fur trade, and the French would arm only the converted. Clearly, conversion meant protection in stormy times. But there was more here than Indians trading belief for guns and pots. Many Hurons were genuinely impressed with Jesuit piety. More important, Huron confidence in traditional ways had been shaken when the shamans failed to protect the villages against disease. Since healing was at the center of so much Native religious belief, Hurons looked at Christianity as a more certain way to survive. In the same way, Jesuit priests presented themselves as substitute shamans.

Those converts, so eagerly welcomed and counted by the Jesuits, sparked an immediate response from Huron shamans. In 1645–1646 there appeared in several Huron villages what might aptly be termed revitalization movements. Such movements were an attempt to regain lost power by reemphasizing and returning to traditional ways. Huron revitalization focused on visions of Native prophets and a renewed zeal for the ceremonies that were the onderha. But despite these efforts, the revitalization movement failed. It could not blunt the pain of constant Iroquois raids, nor could it restore confidence in ancient patterns of life. The Hurons were now living in an Indian new world—a world over which they no longer had much control.

Indeed, danger and dependence marked that new world—as did division. For the first time Hurons were pitted against each other in an ideological conflict. Traditionalists insisted that the old ways were sufficient and that abandoning them was the cause for all the disease and suffering. Huron converts were just as militant in their counterclaims. At the very time when the villages needed to unite to face the Iroquois onslaught, deep divisions weakened Huronia.

What Trigger has called "the bitter harvest" came between 1647 and 1650, years of tragedy and destruction. They marked the virtual end of Huronia as a sovereign political entity. Having failed to intimidate the Hurons, the Iroquois developed a new and effective strategy. Mohawk and Seneca warriors engaged in constant attacks on Huron villages and often drove deep into the heart of Huronia. While Hurons put up a spirited defense, guns obtained from Dutch traders gave the Iroquois a distinct edge. A Huron attempt to find allies among the Onondagas failed when Huron diplomats were ambushed and killed in January 1648. Throughout the period the Jesuits counted many new converts, all seeking refuge in a dying world.

The deathwatch formally began in the spring of 1649, when the Iroquois mounted an extraordinary assault on the Huron settlements. Some one thousand warriors were involved in the attacks. The villages of St. Ignace and St. Louis were destroyed, and soon afterward fifteen other villages were abandoned. Huronia was choked with refugees, as most fled to Jesuit protection. Unsure of what course to follow, the missionaries resettled some 300 families on Christian Island in the Georgian Bay. By the coming of winter, nearly 6,000 people were on the island, where, with little food and inadequate shelter, thousands died. Fewer than 300 people lived to see spring. What had once seemed so prosperous and secure had vanished during the bitter winter on Christian Island.

Because the destruction of Huronia is a crucial event in the history of the colonial Northeast, it is worth taking a moment to explore causes and consequences. What happened in the last generation of Huronia is a classic case of cultures, both Native and European, in collision. It is possible to isolate three central forces that led to the collapse of Huronia. Students of Huronia's fall often point to Indian-white relations as the culprit in producing dependency and weakness. There is no doubt that Hurons welcomed the chance to participate in a trade system that brought many material rewards. But as skilled traders long before the advent of the French, the Hurons could well have managed commerce without losing cultural identity. And while the fur business did make Hurons dependent on the French for firearms, the fur trade itself did not plant the seeds of the bitter harvest.

We come closer to the root problem by looking at disease. Throughout the northeastern woodlands, disease was one of the central forces for change in Native life. As historian Francis Jennings so aptly characterized it in *The Invasion of America,* the European invaders of America found not a virgin land but a widowed one. The shattering epidemics in Huronia destroyed more than thousands of lives. The waves of disease engulfed Huron culture, severed links with the past, and effectively killed much of the future. The epidemics also prompted a crisis of confidence in faith that allowed Jesuit missionaries to gain converts.

The Jesuits themselves were unwitting agents of chaos in Huronia. The mission dream was to produce a Huron society purified of its cultural sins and united by Roman Catholicism. What the dream became was a nightmarishly divided society, half Christian and half traditionalist, one fully at war with itself. The Jesuits believed that they could replace the onderha with Catholic belief and practice without doing any social damage in the process. But the Jesuits succeeded in promoting the very conflicts and divisions they sought to avoid. All of this was done in villages under attack by disease and implacable foes.

Had the Hurons not been facing a massive Iroquois invasion during the 1640s there might have been time to cope with the changes wrought by disease and the missions. But Iroquois raiders gave no respite. Their spring offensive of 1649 was only slowed by valiant Huron defensive efforts.

The demolition of Huronia was not only a shattering blow to Native people, it also had immediate consequences for the French. The fur trade, the life-support system for New France, had been severely hurt by the Iroquois blockade. Jesuit missions were destroyed and missionaries were killed, forcing a thorough reappraisal of conversion tactics. Throughout the 1650s, Iroquois warriors continued to threaten the very existence of New France as well.

By 1663 it was plain that New France was on the edge of collapse. Such a collapse would hardly endanger the French national economy, but it would be a blow to the growing prestige of the Sun King, Louis XIV. If New France was to survive, aid and direction had to come from the crown. With empire in mind, Jean Baptiste Colbert, French minister of marine, began to develop a grand strategy for the colony and all its peoples. That strategy was to create a North Ameican empire founded on a diversified economy. Colbert sought to encourage agriculture and light manufacturing along the St. Lawrence River, believing that the fur trade diverted men and capital away from the central colony and also invited further Iroquois conflict. Colbert understood the imperial value of trade as a means to secure Indian allies, but he feared that trade alone could never provide a reliable foundation for French power in North America.

But none of Colbert's grand plans could ever come to pass so long as New France lacked competent leadership and sufficient military force to break the Iroquois stranglehold. To that end, Colbert and the king sent to Quebec Jean Baptiste Talon as intendant (civil administrator) and Alexandre de Prouville, seigneur de Tracy, to take charge of military affairs. De Tracy was given substantial numbers of troops, including the experienced Carignan-Salieres regiment. In 1666 the French inflicted sufficient pain on the Mohawks that the Iroquois fur-trade blockade was temporarily lifted. The essential problem for New France—its geographical location in relation to that of the Iroquois League—could not be altered, but at least the situation had been eased.

Colbert imagined that a lessening of tensions with the Iroquois might allow the St. Lawrence colony to develop as he had planned. The irony was that once there was a measure of security from the Mohawk and Seneca raids, the fur trade sprang back to life. Even though a glut of fur from northern Indians depressed market prices some 50 percent, the profits furs brought were still handsome. By the 1670s Montreal merchants and Jesuit missionaries were extending French influence into the western Great Lakes region; it was an expansion filled with danger for both the French and Native peoples.

The central figure in that expansion was the governor general of New France, Louis de Buade, compte de Frontenac. Frontenac's vision of New France was every bit as expansive as was Colbert's, but it was fundamentally different in character. While Colbert thought in terms of a balanced economy focused on the St. Lawrence settlements, Frontenac sought an extensive fur-trade empire that would dominate the Great Lakes and outflank the English by finding water routes south from the Great Lakes to the sea. Frontenac's commercial empire would be built on fur-trade posts and Jesuit mission stations. For all their drama and romance, the explorations of Marquette and Joliet, to find the Mississippi River, and of La Salle, who explored that essential waterway and claimed the heart of the continent for France, were simply designed to extend the trade system and bring more Indians into it.

Frontenac's success was not without a price. At the very time when the French were bidding to monopolize the western trade, the Iroquois were thinking of doing the same thing. Having annihilated the Hurons, but with a temporary check to their designs by de Tracy, the Iroquois were now intent on expanding their power into the Ohio Valley and the Illinois country. Once the Five Nations made peace with their neighbors in 1676, they were free to surge westward toward the Great Lakes.

The storm broke in September 1680, when a flotilla of Iroquois war canoes invaded the Illinois country. The Jesuits had warned Frontenac of the invasion, but he ignored the warnings. Although most French traders and missionaries managed to escape, one large Illinois Indian village was destroyed. The next twenty years were some of the most troubled in the long history of French-Indian relations. In the summer of 1684 a French force under Governor General Joseph-Antoine le Febvre de La Barre was humiliated in an abortive invasion of the Iroquois League's homeland. Despite the best efforts of skilled soldiers such as the Marquis de Denonville, New France seemed ever closer to disaster at the hands of the Iroquois. In August 1689, when a force of some 1,500 warriors attacked Lachine, a French settlement just outside Montreal, the end seemed very near indeed.

What lay ahead instead was a ten-year round of bloody raid and counterraid between the French and the Five Nations, a conflict that even spilled over into English territories of New York and New England. The common brutalities of the conflict had a sobering effect on both the French and the Iroquois. For their part, the Iroquois gradually realized that in an effort to achieve Great Lakes hegemony they had overextended their forces. The French undertook a similar re-evaluation of their role in North America but reached a very different conclusion: if the Iroquois after 1701 would pursue a policy of militant neutrality, the French were determined to challenge their English rivals situated along the Atlantic corridor and win the race for empire and eastern North America. In August 1701 a throng of Indian diplomats met with French officials at Montreal to negotiate a lasting peace. The Iroquois gained security, and the French were free to exploit the western fur trade. Only the English seemed the losers, having depended on the Iroquois to shield them from French attack. The treaty of 1701 marked the end of a century of the French-Iroquois conflict. It also heralded the coming age of imperial wars between France and England and their respective colonies.

It has become historical wisdom to insist that the French had better relations with Native peoples of North America than did the English. The argument usually runs that the Gallic temper was better suited to Native ways and even found intermarriage attractive. Such an interpretation would have surprised the French and their longtime foes the Iroquois. The French were every bit as ethnocentric as their English rivals. But certain accidents of geography and history did give French traders, soldiers, and missionaries a distinct edge in the struggle to win Indian hearts and bodies.

First, the French central colony along the St. Lawrence River in Canada was built on lands not currently occupied by any Indian group. The French, unlike the English, did not begin their colony with an act of dispossession.

Second, Jesuit mission theology after the fall of Huronia tended to downplay the disruptive "civilization" program pursued by earlier missionaries. Jesuits sought converts but did not demand cultural suicide.

Third, unlike the English, the French economic strategy did not require occupation of the land.

Fourth, the nature of the fur trade required active Indian cooperation. Whatever Frenchmen thought of Indians and Native ways, the traders needed Indians as partners.

Fifth, the fur trade created a large number of men with personal and family ties to Native groups. Such links worked against overt violence toward Indians.

There are few more enduring images in United States history than Pilgrims and Indians enjoying a peaceful first Thanksgiving together. That event has become part of national mythology, perhaps, because we all have the uneasy feeling that violent conflicts, death, and dispossession will all too soon shatter the peace. Few parts of the history of Indian-white relations in North America have produced more passion and passionate writing than the troubled dealings of coastal Algonquians with the Pilgrims (or Separatists) of Plymouth Colony and the Puritans of Massachusetts Bay Colony. Apologists have described the New English as evenhanded dispensers of justice, while critics have characterized the same people as backwoods thugs and murderers. In the process of defining heroes and villains, historical truth—rarely a clear-cut commodity—has been a casualty. The concluding portion of this chapter will examine the lives of Indians and English New Englanders as they groped toward an uncertain future.

English interest in what became known as New England began long before there was any thought of permanent settlement in the region. John Cabot made his 1497 voyage for the English crown from Bristol to northeastern North America. Cabot's landfalls are as uncertain as the identities of those Native people he met. But whatever his misconceptions about North America as part of Asia, Cabot brought Micmacs and Beothuks into the path of venturesome and enterprising Englishmen. In the 1580s English adventurer and Renaissance man Sir Humphrey Gilbert turned his attention to the region he called Norumbega. Interested in the economic possibilities around what is now Narragansett Bay, Gilbert sent a ship to the bay in 1580. Gilbert's death at sea in 1583, however, put an effective damper on English efforts to do any more than fish in New England's bountiful waters.

English activities along the coast began to change in both frequency and character in the years after 1602. A series of important but often-overlooked expeditions established an English presence on the coast and had far-reaching consequences for Indian-English relations. The first of those probes came in the spring of 1602, when the enterprising earl of Southhampton hired Captain Bartholomew Gosnold and the ship *Concord* for a trading venture to the coast. The Southhampton plan was to have at least some of the crew winter on the coast as the seeds of a future settlement. When the *Concord* reached Cape Neddick on the coast of southern Maine, the ship's company was astounded to meet Indians sailing a Basque shallop and dressed in European clothing. The Indians' dress and their use of broken English were plain evidence for long contact with Europeans. Gosnold decided to sail south toward what he eventually named Cape Cod. While the journey was an economic success, relations with the Pokanoket Indians were less than tranquil. When *Concord* sailors built a fortified camp on Cuttybunk Island and refused to trade, Indians took those actions as a sign of hostility. for while the English saw trade in purely economic terms, Native people viewed the same as a means to establish friendship and balance between strangers. In early

June, relations were tense enough to produce an attack on an English party foraging for food. One English sailor was wounded. That affair was sufficient to convince Gosnold to abandon any plan to winter on the coast. With his stores of sassafras (believed to be an effective remedy for syphilis), fur, and cod, Gosnold could claim success and downplay any Native troubles.

The *Concord* expedition, with its promise of economic reward, prompted a syndicate of Bristol merchants in 1603 to organize a follow-up voyage. Led by Captain Martin Pring, two trading vessels made the Atlantic crossing and landed at what is now Provincetown harbor. Pring was prudent enough to know that images in promotional pamphlets might not square with New England realities. His first move, therefore, was to build a fortified camp. Pring intended the fortress to serve as a base for gathering sassafras. Early contacts between Pring's men and Nauset Indians were friendly despite English worries about sudden attack. In one particularly charming encounter, Indians and English gathered around a blazing fire to sing and dance while a cabin boy played his guitar. But for reasons that are no longer clear, initial friendship dissolved into mutual suspicion and hostility. As the Pring party was ready to leave and return to England, large numbers of armed Nausets surrounded the English camp, seemingly ready to attack. Pring managed to escape, leaving behind yet another component of English-Indian antagonism and distrust.

Once again the profits produced by the Pring enterprise spoke louder than did any troublesome relations with Native people. In 1605 George Weymouth was hired by an odd assortment of Plymouth fish merchants and English Catholics to take the ship *Archangel* on a voyage to northern New England. For some two weeks, there was an active trade between the English and Kennebec and Abenaki Indians. This sort of trade—primarily of tobacco and furs—was nothing new to coastal people who had already enjoyed a brisk exchange with French traders. The powerful Penobscot *sachem*, or political leader, went so far as to invite Weymouth to visit his Penobscot River settlement. But Weymouth feared ambush and rejected what might have become a diplomatic triumph. Instead, the English kidnapped five Indians for use as informants on future voyages.

In the period immediately following the Gosnold-Pring-Weymouth voyages, English merchants and colonial promoters continued to focus on the New England coast. But despite that interest, by 1614 there still was no permanent English presence in New England. More important, the English image current among many coastal indigenous peoples was a decidedly negative one. The English were viewed as dangerous, unpredictable men who might suddenly kidnap unsuspecting Indians. Even more significant for Indians, the English did not seem to understand the noneconomic aspects of trade.

The pace of English activity in New England quickened in 1614 with the arrival of John Smith, who coined the term "New England." So often identified with the history of early Virginia, in 1614 Smith was engaged by merchant Marmaduke Rawdon to direct a New England voyage searching for whales and precious metals. If whales and gold proved elusive, Smith's instructions allowed him to search for fur and fish. Smith did not find whales, and, while most of his crew traded for furs, Smith took a small detachment on an exploring jaunt down the coast. That reconnaissance produced a detailed map of the southern New England coast and a full description of the Native peoples of the region. Smith named the region "New England," providing a clue to the shape of the future. While he was certain that hordes of gold and mountains of copper were to be found somewhere in North America, Smith had a very different vision for New England. Attracted by the obvious prosperity of Indian villages and the richness of the land, Smith proposed the extension of an English landed domain, a "new" England, to challenge Native occupation. To that end, Smith's map illustrated that vision by replacing Indian place and town names with English ones.

Smith knew that his plans for an agrarian New England would be a frontal assault on Native people. Drawing on his Virginia experience and his self-image as an English Hernando Cortés, Smith proposed strong means for dealing with Native reactions to an English invasion. Historian Neal Salisbury has summed up Smith's Indian policy as "the proper combination of deception, intimidation, and brute force." Smith believed that a stoutly armed force would be necessary not only for the protection of any future colony, but also as a means to extort corn from Native neighbors. Smith's dream of an agricultural, heavily armed New England ready to use force against its neighbors did not come to pass under his leadership. But Smith's prescription did not go unnoticed by those English folk who soon founded the Plymouth and Massachusetts Bay colonies.

In the typical telling of the growth of English New England, there is hardly a missed step between John Smith's landed vision and the Pilgrim landing in 1620. But the years between John Smith's and Pilgrim leader William Bradford's arrival in North America were ones of terrifying change for Native people. Between 1616 and 1618, epidemic diseases had devastated parts of the New England coast. The nature of that disease has always been a source of controversy. Salisbury has argued that the killer was a "variety of plague," while ecological historian William Cronon maintains that the disease was chicken pox, since Native New England lacked the rats and human population densities required for the spread of the plague. Whatever the precise nature of the epidemics, the consequences were plain. The coastal Abenakis lost most of their population. But the region that suffered the most dramatic population lost was the southern coast from Massachusetts Bay to Plymouth Bay. Whole villages recorded by Champlain and Smith simply vanished. Entire tribes such as the Patuxets were annihilated. The diseases not only visited horror on one generation but also gravely weakened subsequent ones. The epidemics reoccurred after 1618, and each wave of sickness made Indians less able to resist the growing power of English settlers intent on occupying their land.

The potent image of the first Thanksgiving thus tends to obscure the tension and violence between the English and coastal Indians from the moment of the Plymouth colony's founding in 1620. That the Pilgrims expected trouble was plain in their hiring of Miles Standish as military adviser. Like his contemporary John Smith, Standish believed that Indians would respond only to massive shows of force and firepower. Standish molded Pilgrim Indian policy to suit his perceptions of Natives as hostile savages. Standish made Plymouth an armed camp, from which fortress Separatist militiamen sallied forth to rob Indian graves and extort corn from their neighbors.

Indeed, to the Pokanoket sachem Massasoit, the English must have seemed bewildering neighbors. He realized that some sort of balance had to be achieved with the bearded strangers. Because the Pokanokets had suffered severely in the recent epidemics, Massasoit may well have seen the troublesome English as protectors against the always dangerous Narragansetts. In March 1621, Samoset and Squanto, two English-speaking Indians, arranged a meeting between Plymouth officials and Pokanoket representatives. Samoset, an Algonquin from Pemaquid (now Bristol) in eastern Maine, had learned the newcomers' language from Englishmen who fished the Maine coast. Squanto, the only survivor of the village of Patuxet (where Plymouth stood), had been kidnapped in 1614 by coastal traders and carried to England. He had just returned home to find that his people had been wiped out by disease in 1617. The treaty that emerged from the gathering is worthy of notice since it reveals the unequal measure of power already present in New England Indian–white relations. Both parties promised to aid each other in case of attack and agreed to attend subsequent meetings unarmed. Reflecting the constant fear that they were about to be overwhelmed by Indian warriors, Pilgrim diplomats drafted the first treaty provision declaring that Natives were not to "injure or do hurt" to the English. Significantly, nothing substantive was said about possible English assaults on Indians. The next stipulation of the treaty made it even clearer that Plymouth was to be the fountainhead of all law and justice. Revealing the powerful ethnocentrism that would dominate virtually all Indian–Anglo American relations thereafter, the 1621 treaty required Indians guilty of crimes against the English to be sent to Plymouth for punishment. It would have been unthinkable for Pilgrim lawmakers to suggest that the Native justice system punish those who wronged Indians. It was only at the conclusion of the treaty that some provision was made for the punishment of those English who took Indian goods. After making clear Native responsibility for theft, the treaty added that English settlers would be punished by the colony for infractions against Indians. According to Salisbury, the English "regarded the treaty as one not of alliance and friendship between equals but of submission by one party to the domination of the other."

In the years that followed the 1621 treaty, relations between the New English and Native peoples grew in tension, complexity, and potential for violence. Weakened by disease and threatened with constant demands for more land, New England Indians faced an uncertain future. While they had not yet fully lost political sovereignty and cultural integrity, both were under steady attack. That as-

Illustration showing the return of Miles Standish to Wessagusset following a raid on an Indian camp. His men are armed with muskets and one displays the head of an Indian on a stick.
©Bettmann/CORBIS

sault was a three-pronged invasion, pressing Indians on the flanks of land, law, and cultural values.

In so many ways the English invasion of North America was a contest for natural resources waged by two agricultural peoples. Steady pressure on the Native land base became one of the major sources of friction between English and Native farmers. That tension exploded into violence in 1637 in the Pequot War. Intent on extending both political sovereignty and land claims into the Connecticut River valley, colonial forces from Connecticut and Massachusetts Bay engaged in a virtual slaughter of Pequots at their Mystic River village. The treaty of Hartford (1638) proclaimed both English victory and the dissolution of the Pequot nation. It was a measure that other Native people could not ignore: land-hungry English settlers would make war on any who stood in their path and would with no hesitation proclaim such violence as the will of God. Faced with increased English population and the threat of violence, many New England sachems made land cessions that could only spell economic ruin. The New English conveniently saw themselves as productive workers of the land while denying the same description to Indian farmers.

Closely linked to land troubles were heightened tensions resulting from different perceptions of law. The treaty of 1621 had lasting legal influence in Plymouth Indian–white relations. It established legal practices and fixed attitudes that would be fleshed out by subsequent legislation and court action. More important, the Plymouth treaty makers assumed that the English colony would be the center of justice and that Native deeds would have to conform to English standards. The treaty assured Indians that they could gain equal justice but assumed that such justice would be English in both form and substance, to say nothing of execution. All told, the treaty implied that Native custom law, one of the central bonds of traditional society, was no longer valid.

The first test of legal arrangements between Pilgrims and Indians came in 1638. Late in the summer of that year a band of runaway Plymouth servants led by Arthur Peach, "a lusty and desperate young man," murdered a Narragansett Indian boy who had been trading at the Massachusetts Bay Colony. After robbing the lad, Peach and his gang attempted to escape to New Netherland. Their flight was thwarted when the dying boy found aid among other Indians who in turn apprehended the killers. After some debate that involved colonial and Indian leaders, it was decided to try Peach and the others in Plymouth.

On September 4, 1638, the General Court of the Colony of New Plymouth was the stage for one of the most important legal actions in the history of the colony. Governor Thomas Prence and his assistants closely questioned Peach, Thomas Jackson, and Richard Stinnings. Testimony was also taken from several Narragansetts. The evidence left little doubt that Peach and his cohorts were guilty of murder. The government knew that such a crime, if unpunished, might encourage future assaults and would surely provoke a strong Native response. However, the trial and its obvious verdict raised a troubling question in the minds of many colonists: should an Englishman be tried and executed for the murder of an Indian? Driven by expediency and a genuine concern for justice, the jury sentenced all three men to death, but the decision was not without its critics. Colony historian William Bradford reported that "some of the rude and ignorant sort murmured [unapprovingly] that any English should be put to death for [having killed] the Indians." In spite of adverse public feelings, the executions were carried out.

The Peach case had significance far beyond its sordid details and potent outcome, for it suggests that even at this early date there were two contradictory trends present within Indian-white legal relations. The government did act quickly and forcefully to bring Peach and his men to justice. On the other hand, and perhaps more important for the future, there were many voices in the colony questioning equal legal treatment for Native people. As the English colony expanded in population and geography, those voices would become louder and eventually gain the force of both law and court practice.

In the years between the Peach case (1638) and King Philip's War (1675), legal affairs continued as a source of friction between Indians and their neighbors. The Plymouth government did struggle to use law to protect Native interests, as in the case of trespass by English animals on Native cornfields. And the surviving evidence suggests that until the decade of the 1660s, legal relations between the two peoples was characterized by almost equal measures of protection and subjugation. But as the troubles that would finally spark war grew, the scales of justice began to tip toward law as a means to intimidate. As in racial slavery, law became a means for social control.

In the five years before King Philip's War, Plymouth authorities acted to broaden legal jurisdiction over Indian life. As the colony expanded nearer Indian settlements and fields, the number of cases involving land disputes and trespass increased. To deal with this caseload the General Court of Plymouth developed special procedures for handling these suits. In 1670 the Court ordered that all matters between Indians and English not touching capital offenses be brought first to local selectmen for a decision. This regulation did not, however, dissuade Indians from coming to Plymouth on court days to press their claims. Faced with throngs of Natives in town on court days, the colonial government decided in 1673 to ban Indians from the town of Plymouth during regular court sessions. Indians were permitted to attend only the July and October meetings. The 1673 act was one more step in creating a separate legal system for Indians.

Joining the troubles promoted by territorial expansion and legal distinctions was the tension generated by English mission activities among the Indians. While Protestant missionaries such as John Eliot would have vehemently denied it, Puritan and Jesuit missions shared similar approaches to conversion. Jesuits seeking Huron converts and Puritans preaching to Bay Indians assumed that cultural transformation—"civilization" as they termed it—was a necessary precondition to salvation. In southern New England the civilization program fashioned by Eliot and Massachusetts Bay Colony Indian superintendent Daniel Gookin focused on what they termed the "praying towns." These towns were to be model Christian Indian communities in which converts and their own pacified leaders could pursue the arts of agriculture and faith without interruption from those Natives yet unwashed by the adoption of civilization and the gospel. By the end of the eighteenth century at least ninety-one praying towns had flourished at one time or another. More important, some 133 Indian preachers and lay leaders had given Natives directions to convert to Christianity. The praying towns were, in historian James Axtell's phrase, an Indian Marshall Plan.

The growth of the number of praying towns and the number of their Native residents did not mean that massive numbers of New England Indians had seen the Puritan light and abandoned traditional beliefs for what one Native woman called "the new wise sayings." In fact, Indian responses to the Christian mission reveal the full complexity of Native-English relations in early New England. Praying towns attracted followers from those villages and bands that had suffered the most substantial population losses. Epidemics produced not only weakened leadership but also a crisis of spiritual confidence. Much of Native religious belief and practice centered on healing. Indian priests, called "Powwows," saw their principal function as maintaining a healthy balance between individuals and supernatural forces. When the shamans could not restore health to those stricken by smallpox or other scourges, many Indians turned to Christianity for what seemed the next best remedy. Christianity thereby became a survival ideology, a protective covering in an increasingly hostile world. This is not to imply that Indians who became Christians were somehow insincere in their professions of faith. Native believers on Martha's Vineyard, for example, accepted Christianity but adapted it to their own needs, creating vigorous towns and churches. For many New England Indians, Christianity actually was a way to preserve cultural identity, as well as a means to save their souls and, frequently, their lives.

While some New England Natives found Christianity attractive, others firmly rejected it. That rejection, voiced by shamans, sachems, and ordinary people, amounted to a thorough critique of English Puritan practices and beliefs. In a series of forceful exchanges, Indian shamans challenged many of the theological ideas proposed by Puritan divines. One Indian asked, "May a good man sin sometimes?" Another wished to know "If a man be almost a good man and dyeth; whither goeth his soule?" Indian theologians questioned heaven and hell, punishment after death, and the view of sin. Native political leaders were also critical of the mission. Sachems and village elders saw the missionaries as the advance guard of English political and territorial domination. One sachem pointedly explained what conversion would mean to his own powers. "If I be a praying Sachem, I shall be a poor and weak one, and easily be trod upon by others, who are like to be more potent and numerous; and by this means my tribute will be small, and I shall be a great loser by praying to God." One Indian woman, neither shaman nor sachem, put the Native critique best when she declared, "We are well as we are, and desire not to be troubled with these new wise sayings."

But the new wise sayings, the people who spread them, and the economic and political system that sustained them could not be stopped by words no matter how eloquent or pointed. The tensions produced by demands for land, legal inequities, and ideological assaults all edged Native and English New Englanders closer to conflict. Despite rivalries, arguments, and misunderstandings, a general war did not come until the 1670s. Part of the explanation for that long period of uneasy peace rests in the efforts of the Pokanoket sachem Massasoit. Unlike the Narragansett sachem Miantonomi who had early warned against English influence, Massasoit believed some measure of peaceful coexistence with the English possible. He saw the English as valuable allies against the Narragansetts and important sources of trade goods. With those material benefits in mind, Massasoit was willing to tolerate having troublesome English for neighbors as the price for security and prosperity. The sachem thought in terms of cooperation; the English, however, had visions of domination in a world with no Indians to restrain expansion.

By the time Massasoit died in 1661, the Indians of New England were living in a new world not of their own making. English farmers were changing the face of the land, colonial bureaucrats were pressing for increased political control over Native people, and Puritan missionaries were intent on spreading what seemed to many Indians a subversive faith. At Massasoit's death substantial political leadership in the Pokanoket bands passed to his eldest son Wamsutta, or Alexander. Wamsutta found himself in a difficult position. As English fields and animals steadily encroached on Native lands, the new sachem could not ignore the voices calling for some measure of resistance to the English. When Wamsutta indicated in 1662 that he would be unwilling to travel to Plymouth to assure colonial authorities of his loyalty, English officials reacted swiftly. Militia forces were dispatched, and Wamsutta was brought to Plymouth under guard. At Plymouth, Wamsutta was compelled to swear loyalty to the English regime. After being released, Wamsutta, on the way back to his village, fell ill and quickly died. While his untimely death was surely the result of some disease, many Pokanokets found that explanation unpersuasive. Wamsutta's death seemed only the most recent in a string of disasters that had dogged their people since the arrival of the English.

It was into this atmosphere of fear, anger, and distrust that Metacomet, or Philip, became the new sachem of the Pokanokets. Philip was now confronted with a dilemma that would become increasingly commonplace for Native leaders in the years to come. He could either acquiesce to English demands for land and claims on band sovereignty or risk resistance and face the Pequot fate. The alternatives seemed stark—survival under foreign domination or resort to some kind of violent action. Philip did not pursue a single policy. At various times he sought compromise, while at other moments there was open talk of war. At root, Philip accepted Miantonomi's view that "for so are we all Indians as the English are, and say brother to one another; so must we be one as they are, otherwise we shall all be gone shortly."

Throughout the 1660s and into the 1670s, Philip attempted to export his brand of pan-Indianism and force it into a military alliance. Despite his best efforts, Philip found his message either rejected or ignored. Tribal and band rivalries, old quarrels, and Philip's relative youth all worked to effect what can only be called a failure. When the struggle did finally erupt, Native forces were unified in neither leadership nor cause.

It is one of the great seductions in the study of history to assume that events of great consequence have equally grand causes. King Philip's War was surely the product of forces set in motion long before 1675. But "forces set in motion" is a phrase that tends to obscure the faces of the past and the decisions made, the alternatives chosen or rejected. The conflict was the result not of nameless forces but of human beings. The immediate spark for the war was the death of John Sassamon and the execution of three Pokanokets charged with his murder.

In December 1674, a Natick Indian named John Sassamon warned Plymouth officials of an imminent attack on the settlement by Philip and his warriors. Sassamon, who had served as a Christian preacher and secretary to Philip, was evidently bent on spreading rumors about the young sachem. A recent argument between the two men was behind Sassamon's falsehood. Plymouth authorities discounted Sassamon's warning and promptly forgot about his winter visit.

In January 1675, a group of hunters stumbled on Sassamon's body under the ice of a local pond. Once identified as Sassamon, the body was buried without further examination.

Not until the spring did Plymouth officials grasp the full import of Sassamon's death. They evidently recalled Sassamon's claim that if Philip discovered his role as an informer, his death would be certain. Now Plymouth governor Josiah Winslow and his assistants took this to mean that Sassamon had been murdered at Philip's order. With neither witnesses nor physical evidence, colonial officials arrested and charged three Pokanokets for Sassamon's murder. Among those charged was one of Philip's closest friends and advisers. It now seems plain that Governor Winslow seized on Sassamon's death as an excuse to intimidate Philip. Early in June 1675 the three men were tried at Plymouth. Mindful of the gravity of the situation, colonial officials took the unprecedented step of impaneling an Indian jury along with an English one. But the verdict was never in doubt. The Indians were found guilty and executed soon thereafter.

The executions were a challenge that Philip could not ignore. By what right did English law extend to Indians involved in a case with no English principals? Many of Philip's warriors quickly saw the executions for what they were—judicial murder with a political motive. Those warriors began to pressure Philip for an immediate and violent response. John Easton, deputy governor of Rhode Island and an important actor in the events of the summer of 1675, caught wind of the mounting tension after the execution. "So the English were afraid," wrote Easton, "and Philip was afraid and both increased in arms." Fearing that a general war was almost upon them, Easton and others in Rhode Island attempted to mediate Indian-English differences. The Rhode Islanders, encouraged by Philip's initial acceptance of the mediation proposal, suggested that an Indian representative meet with Governor Edmund Andros of New York. What might have proved a means to air and resolve a wide variety of troubles failed when Plymouth abruptly rejected any thought of negotiations. By the end of June war exploded in a burst of violence that would change forever both Indians and the English.

King Philip's War was a two-summer-long fury of raid and ambush. In the first summer of the conflict, Philip's warriors waged a lightening war against outlying settlements in Plymouth and Massachusetts. Ill-equipped to fight this kind of war, the English suffered substantial casualties and were forced to abandon several towns. The campaign was going so well that Philip opened a second front in the Connecticut River valley. But as winter approached, many of Philip's warriors left the field to support their families. As Philip's forces faded away, it was plain that his call for Native unity had gone largely unheeded. Desperate for fresh warriors, Philip traveled to New York seeking Iroquois support. Mohawk elders listened patiently and then rejected Philip's pleas. The Mohawks saw no reason to become involved in a distant conflict. They also feared that such involvement might endanger their crucial Albany trade connections.

But even as Philip's personal diplomacy failed to produce results, events on the battlefield breathed new life into the struggle. English officials were furious when they discovered that the powerful Narragansetts were openly supporting Philip. In mid-December 1675, colonial militia forces staged a daring raid on a fortified Narragansett settlement deep in the Great Swamp of Rhode Island. In the fierce fighting that followed, scores of Indians and militiamen died. The Great Swamp Fight was an English victory, but it had unexpected and unwelcome consequences for the colonial cause. Stunned by the ferocity of war waged against women and children, Narragansett warriors drew even closer to Philip.

Success in war has often been the product of chance, time, and momentum. In the second summer of King Philip's War those factors were increasingly sliding toward English advantage. After the initial shock of war had worn off, the English began to learn how to fight in the woods. Men like Benjamin Church emerged as disciplined, skilled soldiers. And in the summer of 1676, Nipmuck and Narragansett forces suffered serious defeats. As the numbers of Philip's warriors dwindled and many Indians joined the English, the tide of war turned. By August 1676, Philip was a man hunted and haunted—hunted by a force led by Captain Benjamin Church and Roger Goulding and haunted by what might have been.

The end came for Philip in the cold dawn hours of August 12, 1676. Guided by an Indian informer, colonial forces under Church and Goulding trapped the sachem in swampy ground at Mount Hope. In a flurry of shots Philip was killed. Church ordered the Indian's body quartered and the head taken back to Plymouth. Philip's death and the capture some time later of the influential elder Annawon effectively ended the conflict in southern New England.

The consequences of King Philip's War were shattering for both the English and the Indians. The war broke the political power of the southern New England bands, their leaders either killed in combat or, like Annawon, executed by the vengeful victors. Indian villages and fields lay in smoldering ruins. Many of those Indians who survived and surrendered found themselves sold into slavery in the West Indies to help defray the colonial war debt. The war, with all its political and cultural devastation, made Christianity and the praying towns look even more attractive.

At the same time, the price of victory for the English had been very high. The war shook Puritan confidence in the righteousness of their errand into the wilderness. Many Puritan divines preached that the war was the judgment of an angry God visited on the wayward and unworthy English. But now, not even victory could restore a sense of special providence lost in two years of bitter forest fighting. English casualties were very high. The Plymouth Colony lost in proportion to its population more men than the United States lost in World War II. King Philip's War so disrupted Plymouth that the colony eventually ceased to exist as a distinct polity and became part of Massachusetts Bay. Burned villages, unmarked forest graves, and innocence lost were all part of the price.

Native people did not vanish from southern New England after 1676, but much had been lost and life became harder than ever in a country grown hostile. With many leaders dead and land taken, New England Indians faced a bleak future.

Suggested Reading

Historical writing on Indian–white relations in New France and southern New England ranges from the superb to the ridiculous, from jargon-choked monographs to well-crafted essays. The beginning student can do no better than to start with James Axtell's *The European and the Indian: Essays in Ethnohistory of Colonial America* (New York, 1981). In these graceful, challenging essays Axtell treats subjects as diverse as Indian missions, burial practices, and scalping. Some of Axtell's essays have become classics, including those on scalping and the white Indians. Because most of the examples are drawn from French and New English sources, the collection is especially appropriate. With Axtell as background, students can turn to the fine topical and chronological articles in the *Handbook of North American Indians*, vol.15: *Northeast*, Bruce Trigger, ed., (Washington, D.C., 1978).

Students undertaking readings in the history of New France can profitably begin with three books by William J. Eccles. His short *The Ordeal of New France* (Toronto, 1967) is a good introduction to the subject. More valuable for Indian affairs is Eccles' *The Canadian Frontier, 1534–1760* (New York, 1969). Also useful is his France in America (New York, 1972). No two scholars have done more to illuminate Indian-white relations in New France than Bruce Trigger and Cornelius J. Jaenen. Trigger's magisterial *The Children of Aataentsic: A History of the Huron People to 1660*, 2 vols. (Montreal, 1976) is a landmark in ethnohistorical scholarship. Perhaps more accessible for students is Trigger's *The Huron: Farmers of the North* (New York, 1969). Trigger's Natives and Newcomers: Canada's "Heroic Age" Reconsidered (Montreal, 1986) is an encyclopedic reevaluation of myths and realities in the racial history of New France. Denys Delage's *Bitter Feast: Amerindians and Europeans in Northeastern North America* (Vancouver, 1993) is another penetrating look at the relationships between native people and those recent arrivals who sought to crate a "new" France. For its unique blend of ethnohistory and intellectual history, no student should miss Jaenen, *Friend and Foe: Aspects of French-Amerindian Cultural Contact in the Sixteenth and Seventeenth Centuries* (New York, 1976).

Studies of Indian-white relations in New England have often become polemics either championing the Puritans as dispensers of justice and the true faith or damning them as swindlers and thugs. Alden Vaughan, *New England Frontier: Puritans and Indians, 1620–1675*, rev. ed. (New York, 1979) attempts to exonerate Puritans of charges of oppression, imperialism, and towering hypocrisy. No historian has been more critical of that approach than Francis Jennings. His *The Invasion of America: Indians, Colonialism, and the Cant of Conquest* (Chapel Hill, N.C., 1975) is a slashing attack on Puritan Indian policy and its latter-day apologists. Jennings' book sparked a whole round of new books, articles, and sessions at professional meetings. More important, it signaled a thorough reappraisal of New England Indian-white relations. Perhaps the most important of those books is Neal Salisbury's *Manitou and Providence: Indians, Europeans, and the Making of New England, 1500–1643* (New York, 1982). Recently, three books have significantly advanced that reevaluation of early New England history. Alfred Cave's *The Pequot War* (Amherst, Mass., 1996) is a thoughtful study of what was in so many ways the prototype New England Indian war. Russell Bourne, *The Red King's Rebellion: Racial Politics in New England, 1675–1678* (New York, 1990) is the first thorough examination of the origins and course of what is often called King Philips War. Jill Lepore's superb *The Name of War: King Philip's War and the Origins of American Identity* (New York, 1998) shows the many ways the conflict shaped a growing sense of national selfhood. Identity more narrowly defined is the subject of Jean O'Brien's *Dispossession by Degrees: Indian Land and Identity in Natick, Massachusetts, 1650–1790* (Cambridge, Mass., 1997).

Several recent books represent an attempt to look at New England Indian affairs outside the realm of official policy and diplomacy. Howard S. Russell's *Indian New England Before the Mayflower* (Hanover, N.H., 1980) is a fine introduction to the material culture and lifeways of New England coastal Algonkins. Students with more anthropological background may find Dean R. Snow's *The Archaeology of New England* (New York, 1980) rewarding. Surely the most arresting and innovative new book in the field is William Cronon's *Changes in the Land: Indians, Colonists, and the Ecology of New England* (New York, 1983). Moving away from the Jennings-Vaughan debate about Indian policy, Cronon takes a penetrating look at how native people used the Northeast's rich natural resources. He then analyzes the impact of English agricultural practices on the landscape. Nearly two decades after its initial publication, Cronon's book remains lively and challenging. To gain some comparative perspective on events in the Northeast, students will find Frederic W. Gleach's *Powhatan's World and Colonial Virginia: A Conflict of Cultures* (Lincoln, Nebr., 1997) very helpful.

Students with an eye for native American art and material culture will be interested in looking at the illustrated catalogs of several important museum exhibitions. T. J. Brasser, ed., "Bo'jou, Neejee!" Profiles of Canadian Indian Art (Ottawa, 1976), J. C. H. King, ed., *Thunderbird and Lightening: Indian Life of Northeastern North America, 1600–1900* (London, 1982), and Evan M. Maurer, ed., *The Native American Heritage: A Survey of North American Indian Art* (Chicago, 1977) are all of great value. While somewhat outside the geographical and chronological scope of this essay, Carolyn Gilman's *Where Two Worlds Meet: The Great Lakes Fur Trade* (St. Paul, Minn., 1982) is so splendid in its scholarship and photography that it deserves the widest possible audience.

Chapter 2 ❧
Mutual Distrust and Mutual Dependency

Indian-White Relations in the Era of the Anglo-French Wars for Empire, 1689–1763

Dwight L. Smith

*A*t the close of the seventeenth century, mainland British North America consisted of twelve colonies spread along the Atlantic coastline from New Hampshire to South Carolina. Georgia would be established some three decades later. Roughly half of the colonies—Massachusetts, Connecticut, New York, Virginia, North Carolina, South Carolina, and Georgia—had charter-defined boundaries that extended their territorial jurisdiction westward into Indian lands in the North American interior. In New England, New York also claimed present-day Vermont, and Maine was part of Massachusetts. The British colonies were encircled to the north and west by the French in the Maritimes, the St. Lawrence Valley, the Great Lakes, and the trans-Appalachian interior, and to the west and south by the Spanish in the lower Mississippi Valley and Florida.

Forces of change were in process by the late seventeenth century that would substantially redraw the political boundaries of North America. In 1689, when Protestants William and Mary ascended the throne of England against the wishes of France's Catholic king, Louis XIV, war erupted in which the three North American colonial powers—England, France, and Spain—became antagonists. From then until 1763, this and the three other wars involved their empires in varying degrees. The second war, ending in 1713, expanded the British empire by pushing the French out of the Hudson Bay country, Acadia (Nova Scotia), and Newfoundland in Canada. The fourth and final war, the most consequential to the peoples of North America, was launched over Anglo-French territorial rivalry in the Pennsylvania wilderness. At its conclusion in 1763, the map was redrawn to erase all French claims to the continent, with Great Britain now having treaty title to North America from Hudson Bay to the Gulf of Mexico and from the Atlantic Ocean to the Mississippi River. Except for Russian activity in Alaska and the far Northwest, the rest of the continent remained part of Spain's empire.

In these tumultuous decades between 1689 and 1763, what, then, was the situation with respect to the North American Indians as the English were push-

René-Robert Cavalier, Sieur De La Salle, shown with Indian guides, proclaiming the French empire in America. Library of Congress #LC-USZ62-15933

ing their colonies from enclaves along the Atlantic coast into the interior of the continent as far west a the Mississippi? How and why were various groups of Native American people involved in these imperial wars? How did Indians respond to these events? Were Indians united in their reactions? Was the Indian situation improved or worsened as a consequence of these wars? What was the relationship between the respective colonial governments and the Indians, and between the British government and the Indians? At ground level, did accommodations between Indians and white colonists emerge as each sought to carry out their daily lives? Finally, who shaped and controlled colonial American Indian policy?

As with much of post-Columbian Indian history, many student readers can best understand what is known within the framework of white history. Era by era, period by period, it is not easy to generalize, for the history of Indian-white relations in what became the United States reveals a relationship in a constant state of flux, with some policies succeeding, others failing, and still others phasing in and out. It is as if continuous experimentation was going on trying to find solutions to what white Americans would for nearly 300 years refer to as the "Indian problem." Frequently British and then American Indian policy was formulated and implemented under the assumption that all Indian peoples were culturally similar. And usually all such policy was formulated from the white rather than the Native perspective. And all too often, political considerations, misguided humanitarian conceptions, avarice and greed, or other human failings shaped Indian policy. Finally there was, as always the discrepancy, sometimes great, between policy and practice, with very little awareness, understanding, or concern for the consequences. These things make it exceedingly difficult to chronicle and assess any period of Indian-white history. The eighteenth century is no exception.

It should be noted that the British established their thirteen mainland colonies over a span of 125 years. For much of that time the colonies were better able to maintain communications with England than with one another. Therefore it was not until about mid-eighteenth century that intercolonial considerations carried much import. Hence, as in other matters prior to that time, each colony tended to formulate its own policies concerning the Indians, with varying results in their implementation. At the same time, except for instructions in specific cases concerning Indian relations, there was no British imperial or national policy. With variable action, reaction, and perception on the part of both Indians and whites, the overall picture may be likened to a vast jigsaw puzzle whose hundreds of pieces seldom fit together in part and never totally to form the entire picture. Indeed, to complicate things further, the pieces themselves often changed in configuration. Despite this chaotic confusion, it is possible to chronicle the course of Indian-white relations during the first half of the eighteenth century to the point where meaningful generalizations can be made and some perspective on historical trends discerned.

Aside from the search for the Northwest Passage, an all-water route across the continent to the Pacific Ocean and on to the riches of the Far East, Europeans were motivated to explore and control the newfound North American continent by the immediate compulsion to exploit the land's rich natural resources. Gold, silver, and precious stones at first, and then other natural commodities such as the soil, timber, naval stores, furs, game, and fish, commonly sparked the Europeans' avarice. From first contact with white people, the Native peoples of North America aided and abetted, deterred and discouraged, and benefited or suffered from the newcomers' commercial pursuits.

Of the European peoples who came to the shores of North America, only the English, who also engaged in utilizing nature's bounty to their own commercial advantage, came primarily to settle and to farm. While the Indians gave Europeans basic training in wilderness survival and helped them to establish themselves on their newly occupied lands, the increasing success of the white venture soon placed the Indians's very survival in jeopardy. Rapidly Europeans began to perceive Indians as obstacles in their seemingly insatiable drive to exploit natural resources for profit and to acquire more land. All of this, at first, hopelessly confused the Indians, whose cultural conditioning held that land was a communal entity that no one could possibly "own." Naturally, this stood in sharp contrast to the European concept of private property. Nevertheless, as whites began to gain the upper hand throughout increasing acreage of the continent, they imposed their concept of land ownership on the Indians, whether or not they understood it, and whether or not they could reconcile themselves to it. Even as whites relied on Indians in survival and trade matters and used them for labor or military services whenever that seemed feasible, whites made very little effort to reconcile cultural differences or to accommodate themselves to Indian culture or needs, and otherwise considered tribes as stumbling blocks to white progress into the "wilderness."

In the seventeenth century English settlers had pushed westward beyond their original seaboard beachheads, occupied the coastal lowlands, and then started to establish farms in the upland area beyond the fall lines of the rivers. By one means or another, the Indians were largely displaced, reduced in number, or forced into westward retreat to the extent that the English agriculturists gained control of much formerly tribal lands. The Appalachian Mountains might well be considered as the effective western border of the English colonies by 1800. By this time, trans-Appalachia had become the stronghold of displaced Indian tribes, some hostile to the tide of westward progressing English settlement and some friendly to the French, who regarded the heartland as their vast fur-trading domain. To a lesser extent, the Spanish factor with tribes and American colonials was present in the Floridas and along the Gulf coast. While oversimplified, this is the essential picture in the closing years of the seventeenth century.

In the European nations' contest for control of North America Indians played roles of varying significance and consequence. They were certainly more than interested bystanders. Often they were direct participants in this imperial struggle. Always they had much at stake—their survival and future. As the European powers moved into the continent's interior and tried to control it, the tribes were forced to assess, and usually reassess, their policies regarding the Europeans.

Besides the magnetic attraction of vast stretches of fertile land pulling colonial farmers westward, another principal force in Euro-Indian relations was the fur trade. The increasing demand for furs in Europe and the profits to be gained from that trade brought Indians and whites into economic interdependency, albeit not one strong enough in the long run to counteract the displacement of tribes in the wake of advancing white settlement. Moreover, the competition for furs and the resulting decline of the fur-bearing animal population exacerbated bitter rivalry among the competing Indian groups. This in turn made it ever more difficult for the many tribes to present a united front against whites in the process of moving the colonial agricultural frontier line.

The North

European penetration into the interior of the continent resulted in shifting tribal locations and loyalties. Except for precise moments or dates, only generalizations will serve to designate tribal locations, many of which changed frequently over time.

In the North, the Indian population was composed of the Iroquois Confederacy and various loosely related Algonquian tribes. Intra-Algonquian hostility was all too common, and the Iroquois-Algonquian rivalry was a bitter and longstanding one. The Iroquois Confederacy by virtue of its cohesiveness and its location figured prominently and actively in the affairs of the northern British colonies and the French Canadians. The Cayuga, Mohawk, Oneida, Onondaga, and Seneca, five powerful tribes occupying the Mohawk and Hudson River valleys in present-day New York, the most feasible routes out to the Great Lakes country, had forged their defensive alliance in the sixteenth century. Tribal representatives in council made the key decisions of peace and war for the Confederacy, but each of the five tribes retained some autonomy. Later, in 1711, the Tuscarora, another linguistically related tribe, moved up from the South to join the Confederacy. The Six Nations, as the Confederacy came to be known, ably defended their homeland against all threats, Indian and white alike. They further tried, with remarkable success, to subjugate or destroy potential Native rivals, including other non-Confederation Iroquoian tribes like the Huron and the Erie.

An accident of geography had thrust the Iroquois into the midst of the European imperial rivalry, the Five Nations flanked by the English on the east and by the French on the north and west. In the early 1600s the Iroquois had become the middlemen for the New Netherland colony's Dutch traders along the Hudson River. Since guns were a principal trade item, the Iroquois Confederacy soon gained a crucial technological advantage over its French-backed Algonquian and Huron enemies. After England conquered New Netherland in 1664, the English came to similar commercial terms with the Iroquois. The French in Canada, with the fur trade as their principal economic base, moved to establish trading posts over great wilderness distances in order to connect French posts in the St. Lawrence Valley with those in the Mississippi Valley. As had the Indians long since traveled, the French used portages from the rivers flowing northward into the Great Lakes, such as the Maumee in Ohio, to those flowing southward into the Mississippi and its tributaries, such as the Wabash in Indiana, as their communications and supply lifeline to connect the extremities of their North American empire.

The Iroquois Confederacy launched wars in the seventeenth century to challenge the French and their Indian allies' domination of the Great Lakes–country fur trade, as well as the French penetration of the Mississippi Valley. In 1684, at the urging of the colonial governor of New York, the Iroquois again lashed out against the French and their Indian allies, with assaults so devastating that they even threatened the very French presence in Canada along the St. Lawrence. When King Louis XIV sought to save his colonial empire, and later when his successor tried to expand it, England moved to thwart France's plans, thus triggering four wars for empire between 1689 and 1763, fought mainly in Europe but also in North American theaters among the French, the English, and, to a lesser extent, the Spanish.

The Iroquois Wars broadened into King William's War (1689–1697), the first of the four imperial wars. The French became more generous with their trade goods so as to counter English competition with the tribes of the Great Lakes region. After rebuilding their disintegrating Indian alliances, the French

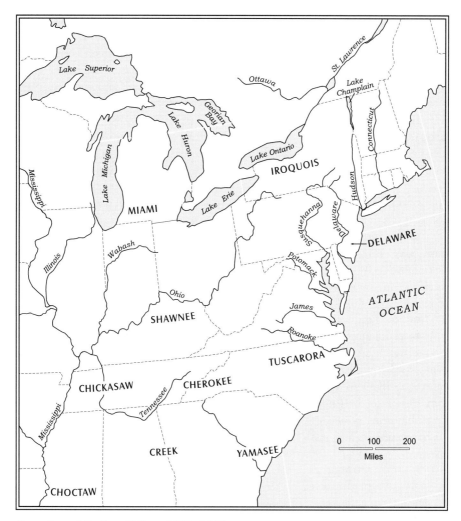

Location of Indian Tribes, 1689–1783

raided backwoods settlements of New England and New York. The attacks had little long-term strategic effects, but they did serve to convince the otherwise divided English colonies to cooperate somewhat in the war effort against the French and Indian enemies to the north. The Treaty of Ryswick ending King William's War was an indecisive arrangement whereby the English and French gave up any gains of the conflict, reaffirming the prewar territorial status.

By the close of King William's War in 1697, the Iroquois came to the conclusion that to continue the fur-trade wars and to take part further in the French-English imperial struggle were exercises in futility. Thereafter the Six Nations adopted a policy of armed neutrality as their stance in the French-English struggle, of political manipulation rather than armed aggression with neighboring tribes, and of peace with tribes removed from the lands over which they claimed hegemony. Surviving until the American Revolution, this policy assured the Confederacy the balance of power and brought them commercial prosperity.

The Iroquois Confederacy became rather astute in its diplomatic duplicity, playing one power against the other. At times the French believed the Iroquois were on their side, at other times on the side of their English enemies. Similarly, the English sometimes viewed the Iroquois as pro-English, sometimes as pro-French. Consequently, both European powers proffered political and economic concessions to the Confederation to try to maintain Iroquois neutrality. When the competing European powers occasionally departed from this basic policy and forged alliances with the Iroquois, they were almost always disappointed.

The Ohio country, situated between the English and French colonial positions, was a no man's-land of political sovereignty. The Iroquois asserted jurisdiction over it by virtue of conquest and, since the seventeenth century used it as their personal hunting grounds. In time the Ohio country became the residence of other tribes, mostly Algonquians, whose status was political subordination to the Iroquois Confederation, a status the French and the English both recognized. In 1744 an alliance was worked out between the English and the Six Nations. The Iroquois appointed local officials and assigned certain tracts to the dependent tribes. As the English pushed their trade initiative into the Ohio Valley, the Iroquois and the resident Algonquian tribes, even French-oriented tribes like the Miami, were drawn to the English traders and their goods. With Iroquois permission, English trading posts and traders expanded in the Ohio country. Ominously, English speculators and settlers were covetously eyeing the western country. The crown even granted a 200,000-acre tract to a company to fortify and establish a settlement of 200 families.

The French believed the Six Nations had overextended themselves and proceeded to challenge the English-Iroquois threat to their St. Lawrence to Mississippi Valley lifeline. Posting claim to the Ohio country in 1749, the French duly warned the English traders and Indians to respect French hegemony in the area, an admonition that served neither to frighten the merchants away nor intimidate the Indians. The French response was direct and decisive. In 1752, they destroyed the principal British post in the heart of the Miami trading area in what is today southwestern Ohio and literally ate the local pro-Iroquois chief with great ceremony. Two years later the French seized the forks of the Ohio River, at the present site of Pittsburgh, and there constructed Fort Duquesne, the southern anchor in a chain of forts stretching northward to Lake Erie that the French anticipated would help them control the Ohio country and the Ohio River valley. The British and colonials from Virginia and Pennsylvania, however, disagreed. The governor of Virginia sent a young officer in the Virginia militia, George Washington, to challenge the French at Fort Duquesne in 1754. Fighting erupted and quickly escalated into the fourth imperial war, one the American colonists called the French and Indian War.

The Iroquois tried, unsuccessfully, to regain their lost leverage between the French and English, but neutrality no longer worked for them; neither did joining war parties of one side and then the other under the rationale that they were trying to defend their lands. The English hoped for a firm alliance with the Iroquois Confederacy, but did not get it. At the war's end, the French were ousted and the English occupied posts within the Iroquois sphere of influence. The Iroquois position and power had now been seriously compromised. Whether the former role of the Iroquois in wilderness diplomacy could ever be resumed remained, for the time being, an open question.

Pennsylvania

For awhile, the Pennsylvania Indian situation was an exception among the British colonies' relations with Indians. As has been noted, the Iroquois Confederacy and the Algonquian tribes it sought to incorporate into its sphere of influence dominated much of the chronicle of Indians in the northern colonies during the first two-thirds of the eighteenth century. The situation in the colony of Pennsylvania presented a notable exception to this generalization, particularly in the early years after its founding.

When the Quakers moved into the area that became Pennsylvania to establish their colony in the early 1680s, among the Indians they found there were the Delaware, a tribe that had been subjugated by the Iroquois Confederation. The Delaware regularly paid tribute to their Native overlords and were forbidden to wage war. William Penn made a land purchase treaty with them. So long as the Quakers dominated the Pennsylvania colony's government, sincere efforts were made to treat the Indians in the spirit of brotherhood. The Quakers were generous with money and gifts, and they acquired Indian lands by treaty and purchase rather than by conquest and diplomatic subterfuge.

By the mid-1720s, as the components in this happy arrangement began to change, erosion of Pennsylvania-Indian relations set in. The Iroquois overlords of the Delaware sought and got an increasing share of the presents and other considerations dispensed by the colonial government. Now the Shawnee and other tribes to the west of the Delaware objected to the stepped-up acquisitive intrusion of the Iroquois, as well as to the westward advance of white settlement. While the Quakers continued to practice their altruism, the non-Quaker proprietors who succeeded William Penn increasingly favored the Iroquois over the other Indian groups.

Pennsylvania's expanding involvement in the fur trade, the French competition factor, the dispute with Virginia over the ownership of the forks of the Ohio River country, and the geopolitics of the French-English struggle all made it increasingly difficult for the Pennsylvania colonial government to continue its peaceful policy with the Indians. It is noteworthy that prior to 1754 when the English had attempted to dislodge the French from their presence in the Ohio

River headwaters country, thus triggering the French and Indian War, no consequential Indian raid or attack on a frontier settlement had occurred on Pennsylvania soil.

The South

During the seventeenth century, the southern coastal tribes, like those in New England, had been crushed, subjected, or pushed aside. The westward-advancing English frontier, once it pushed beyond the coastal tribes, had to deal next with the Indians of the interior. As the English and French battled in the closing decade of the eighteenth century, the southern colonial frontier was not the scene of Euro-Indian involvement during King William's War and so remained relatively calm during that conflict. The Florida-based Spanish, because they were then an English ally, refrained from attacking the southern colonies from bases in Florida and along the Gulf of Mexico. The French presence was too remote from the English southern colonial frontier to cause any serious friction during King William's War.

This situation changed in the eighteenth century, as southern Indians found themselves in increasingly difficult positions as European rivalry for control of the interior grew in magnitude and intensity. Early in that century, the French established posts along the Gulf of Mexico coast, from them they hoped to increase trade and influence with the lower Mississippi Valley Indians. Moreover, they sought to link their new Gulf posts with their positions in the Great Lakes and St. Lawrence Valley. The neutrality of the Iroquois Confederacy in the north combined with a new alliance with the Florida-based Spanish, also encouraged France to pursue the goal of completely encircling the English colonies based on the Atlantic coast.

As the English-French rivalry once more exploded into war, the southern colonial frontier became a theater in this second conflict, known as Queen Anne's War (1702–1713). The French, seeking to stem the tide of westward-looking American settlers and the English commercial advance into the headwaters of the Gulf-flowing streams and lower Mississippi Valley, tried to forge a Franco-Indian military alliance among the four dominant southern interior tribes. In this they were only partially successful. Two of the four tribes, the Choctaw and the Creek, joined the French because they hoped to thwart the activities of Charleston, South Carolina-based traders who had penetrated their lower trans-Appalachian homelands. The third tribe, the Chickasaw, as on previous occasions, rejected French overtures and actively supported English efforts. The Chickasaw thus effectively served as a counterforce to the pro-French Choctaw and Creek. The Cherokee, the fourth dominant southern Indian tribe, simply declined the French overtures. By the close of Queen Anne's War, the French position in North America had suffered severely by the loss of the Hudson Bay area, Newfoundland, and Acadia in Canada, a portent of French erosion and decline in the New World.

Simultaneously, the Tuscarora on the Carolina-Virginia frontier were chafing from exploitation encouraged by Charleston merchants. To compound their woes, bands of traders and Indians made raids into Tuscarora towns to acquire slaves. The tribe was also losing some of its choice lands to colonial settlers. In 1711, the Tuscarora turned on settlers on the Carolina frontier with such fury that it was two years before an intercolonial militia combined with Indian forces could defeat them. Nevertheless, by the time hostilities ended, the Tuscarora lands had been devastated, the tribe had sustained heavy casualties, and hundreds of Tuscarora were taken prisoner. The remnants fled northward to join with their Iroquois cousins in their New York-based coalition: the Iroquois Confederacy was henceforth known as the Six Nations.

Close on the heels of the Tuscarora War, which presented such a serious threat to whites in North Carolina and adjacent Virginia had a devastating impact on the Tuscarora, a conflict erupted in South Carolina. Its seriousness would force the colonials to restructure their policies bearing on their relations with the Indians. This was the Yamasee War. The Yamasee, a Muskhogean-speaking tribe, lived in northeastern Florida. Dissatisfied with the Spanish environment and policies there, they had lately moved into proximity of the South Carolina frontier. Not long thereafter they came to feel their position in their new territory untenable as well: they sustained shoddy treatment from traders, and they were pressured and unnerved by the unremitting penetration of white settlers into areas specifically designated as their own by the Carolina colony. Hoping to improve their relations with the Carolinians, the Yamasee had provided sorely needed manpower and support to colonials in the recent Tuscarora War. But the cumulative and continued abuse over the next four years became more than they could bear. In 1715 the Yamasee rose up in a fury. Neighboring tribes joined them, and the very existence of the colony seemed to hang in the balance. The tide of war turned, however, after the Cherokee joined the side of the Carolinians, which then managed to defeat the Yamasee and their allies.

The principal consequence of these wars was to make the English colonies face the reality of the inadequacy of their defense and trade policies on the southern colonial frontier. Soon they also had to contend with the strengthened Spanish and French influence with the Indians, which increased the threat to their territorial and economic ambitions westward and southward.

With the lower Mississippi Valley a point of contention among France, Spain, and England, the Indians in the region were caught in a position of trying to maintain their own best interests by accommodating themselves to what they perceived to be the predominant European imperial power at any given time. This produced intra- and intertribal rivalry and tensions. Initially to tribes it appeared the French were in the ascendancy. Prospering in the Gulf coastal trade, they had established New Orleans in 1718 and other coastal settlements. French traders and settlers were moving up the coastal rivers into the interior. And when they built a new post in central Alabama among the Creek, French influence became more pronounced. Certain Creek villages in central Georgia actually relocated westward to be closer to the new French outpost. Other Creek, Choctaw, and some lesser tribes closed their villages to English traders. Finally, the Yamasee resumed their attacks on Carolina frontier settlements.

To defend themselves the English seaboard colonies ringed their frontier with fortifications and then began to rebuild their deteriorated relations with the Indians. They won over vacillating tribes with presents, low-priced trade goods, and promised rewards for allegiance. Now the Creek, and even some of the Chickasaw, recognized the advantages of becoming more friendly with the English. There were holdouts to the English blandishments, however, particularly the Yamasee, who remembered their fate at the hands of Anglo Americans in the Yamasee War a decade earlier.

Some tribes, motivated by recent developments, assaulted the French in the South. Unhappy with the administration of a French commander at Fort Rosalie (at present-day Natchez, Mississippi), which along with Fort St. Peter (about seventy-five miles north of Natchez) guarded French settlements along the Mississippi, and increasingly envious of the superior goods other tribes were getting from English traders, the Natchez joined with the Chickasaw in 1729 to annihilate the French garrison and settlements. This sparked the bitter Natchez War of the 1730s, with the French and their Choctaw allies pitted against the tribes of the lower Mississippi Valley. Now the French had been put on the defensive. Taking advantage of this shifting situation, the English successfully established their thirteenth colony, Georgia, in 1733, which had already spread beyond a coastline beachhead when the attacks came. With the Choctaw busy helping the French and with the Cherokee, Creek, and Chickasaw friendly to the English, the Indian assault against this new colony came from the Yamasee. They joined with the Florida-based Spanish in an effort, unsuccessfully, to drive out the Georgians.

In 1744 the third imperial war between Great Britain and France for mastery of eastern North America, King George's War, began. With most of the Indians on the southern frontiers in the English camp, and with the Spanish and French threats to their colonies minimized, the region witnessed only minor skirmishing. Most of the European activity in the South concerned gaining Indian alignment. The Chickasaw helped the English by making it difficult for the French to use the lower Mississippi for communications between the St. Lawrence Valley and the Gulf of Mexico. And the Cherokee sided with the English in their attacks on pro-French Creek factions and Choctaw. When this third Anglo-French imperial war ended with the Treaty of Aix-la-Chapelle, no land in America changed hands, and the Indians remained pragmatists in their allegiances, espousing whatever posture seemed at the moment the most advantageous.

During the early 1750s, in the aftermath of the indecisive King George's War, the English and the French increased their efforts to enlist Indian assistance. For the English, Indian aid was judged as crucial in dislodging the French from the interior and opening up the area to increased trade opportunities. For the French, who were equally as determined to contain their English rivals east of the Appalachian Mountains, Indian assistance became even more crucial. The French labored hard to mend their fences with the southern Indians. They made peace with the Chickasaw and established friendly relations with the Cherokee and Creek. These diplomatic moves, along with the traditional Choctaw support, put the French in a presumed position of strength. And when the French and Indian War exploded in 1754, the preponderance of the Indian factor was either neutral or weighted on the side of the French throughout the southern interior. The notable exception to this was the Chickasaw, who had come to believe that their English connection was more advantageous than their recent friendly relations with the French. The Chickasaw therefore pushed westward to occupy the lower Mississippi country. In 1752, after failing in this last of three attempts to dislodge them, the French withdrew from the area. Effectively they had lost their control over the lower end of their mid-continent lifeline. The French and Indian War ended in 1763. By terms of the Treaty of Paris, France ceded Canada and virtually all of its North American territory east of the Mississippi to Great Britain.

After the Wars for Empire

The triumph of the English and the demise of the French as a New World power did not however signal a new era for the Indians in British North America. The English had long since learned that neither the wilderness nor the Indians could be exploited and controlled to their expectations. British Indian policy had long been neglected, confused, and contradictory, resulting in a mixture of successes and failures. The Indians were important factors in Euro-American affairs, they played roles in intercolonial rivalries, and their mere presence figured in English penetration into the North American wilderness. At various times the Indians were aggressors. Anglo-Indian relations at the close of the French and Indian War were as volatile as they had ever been.

Meanwhile Anglo-Cherokee relations along the southern frontier were becoming uneasy, this after many years of reasonably good relations that had brought them under English influence, even though the French traders had continued to deal with them to a limited extent. Indeed, trade rivalries among the English mainland colonies helped set the stage for a serious threat to Great Britain. Enjoying a near monopoly of trade with the western Indians, the Charleston merchants perceived an increasing challenge by mercantile interests in the other southern colonies. The price of deerskins and trade goods had become a matter of serious contention between the Cherokee hunters and the Charleston traders. When the traders tried to dictate terms, the Cherokee invited the business of merchants from other colonies.

Anxious to enlist Cherokee fighting men against French-backed Indians in the Ohio Valley during the French and Indian War, the English had agreed to build and garrison posts in Cherokee country as protection against French and Creek raiders in the absence of the Cherokee warriors. This was a mistake. Not only had the English stepped-up their interference in Cherokee affairs, but aggressive traders increasingly exploited the Cherokee, and frontier settlement steadily encroached on their territory.

Homeward-bound Cherokee warriors who had completed their service in the British army in the Ohio Valley quarreled with settlers along the Virginia and Carolina frontiers, sometimes stealing horses. Frontierspeople and Cherokee clashed, with casualties on both sides. Attempts to defuse the tension failed as mutual misunderstandings worsened the situation. In 1759, when the whites took Cherokee hostages and sent an armed force toward their villages, the Cherokee War erupted. With each side wearying of war as it escalated and dragged on, a truce was struck in 1760. But the next year a colonial-British-Indian force assaulted and wreaked systematic havoc on Cherokee settlements and their crops. Lacking the means of continuing resistance, the Cherokee agreed to a peace pact and surrendered a large tract of their territory bordering on the white frontier. Beyond the treaty specifics, the main effect of the treaty was to solidify Cherokee hatred of the English.

While the Cherokee War raged along the southern frontier, the Indians to the north of the Ohio River were becoming increasingly unhappy with the English, who were now presuming to be their masters and protectors. With the French removed as a consequence of the recent French and Indian War, the Indians could no longer bargain for the best concessions by playing the English against the French. With French competition for their trade and support gone, the English traders now dictated the terms for doing business. Furthermore, the Indians could no longer get supplies—particularly gunpowder for subsistence hunting—on credit from the English posts. Certain tribes charged that they were being denied credit as punishment for their anti-British efforts in the late war. Whether or not these allegations were true, British appropriations for Indian affairs were reduced and the practice of giving gifts to tribes was suspended.

Indian discontent was fueled by rumors that the English were bent on exterminating the Indians. War had already reduced their ranks by serious proportions and Indians' fears had been confirmed when the British army used germ warfare and dogs against them. The 1763 smallpox blanket incident that occurred at Fort Pitt is the most famous example of this practice. Speculators were already spying out their lands and explaining that whites by the hundreds eagerly anticipated moving westward. French traders who lingered in the region whispered to the Indians that French expulsion was only temporary and that their countrymen were coming back in force to help them overthrow their English oppressors. A Delaware mystic was proclaiming that if the Indians would renounce their cultural dependence on the whites and return to the ways of life of their ancestors they could regain control of their homelands and their own destiny.

Unrest and discontent spread through the tribes to the north of the Ohio River, especially among those in the vicinity of the several posts the English occupied as they gained control of the country from the French. One of the interesting debates about frontier history is whether what happened next was carefully planned and masterminded by Pontiac, an Ottawa chief. It has typically been called "Pontiac's Conspiracy," but revisionist historians are no longer willing to accept such a label. What is beyond dispute is that on May 7, 1763, Pontiac led an attack on British forces at Fort Detroit from his nearby village. When the stronghold did not capitulate, the Indians ravaged adjacent farms and laid siege to the stronghold.

As the news spread through the wilderness, other tribes sought convenient targets; fierce and bloody warfare engulfed the western frontier in an effort to forestall the British presence. Along with Detroit, only Forts Pitt and Niagara escaped destruction in this widespread but not coordinated resistance movement, though even these posts were seriously threatened. Military expeditions relieved the besieged and crushed the movement. Now the Great Lakes tribes, so buoyed by their initial victories, were demoralized.

The British government had been wrestling with the problem of the Indians in the western wilderness even before the end of the French and Indian War. Traders and speculators and land-hungry pioneers were pressuring for permission to move full force into the trans-Appalchian country. In the summer of 1763, the government received the news of Pontiac's attack and the turn of events on the American frontier, and the king issued a royal proclamation that ordered a demarcation line between white settlers and Indian lands following the crest of the Appalachian Mountains from Maine to Georgia. Any settlers west of the line were to remove to its east, and the private purchase of Indian lands was forbidden. This, presumably, would reduce tension and Indian apprehension of American colonists pushing westward onto their lands. Only traders with licenses issued by colonial governors or military commanders could do business with the Indians. Perhaps the Indians would appreciate the good intentions of the British and some measure of control over the traders would lessen their malpractices. Administratively, the proclamation also established colonies out of the real estate gained in the late war: Quebec from the French, and East and West Florida from the Spanish. These were opened to American colonials in the hopes of deflecting settlement from the prevailing westward orientation, thus relieving pressure and reducing friction with the trans-Appalachian Indians.

In the midst of these tumultuous years, sometimes a different type of attitude and relationship emerged between the colonists and the Indians as they sought to carry on their daily lives. It is now recognized that from the early encounters of Europeans with the New World's aboriginal peoples, whenever interpenetration occurred, the interaction of these diverse or distinctly different societies did not always, or necessarily, result in violence or geopolitical maneuvering. Scholars are increasingly identifying examples of mutual cultural accommodation and modification. In some areas this was of such extent as to mark the emergence of what is sometimes now called "the middle ground," where the challenge of living between competing empires and colonies was confronted. Instead of at tribal and imperial levels, individuals and small groups of Indians and whites cooperatively established their own mixed ethnic villages where they met and traded and socialized. Gift exchange, calumet ceremony, and other rituals and ceremonies generally replaced coercion. Middle ground situations functioned with some immediate benefit to the parties concerned, but their influence had little effect on the course of Indian-white relations in eighteenth century British North America.

Throughout American colonial history, Indian-white relations remained confused and often unsatisfactory to all parties concerned, in part simply because each colony exercised its own Indian policy, thereby lessening the chances of the success of any one and confusing efforts to establish a British or national Indian policy. Occasionally, intercolonial efforts met with some limited success, but the most promising effort to establish a unified or national Indian policy resulted from the interests and efforts of Edmond Atkin. As a successful Charleston merchant and member of the governor's council of South Carolina, Atkin had become very knowledgeable about the Indians and was expert in Indian-white relations. In a long report, which he presented to the Board of Trade in London in the early 1750s, Atkin outlined a plan for the management of Indian affairs. He gave high praise to the French system of Indian control through the judicious use of presents, the ready availability of gunsmiths to keep their knives and hatchets sharpened and their guns in good repair, and a centralized administration that would not tolerate injustice to the Indians. He severely censured British and colonial methods, especially those employed by his own South Carolina. The self-interest of each faction that had dealings with the Indians, whether imperial, colonial, or individual traders, came before the general good. Who were the Indians to believe when rival traders lied about each other? Such continued chaos and mismanagement could only move towards complete alienation of the Indians, persuading them to look to the French for their survival.

Atkin's scheme provided for a detailed administrative hierarchy under a northern and a southern superintendent, an elaborate system of uniform trade regulations, a penurious use of rum, an extensive system of factory-forts, and such other support personnel as interpreters, missionaries, and gunsmiths. In effect, this would nationalize Indian policy. His recommendations were followed somewhat. The British government appointed Atkin as the southern superintendent, and Sir William Johnson as his northern counterpart. Atkin's ideas, however, were beyond his abilities, and he failed to establish a strong southern Indian department. After he died he was replaced in 1761 by John Stuart. While Johnson, on the other hand, was able and astute, his success was not matched by the realization of the centralized, national Indian policy that Atkin had envisioned.

Indian-white relations in eighteenth century colonial British North America were not easy. Neither the Indians nor the whites spoke with one voice. Inter- and intratribal, inter- and intraIndian confederation, inter- and intracolonial, private versus public white sectors, and international considerations, interests, and forces all affected Indian-white relations in the years 1689-1763. Whatever happened in those eight decades, one must take these many factors into consideration.

Britain's absolute triumph over the French in 1763 in eastern North America proved to be short lived. And, no matter what the maps delineated or which flag flew over them, the Indians were engulfed in an uneven struggle with a white culture that had the resources and the will to predominate. Based on their troubled history, the eighteenth-century Indians must have viewed the future with apprehension, a mixture of dubious optimism and resigned futility.

Suggested Reading

Anyone who wishes to flesh out the details of Indian-white relations in British North America between 1701 and 1763 should progress from the general to the specific. If one's understanding of colonial American history is wanting or incomplete, the reader should first gain a survey knowledge of that history. I would suggest reading appropriate chapters in all three types of books in this consecutive order: any standard United States history textbook; a history of the American frontier; and a survey history of the American Indians, such as Arrell Morgan Gibson, *The American Indian: Prehistory to the Present* (Lexington, Mass., 1980). Gibson's text can profitably be supplemented with Roger L. Nichols, *Indians in the United States and Canada: A Comparative History* (Lincoln, Nebr., 1998). As the international wars of these years are so much a part of the setting for Indian-white relations, the reader will find a convenient summary in Howard H. Peckham, *The Colonial Wars, 1689–1762* (Chicago, 1964).

Building on the general knowledge that such references offer, it is profitable to move into a more specialized and detailed look at the topic. Three excellent monographs are essential requirements for this: Douglas Edward Leach, *The Northern Colonial Frontier, 1607–1763* (New York, 1966); W. Stitt Robinson, *The Southern Colonial Frontier, 1607–1763* (Albuquerque, N. Mex., 1979); and a similar volume from another vantagepoint, William J. Eccles, *The Canadian Frontier, 1534–1760* (New York, 1969). The essays in Howard Peckham and Charles Gibson, eds., *Attitudes of Colonial Powers Toward the American Indian* (Salt Lake City, Utah, 1969) will be of interest. Appropriate chapters in William C. Sturtevant, ed., *Handbook of North American Indians*, vol. 4: *History of Indian White Relations* (Washington, 1988) also are helpful.

Three provocative monographs reflect some current revisionist thinking. In his forceful *Empire of Fortune: Crowns, Colonies, and Tribes in the Seven Years War in America* (New York, 1988), Francis Jennings reflects on Indian-white relations in eighteenth-century colonial British America. Richard White offers another perspective in his *The Middle Ground: Indians, Empires, and Republics in the Great*

Lakes Region, 1650–1815 (New York, 1991). Michael N. McConnell examines a major defensive Indian restructuring occasioned by the successes of the geopolitical and colonial side of the Indian–white relations equation in his *A Country Between: The Upper Ohio Valley and Its Peoples, 1724–1774* (Lincoln, Nebr., 1992).

One can identify the published literature in two fundamental ways. First, any one of the items in this brief list will cite the sources of information its author has consulted. Second, standard bibliographies identify much of the published literature. I highly recommend Francis Paul Prucha, *A Bibliographical Guide to the History of Indian-White Relations in the United States* (Chicago, 1977) and its supplement, *Indian-White Relations in the United States: A Bibliography of Works Published 1975–1980* (Lincoln, Nebr., 1982). Another suggestion: Arlene B. Hirschfelder, Mary Gloyne Byler, and Michael A. Dorris, *Guide to Research on North American Indians* (Chicago, 1983) offers a helpful annotated bibliography of a selection of some 1,000 books, articles, and government documents.

While much more than is generally believed has been published about Indian-white relations in British North America in the eighteenth century, much more remains to be done, both to add to our present knowledge and possibly to invite revisionist interpretation.

Chapter 3 ✒
Facing Off

Indian-Spanish Rivalry in the Greater Southwest, 1528–1821

David La Vere

*E*verything had gone horribly wrong. The fabulous riches discovered by Spanish explorers in Mexico, Central America, and South America had inspired a search for more, and in 1528, Pañfilo de Narvaez landed with a small army on the west coast of the Florida Peninsula to continue the pursuit. But Spain's Florida "conquest" could only be considered a miserable failure. Indian attacks picked off soldier after soldier. Relief ships never arrived. Starvation set in. Attrition took its toll. In a desperate effort to get back to New Spain (Mexico), the survivors built crude boats that they paddled west along the Gulf of Mexico coast. Storms and miscalculations further reduced their number. One by one the small boats sank until the last two washed ashore on the upper Texas coast near Galveston Bay in November 1528, spilling Álvar Núñez Cabeza de Vaca and his nearly dead companions into the arms of the Karankawa Indians. So began the long rivalry between the Indians of the American Southwest and the peoples of Europe.

The strangers who had suddenly appeared among them hardly awed the Karankawas. Certainly, they did not think them gods. Rather, they pitied them, rescued them, and nursed them back to health. But when, after weeks, the Spaniards had done nothing but eat, the Karankawas, like any exasperated hosts, decided to make their boarders work for their dinner. The Europeans complained, characterizing such treatment as abuse, and in time, a few of the remaining survivors decided to trudge back to New Spain. In all, their challenging trek—from landfall in Texas to homecoming in Mexico—took seven years and only four Spaniards lived to complete it, Cabeza de Vaca being one of them. During their years in Texas, the Indians killed a few of the Spaniards. Some allowed themselves to become Karankawa slaves, while others simply gave up and died. For his part, Cabeza de Vaca experienced amazing things and learned how to live in the Indian world. Although he, too, grumbled that the Karankawas had mistreated him, he spent a substantial amount of time as a trader between the coastal Karankawas and the Caddos, Attakapas, and Coahuiltecans farther inland. He also became a formidable shaman, known for his healing powers and recognized as a religious leader, with hundreds of Indian followers trailing him back to Mexico City. In many ways, Cabeza de Vaca's sojourn in Texas was a microcosm of the Spanish experience in the Indian Southwest: the Spanish arrived in the land with visions of its potential profits and blessings, but, despite their few successes, they soon realized the land was one in which Indian power and diplomacy matched that of Spain, one in which Europeans had no choice but to work within the dictates of Indian society.

By the time Cabeza de Vaca washed ashore at Galveston Island in 1528, the Indian peoples of the American Southwest had already passed their "Classical Period" and were living in what might be termed their "Middle Ages." Between the tenth and fourteenth centuries, the Anasazi, Mogollon, and Hohokam cultures of present-day New Mexico and Arizona flourished. They cut irrigation canals for their cornfields; constructed immense, multistoried apartment buildings such as Pueblo Bonito and Chaco Canyon; worshipped in underground temples called *kivas;* and created an ornate style of pottery that rivaled anything produced in Europe. At the same time, on the eastern side of the Southern Plains, the cultures of the Caddos and other peoples of the Mississippian tradition equaled the Anasazi in sophistication and splendor. From the Arkansas River in the north to the Red, Sabine, and Neches Rivers in the South, the Caddos and Wichitas founded cities of haystack-shaped houses surrounded by enormous cornfields and ruled by priest-chiefs who professed lineage back to the moon and stars. To solidify their link to the gods, the Mississippians built gigantic earthen temple mounds, which placed the priest-chief physically closer to his celestial kin. By 1400, for reasons not altogether clear but probably linked to climatic changes, both these great cultures had declined. The Anasazi, Mogollons, and Hohokams abandoned their great houses and dispersed across Arizona and New Mexico to live in small towns the Spanish would later call *pueblos.* The Hopis, Zunis, and all the other peoples referred to as Pueblo Indians, arose out of these cultures. On the eastern border, Caddo and Wichita mound building came to an end, and, like the Pueblos, these groups abandoned their ceremonial centers for smaller, more dispersed villages and towns.

Between these two great civilizations, on the Southern Plains and the Texas coast, lived a host of other Indian nations that could not grow extensive cornfields and relied heavily on hunting and gathering. South of the Caddos, on the upper Texas coast, lived the Attakapas. On the middle coast, between Galveston Island and Matagorda Bay, lived Cabeza de Vaca's Karankawas. On the lower coast and straddling the Rio Grande across South Texas and Northern Mexico, roamed over 300 different bands of peoples collectively known as the Coahuiltecans. On the middle Rio Grande, between its confluence with the Concho River and the site of present-day El Paso, lived the Jumanos. Some Jumano bands hunted buffalo between the Pecos River and Rio Grande, while others lived in flat-roofed adobe houses along the big river, where they grew corn and beans. North of them,

An early Spanish illustration of the "Heathen Seris" who came to the Jesuit missions near the Arizona-Mexico border in the early eighteenth century. Courtesy, Newberry Library

on the upper Rio Grande and Pecos River, spread an arc of Pueblo towns such as Pecos, Taos, Zuni, and Acoma, the latter the oldest permanently occupied town in North America. A few Caddoan and Tonkawa villages lay scattered along the rivers of the Southern Plains, but by 1500, buffalo-hunting Apaches, trudging down the face of the Rockies from Canada, were already pushing them off the plains, or absorbing them into their Apache bands.

Had the Spanish been able to look beyond the outward appearances of the Indians they encountered in North America, they would have comprehended a world not all that different from the one they had known in Europe. Certainly, the Indians were technologically unsophisticated in relation to the Spaniards— they possessed no iron tools or machinery—but in other ways they were similar. The Southwest peoples utilized diplomacy, sending and receiving ambassadors, and had relations with each other that ranged from negotiated alliances to out-right war. Trade was common and far ranging, with Caddo pottery spreading across the American South and Southwest, and Pueblo turquoise and cotton blankets finding their way into East Texas. Warfare could consist of huge battles of regimented warriors as well as lightning-quick raids and ambushes conducted by just a few men. Europeans understood divinely appointed aristocrats and class distinctions and therefore felt comfortable around the Caddo's priest-chiefs and their hierarchical society. Furthermore, Pueblo religious practices, with their priests, altars, chants, and baptism-like head washings, seemed eerily familiar to the Spaniards, who might easily have mistaken *kachinas* for Indian saints.

And the same things that motivated the European settlers—the quest for status and power—drove Indian men. Europeans gained status through the accumulation of goods such as horses, cattle, hides, gold, and money: the more one possessed of these forms of capital, the more one's status grew, which in turn translated into power. Conversely, Indian men gained status through generosity: the more one gave away, the more debts of gratitude one created. By complementing this generosity with displays of bravery, fortitude, and wisdom, one acquired status, even a following. Therefore, while they took slightly different paths to power, Europeans and Indians understood each other on a basic level, and each group tried to manipulate the other.

Rather than a conquering empire of a powerful people over weaker peoples, it may be more accurate to think of the Spanish entry into the American Southwest merely as the migration of a powerful nation into a region already containing powerful nations. And the opportunities to be found in the Southwest only attracted more. That said, the first Spaniards to enter the Southwest after Cabeza de Vaca did so as conquerors. Believing contemporary legends of the existence of cities of gold, in 1540, Francisco Coronado led an expedition of 1,300 Spaniards and Indian allies into Pueblo country. Metal swords and lances, horse-mounted cavalry, a willingness to use deception in his negotiations, and superior military tactics passed down to him from generations of battles against the Moors of Spain and then the Aztecs of Mexico gave Coronado an advantage. Firearms, though highly inaccurate and almost useless as weapons of destruction, produced enough noise and smoke to make them psychologically valuable. Conversely, the Pueblos' un-walled villages and immediate need to defend their wives and children put the Indian defenders at a disadvantage. When the Pueblos resisted Spanish demands for food, shelter, and women, Coronado attacked and rather easily defeated them. Fortunately for the Pueblos, Coronado's expedition moved on in its search for gold, finally reaching the Wichita villages on the Arkansas River in present-day Kansas before returning to Mexico. At the same time that Coronado was crossing the Southern Plains, the remnants of Hernando De Soto's Southeastern expedition were smashing Caddo villages on the Red River. Fearing the rigors of an overland trek back to New Spain, De Soto's men turned around, sacked the Caddos a second time, then marched back to the Mississippi River, built boats, and sailed donwriver and home to Mexico.

Coronado, however, proved merely a foreshadowing for the Pueblos. Juan de Oñate, ordered by Spanish officials to settle and develop the interior of the northern Rio Grande frontier, invaded Pueblo country in 1598 with the express purpose of subjugating the Pueblo peoples to the Spanish Crown. Although the Pueblo city-states resisted this second instrusion, the same advantages and disadvantages prevailed and, after much loss of life, they fell to the Spanish. Now, Oñate founded the Spanish colony of New Mexico and its capital city of Santa Fe, from which the Spanish solidified their control over the Pueblos and tried to expand their power in other directions. The Spanish were very fortunate that the Pueblos lived in settled villages and towns, as this made them much easier to conquer and exploit. Using the *ecomienda,* an institution resembling the old European manorial system, the Spanish divided up Pueblo towns, "giving" choice lands to high-ranking Spaniards. In return for his protection and instruction in Roman Catholic Christianity, the Spanish *ecomendaro* taxed "his" Indians, demanding regular payments of corn or cotton blankets. He could also conscript Indians' labor, making them work on his own farm or ranch for so many days a month. While not exactly slavery, the ecomienda was not far from it, and New the Mexican ecomendaros demanded much from their Indian charges.

Catholic missionaries also benefited from Pueblo urban life. They built churches in virtually every pueblo and stationed a Franciscan padre there to compel the "savages" to accept Roman Catholicism. For the missionaries, Catholicism did not merely mean conversion and attendance at Mass, but the eradication of Indian culture too. Pueblo religion, deemed satanic, had to be uprooted. Consequently, traditional ceremonies were prohibited, shrines destroyed, and Pueblo priests tortured, while Catholic priests burned every mask, kachina, and prayer stick on which they could lay their hands. Additionally, the padres demanded the Indians work for them. Eventually this brought the colonial government and its ecomendaro supporters into conflict with the missionaries. Like male buffaloes, Spanish colonial governors and priests butted heads, while it was the Pueblo grass that got trampled.

On the heels of subjugation came disease, which ravaged Pueblos and all other Indian peoples across the Southwest. Having never before faced eastern hemispheric germs and viruses, to which the Indians possessed no immunities, epidemics of smallpox, diphtheria, measles, mumps, and a host of other ills raced through their communities. Wherever Spaniards and their goods went, disease followed. Just weeks after Cabeza de Vaca washed ashore, he reported a deadly flux among the Karankawas and the Coahuiltecans. And, the situation only grew worse over the next four hundred years. Not a single Indian nation across the Southwest, probably not a single family, was spared the ravages of these diseases, which decimated their populations. As nations and peoples, it made them weaker and less able to stand up to Europeans. It disrupted their societies by removing valuable, productive members. When large numbers of farmers and hunters suddenly died, mass starvation ensued. The loss of warriors, diplomats, and chiefs exposed the nations to raids and invasions, while the death of midwives and healers made it difficult to maintain or replenish their populations. And when disease took shamans and priests before they could pass on their knowledge, then no one knew how to appease the gods or to get to one's home in the afterlife. Some Indian nations, such as many of the Coahuiltecan and Jumano bands, never recovered and disappeared altogether, with only their names scratched on a piece of paper in a Spanish archive to testify that they had ever existed. Fortunately for the Indians, the number of Spanish soldiers and settlers in the Southwest never matched or overwhelmed the much-depleted Indian population.

In addition to encountering new diseases and the effects thereof, the Indians saw their lives quickly changing in many other ways . The horses, cattle, pigs, and sheep that the Spanish brought into the region soon found their way into Pueblo corrals and Pueblo stomachs. Increasing numbers of these animals escaped Spanish pastures or were taken in raids, and the livestock soon diffused out to Indian peoples across the Southwest. Horses became particularly valued. The Spanish knew the great value of horses and soon passed laws prohibiting Indians from riding them, but the Pueblos and other Indians quickly learned how. Horses made warriors more formidable and hunters more productive. Horses could carry or drag much more than could dogs, and they allowed camps to move faster and evade enemies more quickly. They also became status goods, making those who owned them wealthy. Conversely, the constant need for forage meant that bands and camps needed to be smaller and even more mobile. By the end of the seventeenth century, Apaches, Caddos, Wichitas, and Comanches possessed horses, while those Indians who did not certainly wished to. Besides European livestock, wheat, oats, peaches, and watermelons sprang up in Indian fields. In addition, manufactured goods, particularly metal ware, quickly went from being luxuries to necessary parts of Indian life. Iron points and blades soon tipped Indian arrows and lances. Kettles proved much more durable than earthen cookware. Shovels, axes, hoes, and picks made farming more efficient. Indians added cotton and woolen clothes to their wardrobes, while glass beads and metal needles could make virtually any piece of clothing a work of art. And muskets, though still just as inaccurate as ever, became prizes wanted by every warrior in the Southwest. Because of their value and scarcity, manufactured goods, like horses, conferred status to their owner, and to give away these goods generated great obligations of reciprocity bringing the giver much prestige and power. As horses and manufactured goods made their way into the existing trade networks, Indian peoples tried to find ways to acquire a steady supply of them.

One way was through exchange and trade. Taos Pueblo, Pecos Pueblo, and the Jumano village of La Junta de los Rios on the Rio Grande all expanded into major Southern Plains trading centers. For a while, the Jumanos became the masters of the Southern Plains trade, taking caravans of horses, salt, pottery, and Spanish manufactured goods to the Caddo cities of East Texas, where they exchanged them for deer and buffalo hides, bows made of bois d'arc wood, and other items. Apache trading parties visited Pueblo and Spanish traders at Taos and Pecos, exchanging buffalo hides, buffalo meat, and Wichita and Caddo captives, for corn, bread, and manufactured items. The Spanish realized the value

Indians placed on this merchandise and tried to use it to their advantage. While they consistently maintained a policy that prohibited giving guns to Indians, Spanish officials provided them gifts of manufactured goods. Indeed, merely the promise to provide such goods, or the threat to withhold them, gave the Spanish much power to influence the Indians. Sometimes such tactics worked; sometimes they did not. One way around this strategy was raiding, and Spanish and Pueblo corrals and villages soon became the targets of Apache warriors.

European goods and infomation about them spread rapidly across the region. While Pueblos could curse Apache raiders, they also sought refuge among them when Spanish oppression became too harsh. The Apaches welcomed these Pueblo refugees, for they brought horses, cattle, and sheep, as well as the knowledge of farming and reliable information about the Spaniards with them. Some Apache bands, such as the Diné, better known as the Navajo, took up farming and herding sheep and eventually settled down among their Pueblo neighbors. Out on the plains, a community of Apaches and Pueblo refugees sprang up north of the Arkansas River in present-day Colorado. The Spanish called it *El Cuartelejo,* and during the seventeenth and early eighteenth centuries it flourished as one of the largest settlements on the Great Plains, with hundreds of Pueblos and Apaches planting corn side by side.

That the Pueblos felt the Spanish whip so keenly boded ill for the colony of New Mexico. Finally, in 1680, after years of brooding servitude, the Pueblos exploded in rebellion. Popé, a Tewa Pueblo priest, managed to unite most of the Pueblo peoples and in early August, they rose up, killing over 375 Spaniards, including twenty-one priests. The surviving Spaniards and loyal Pueblo refugees retreated south and set up a government in exile at El Paso. Meanwhile, the Pueblo peoples of New Mexico declared their independence and a rededication to the old ways. Nevertheless, the Pueblo world already had changed too much for them to ever fully go back.

The retreat of the Spanish created a severe shortage of horses and manufactured goods in the Southwest. The Apaches particularly felt the pinch. Embroiled in a war for control of the Southern Plains economy, they constantly battled Jumanos, Caddos, and Wichitas. The Apaches had depended on the Spanish, through both trade and raids, to replenish supplies of horses and goods lost in battle. Now, with the Spanish out of the picture, the Apaches stepped up their raids on the Pueblos, as did the Navajos and Utes to the north. Then, the arrival of an Indian people new to the Southwest only roiled the waters even more. The Comanches now galloped down the plains, hard on the heels of the Apaches and contested their claim to the Southern Plains. Popé himself did not make things better by trying to set himself up as ruler of a unified Pueblo nation, an idea strongly resisted by the stubbornly independent city-states. Popé became so dangerous that his own people assassinated him. In fact, a virtual civil war broke out among the Pueblo towns during the Spanish absence. Now, amidst all the short-

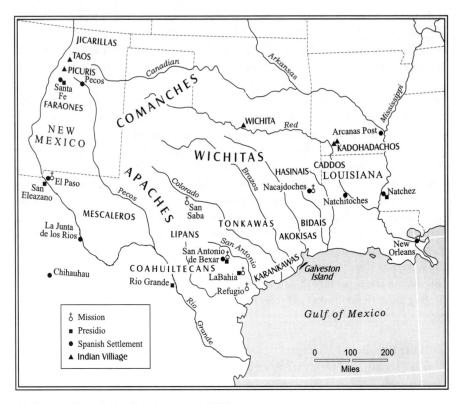

Indian Tribes of the Southwest, c. 1700

ages and troubles, some Pueblos longed for the return of the Spanish. Over the next few years, and without too much trouble, Spanish authority returned to New Mexico until 1696 when they could again claim full control of the province. But the Spanish had learned their lesson well. Gone was the ecomienda, while the authority of the missionaries was extremely curtailed. Pueblo religion, while still not accepted by the Spanish, was at least henceforth tolerated. Pueblo towns might still owe taxes and labor, but Spanish officials now worked through a pueblo *cacique,* who represented his town and spoke for his people. While troublesome pueblos might still feel the cut of Spanish Toledo steel, generally both the Spaniards and the Pueblos found it in their best interest to work together to stem Apache, Ute, and Comanche raids.

During the period of its expulsion from Mexico, Spain turned its attention eastward to Texas. The Caddos of East Texas, their appetites whetted for horses and manufactured goods, sent word through their Jumano trade partners that they would welcome a Spanish presence in their lands. The Caddo city-states looked very appealing to the Spanish, but they dawdled. Then, in 1685, French explorer Sieur de La Salle established a French colony at Matagorda Bay. From the very first everything went wrong for the small settlement of French men, women, and children. Hungry and lacking supplies, they also angered the nearby Karankawas by stealing their canoes. La Salle was murdered by his own men. Some men deserted, marching back to the Mississippi River and then on to New France. Finally, in 1688, the Karankawas attacked, overrunning the fort, killing most of the settlers, while adopting the survivors. French activities spurred Spain to take a much more active interest in Texas. In the 1690s, several Spanish expeditions marched into East Texas, where they rounded up the La Salle expedition's survivors and established a clutch of missions among the Tejas Caddos on the Neches and Angelina Rivers. Although visions of vast quantities of manufactured goods danced in Caddo heads, the East Texas missions, far from the supply centers of New Spain, remained poor. Disappointed and receiving little benefit from the new Spanish missions, the Caddos refused to settle around them. And with no Caddo converts or workers, the East Texas missions closed after only a few years.

From the Spanish point of view, missions were an innovative religious and economic institution that could build cities in frontier areas by transforming wandering hunting and gathering Indians into Catholic, Hispanic peasants. Indian labor might make the missions self-supporting, perhaps even profitable. Spain had used the missions with some success in northern Mexico. Now, with the growing French presence in western Louisiana during the early eighteenth century, Spain again moved them into Texas. Between 1718 and 1793, Spain built a group of missions for the Coahuiltecans where San Antonio sits today. It also re-established the East Texas missions among the Caddos, founded some additional missions along the Texas coast for the Karankawas and Attakapas, established a few short-lived ones for the Tonkawas in Central Texas, and even built a few for the Apaches, the most important being Mission Santa Cruz de San Sabá on the San Sabá River in Central Texas. The San Antonio missions could be judged as successful enterprises. The Caddos still ignored the revamped East Texas missions, which faced the same shortages as in the past. The San Sabá mission built for the Apaches was a spectacular failure.

Many Indians, such as the Coahuiltecans and Tonkawas, flocked to the Spanish missions to escape Apache raids or drought conditions or to acquire European goods. While some Indians did settle in to the mission routine, accept Roman Catholicism, and adopt Hispanic culture, unintended changes often resulted. Disease stalked the crowded missions, which soon became deathtraps, periodically needing to be "re-stocked" with Indians. Thousands of Coahuiltecans entered the missions of Texas and Mexico never to emerge. Not all missionized Indians died, however. Many Indian residents exchanged ideas and intermarried with other peoples and so created wholly new Indian nations. These mixed, Hispanized Indians, such as the Yverpiames and Xaranames, understood the workings of Spanish society and sometimes abandoned the missions to strike out on their own. Called "apostates" by the Spanish, these acculturated bands could be particularly dangerous when they shared their knowledge of Spanish strengths and weaknesses with the more powerful Apaches, Comanches, or Wichitas. Because of this, Spain made every effort to return "apostates" to the fold. Other Indians, such as the Karankawas, Attakapas, and Tonkawas, used the missions as temporary oases, living in them during hard times and then abandoning them when conditions improved. While Tonkawas might ask for a mission to protect them from Apaches, and Apaches might ask for one to protect them from the Comanches, for the most part, all Indian peoples largely viewed the missions as larders to be raided for horses or goods.

One of Spain's greatest strengths lay in its ability to be the main, if not sole, supplier of manufactured goods to Indians. Providing goods to allies and withholding them from enemies had long been a cornerstone of Spanish Indian policy. As the French presence in Louisiana grew during the eighteenth century, Spain found it had lost its monopoly but was slow to respond with a counterstrategy. The adroit French officer Louis Juchereau de St. Denis founded the outpost of Natchitoches on the Red River in 1713, while Bénard de la Harpe established what would become Fort St. Louis de Cadodaquoix among the Caddos at the Great Bend of the Red River in 1720. St. Denis showered the Caddos with gifts and they in turn made strong kinship ties and alliances with him. The Caddos in Louisiana and Texas developed a loyalty not only to St. Denis, but also to his son, sons-in-law, and grandchildren for years to come. By 1740, virtually every Caddo, Wichita, and Attakapa village had a French trader living among them for several months of the year. The Comanches and the Tonkawas received regular visits, as well. To the north, French traders from the Arkansas Post and St. Louis, Missouri, made their own economic ties to the Osages, Quapaws, and Pawnees. Since it was mercantile capitalism that drove the French, they never hesitated to provide firearms and metal weapons to the Indians in exchange for hides and horses. The imperial and economic rivalry between the French and the Spanish gave the Indians great leverage and allowed them to play one European power against the other. By the 1750s, many Indian peoples of the Southern Plains, particularly the Apaches, Comanches and Wichitas, were every bit as well armed as were the Spanish.

While Spanish officials constantly complained about French traders in Texas, they never fully grasped that Indian power was growing, while their own military power was waning. Because of this, during the 1750s, Spain blundered into a vicious Indian war. Apaches, who had controlled the Southern Plains economy since the late 1500s, now found themselves under attack, not only from their old Caddo enemies, but also from southward migrating Comanches and Wichitas. A Caddo-Wichita-Comanche alliance formed, becoming so close that the Spanish referred to them collectively as the *Norteños*, or Northerners. Fueled by a steady supply of guns and goods out of French Louisiana, the Norteños began to drive the Apaches off the plains. As economics and the dictates of blood revenge demanded, the Apaches fought back as best they could, but found themselves pushed ever farther south, directly into the Spanish settlements of South Texas and northern Mexico. Continued Spanish refusals to provide guns to Indians only made the conflicts more lethal, as desperate Apaches not only began to attack towns but killed individual citizens caught out alone for their guns, horses, and goods. Making matters worse, Osages out of Missouri and Arkansas, in their attempt to break out to the buffalo- and horse-rich Southern Plains, attacked Norteños villages. Needing to replace their own lost horses and goods, the Caddo, Wichita, and Comanche stepped up their raiding of Spanish towns and Pueblo villages in Texas and New Mexico. Complicating matters even further, all the Indian powers used various diplomatic means to try to entice the Spanish onto their side and against their enemies.

Then, in a fatal, inadvertent decision, and one certainly taken without proper consideration, the Spanish declared on the side of the Apaches in the on-going struggle among the Indians of the region. Curiously, the Spanish may not have even realized they had done so. The Apaches had long asked for a mission to protect them from their Comanche and Wichita enemies. Finally, the Spanish agreed, building Mission Santa Cruz de San Sabá in 1757. The San Sabá mission was a dangerous place, an inviting target too far north and within easy striking distance of Norteños raiding parties. The Apaches realized it and never settled at San Sabá, visiting the mission only briefly before hurriedly moving on. For the Wichitas, Caddos, and Comanches, the San Sabá mission, with its nearby *presidio* (garrisoned fort), stood as proof that Spain had allied with the Norteños' Apache enemies. The Norteños, therefore, decided to teach the Spanish a lesson in Indian diplomacy. On March 16, 1758, a force of perhaps 2,000 Wichita, Caddo, Tonkawa, and Comanche warriors struck the San Sabá mission. This was no horse raid, but a major attack. The warriors managed to get inside the complex, wherein they killed the two missionaries and six other occupants. After looting the buildings, the war party headed back north. For all intents and purposes, Mission San Sabá now ceased to exist. It was officially abandoned a few years later.

Spanish pride and politics demanded a retaliatory expedition against the Norteños. The next year, in August 1759, Colonel Diego Ortiz Parilla, at the head of 139 soldiers, 241 militiamen, 254 Apache, Tlaxcaltecan, and mission Indian auxiliaries, and hauling two cannons, marched out of San Antonio and headed north toward the main Wichita village on the Red River. Along the way, Parilla's men attacked a band of Tonkawas who had been at San Sabá, killing scores and taking 149 persons captive. If the victory over the Tonkawas at once buoyed Parilla's confidence, the reality of Norteño power deflated it just as quickly. Reaching the Red River in early October, Parilla found the Wichita village enclosed within a wooden stockade complete with firing ports and surrounded by a moat. Hundreds of well-armed Norteños manned the walls, while a seventy-man detachment of Indian cavalry prevented the Spanish from laying siege. The Battle of the Wichita Fort on October 7, 1759, often not mentioned in history books, was one of the most spectacular battles of the American West. Heavy fire from the Indians in the fort kept the Spanish troops at bay, while the Indian cavalry constantly probed and attacked Parilla's flanks, never letting him position his cannons effectively. Although a few French traders were to be found in the fort, this was a Norteño battle and it was their disciplined battle tactics along with their large supply of ammunition that carried the day. That night, Parilla and his men declared that they had taught the Indians a lesson and, abandoning the two cannons to the Wichitas but taking their Tonkawa captives with them, retreated back to San Antonio.

The Battle of the Wichita Fort might well mark the true ascendancy of the Comanches as the "lords of the Southern Plains." For the remainder of the eighteenth century, the Caddos and Wichitas, though still powers to be reckoned with, increasingly found themselves either trying to stave off Osage and Choctaw attacks or recovering from diseases that regularly swept through their villages. Contrasting this, the Comanche population seemed to be growing, as was their presence and strength on the Southern Plains. By the mid-eighteenth century, two concentrations of Comanches had appeared: a southeastern division of Kotsotekas who roamed through much of North and Central Texas, and a more northwesterly group of Jupes and Yamparikas who spent more time in and around New Mexico. The "Orientales," or eastern Comanches, in Texas maintained their alliance with the Wichitas and Caddos, for the most part, and through them their connection to the traders and merchandise in Louisiana. The western Comanches living north of the Arkansas River and therefore farther from Louisiana and the goods that flowed from there, depended more heavily on securing trading privileges from the Spanish in New Mexico.

San Sabá and the Wichita Fort certainly taught Spain the consequences of intemperate actions and forced it to rethink its Indian policy in the Southwest. France's defeat in the French and Indian War, which ended in 1763, furthered this determination, as the Louisiana Territory west of the Mississippi River now became a Spanish possession. Needing to cut administrative costs, Spain did not replace French officials and soldiers in the vast Louisiana Territory but merely transformed them into Spanish citizens by making them swear allegiance to His Catholic Majesty of Spain. This brought to the fore such young, capable officers as Athanase De Mézières, the commandant of Natchitoches, who firmly understood the nuances of Indian diplomacy. De Mézières had married the daughter of St. Denis, the French officer who had made such close alliances with the Caddos and the Wichitas. As heir to St. Denis and with his own ability to work within Indian society, De Mézières prospered in the hide trade. Now, as a Spanish official, De Mézières advocated a pro-Norteño policy, which was not surprising considering his strong ties to the Caddos and the Wichitas. De Mézières and other officers argued that rather than trying to be all things to all Indians, Spain should declare in favor of the Norteños, make peace with them, supply them with annual gifts of merchandise and maintain a regular trade, including in guns, and then join them in waging total war on the Apaches and the Osages. The Caddos, Wichitas, and Comanches had long urged such a plan and could not have been happier with the Frenchman's ideas. Spanish officials, fearing the land-hungry Anglo-Americans who sat to their east across the Mississippi River, saw the need for an Indian buffer against English and American expansion. Therefore, they gave De Mézières' plan a tentative go-ahead. Things looked favorable in 1771, when De Mézières, with the help of the Caddo "Great Chief" Tinhiouen, signed peace treaties with a few Wichita and Comanche bands.

De Mézières' untimely death in 1780 deprived the Norteños of a valued kinsman and Spain of a capable officer but it did nothing to alter the new anti-Apache direction of Spanish diplomacy. Although they now provided firearms in limited quantities to the Norteños, Spanish officials still relied on the old tactic of giving and withholding gifts and trade to coerce the Indians to quit raiding and settle down, but continued to wage all-out war on the Apaches. In Texas, Indian economics and kinship undercut the Spanish position, as it had ever since the French had appeared in the province early in the eighteenth century. Although Spain since 1763 had controlled Louisiana, French creole traders and merchants there had long been making their living in the Indian trade. Over the years, these Frenchmen had established strong, long-lasting relationships with the Indians. Many of them had married Indian women or had been adopted by Indian families, and thereby had their own obligations of reciprocity to uphold. And as businessmen, they needed to pay their debts contracted with merchants in Natchitoches, St. Louis, New Orleans, even British Natchez and Pensacola. Therefore, while Spain might demand that only licensed traders visit Indian villages, in reality, *contrabandistas* out of Louisiana, as well as British and colonial American traders east of the Mississippi from the thirteen colonies, continually supplied the Indians of the Southwest with guns and manufactured goods—and often at prices below the Spaniards' best offer.

Despite their continued access to merchandise from Louisiana, the Indians' demand for goods was never met. The continual wars between the Norteños and the Apaches, attacks by the Osages, skirmishes between the Wichitas and their distant Pawnee cousins to the north, and day-to-day wear and tear meant that Indians continually needed large quantities of manufactured goods. Spain could not always supply that demand. Bureaucratic red tape, its involvement in costly European wars and then the American Revolution, and the generally unreliable transportation system then in place made for periodic shortages. Indians did not want to hear any such rationalizations, regardless of their validity, and they often grew angry when Spanish promises of goods went unfulfilled. On the other hand, it was essential for the Indians to find supplies of merchandise, and with France gone, they could not just turn their backs on the Spanish. Recognizing their own need for goods, in 1785 most Comanche bands made peace with Spanish Texas, a peace that except for an occasional horse raid lasted almost until the end of the eighteenth century. Even so, the need for goods often made for strange bedfellows. The Apaches, finding themselves politically and economically isolated and under constant attack, reached out to the Tejas Caddos and the

Tonkawas, their former enemies, in an effort to secure trade partners. El Mocho, an Apache who had been captured and adopted by the Tonkawas, had risen to become Tonkawa chief. No friend of Spain, El Mocho advocated a Tonkawa alliance with the Apaches, and soon firearms and merchandise flowed through the Tonkawas to the Apaches. This horrified the Spanish, and in 1784 they managed to have El Mocho assassinated by a rival and replaced with a more anti-Apache chief.

Particularly galling to the Norteños, meanwhile, were the Osage attacks. Since the early eighteenth century, the Osages had been trying to break out onto the Southern Plains, where they might tap into the enormous buffalo herds, but the Comanches and the Wichitas blocked their access. Now firmly connected to the French creole traders in present-day Arkansas and Missouri, the well-armed Osages struck westward and battled the Wichitas and the Comanches for a place on the plains. But skirmishes could prove costly. In order to pay their debts and replenish their supplies of merchandise, the Osages needed to acquire ever more horses, more hides, and more captives. To do so, they increased their raids on Caddo villages, driving these people ever southward. As discussed previously, it had been these raids that had prompted De Mézières to urge that Spain make war on the Osages. The Osages, however, were simply too powerful. Spanish officials ran the numbers and reckoned it would cost too much blood and money to subdue them. Just as bad, a punitive strike would probably anger the Osages into allying with the newly formed United States. Perplexed, Spain did nothing, while Caddo villages burned. In 1789, 700 Comanche and Wichita warriors repelled a major Osage attack and then countered by raiding Osage villages in Arkansas. This halted Osage westward expansion. To solidify their control of the Southern Plains, beginning in 1790, the Comanches initiated an ever-expanding alliance with the Kiowas and Kiowa-Apaches then migrating south from the Yellowstone country. The Osages, prevented from securing a place on the Plains, redoubled their attacks on the hapless Caddos. Making things worse for the Caddos, they found their villages coming under attack from Choctaws too. The latter had been invited into the area by Spain in an attempt to build an Indian barrier against Anglo expansion.

Their increasing need for manufactured goods made the Comanches recognize the benefits of peace with Spanish New Mexico. For a brief time, this effected an astonishing change in Comanche politics, one in which a single man rose to become chief of all Comanche bands. The Comanches, as with most hunter-gatherers, had never been a unified nation, but a collection of autonomous bands each led by its own chief. Spanish officials in New Mexico found this confusing, as one Comanche band might come to Pecos pueblo to trade, while another might come to raid it. With Spain's anti-Apache policy in force, Spanish officials in New Mexico now held an olive branch out to the Comanches with the promise of unlimited trade, while urging them to select a single man who could speak for the entire Comanche people. Kotsoteka Comanche chief Ecueracapa, known alternately as *Cota de Mallo* (Mail Coat) and *Camisa de Fierro* (Iron Shirt), seized the moment. Known and respected across the Southwest, Ecueracapa, through his own bravery, influence, and force of personality, rose to become the spokesman for all Comanches. In 1786, Ecueracapa forged a peace with New Mexico governor Juan Bautista de Anza and displayed his newly acquired power by executing a band chief who refused to abide by the agreement. The single leader position would not last as it went against the autonomy stressed by Comanche society and would die with Ecueracapa in 1793.

Fortunately for Spain, Anza proved himself a highly capable officer who understood Indian society. He could be a tenacious fighter when necessary. In 1779, he had taken the war to the Comanches. Leading a force of Spanish soldiers, militia, and Pueblo, Ute, and Jicarilla Apache auxiliaries, he attacked the village of Comanche chief Cuerno Verde, long an enemy of Spain. Realizing Cuerno Verde was at the moment leading a raid into New Mexico, Anza set up an ambush. Although the Comanches evaded the trap, a battle resulted in which Cuerno Verde and many of his best warriors were killed, thereby paving the way for the rise of Ecueracapa. Anza's abilities gained him the respect of Indians throughout the Southwest, which naturally gave him an advantage in peacemaking. Anza knew the Indians put great stock in Spanish governors visiting their villages. So rather than sitting comfortably in the capital of Santa Fe, Anza ventured into the heart of Comanche, Ute, and Navajo territories, thereby bringing about amazing results. Not only did Anza forge an alliance with Ecueracapa's Comanches, he also forged a peace between them and the Utes. He broke up an alliance between the Navajos and the Gila Apaches, even persuading the Navajos to make war on their one-time friends. Various bands of hard-pressed Apaches also appealed for peace, but remembering the failure at San Sabá, Spain remained adamant in its anti-Apache diplomacy, especially as Comanche chiefs spoke out against any alliance with their long-time enemies. When Anza died in 1790, his abilities were sorely missed. His successors were not nearly as competent or active as he. Opportunities for further peace ventures slipped from Spain's grasp, and warfare between various Indian nations soon sparked up again.

By 1800, Spain may have imagined that its Indian policy in the Southwest was bearing fruit. Pueblo farmers had remained loyal allies for over a century. Although Utes, Navajos, and Comanches had again started raiding each other, the alliances they had made with Spain in the 1780s remained solid. Even the Wichitas, Caddos, and Osages, though they might periodically receive goods from creole or American traders, still looked to Spain for most of their merchandise. These diplomatic successes came not from Spanish military power, but from Spain finally accepting the idea that the more goods it could provide the Indians, the fewer raids the Indians would conduct on Spanish citizens. Spain now hired loyal Anglo-American traders in Louisiana to supply merchandise to Indians in East Texas. Similarly, groups of Pueblo and Spanish traders in New Mexico, known as the

Comancheros, periodically drove their carts, loaded with goods, out onto the plains to trade with the Comanches, Kiowas, and other Indians. Disease and warfare between Indian peoples also played into Spain's hands, decimating the Attakapas, Tonkawas, Karankawas, Coahuiltecans, and Jumanos. Meanwhile, the missions on the lower Texas coast, at San Antonio, along the Rio Grande, and in New Mexico, despite high death rates among the neophytes, played their own role in turning Indians into Hispanic peasants. Spain even began to note success among the Apaches. The use of Indian auxiliaries, even friendly Apache scouts, helped bring Apache raiders to heel. A new policy of deporting Apache captives to far-off Cuba, so they could not be exchanged, made many bands sue for peace. Some Apache bands even settled down to plant fields of corn. Not all was perfect tranquillity, however, as any shortage of goods or the desire of young men to acquire prestige could trigger a raid on a village horse herd or an attack on an isolated ranch or farm.

Then, in 1803, it all began falling apart after the United States acquired the Louisiana Territory. Americans, such as Philip Nolan and Anthony Glass, at once slipped into Spanish Texas to begin trading with the Indians. The United States set up a trading post in Natchitoches, inviting Indians from across Texas to visit it. Many did just that and were delighted with the quantities of high-quality manufactured goods they received there. American flags soon appeared in Texas Indian villages, and Spain worried that it was fast losing its allies. Raids picked up again, as Indians sought to acquire horses and hides to provide to American traders. The Mexican Revolution began in 1810, and a decade of hard and bloody warfare virtually stripped Texas of Spanish settlers and officials. The province was essentially abandoned to the Indians. When Mexico gained its independence from Spain in 1821, the Southwest was a different place than it had been a decade earlier, yet it was still a place that Cabeza de Vaca might have recognized from 1528. Pueblos farmed and worshipped in New Mexico, much as they had for centuries. Powerful Indian nations, such as the Apaches, Comanches, Wichitas, and Kiowas, roamed the Southwest, afraid of no one but each other. Karankawas, Attakapas, and Coahuiltecans, though much diminished, still inhabited the coastal plains. And the Southwest still attracted new immigrant groups, just as it always had. Some of these newcomers were sophisticated Indian peoples who had been removed from their homelands in the East, such as the Cherokees, Creeks, and Shawnees. Others were land-hungry Americans, with whose arrival a climactic new day dawned for the Indians of the Southwest. In the next fifty years, they would experience defeat and subjugation at the hands of these Americans and their government, something that Spain had not accomplished over the course of three centuries.

Suggested Reading

The single best work on Indian history of the Southwest is Gary Clayton Anderson's ethnohistorical *The Indian Southwest, 1580–1830: Ethnogenesis and Reinvention* (Norman, Okla., 1999), which examines how Indians created and re-created themselves in order to counter the coming of the Spanish. Elizabeth A. H. John, *Storms Brewed in Other Men's Worlds: The Confrontation of Indians, Spanish, and French in the Southwest, 1540–1795* (College Station, Tex., 1975) remains the classic, single most complete examination of Spanish Indian policy in the Southwest. Other books providing excellent overviews of Spain in the Southwest include David J. Weber, *The Spanish Frontier in North America* (New Haven, Conn., 1992); Donald Chipman, *Spanish Texas, 1519–1821* (Austin, Tex., 1992); and Thomas D. Hall, *Social Change in the Southwest, 1350–1880* (Lawrence, Kan., 1989). Ramón A. Gutiérrez, *When Jesus Came, the Corn Mothers Went Away: Marriage, Sexuality, and Power in New Mexico, 1500–1846* (Stanford, Calif., 1991), examines the interdependent relationship that developed between the Pueblos and the Spanish. Robert Weddle, *The French Thorn: Rival Explorers in the Spanish Sea, 1682–1762* (College Station, Tex., 1991) details French efforts in the Southwest. Some excellent anthologies on the Indians of the Southwest and their relations with the Spanish include volume 1 of David Hurst Thomas, ed., *Columbian Consequences*, 3 vols., (Washington, D.C., 1989–1991) and volume 10 of Alfonso Ortiz, ed., *Handbook of North American Indians: Southwest* (Washington, D.C., 1983). Older works, such as Herbert Eugene Bolton, *Texas in the Middle Eighteenth Century: Studies in Spanish Colonial History and Administration* (Austin, Tex., 1915, 1970); Jack D. Forbes, *Apache, Navaho, and Spaniard* (Norman, Okla., 1960); and Max L. Moorhead, *The Apache Frontier: Jocobo Ugarte and Spanish-Indian Relations in Northern New Spain, 1769–1791* (Norman, Okla., 1968) present fine scholarship, mainly from a Spanish point of view.

Over the past decade or so, many fine books have been published on particular Indian nations. Thomas W. Kavanagh, *The Comanches: A History, 1706–1875* (Lincoln, Nebr., 1996) is an intense study of changing Comanche politics, while Stanley Noyes, *Los Comanches: The Horse People, 1751–1845* (Albuquerque, N. Mex., 1993) is a general history. Ernest Wallace and E. Admanson Hoebel, *The Comanches: Lords of the Southern Plains* (Norman, Okla., 1952) remains the classic Comanche anthropology. F. Todd Smith, *The Wichita Indians: Traders of Texas and the Southern Plains, 1540–1845* (College Station, Tex., 2000) is a historical overview; while David La Vere, *The Caddo Chiefdoms: Caddo Economics and Politics, 700–1835* (Lincoln, Nebr., 1998) focuses on how ancient Caddo institutions and kinship allowed them to counter the French and Spanish. The Osage point of view is provided in Willard H. Rollings, *The Osage: An Ethnohistorical Study of Hegemony on the Prairie-Plains* (Columbia, Mo., 1992). Several good overviews on the Apaches include Donald E. Worcester, *The Apaches: Eagles of the Southwest* (Norman, Okla., 1979); John Upton Terrell, *The Plains Apache* (New York, 1975); and William H. Perry, *Western Apache Heritage: People of the Mountain Corridor* (Austin, Tex., 1991). Unfortunately, the Indian peoples of South Texas and the Texas coast have often been overlooked, but a few fine books do exist. Robert A. Ricklis, *The Karankawa Indians of Texas: An Ecological Study of Cultural Tradition and Change* (Austin, Tex., 1996); Martín Salinas, *Indians of the Rio Grande Delta: Their Role in the History of Southern Texas and Northeast-*

ern Mexico (Austin, Tex., 1990); Lawrence E. Aten, *Indians of the Upper Texas Coast* (New York, 1983); and a collection of articles by Thomas N. Campbell, *The Indians of Southern Texas and Northeastern Mexico: Selected Writings of Thomas Nolan Campbell* (Austin, Tex., 1988) all provide some of the best and most recent anthropological work on the Karankawas, Attakapas, and Coahuiltecans. Much has been written on the Pueblos. A classic is John L. Kessell, *Kiva, Cross, and Crown: The Pecos Indians of New Mexico, 1540–1840* (Washington, D.C., 1979), which examines the economics of this Pueblo-Plains gateway community. The effects of the Spanish conquest of the Pueblos can best be seen in Marc Simmons, *The Last Conquistador: Juan de Oñate and the Settling of the Southwest* (Norman, Okla., 1991) and Robert H. Jackson, *Indian Population Decline: The Missions of Northwestern New Spain, 1687–1840* (Albuquerque, New Mex., 1993). An excellent work on the Pueblo Revolt is Andrew L. Knaut, *The Pueblo Revolt of 1680: Conquest and Resistance in Seventeenth Century New Mexico* (Norman, Okla., 1995).

Chapter 4 ❧
The Trail of Tears

Removal of the Southern Indians in the Jeffersonian-Jacksonian Era

Theda Perdue

*O*ne of the great tragedies in American history is the United States government's removal of the southern Indians from their traditional homelands. The genuine effort that many of these Indians made to adapt to the presence of Euro-Americans and even to conform to the invaders' culture failed to protect them from insatiably land-hungry whites. Indeed, with greed masquerading as philanthropy, white Americans claimed that removal was in the best interest of Native peoples. When Indians lived close to whites, the argument ran, they tended to acquire the vices rather than the virtues of "civilization." Corrupted by alcohol and other features of Euro-American culture, Indians faced certain destruction unless they moved beyond the reach of "civilization." If the Indians resisted the westward path to salvation, whites felt legally as well as morally justified in forcibly evicting them from their southeastern homeland. Indians, whites believed, were only wandering hunters who failed to make proper use of the land. Moreover, they asserted that the European right of discovery took precedence over the Indians' limited right to temporary occupancy. The Frenchman Alexis de Tocqueville, a celebrated visitor to the United States in the nineteenth century, astutely observed that through removal the United States succeeded in exterminating Native peoples and denying Indian rights "with wonderful ease, quietly, legally, philanthropically, without spilling blood and without violating a single one of the great principles of morality in the eyes of the world. It is impossible to destroy men with more respect to the laws of humanity." While many whites congratulated themselves on their humane handling of the "Indian problem," the displaced Native peoples regarded removal as a "Trail of Tears." Individually, socially, and culturally they suffered, they changed, and they rebuilt. But their lives would never again be quite the same.

When the United States government began implementing the removal policy in the early nineteenth century, five major Indian groups lived in the Southeast. The Chickasaws occupied territory in western Tennessee, northern Mississippi, and northwestern Alabama. The Choctaws, who spoke a language very similar to

Chickasaw, lived to the south, in central Mississippi and Alabama. East of the Choctaws lay the Creek Confederacy of Alabama and Georgia. In northern Georgia, northwestern Alabama, eastern Tennessee, and southwestern North Carolina lay the Cherokee country, and in Florida lived the Seminoles, a tribe comprising disaffected Creeks, Native Florida tribes, and runaway African slaves. While each of these tribes was a separate political entity with its own cultural peculiarities, all of them participated in the same broad cultural tradition, just as all Europeans were a part of "Western civilization." At the time of European contact, this southeastern Indian culture was known as Mississippian. Over several centuries, Mississippian peoples had developed a complex culture characterized by permanent villages, an agricultural economy, hierarchical political systems called chiefdoms, and social organizations that emphasized the community rather than the individual, a belief system aimed at preserving order and harmony in the world, and a ceremonial life that reflected the values and aspirations of the society. Interestingly, upon first contact and for many years thereafter, Europeans failed to understand a great deal about southern Indians and Mississippian culture. Perhaps self-interest continuously clouded their view, but, for whatever reason, they often overlooked or distorted these Natives' major cultural characteristics. Therefore, the claim of cultural inferiority and inadequacy that whites used to justify Indian removal was not, and never had been true.

The notorious "Trail of Tears" along which the Cherokees were forced to march to their new residence in the Indian Territory, 1838. Painting by Robert Lindneux. Courtesy, Woolaroc Museum, Bartlesville, Oklahoma

Although they had been interacting with white people—explorers, traders, colonial agents, and soldiers—for quite some time, the major southeastern tribes began to feel the pressure of expanding European settlement in the late eighteenth century. By this time the tribes had extensive contact with three European powers—the French, Spanish, and British—who were vying for control of the North American continent. The British triumphed, which set in motion a series of events that culminated in the removal of the southern Indians from their ancient homeland in the nineteenth century.

Initially, British relations with American Indians resembled those of the Spanish and French: the colonial power sought military alliances and trading relationships among the Native peoples. Because southern forests sheltered large herds of deer, Europeans first viewed the Southeast as a good source of raw material for the leather market. In exchange for the deerskins the Indian hunters brought to trading posts each spring, white traders provided them with a variety of European manufactured goods. Metal tools such as hoes, knives, scissors, needles, hatchets, and axes were in great demand among Native peoples, as were guns and ammunition, copper kettles, and European textiles. As the volume of trade increased, many Indians developed a dependence on European goods. Guns, powder, and ammunition became essential not only for hunting but for protection against well-armed Native enemies, and other items were incorporated fully into Native life. The Europeans' desire for deerskins seemed limitless, and they pressured Indian hunters to provide increasingly more skins. In time, the hunters also became acquisitive, many of them no longer satisfied with mere subsistence.

As their material desires increased, Indians became embroiled in colonial rivalries. European powers on the North American continent sought Indian allies, whom they often recruited through gifts of guns, ammunition, sugar, rum, and other desirable commodities. Some warriors became more concerned about their own material well-being than about community welfare, and they sometimes jeopardized the safety of entire villages for personal gain. As a result, many southern Indians began to see advantages to centralized and coercive governments that could control individual actions. While such governments did not materialize during the colonial period, tribes moved in that direction in order to cope with the erosion of the communitarian ethic.

With the aid of Indian allies, the British ultimately won the imperial contest for North America. Unlike their European rivals on the continents, the British had a large and restless population, many of whom wanted to migrate to North America. Consequently, the British could not be content with forts, missions, trading posts, and scattered settlements; they needed vast tracts of Indian land. The South, in particular, attracted English colonists because the climate permitted cultivation of extremely profitable crops such as tobacco and rice. Reluctant simply to seize the land, the British sought to relieve the Indians of their territory through treaties in which the Indians sold or merely relinquished as war reparations their right to occupy the land. Such transactions proved difficult because

Indians insisted that an individual could cede only his own right to the land. Because delegated political power did not truly exist in eighteenth-century Native societies, even a respected leader could only speak for himself. Consequently, the British began to demand a reorganization of Indian politics and, in some cases, even appointed chiefs to act for villages or for the tribe as a whole. Although this practice was alien to Indian jurisprudence, the British defended the legitimacy of land cessions negotiated by such chiefs.

From the British perspective, the land had never really belong to the Indians in the first place. The British based their claim to North America on the discoveries of the Cabots and others who explored the New World under the auspices of the British Crown. People, of course, lived in this "newfound" land, but the British insisted that the Natives had only the right to occupy the land temporarily. This limited right of occupancy stemmed from the perception of Indian peoples as wandering hunters and gatherers who did not cultivate the soil or permanently inhabit a particular tract of land. Discovery entailed the right of preemption, that is, the right to possess the land when the Indians no longer occupied it. The immediate problem for the British was how to remove the Indians from tracts of land so that colonists could exercise their right of preemption. The solution lay in treaties whereby the Indians surrendered their right to live on the land. When the Indians relinquished their right of occupancy, the "civilized" nation that had discovered the land could then settle, put it to proper use, and establish legitimate ownership. The British, therefore, viewed Indian land titles as transitory and European land titles as genuine and permanent.

The British policy of acquiring specific tracts of land led to a formal distinction between Indian and British territory. Normally Natives and colonists did not share tracts of land: if the British acquired the land, the Indians left and whites moved in. In one sense, this was the beginning of Indian removal. Although Indian enclaves existed in the colonies, the British tended to push Native peoples westward and to create a "frontier," a boundary, between Indians and whites. In 1763, after the British victory in the French and Indian War, George III formalized the boundary and prohibited migration of British colonists beyond the crest of the Appalachians. The Crown and its colonial governments also carefully regulated intercourse between the colonies and the Indians by appointing agents and licensing traders. Therefore, the British regarded the Indians as sovereign for the purpose of negotiating treaties but did not view Native peoples living on land "discovered" by British subjects as permanently entitled to it. When the United States achieved its independence, the new country inherited the British right of discovery and a well-established method for dealing with the Native peoples who temporarily resided within that domain.

The Articles of Confederation, under which the United States was governed from 1779 to 1789, placed Indian relations within the province of Congress, but states often conducted their own negotiations that placed them at odds with the federal government. Congress nevertheless established an Indian policy that asserted the federal government's right to regulate trade with and travel within the Indian nations. The architects of early Indian policy clearly considered the tribes in the Northwest Territory and the old Southwest to be residing on United States land; that is, they believed that Indians merely lived on land actually owned by the United States. Under the Articles of Confederation, the United States also set up a procedure for disposing of all such land once the Indians ceased to occupy it: U.S. agents surveyed tracts and then sold them at minimal price in order to encourage rapid white settlement and ultimate statehood. Even in its infancy, the nation prepared to move westward, and the justifications and machinery for dispossessing the Indians were well in place by the meeting of the Constitutional Convention.

The Federal Constitution of 1789 reserved the conduct of Indian affairs to the federal government. The first chief executive under the Constitution, George Washington, delegated his authority to various cabinet officials. Indian affairs fell under the oversight of the War Department, for if a major policy objective failed, the alternative was military defeat. Henry Knox, Washington's secretary of war, advocated the British concept of proprietorship and their practice of purchasing the Indians' occupancy claims. He also maintained that the privilege of acquiring Indian land belonged exclusively to the federal government rather than to individuals or states. Overcoming opposition from Georgia and other states, Congress concurred with Knox and passed a series of laws called the Indian Trade and Intercourse Acts. Through these laws, the federal government established Indian boundaries, regulated trade with and travel in the Indian nations, controlled the liquor traffic, restricted the purchase of Indian land to the federal government, and provided funds for the education and "civilization" of the Indians.

The Indian policy established by the new nation reflects a dichotomy in American attitudes toward the Indians. On the one hand, many white Americans wanted Indian land: they believed that they could make better use of that resource than could the Indians, and that they were, as American citizens, its rightful owners. On the other hand, many Americans were committed to "civilizing" the Indians. These people believed that Indians could be transformed culturally and assimilated into white society. The belief that Indian farmers would no longer need their vast hunting grounds, which could be opened to white occupancy, no doubt accounts for some of the interest in "civilizing" Indians, but genuine altruism motivated many whites. Convinced that "savage" peoples could not compete with "civilized" ones and consequently were doomed to destruction, these individuals sought to "save" American Indians by convincing them to give up their traditional lifestyles.

For its part, the federal government sought to promote "civilization" in two ways. First, it dispatched agents to live among the Indians and introduce them to the principles of commercial agriculture, animal husbandry, and the domestic arts. Second, it provided financial assistance to missionary societies willing to send people into this particular mission field. Such aid was compatible with the government's goals because most Protestants considered "civilization" and Christianity intrinsically linked—a good Christian life was a "civilized" one. Similarly, the architects of federal Indian policy believed that "civilization" entailed not only an agricultural economy, a republican government, and an English education, but conversion to Christianity as well.

While little of a religious nature was accomplished with the southern tribes during the Federalist era (and the Creeks actually resisted the establishment of a school), federal agents did entrench themselves among them. They encouraged the southern Indians to abandon their traditional towns and communal work habits and to settle on isolated homesteads in preparation for individual ownership of land parcels. Contrary to the Indians' traditional division of labor in which women farmed, the agents furnished the men with plows and hoes and relegated women to the domestic chores of spinning and weaving on newly acquired wheels and looms.

Nevertheless, many southern Indians readily accepted the government's "civilization" program, which was aided considerably by the erosion of traditional Native culture in the eighteenth century. Moreover, the descendants of white traders and Indian women already were accustomed to the white people's ways and capitalized on the material aspects of the program. In addition, many men who formerly had engaged in hunting and war found an avenue for self-fulfillment and an outlet for aggression in the individualistic economic system and acquisitive values that the agents introduced. In the government's view, these men, whose ancestry was Indian, as well as others of mixed ancestry became "civilized," or at least acquired that "love for exclusive property" on which Knox believed civilization rested. In the late eighteenth and early nineteenth centuries, leadership of the southern tribes fell increasingly to individuals who were well on their way to acculturation. These were the people with whom U.S. agents and treaty commissioners interacted most easily and comfortably. In some cases, more traditional Indians deferred to these "progressives" and looked to them as interpreters of U.S. policies and mediators of American culture. In other cases, however, government officials grossly overestimated the power of those Native people who supported federal policies and failed to realize that they had little support within their respective tribes.

Most federal officials viewed the "civilization" program as a means to an end: the real objective of U.S. Indian policy was the acquisition of Indian land. The United States pressured southern Indians to relinquish "surplus" land in a variety of ways. The War Department authorized the construction of government-owned trading posts, or factories, and instructed traders to permit Indians to run up sizable accounts. Once this happened, the authorities demanded payment in land. In 1802, for example, the federal government built a factory among the Chickasaws who within three years owed $12,000; they paid their debts by ceding their territory north of the Tennessee River. Alternatively, treaty commissioners sent by the federal government to negotiate land cessions bribed chiefs and exploited tribal factionalism. In the Cherokee removal crisis of 1806–1809, for example, the U.S. government took advantage of discord between the upper towns of eastern Tennessee and western North Carolina and the lower towns of Alabama and Georgia. Those in the lower towns were more committed to civilization and ultimate assimilation into white society. Espousing the political fiction of tribal unity, federal officials negotiated land cessions and exchanges with lower-town chiefs in the name of the entire tribe. They also lubricated the process by bribing lower-town chiefs with the inclusion of secret treaty provisions appropriating funds to particularly cooperative chiefs. Treaty commissioners employed the same tactic in 1825 when they bribed William McIntosh and other progressive lower Creeks to cede tribal lands in Georgia. In both cases, the Indian nations executed the miscreants, but considerable damage had already been done. While the president of the United States set aside the treaty McIntosh signed, a subsequent treaty achieved the same cession. Furthermore, the willingness of the federal government to use bribery and factionalism demoralized southern Indians and encouraged self-serving individuals to cede tribal land.

In response to these tactics, southern tribes began to devise ways of coping with incessant demands for their land. With the hearty approval of the civilizers, agents, and missionaries, southern tribes began to adopt Anglo-American political institutions. The Cherokees, Creeks, Choctaws, and Chickasaws began to centralize their tribal governments, to formalize political processes and structures, to delegate authority to clearly designated chiefs, and to hold those chiefs accountable for their actions. Between 1808 and 1810, the Cherokees established a national police force, created an executive committee to transact tribal business between council meetings, and made murder a national crime (instead of a family matter) by abolishing blood vengeance. In 1829, they committed to writing a previously unwritten but well-known law making the cession of tribal land a capital offense. The Creeks enacted such a law in 1811, and, as demands for tribal land increased, gradually shifted responsibility for the conduct of foreign affairs to a national council, which alternated its annual meetings between upper and lower Creek towns. The Choctaws and Chickasaws also renounced the practice of blood vengeance and made murder a national crime. In 1826, the Choctaws enacted a written law code and a system of elective chiefs that replaced the old informal system in which chiefs of three districts acted in concert. The Chickasaws extended their system of national laws and committed them to writing in 1829, four years after they established judicial districts.

These political changes did not have unanimous support. A large number of Creeks, in particular, disapproved of the Europeanization of political institutions and the attempt by elected officials to placate whites. This dissatisfaction contributed to the eruption of civil war in 1813. The United States, embroiled in the War of 1812, invaded Creek country and allied itself with friendly Creeks against the "Red Sticks," as those opposed to rapid cultural change were called. Following their defeat, many Red Sticks migrated south and joined with remnant Florida tribes to form the Seminoles. Subsequently they accepted runaway African slaves. This hybrid tribe clung to old ways of governing, leaders deriving their power from personal accomplishment and charisma, and the Seminoles became the most united in purpose of all southern tribes.

Among southern Indians, a significant number of people rejected or, perhaps more appropriately, ignored aspects of "civilization." They preferred their traditional town councils to centralized governments, the lessons taught by elders and family members to those imparted by teachers in mission schools, and their own religion to Christianity. The persistence of traditional culture troubled missionaries and U.S. agents who mistakenly had believed that "civilizing" the Indians would be a fairly simple task. They feared for those recalcitrant "savages" whose days, they felt certain, were numbered by the onrush of "civilization."

Some conditions in the Indian nations in the early nineteenth century seemed to confirm these fears. In the view of many whites, exposure to "civilization" only further corrupted these "savages." Equally distressing to them was the inability of other Indians who acknowledged the virtue of "civilization" but proved unable to resist its vices. Many Indians lived on credit, and their wants far exceeded their means. Some discovered a "civilized" way to avoid manual labor: they bought African slaves to work for them. Southern Indians also liked to gamble. Although gambling was a long-held aboriginal practice, "civilization" introduced new contests such as horseracing on which Indians might wager. But most tragically, many Indians acquired a taste for alcohol. Faced with the weakening of cultural traditions, economic and political changes, and an uncertain future, they overindulged, and alcoholism became a serious problem among a number of tribes.

Soon, all such difficulties in implementing the "civilization" program led philanthropists to question just how quickly and easily the southern Indians could be assimilated into white society. And these doubts opened the door for those whites who desired the Indians' land rather than their "civilization." Reconciliation of these opposing positions came in the proposal to move the Indians beyond the reach of "civilization," where they would have more time in which to adjust to the problems that "civilization" brought. And once the southern tribes were relocated, the Indians would be safe and their land opened for white settlement. The immediate problem was where to send the Indians.

The answer actually preceded the recognition of a pressing problem. Thomas Jefferson may not have had Indian emigration in mind when he made the Louisiana Purchase in 1803, but his political opponents (and even some supporters) demanded to know exactly what he intended to do with this vast wilderness. Jefferson, a great advocate of assimilating Native Americans into the mainstream society, responded that the eastern Indians could now be moved west of the Mississippi River and "civilized" at their own pace. Thus the U.S. governments' removal policy officially was born. Troubled by the constitutionality of the acquisition of Louisiana, Jefferson contemplated a constitutional amendment to validate his actions. The amendment he proposed recognized only the Indians' right of occupancy (not ownership) of their current lands, affirmed the U.S. right of preemption, and gave Congress the authority to exchange the right of occupancy of lands in the East for the same right to lands in the West. Although the provision never became a part of the Constitution, the Louisiana Territorial Act of the following year authorized the president to negotiate just such an exchange of land for removal of the southern tribes. Exchanges were, of course, supposed to be entirely voluntary. Therefore, Jefferson did not persist when the Chickasaws rejected a proposal that they move west of the Mississippi in 1805, or three years later, when overtures to the Choctaws received an equally cool response.

Despite these early rebuffs, the Jefferson administration did develop the first technique for transferring the Indian population of the Southeast beyond the line of white settlement: officials simply offered to exchange land west of the Mississippi for tracts ceded in the Southeast. They believed that as white "civilization" encroached, those Indians who did not want to assimilate could move west. Some southern Indians, in fact, already had elected to do so. In the late eighteenth century, a band of Cherokees moved beyond the Mississippi after their massacre of a party of pioneers. Chickasaws hunted regularly in the trans-Mississippi West, and one group apparently settled permanently in Louisiana about the turn of the century. During the same period, other Indians also went west to hunt or to fight the enemy Osage and then returned to their homes in the Southeast.

The Jefferson administration succeeded only in convincing the lower Cherokees to exchange land, and in 1810 about 1,000 Cherokees moved to Arkansas. Subsequent administrations followed the Jeffersonian model and arranged territorial exchanges. Another Cherokee emigration took place in 1817–1819, after a group of Cherokees (who received private reservations that could be sold at considerable profit) ceded land in the Southeast to compensate the federal government for additional land the Arkansas Cherokees had settled. In 1820, the Choctaws agreed to the Treaty of Doak's Stand, under which they relinquished one-third of their eastern domain for a larger tract in Arkansas. Because of protest from white residents of Arkansas, however, the treaty had to be renegotiated in Washington in 1825, after which the Choctaws received a tract of land in what is today southeastern Oklahoma. In 1826, the Creeks grudgingly acceded to an exchange of land in Georgia for a tract north of that held by Choctaws so that the discredited and despised followers of William McIntosh, who had been executed, could emigrate.

The consequences of these exchanges were not exactly what Jefferson and other proponents of the removal policy had had in mind. Some Indians who moved west were the traditionalists for whom Jefferson originally had proposed removal. A surprisingly large number, however, were highly acculturated Indians. Some of these people moved to escape political enemies, but economics probably motivated most of them. Perhaps they hoped to capitalize on the westward movement, or they may simply have felt the same urge to go west as did many white Americans. These progressives experienced little remorse in leaving their homeland, but the traditionalists, who were the intended beneficiaries of the policy of removal, felt a profound attachment to their homeland and refused to leave it. Indeed, those who still practiced traditional religion regarded their own territory as the center of the world and associated the West with death. In addition, their mythology incorporated familiar land forms. The Choctaws, for example, believed that they came originally from the Nanih Waiya mound in Mississippi, and the Cherokees thought that they could see and influence the future through the crystal forelock of the Uktena, a monster that lived in the high mountain passes of their country. Sacred medicine, which southern Indians used to cure physical and spiritual ills, came from native plants that did not necessarily grow in the trans-Mississippi West. For these traditionalists, removal meant not only physical relocation, but also spiritual reorientation.

Exchanges of land and piecemeal removal had an additional unforeseen effect. Instead of the trickle of emigrants swelling to a stream, a burst of enthusiasm for removal was followed by long periods of almost total disinterest. Those inclined to go west took advantage of the opportunity afforded by exchanges and departed. Their removal siphoned off the very people who might have been inclined to negotiate further exchanges. So with every migration west, public opinion in the southern tribes became increasingly opposed to removal. There was little that U.S. officials could do about this situation because, until 1829, presidents refused to force Indians to go west against their will.

The slow pace of Indian removal angered many white southerners. As prices for cotton rose, the white population in the South grew, and as the Cotton Kingdom expanded, the desire for additional land suitable for cultivating cotton increased. Consequently, southern states began to demand that the federal government, which controlled Indian relations, liquidate Indian title to land within their borders. Georgia, in particular, insisted on federal compliance with the Compact of 1802. In this agreement, the state relinquished claims to its original charter's western land, which became Alabama and Mississippi, in exchange for the federal government promise to extinguish Indian land titles within the state at some unspecified time. In the 1820s, Georgians thought that the federal government had delayed long enough. Indian land promptly became a political issue. Constitutional changes in 1825 that provided for the direct election of governors (previously elected by the state senate) contributed to the uproar. Politicians seized on Indian land as an issue with broad popular appeal. In 1826, Georgians rejoiced when the Creeks gave up their remaining land in the state and withdrew to Alabama. Then they turned their attention to the Cherokees.

In 1827, the Cherokees established a republican government with a written constitution patterned after that of the United States. Georgia interpreted this act as a violation of state sovereignty and renewed demands for the extinction of Indian land titles. The state legislature enacted a series of laws intended to establish state control over Cherokee country and to make life so miserable for the Indians that they would leave willingly. The legislature extended Georgia law over the Cherokees and created a special militia, the Georgia Guard, to enforce state law in the Cherokee country. One legislative act prohibited Indians from mining gold, deposits of which had been discovered in their territory. Other laws prevented Indians from testifying against whites in court and required all whites, including missionaries, to take an oath of allegiance to the state. The Georgia legislature enjoined the Cherokee council from meeting and leaders from speaking publicly against removal. Finally, legislators formulated plans for a survey and division of Cherokee lands in preparation for their distribution by lottery to whites. Other southern states soon followed Georgia's lead and extended oppressive state laws over their Indian populations.

President John Quincy Adams had little sympathy for southerners in their struggle for Indian lands, but in the presidential election of 1828 Adams lost to Andrew Jackson. Jackson brought to the high office long experience fighting and negotiating with southern Indians. Soon after moving into the White House, Jackson made clear his intention to acquire and open to white settlement all Indian land in the Southeast. In his 1829 message to Congress, the president offered southern Indians two alternatives—they could become subject to the discriminatory laws of the states or move west and continue their own tribal governments. The president and most southerners believed that they should move. In 1830, Congress passed the Indian Removal Act, which authorized the president to negotiate exchanges of territory and appropriated $500,000 for that purpose. Under the proposed removal treaties, the federal government would compensate emigrants for improvements made to the property (such as houses, cleared and fenced fields, barns, orchards, and ferries) and assist them in their journey west.

The Choctaws were the first tribe to remove under the provisions of the Indian Removal Act. In the fall of 1830, a group of Choctaw chiefs agreed to the Treaty of Dancing Rabbit Creek. In this treaty, the Choctaws ceded their land in the Southeast, but those who wished to remain in Mississippi (or could not pay their debts to citizens of the state) would receive fee simple title to individual allotments of land and become citizens of the state. The federal government promised those who removed reimbursement for improvements, transportation to the West, subsistence for one year after removal, and an annuity for the support of education and other tribal services. There was much dissatisfaction with the treaty, particularly among Choctaw traditionalists who did not want to go west under any condition. Opponents, however, had little opportunity to protest formally because the U.S. government refused to recognize any chief as long as the Choctaws remained in Mississippi. Consequently, the Choctaws began preparations for their westward migration.

Confusion surrounded these preparations as well as the journey west. After a dispute over routes, the Choctaws and the government agreed on a combination water and land route. Finally, in late fall 1831, the first detachment of Choctaws left Mississippi. The War Department had divided the supervision of this group's removal between the Indian trader George Gaines, who conducted the Indians to the Mississippi River, and the Jacksonian Democrat Francis Armstrong, who then assumed control. These men, however, delegated their authority to supply the Indians en route to agents in the field, many of whom viewed removal only as an opportunity to increase their own fortunes. Therefore, Choctaws often failed to receive the rations promised. The Indians who removed under government supervision suffered greatly as a result of exposure to harsh winter weather, the corruption and greed of conducting field agents, and bureaucratic bungling, but so did those who received a $10.00 commutation fee from the United States with which they paid fellow Choctaws to conduct them west. The subsequent Choctaw removals of 1832 and 1833 were not as plagued by corruption and confusion, in part because military officials replaced civilian speculators as field agents. By the spring of 1834, between 13,000 and 15,000 Choctaws had removed.

About 7,000 Choctaws remained in Mississippi under provisions of the Treaty of Dancing Rabbit Creek; these were either heads of households who had registered to receive an allotment or those barred from leaving the state because of indebtedness. Some Choctaws who remained in Mississippi were highly acculturated, such as Greenwood LeFlore, who subsequently embarked on a successful career in Mississippi politics. Others, however, were traditionalists accustomed to communal ownership of land who did not understand titles, deeds, or the individual ownership of land. Many such these traditionalists knew only their Native language and, as a result, became the unwitting victims of unscrupulous speculators. Often tricked into running up debts or signing their deeds over to these men, the traditionalists appealed to the government for help. U.S. officials, however, turned a deaf ear to their pleas and insisted that the fraudulently obtained contracts be honored. No longer entitled after 1834 to emigrate at government expense, these landless Mississippi Choctaws either straggled to Indian territory on their own or remained in the state as an impoverished minority.

The federal government made allotment a major feature of the treaties it concluded with the Creeks and Chickasaws in 1832. The Creek chiefs agreed to cede much of their land in Alabama and to permit some Creeks to receive the remainder in allotments. Soon thereafter, white land speculators descended on these tribes and once again defrauded many out of their individual allotments. Evicted from their homes and farms, many Creeks still refused to go west. Tension between white intruders and foraging Indians escalated and finally erupted into violence. In 1836, the War Department responded by forcibly removing thousands of Creeks as a military measure. Although many of these Creeks died during their westward trek, casualites of the sinking of a steamboat, disease, hunger, and exposure, about 14,500 of them finally assembled in their new nation in the west.

While the Chickasaws avoided some of the suffering of the Creeks, once again, corruption and fraud characterized their removal. Under the terms of the Treaty of Pontotoc, they ceded their eastern homeland, but the federal government delayed removal of the tribe until officials could locate a suitable tract of land in the West. In the interim, the Chickasaws received individual plots, and the federal government opened the remaining two-thirds of the Chickasaw territory to white settlement. Speculators promptly poured into the Chickasaw country, defrauding hapless Indians of their property. Finally, in desperation, the Chickasaws agreed to purchase a tract of land from the Choctaws, and in 1837–1838, about 4,000 Chickasaws migrated beyond the Mississippi.

The scandal generated by allotment failed to temper Georgia's demands that the federal government extinguish Indian land titles within the state. The widespread suffering, however, did strengthen the Cherokees' resolve to resist removal negotiations. When Georgia courts sentenced two white missionaries to prison for their failure to take an oath of allegiance that the state required of white residents of the Cherokee Nation, the Cherokees turned to the U.S. Supreme Court for a ruling on whether or not Georgia law could be extended over that part of the Cherokee Nation that lay within the chartered limit of Georgia. In *Worcester* v. *Georgia*, the Court enjoined Georgia from enforcing state law in the Cherokee Nation and ordered the release of the missionaries. Nevertheless, the state refused to comply. Legal technicalities and President Jackson's disinclination to interfere in the matter precluded federal enforcement of the decision. The missionaries remained in prison, and Georgians continued to harass the Cherokees.

Once it became obvious that even a Supreme Court decision would have little impact on the situation in the Cherokee Nation, a group within the Nation began to consider negotiations with the federal government. This group came to be known as the Treaty Party. Its leaders included Major Ridge, who had fought with the United States in the War of 1812 and had risen to a prominent leadership role in the Nation, his New England–educated son, John, and Elias Boudinot, editor of the bilingual newspaper *The Cherokee Phoenix*. Motivated at least as much by economic and political ambitions as by concern for the Cherokee people, the Treaty Party enjoyed little popular support. The vast majority of Cherokees supported Principal Chief John Ross in his steadfast opposition to removal. Nevertheless, the U.S. treaty commissioner met with about one hundred Treaty Party members in December 1835, and they negotiated the Treaty of New Echota. This treaty provided for the exchange of Cherokee territory in the Southeast for a tract of land in what is today northeastern Oklahoma. While the original document gave acculturated Cherokees such as those who signed it preemption rights (that is, the right to stay in the East and come under state law), supplemental articles eliminated this provision. Therefore, no Cherokees received individual allotments; removal encompassed the entire tribe. Although 15,000 Cherokees, almost the total population, signed a petition protesting the treaty, the U.S. Senate ratified the document. In summer 1838, federal troops seized thousands of Cherokees and imprisoned them in stockades in preparation for their westward trek. As the death toll mounted among Cherokees imprisoned without adequate clothing, food, water, or shelter, the Van Buren administration, which had inher-

Osceola, one of the outstanding leaders of the Second Seminole War. Painting by George Catlin, 1837. National Archives #NWDNS-111-SC-93123

ited the removal program, agreed to let the Cherokees conduct their own removal in the winter of 1838–1839. Despite this "humanitarian" gesture, four thousand Cherokees died during that summer and as a result of exposure, tainted water, and the rigors of travel en route to their new home in the West.

The Cherokees had fought violation of their rights in the courts; the Seminoles resisted removal militarily. In 1832, the Seminoles signed a provisional removal treaty in which they agreed to go west if they found a suitable country in which to relocate. The next year, their agent conducted a delegation of Seminoles west in search of such a site, during which journey he reportedly forced the delegation to sign a new treaty guaranteeing removal from Florida by 1837. Although the Seminoles had signed it under duress, the Senate ratified the treaty, and President Jackson, who had fought the Seminoles in the War of 1812, ordered it enforced. Because many Seminoles once had been a part of the Creek confederacy, the U.S. government believed that the two tribes should reunite in the West. The Seminoles strenuously objected to this plan and demanded that their tribal integrity be preserved. Ignoring Seminole objections, the United States sent troops to Florida to round up the Indians for removal. In 1835, desperate Seminole warriors ambushed a company of soldiers, and the massacre sparked the Second Seminole War. Skillfully employing guerrilla tactics in the swamps of southern Florida and led by superb warriors such as Osceola, the Seminoles forced the United States to commit a total of 40,000 men, between $30 million to $40 million, and suffer substantial casualties over the next seven years. In attempting to defeat and remove the Seminoles, the government resorted to even more duplicitous means than bribing chiefs and exploiting tribal factionalism: commanders in the field, with approval from Washington, repeatedly captured Seminole warriors under flags of truce. Even after the official end of the war in 1842, soldiers continued to capture and deport bands of Florida Indians until roughly 3,000 Seminoles resided in the West and only several hundred remained in the Florida Everglades.

Although remnants of all southern tribes continued to live in their ancient homeland, most occupied worthless land from which they barely eked out subsistence. Because these Indians had little that whites wanted, the pressure to remove them diminished. In the 1840s and 1850s, state and federal governments turned their attention to other issues, in particular, the growing sectional conflict over slavery. Many white Americans quickly forgot about the southern Indians and their tragic removal.

Meanwhile, the Indians who had gone west faced a number of problems in adjusting to their new situation. The native tribes of eastern Oklahoma resented the relocation of the southern Indians on their territory. During the initial stages of removal, warfare raged, particularly between the Cherokees and the Osages. In this conflict, the Cherokees abandoned much of the ceremonialism of aboriginal warfare. Instead of fighting primarily for vengeance, they looted and pillaged Osage villages, their tactics coming to resemble those of the U.S. Army: in 1817, while Osage men were away hunting, Cherokees attacked their town, killed women and children, stole livestock and other property, took about 100 captives, and burned down the village. The southern Indians also had experienced problems with other tribes who shared neither their aboriginal heritage nor their adoption of Anglo-American culture. The Seminoles and Chickasaws, who ultimately took up residence to the west of the Creeks and Choctaws, had considerable difficulty with raids by Kickapoos, Shawnees, Kiowas, and Comanches. Many Chickasaws even refused to move out of the Choctaw Nation and onto their own land until the U.S. government built Fort Washita in 1843 to protect them.

Disputes also sprang up between the relocated southern Indian nations themselves. As mentioned, the federal government tried to force the Seminoles to join the Creeks, but many Seminoles refused. Squatting on Cherokee territory, they presented a number of problems for government officials. The Seminoles were afraid that the Creeks would seize their slaves, whose considerable freedom made them hardly slaves at all. They had reason to worry. In the negotiations that followed the War of 1812, the Creeks had agreed to reimburse white planters for slaves who took refuge with them or whom they captured. Most of these blacks, however, actually lived with the Seminoles, and the Seminoles refused to surrender them. Since they had paid for these bondsmen, the Creeks believed that they were entitled to their labor. Both the Creeks and Cherokees had slaves, but their peculiar institution more closely resembled plantation slavery in the white South than the system developed by the Seminoles. In short, the Cherokees objected to Seminole residence in their nation because they feared that the semiautonomous Seminole blacks would be a bad influence on their own bondsmen. Finally, the

Creeks and the U.S. government resolved the difficulties by first permitting the Seminoles to establish their own towns in 1845 and then by severing the two nations in 1856.

Within all southern tribes, removal produced or exacerbated factionalism. Among the Cherokees, civil war erupted. In 1839, unknown Cherokees executed Major Ridge, John Ridge, and Elias Boudinot. Treaty Party members retaliated, and partisans battled intermittently until 1846 when the two sides accepted an uneasy truce. In other nations, voters turned out leaders favorable to removal, and the Creeks banned missionaries because highly acculturated Christian progressives had promoted removal. The disaffection of some Indians became so great that they proposed to move elsewhere; the Seminole warrior Coa-coo-chee (Wild Cat), for example, sought a permanent home in Mexico. Some of the factionalism of the removal reappeared during the American Civil War: the Seminoles as well as Creek and Cherokee factions who opposed removal favored the Union while proremoval factions actively supported the Confederacy.

Following removal, the division between the traditionalists or conservatives and the highly acculturated progressives became more pronounced. Progressives reestablished centralized republican governments and written law codes, built schools, encouraged missionaries, and took advantage of the economic opportunities afforded by the new land. They grew corn, raised cattle, made salt, and engaged in trade. Some amassed fortunes. After the American Civil War, progressives tended to advocate the construction of railroads and the exploitation of natural resources such as timber, asphalt, coal, and oil. They did not oppose the influx of white railroad workers, loggers, and cowboys, and at the turn of the century most supported allotment of land to individuals, dissolution of tribal governments, and Oklahoma statehood.

Conservatives, on the other hand, shunned many of the political, economic, and cultural changes of the progressives. Civilization had not saved their homeland, and now they regarded it with misgivings and even disdain. After removal, conservatives found comfort in what they could preserve of their traditional practices. Family and town continued to be the fundamental relationships of these people who were content with a mere economic subsistence. They found outlets for aggression in the ball play and other traditional games. Medicine men and women still relied on plants and sacred formulas to cure disease, cast spells, and control the natural world. Many conservative communities built square grounds, or stomp grounds, where they performed all-night dances, celebrated the Green Corn Ceremony, and took medicine to cleanse themselves physically and spiritually. The rituals of the stomp ground reinforced their traditional values of kinship, purity, and balance. Some southern Indians even formed secret societies in an attempt to revitalize the culture that embodied these values. The Cherokee Kee-too-wah society, for example, encouraged the abandonment of the white man's way and a return to traditional customs and beliefs. When faced with allotment and statehood, some traditionalists resisted violently, but most simply withdrew to their families, communities, and stomp grounds. These people held on to a cultural tradition created in their native Southeast and transferred west of the Mississippi in removal.

From the white perspective, removal accomplished its goals: the U.S. government "protected" thousands of Indians from the corrupting influence of civilization by moving them west and opened millions of acres of Indian land to white settlement. These successes can be charted in economic, political, and demographic terms, but the human cost is not so easily measured. Thousands died; others suffered permanent mental and physical impairment. Although many of their traditions survived, southern Indians experienced significant cultural modification and even transformation. All of this took place not according to the will of the Indians but by the dictates of white policymakers. Although they exercised considerable agency in adapting to new circumstances, the Indians lost the power to determine their own future within the United States. Perhaps the greatest tragedy of removal is that white Americans used their power over Indians to inflict death and great suffering, after which they congratulated themselves on their humanitarianism.

Suggested Reading

F or a readable account of the southeast's Mississippian chiefdoms at the time of initial European contact, see Charles Hudson, *Knights of Spain, Warriors of the Sun: Hernando de Soto and the South's Ancient Chiefdoms* (Athens, Ga., 1997). Hudson's *The Southeastern Indians* (Knoxville, Tenn., 1976) provides a more general summary of the region's Native cultures. Patricia Galloway, *Choctaw Genesis, 1500–1700* (Lincoln, Nebr., 1995) addresses the emergence of the historic Choctaws while James H. Merrell, *The Indians' New World: Catawbas and Their Neighbors from European Contact Through the Era of Removal* (Chapel Hill, N.C., 1989) describes the process by which remnant peoples coalesced to form the Catawbas.

Relations between Native people and Europeans in the colonial period centered on imperial rivalries and the deerskin trade, but Native people retained considerable autonomy in their economic and diplomatic dealings. See Kathryn E. Holland Braund, *Deerskins and Duffels: The Creek Indian Trade with Anglo-America, 1685–1815* (Lincoln, Nebr., 1993); Tom Hatley, *The Dividing Paths: Cherokees and South Carolinians Through the Era of Revolution* (New York and Oxford, 1993); Daniel H. Usner, Jr., *Indians, Settlers, and Slaves in a Frontier Exchange Economy: The Lower Mississippi Valley Before 1783* (Chapel Hill, N.C., 1992); and Peter H. Wood, Gregory A. Waselkov and M. Thomas Hatley, *Powhatan's Mantle: Indians in the Colonial South* (Lincoln, Nebr., 1989).

The following works focus on early United States Indian policy: Francis Paul Prucha, *Intercourse Acts, 1790–1834* (Cambridge, Mass., 1962); Ronald N. Satz, *American Indian Policy in the Jacksonian Era* (Lincoln, Nebr., 1975); and Mary E. Young, *Redskins, Ruffleshirts, and Rednecks: Indian Allotments in Ala-*

bama and Mississippi, 1830–1860 (Norman, Okla., 1961). The intellectual climate of the early nineteenth century is the subject of Bernard W. Sheehan, *Seeds of Extinction: Jeffersonian Philanthropy and the American Indian* (Chapel Hill, N.C., 1973) and Reginald Horsman, *Race and Manifest Destiny: The Origins of American Racial Anglo-Saxonism* (Cambridge, Mass., 1981).

Tribally specific histories include William G. McLoughlin, *Cherokee Renascence in the Early Republic* (Princeton, N. J., 1986) and *After the Trail of Tears: The Cherokees' Struggle for Sovereignty, 1839–1880* (Chapel Hill, N.C., 1993); Theda Perdue, *Slavery and the Evolution of Cherokee Society, 1540–1866* (Knoxville, Tenn., 1979) and *Cherokee Women: Gender and Culture Change, 1700–1830* (Lincoln, Nebr., 1998); Arrell M. Gibson, *The Chickasaws* (Norman, Okla., 1971); James Taylor Carson, *Searching for the Bright Path: The Mississippi Choctaws from Prehistory to Removal* (Lincoln, Nebr., 1999); Michael D. Green, *The Politics of Indian Removal: Creek Government and Society in Crisis* (Lincoln, Nebr., 1982); Claudio Saunt, *A New Order of Things: Property, Power, and the Transformation of the Creek Indians, 1733–1816* (Cambridge, Mass., 1999); Joel Martin, *Sacred Revolt: The Muskogees' Struggle for a New World* (Boston, 1991); and Patricia Wickman, *The Tree that Bends: Discourse, Power, and the Survival of the Maskoki People* (Tuscaloosa, Ala., 1999). The standard work on the Seminole War is John K. Mahon, *History of the Second Seminole War, 1835–1842* (Gainesville, Fla., 1974).

For removal specifically, see Grant Foreman, *Indian Removal: The Emigration of the Five Civilized Tribes of Indians* (Norman, Okla., 1932); Arthur H. DeRosier, Jr., *Removal of the Choctaw Indians* (Knoxville, Tenn., 1970); and Theda Perdue and Michael D. Green, *The Cherokee Removal: A Brief History with Documents* (Boston, 1995).

Chapter 5 ❧
Blue, Gray, and Red

Indian Affairs during
the American Civil War

Philip Weeks

*T*he combination of military, political, racial, social, cultural, economic, demographic, and constitutional consequences of the Civil War made it pivotal in the national experience. It also proved crucial in Indian affairs. While the West paled in military significance to the eastern theater of the war between the United States and the Confederate States, both countries still considered that region strategically important. The government in Washington was concerned with holding its western domain and protecting the supply of gold and silver from western mines, which it vitally needed to help finance war against the Confederacy. The government in Richmond intended by force of arms to acquire territory in the West for the expansion of its institutions, especially slavery—an endeavor that, to the South's bitter frustration, the federal government had squelched before the war. The Confederacy also intended to secure a land corridor to the Pacific, stretching westward from the Confederate state of Texas across New Mexico and Arizona territories to California. Finally, the Confederacy was determined to seize the Union's western silver and gold mines to shore up its pitiful lack of capital to prosecute its war for independence.

Since early in 1861, Southern officials had extended overtures to leaders of the five Indian republics in the Indian Territory (present-day Oklahoma), hoping to draw the Cherokees, Creeks, Choctaws, Chickasaws, and Seminoles into an alliance with the new Confederate nation. "Our people and yours are natural allies in war," argued Arkansas Governor Henry M. Rector to Principal Chief John Ross of the Cherokees. "Your people, in their institutions, productions, latitude, and natural sympathies, are allied to the common brotherhood of the slaveholding States." The other four tribes received similar appeals. Confederate Indian Commissioner Albert Pike traveled to the Indian Territory in 1861, hoping to draw the so-called Five Civilized Tribes away from the United States. Pike had fertile ground on which to work. Economically the five republics had much stronger ties to the states of the South than to those of the North. Many tribal members still harbored deep animosity toward the United States for the removal trauma of the 1830s, as well as for the federal authority's general nonobservance of treaty obligations in the years following removal. Moreover, a number of the Indian republics' citizens were slaveholders who felt a natural affinity for the Confederate cause and a like dread of the alleged threat posed by Abraham Lincoln and the Republican party to the maintenance of slavery in the United States.

But the case against the United States did not end here. Confederates exploited several other provocative issues, especially the threat the United States posed to the sovereignty of the five Indian republics. Pike and his agents apprised the tribes of the recent campaign promises of William H. Seward, a leading New York Republican who now served as Lincoln's secretary of state. During the 1860 election, Seward had, in a speech at Chicago, advocated the appropriation of the land of the Five Civilized Tribes for white homesteaders. Confederates also reminded the tribes of how the U.S. government had forsaken them when the sectional conflict exploded. In the spring of 1861, the federal Indian Bureau withdrew all Indian service agents from the Indian Territory and Secretary of War Simon Cameron ordered the abandonment of Forts Washita, Arbuckle, and Cobb in the Indian Territory. Confederate forces now occupied the installations. This action left the five tribes vulnerable and fully exposed to assault from the Confederacy, which surrounded them on three sides and maintained troops within their homeland.

There seemed few alternatives for the Five Civilized Tribes. In fact there appeared to be a number of advantages in allying with the Confederates, in part because they promised more liberal treaties than the United States ever had extended them, but also because the Confederacy pledged to preserve and defend the independence of the Indian republics.

The great majority of Chickasaws wanted an alliance with the Confederacy, and on May 25, 1861, their government made its decision. "The Lincoln Government . . . has shown by its course toward us, in withdrawing from our country the protection of the Federal troops, . . . a total disregard of treaty obligations," the Chickasaw legislature proclaimed. It therefore declared independence from the United States. Like the Chickasaws, citizens of the Choctaw republic also overwhelmingly supported the proposed alliance. On July 12, delegates of both nations signed a joint treaty with Albert Pike committing their governments to the Confederate cause.

Not all tribes in the Indian Territory possessed the same certitude of action. The Creeks, Seminoles, and Cherokees, each tribe deeply divided over the question of allying with the Confederacy, split along factional lines with one side supporting an alliance and the other demanding neutrality. Albert Pike, in July 1861, at last won over influential mixed-blood chiefs, among them Daniel McIntosh, who allied the Creek nation with the South. But many other Creeks, those led by the respected full-blooded chief Opothleyahola, resisted interfering in this "white man's war," declared themselves neutral, and sought support from Washington. None came. With their people split over the question of allying with the Confederacy, the neutrals bitterly condemned the federal government's actions as a betrayal. Opothleyahola, in a long letter to Abraham Lincoln, demanded to know why they did not hear from him. The chief reminded the president that previous chief executives promised that "in our new homes, we should be defended from all interference from any people, and that no white people in the whole world should ever molest us unless they came from the sky." Perhaps Southern agents were correct after all. Perhaps the "Government represented by our Great Father at Washington has turned against us," he stated tartly.

The stand of Opothleyahola and his followers put them in a precarious, perhaps even perilous, position. Hoping to avoid a confrontation with the pro-Confederate Indians, the neutrals journeyed into the northern portion of the Creek nation and established a camp along the North Fork of the Canadian River, near the present town of Eufalaula, Oklahoma. The number in camp soon swelled to between 800 and 1,200 people with the arrival of neutral Seminoles under chiefs John Chupco and Billy Bowlegs, who had separated from their pro-Confederate kin.

No less severe was the split among the Cherokees, which fused disagreement over a potential Confederate alliance with a bitter intratribal fight that stretched back three decades to the Removal crisis. One faction, the so-called Ross party, opposed the other, the so-called Ridge, or Treaty party. Back in Georgia during the 1830s, the New England–educated Cherokee John Ridge had painfully come to see the hopelessness of the Cherokees' position in retaining their homeland, especially after President Jackson's refusal to enforce the Supreme Court's ruling in the *Worchester* v. *Georgia* decision. Believing that his nation's only salvation lay in surrendering its land and relocating quietly in the West, Ridge moved cautiously but purposefully to line up influential support within the tribe for a removal treaty. He persuaded his father, Major Ridge, one of the wealthiest Cherokees and speaker of the Cherokee National Council, the nation's ruling body, as well as Stand Watie and his brother Elias Boudinot, editor of the tribal paper, the *Cherokee Phoenix*. The Ross party, led by Principal Chief John Ross, opposed them. They categorically rejected removal, strenuously denounced the Ridge party and federal advances to endorse a removal treaty, and emphatically warned the Ridge party that signing the treaty would be tantamount to signing their death warrants. Understandably, officials in Washington sided with the Ridge party. Disregarding the wishes of the majority of Cherokees, the Ridge party signed the Treaty of New Echota in 1835, which sold the tribe's homeland for $5 million and authorized removal of the Cherokee people to the Indian Territory.

The Cherokees carried the feud from Georgia to the Indian Territory, and now, in 1861, the Ross and Ridge parties again engaged in an intense struggle to chart the national course for the Cherokees. Stand Watie, following the assassinations of the Ridges and Boudinot in retaliation for their signatures at New Echota, inherited leadership of the Ridge party. He supported the Confederacy and pressed for an alliance. John Ross opposed him absolutely. The Civil War terrified Ross.

He worried that the sea of violence currently drowning Americans might also overwhelm his people in a fratricidal conflict. The principal chief saw no option but to declare neutrality. "I am—the Cherokees are—your friends," he reassured Confederates, "but we do not wish to be brought into the feuds between yourselves and your Northern Brethren. Our wish is for peace. Peace at home and Peace among you." Ross requested that his people abstain from "partisan demonstrations."

The Creek and Seminole neutrals applauded Ross's decision, but reaction from within the Cherokee nation was severely divided. Watie, sensing a growing public shift to his pro-Southern position, especially after the Federal military catastrophe at Bull Run in July 1861, moved quickly to shape events. Watie offered military assistance to the Confederacy on behalf of the Cherokees and, in return, on July 12 received a commission in the Confederate Army at the rank of colonel. General Ben McCulloch, Confederate military commander in the Indian Territory, then authorized him to raise a regiment of Cherokees.

The Chickasaws and Choctaws also organized a regiment of "mounted rifles." On August 1, 1861, Commissioner Pike notified Confederate President Jefferson Davis that the Indian regiments stood ready for battle. Later that month they saw their first action at the Battle of Wilson's Creek, fought near Springfield, Missouri. There a Confederate army, with the aid of the Indian regiments (although Watie was not present), mauled Federal forces under General Nathaniel Lyon. The news of victory and the performance of its sons thrilled the Cherokee nation. Just as war fever had swept across the North and the South that spring following the fall of Fort Sumter, martial passion now swelled throughout the Indian Territory in the late summer of 1861.

Watie's actions and the contribution of Cherokee soldiers in the victory at Wilson's Creek invalidated John Ross's declaration of neutrality. Desperately hoping to block Watie's ascendancy among the Cherokee, Ross dramatically altered his position and announced he would seek an alliance with the Confederacy. General McCulloch reported jubilantly on August 31: "The Cherokees have joined the South." Those Cherokees still clinging to a course of impartiality went into exile; bearing the news of Ross's defection, these neutrals sought haven with Opothleyahola's band of Creeks. All too soon, Ross's worst fears came to pass. The specter of civil war among his people became imminent, as Confederate Indians organized an expedition to assault the neutral's encampment, hoping to put the "traitors" to flight. Ross, in a letter that fall to Opothleyahola, pleaded: "Brother—My advice and desire, under the present extraordinary crisis, is for all the red Brethren to be united among themselves in the support of our common rights and interests by forming an alliance of peace and friendship." But time had run out.

The disagreement in the Indian Territory exploded in violence on November 19, 1861, when Confederate Indians supported by Texans under Colonel Douglas H. Cooper assaulted the neutrals at the Battle of Round Mountain. Less than a month later the two sides clashed again at Chusto Talasah. The decisive engagement came on December 26. Reinforced by 1,600 Southern cavalrymen, the Confederate Indians routed Opothleyahola's neutrals, destroying their belongings, supplies, and livestock, and drove them from the Indian Territory. They fled northward, ultimately settling in refugee camps in Kansas, where they faced destitution throughout the next three years. Army surgeon A. B. Campbell witnessed the plight of the refugees. After visiting the Verdigris River camp during the refugees' first winter in Kansas, he tried to convey the distress of the experience: "It is impossible for me to depict the wretchedness of their condition. Their only protection from the snow upon which they lie is prairie grass, and from the wind scraps and rags stretched upon switches; some of them had some personal clothing, most had but shreds and rags, which did not conceal their nakedness; and I saw seven, ranging in age from three to fifteen years, without one thread upon their bodies." After arrival in Kansas, the refugees' leaders cast off neutrality and offered to assist the United States.

The year 1862 proved fateful for both the Southern Confederacy and its Indian allies. In early spring, while General Ulysses S. Grant battered Confederate defenses along the Tennessee and Cumberland rivers, Federal forces to his south prepared to battle for control of Missouri and northern Arkansas. The showdown came on March 6, 1862, near Elkhorn Tavern, Arkansas. General Samuel R. Curtis's 10,000 Federals withstood an assault on the first day of the Battle of Pea Ridge by Earl Van Dorn's 16,000 Confederates, whose troops included 3,500 Indians. Although outnumbered, Curtis counterattacked on the second day, inflicting heavy casualties on the Southerners and forcing them into full retreat. The performance of Colonel Watie's Cherokee Mounted Rifles proved to be one of the few bright spots during the Confederate debacle at Pea Ridge. Watie's men captured a strategic Federal artillery position that raked Southern lines and later skillfully covered the Confederate withdrawal. In his report, General Curtis noted how impressed he and fellow Federal officers had been with "the hordes of Indians, cavalry, and infantry that were arrayed against us" at Pea Ridge.

Thereafter Confederates abandoned conventional tactics in the border states of Kansas, Missouri, and Arkansas and waged their fight through guerilla warfare. General McCulloch relied heavily on Colonel Watie and his Cherokees, whom he ordered to "destroy everything that might be of service to the enemy." Raiders under commanders such as Watie and the white Missourian William Clarke Quantrill attacked Union border settlements and disrupted Federal supply lines and bases. Quantrill and his men, who included future Western outlaws Jesse and Frank James and Cole and Jim Younger, became notorious bushwhackers, killing unarmed soldiers and civilians, whites as well as blacks. One Federal officer assessed that they "kill for the sake of killing and plunder for love of gain." Quantrill's band demonstrated this in August 1863 when they raided Lawrence, Kansas, burning the defenseless town and murdering over 180 male civilians in cold blood. Unlike the atrocities committed by Quantrill, Watie rejected such tactics. In light of his notable war record, in 1864 his superiors promoted him to brigadier general.

The Confederate defeat at the Battle of Pea Ridge also opened the Indian Territory to invasion from Kansas, and the United States saw two principal benefits in such a course. One, as Lincoln told Congress, was to lead the Confederate Indians back into the Union. "It is believed that upon the repossession of the country by the federal forces," the president explained, "the Indians will readily cease all hostile demonstrations, and resume their former relations to the government." The second advantage, one pressed for fervently by the two United States senators from Kansas, James Lane and Samuel Pomeroy, was to hasten the removal of the refugee Indians from that state.

Meanwhile, Opothleyahola and other pro-Union chiefs had met with General David Hunter in February 1862 and agreed to assist with such an invasion. A month later the commander of the Department of the Mississippi received his orders: "It is the desire of the President . . . that you should detail two regiments to act in the Indian country, with a view to open the way for friendly Indians who are now refugees in Southern Kansas to return to their homes and to protect them there. Five thousand friendly Indians will also be armed to aid in their own protection and you will please furnish them with necessary subsistence." By spring, cavalry and infantry regiments from Ohio and Wisconsin arrived, swelling the ranks of the invasion force. Superiors attached them to troops from Kansas and the pro-Union Indians to form the "Indian Expedition."

Pushing southward during the summer of 1862, the Federals and their Indian allies advanced into northeastern Indian Territory as far as Tahlequah, capital of the Cherokee nation, where they arrested John Ross without incident. Thousands of Cherokees, realizing the futility of supporting the Southern cause, defected to the Union. The U.S. government sent Ross to Fort Leavenworth, Kansas, then to Philadelphia. There, with great personal relief, he repudiated his nation's alliance with the Confederate States of America. For the remainder of the war he directed a pro-Union Cherokee government in exile, ultimately serving as emissary to the United States. Stand Watie disavowed Ross's actions and declared himself rightful chief of the Cherokees. A meeting of Cherokees on August 21, 1862, elected Watie principal chief and reaffirmed the treaty of alliance with the Confederacy.

Upon his arrival in Washington, D.C., John Ross immediately sought to develop a cordial relationship with Abraham Lincoln and to secure aid for his people. Interior Secretary Caleb Smith wrote to Lincoln, asking permission for Ross to visit the White House. The president responded coolly. "I will see Mr. Ross at 9 A.M. to-morrow, if he calls." The chilly demeanor continued when the two men met on September 12, 1862. Ross reaffirmed the Cherokees' loyalty to the United States. He also explained to Lincoln that the Cherokees had signed the treaty with the Confederacy under duress, and only after the United States failed to protect his people under obligations set forth in earlier treaties. The president disclaimed any failure on the part of the United States government, and made clear he was not satisfied with Ross's rationale for the alliance. Nevertheless, Lincoln closed the meeting by assuring Ross that he would investigate the matter thoroughly.

Later that year, Ross again approached Lincoln to seek a pardon for the Cherokee people. The president, after a special meeting with his cabinet, assured Ross that he would do everything in his power to protect pro–Union Cherokees; however, any determination of the fate of those who had aided the Southern cause must wait until the war's conclusion, when the issue would be duly placed on the government's Reconstruction agenda. (The United States eventually granted a parole to John Ross, but, to his distress, the victorious Union punished his people and the other Indian republics more harshly than it did the states of the defeated Confederacy.)

Federal troops and pro–Union Indians followed their successful 1862 invasion by launching another operation against the Indian Territory in the summer of 1863. At the Battle of Honey Springs, fought on July 17, the Indian Expedition defeated Confederates and their Indian allies. Then it advanced steadily southward, at last reaching the Canadian River, which separated the Cherokee and Creek nations from the Choctaw and Chickasaw nations. Fleeing Confederate Indians eventually reassembled in refugee camps farther south and west, not unlike those in which their kinsmen languished in Kansas. At this point the Indian Expedition might have pressed deeper into the Confederate Indians' territory and claimed absolute victory had military developments in the East not intervened. Earlier that month in Pennsylvania, Federal and Confederate forces had fought the terrible Battle of Gettysburg. Confederate general Robert E. Lee thereafter withdrew his battered army back into Virginia and prepared for the inevitable Federal counteroffensive. Unsatisfied with his commanders in the East, Lincoln soon ordered General U. S. Grant in from the western theater, assigning him responsibility for directing what the president hoped would be the conclusive operation against the Confederacy. Consequently, Northern and Southern commanders chose to abandon operations in the Indian Territory and the Border States and reassign men to the more critical eastern theater.

With Union and Confederate soldiers elsewhere, the Indian Territory descended into its own bloody and destructive fratricidal struggle, as pro–Union and pro–Confederate Indians assailed one another. For the next two years, each side swept back and forth across the Canadian River, the rough boundary separating the opposing forces, turning the once bountiful Indian Territory into a no-man's-land of terror, disorder, and desolation. At last the Civil War concluded. General Lee surrendered his Army of Northern Virginia on April 9, 1865. Over the next six weeks, other Confederate commanders capitulated to the United States; Stand Watie was the last Confederate general to do so. He signed articles of surrender on June 23, 1865, near Doaksville, the capital of the Choctaw nation.

Like the South, the Indian Territory was prostrate after the terrible fighting of the Civil War years. Great portions of it lay devastated: homes destroyed, fields overrun or untended, stock dead or running loose. The war left countless families bereft, while thousands from the five republics suffered as refugees. One can sense from the words of John Ross the feelings of anguish and dislocation so widespread among members of the Five Civilized Tribes as he traveled back to the Indian Territory. "I know that I am fast approaching my country & my people," he wrote from Arkansas in late August 1865, "but, where is that delightful Home . . . the family Homestead ruthlessly reduced to ashes by the hand of rebel incendiaries. And whilst the surviving members of our family circle are scattered abroad as refugees—I am here journeying as it were, alone to find myself, a stranger & Homeless, in my own country."

Reconstruction under Abraham Lincoln might have been less calamitous for the Five Civilized Tribes and for the South, but by war's end he lay dead from an assassin's bullet. With the succession of Andrew Johnson to the presidency, a spirit of pardon was usurped by one of vindictiveness toward the vanquished, which certainly characterized Washington's postwar dealings with the Five Civilized Tribes. The federal government, virtually charging the tribes with treason, asserted that they "had compromised their rights under existing treaties." James Harlan, Johnson's secretary of war, made clear the government's agenda in reconstructing the Five Civilized Tribes: "The President is willing to grant them peace, but wants land for other Indians, and a civil government for the whole Territory."

To reestablish their relationship with the United States, each of the five tribes was made to sign a Reconstruction treaty. In most respects, all such treaties were similar. They contained five major provisions: first, they established peace with the United States and among the five Indian republics; second, they abolished slavery, granted tribal citizenship to blacks formerly held in bondage, and ordered their integration into the five tribes on an equal footing; third, they acknowledged preliminary steps for a unified government in preparation for territorial status and possibly an Indian state; and fourth, they mandated tribal acquiescence to rights-of-way for future railroad construction across the Indian Territory. The fifth provision dealt with land occupancy. And the Indian Reconstruction treaties contained substantial land cessions by all five tribes; their collective forfeiture amounted virtually to the western half of present-day Oklahoma for future use as federal reservations (on which to put tribes other than those of the five republics).

The burden of peace, like that of the war years, proved heavy for the people of the Indian Territory. John Ross concluded that the "victory perched upon the banners of the United States . . . has been achieved at the sacrafice [sic] of hundreds of precious lives, the loss of wealth and resources of the [Cherokee] Nation and amid pain, suffering and destitution hitherto unknown to our people." Elias C. Boudinot tersely summarized the net effect of the Civil War—the "white man's war" that Ross, Opothleyahola, and others so desperately tried to avoid—on the Five Civilized Tribes in a letter to Stand Watie in 1866: "We have been beaten." The Five Civilized Tribes were the only Indians actually drawn into the Civil

War. The Civil War was not, however, the only arena of Indian-white conflict between 1861 and 1865. The United States government, locked in a struggle with a determined Southern Confederacy, of necessity was forced to give Indian affairs a low priority. Having little effort to spare for policing its own regulations in an area far removed from the principal arenas of the conflict between the states, Indian affairs suffered. Settlement of the trans-Mississippi West, although slackening slightly, continued throughout the war years. Under the buffeting of those Americans looking for land to farm or to strike gold, Washington found it increasingly difficult to maintain the integrity of its treaty obligations to western tribes. Indians, who already had complained of many uncorrected injustices, were now exacerbated by the absence of federal authority. Taking advantage of the recall of army regulars from frontier posts, they took matters into their own hands. This situation twice resulted in eruptions of interracial violence. One involved the Sioux, the other the Southern Cheyenne.

While the United States and Confederate armies battled through the opening years of the war, the first serious outbreak of the trouble occurred in Minnesota between white settlers and the Santee Sioux. The tribe had agreed to two sets of treaties with the United States during the 1850s, both of which influenced to the events in the late summer of 1862. In the first of the treaties, concluded at Traverse des Sioux in 1851, the tribe ceded twenty-four million acres to the United States and, in turn, were allotted two reservations along both sides of the upper Minnesota River, measuring twenty miles wide by 150 miles long. In 1858, the Santee Sioux concluded a second set of treaties that reduced this reservation by half as they forfeited the territory north of the river. Both sets of treaties contained assimilation measures that directed the government to build blacksmith shops and saw mills and establish manual labor schools on the reservations, and introduce the concept of private property among the Santees by allotting eighty-acre farm plots to individual families. "The theory," explained Thomas J. Galbraith, the federal Indian agent assigned to the Santee Sioux, "was to break up the community system among the Sioux; weaken and destroy their tribal relations; individualize them by giving each a separate home and having them subsist by industry— the sweat of their brows; till the soil; make labor honorable and idleness dishonorable; or, as it was expressed in short, 'make white men of them,' and have them adopt the habits and customs of white men."

It did not take long for problems to arise on the reservation. The assimilation measures of the recent treaties provided one source of intratribal tension, triggering antagonism between the "farmer" and "blanket" Santees, who disagreed over whether to shed or keep the old tribal ways. Food shortages among the Santee Sioux caused the second problem. A constantly increasing white population in the rich Minnesota River valley during the 1850s and early 1860s steadily diminished the amount of game on or around the reservation. This development, coupled with the Santees' mounting inability to grow sufficient food to feed themselves on their compressed reservation, made it inevitable that government annuity payments came to mean the difference between survival and starvation. Tribal members typically used annuity monies to purchase food supplies.

The Civil War destroyed many things, among them the federal government's plan for feeding the Santee Sioux. Ever since that conflict broke out, the United States, preoccupied with prosecuting the war and in need of every available dollar, had become increasingly tardy in providing annuity payments. Combined with bad harvests, this development produced severe food shortages for the Indians in the early 1860s. Hunger on the reservation increased, as did the Santee Sioux's hostility toward white settlers who, it seemed, had forged lives of plenty on former Sioux lands while the Santee slipped from deprivation to destitution. By the summer of 1862, the severe hunger precipitated a catastrophe.

By early August 1862, the Sioux were desperate. Santees from the Upper Agency, the northern portion of their reserve, broke into the government's warehouse and, with the reluctant approval of their agent Thomas Galbraith, took enough pork and flour to save their people from starvation. Less than two weeks later, Santees from the Lower Agency requested emergency food allotments. Galbraith, backed by a local contingent of armed traders, rejected their appeal. Andrew Myrick, one of the more vocal traders, closed the discussion contemptuously: "So far as I am concerned, if they are hungry, let them eat grass or their own dung."

Soon many young warriors talked openly of trying to drive white settlers out of the Minnesota River valley and back across the Mississippi River. The Lincoln administration's recall of army units from the region to fight the Confederates made triumph more credible. But this talk was checked by Little Crow, or Taoyateduta, chief of the Mdwekanton, a tribal division of the Santee Sioux. Little Crow gravely warned the angry young men that any engagement would be nothing short of suicide. "We are only little herds of buffalo left scattered, the white men are like the locusts when they fly so thick that the whole sky is a snowstorm," he explained. "You may kill one—two—ten; [but] count your fingers all day long and white men with guns in their hands will come faster than you can count." For the moment, the young warriors heeded Little Crow's warning.

An uncertain peace lasted for two weeks. Then on August 17, the unavoidable explosion occurred—"like a spark of fire, upon a mass of discontent, long accumulated and ready for it," characterized Minnesota Lieutenant-Governor Ignatius Donnelly—near the town of Acton, Minnesota, forty-five miles north of the Santee's reserve. A small Sioux hunting party stole eggs from settlers, quarreled with them, and in a mindless act of reprisal murdered five whites. That evening the hunters returned home and went immediately to Little Crow to recount the deed. He called a meeting of chiefs of the Lower Agency for later that night to decide what course of action should be taken. After heated debate between a war and a peace faction, the majority decided upon a preemptive strike before whites could retaliate for the murders. Little Crow agreed to lead the fight against the settlers of Minnesota, even though he acknowledged it a lost cause.

Refugees from the Sioux Uprising, August 21, 1862. Thousands of settlers abandoned their homesteads virtually depopulating twenty-three counties in southwestern Minnesota. Courtesy, Minnesota Historical Society, Loc. #E91.4S/r16, Neg. #36775

The attacks began during the early morning hours of August 18, 1862. The Santees initially struck at settlers residing at nearby farms. One of the first to die was the trader Andrew Myrick who, when found later, had prairie grass crammed into his mouth. The warriors sent overtures to followers of the peace faction chiefs to join in the rampage, but they firmly rejected the offer. As the day advanced, the range of the massacre, with its accompanying raping and plundering, widened. The Santees' attack caught settlers by surprise. "We were beginning to regard the poetry of the palisades as a thing of the past," one settler recollected, "when, suddenly, our ears were startled by the echo of the warwhoop, and the crack of the rifle, and our hearts appalled by the gleam of the tomahawk and the scalping knife, as they descended in indiscriminate and remorseless slaughter, on defenseless women and children on our border."

Fighting frantically, the Santee Sioux swept down the Minnesota River valley trying to eliminate all settlers. Minnesota Governor Alexander Ramsey wired Secretary of War Edwin Stanton, apprising him with alarm: "The Sioux Indians on our western border have risen, and are murdering men, women, and children." Many in Washington feared, incorrectly, that the uprising was a Confederate conspiracy to disrupt the Union war effort. While the United States and Minnesota prepared a military response, Little Crow, in a wise tactical move, suggested directing a concentrated attack against strategic Fort Ridgely. There, at the compound guarding the populous valley, terrified settlers had sought shelter. The younger warriors overruled him, preferring to continue to loot and plunder, a serious and ultimately fatal error because it allowed reinforcements to swell the number of defenders at the fort. Not until August 20, the third day of the uprising, did the Santees assault Fort Ridgely. After three days of intense fighting, the garrison repelled the attack. With their path to advance through the valley blocked, the Sioux changed direction and raided to the northwest. Between four hundred and eight hundred citizens of Minnesota perished in what Commissioner Dole called "the most atrocious and horrible outbreak to be found in the annals of Indian history."

Responsibility for carrying the war to the Santee Sioux fell to Governor Ramsey and to General John Pope, commander for the newly established military Department of the Northwest. "Attend to the Indians," Lincoln advised upon hearing of the uprising, "necessity knows no law." The general concurred. "It is my purpose utterly to exterminate the Sioux if I have the power to do so." Pope's orders to Colonel Henry Hopkins Sibley, commander of the Third Minnesota Volunteer Regiment, were blunt and explicit: "Destroy everything belonging to them and force them out to the plains, unless, as I suggest, you can capture them." Although there was little need to elaborate on such orders, Pope apparently felt a need to add to the savagery. "They are to be treated as maniacs or wild beasts," he insisted. The Minnesota militia defeated the outmatched Santee Sioux in a pitched battle at Wood Lake, Minnesota, on September 23, 1862. Large numbers of Sioux surrendered. Little Crow and many of the hostiles escaped into the Dakotas to join their plains cousins, the Teton Sioux.

The rest of the Santee Sioux did not flee. For many, staying was the natural choice, since they had been neutrals all along and supposed they would be treated as such. They understood clearly that those who had rampaged could hardly expect much mercy from the Americans. In October John Pope informed the U.S. government that he had taken about 1,500 Santee prisoners. Pope recommended "executing the Indians who have been concerned in these outrages." Minnesotans adamantly agreed, demanding vengeance against the perpetrators. "Exterminate the wild beasts," urged Jane Swisshelm, editor of the *St. Cloud Democrat,* "and make peace with the devil and all his hosts sooner than with these red-jawed tigers whose fangs are dripping with the blood of the innocents." Pope faced a tricky problem in meting out justice. "I don't know how you can discriminate now between Indians who say they are and have been friendly, and those who have not. I distrust them all." Undeterred, he convened a military court of justice that, in ten days, tried 392 Indian prisoners accused of committing crimes during the uprising. When it finished its work the commission had sentenced sixteen to imprisonment and condemned 303 to death by hanging.

Abraham Lincoln was not convinced that justice had been served in Minnesota and ordered that no executions be made without his sanction. On November 10, he sent a request by telegram to General Pope: "Please forward, as soon as possible, the full and complete record of these convictions." Pope obeyed and dispatched the transcripts to Washington so the president and his attorneys could review them. The general also warned Lincoln: "The people of this State . . . are exasperated to the last degree, and if the guilty are not all executed I think it nearly impossible to prevent the indiscriminate massacre of all the Indians— old men, women, and children." Episcopal Bishop Henry B. Whipple, taking an extremely unpopular stand in the eyes of fellow Minnesotans, vigorously interceded with Lincoln on behalf of the condemned Sioux, thereby launching an illustrious career as an Indian reformer. Indian Commissioner William Dole and Interior Secretary Caleb Smith likewise threw their support behind efforts to prevent the mass executions. After a review of the verdicts, Lincoln authorized the hanging of less than forty of the condemned Santee Sioux. All had either participated in the massacre or raped women. Lincoln's goal, as he told the Senate, was neither to act "with so much clemency as to encourage another outbreak, on the one hand, nor with so much severity as to be real cruelty, on the other." A large gathering watched as thirty-eight Santees died on a single scaffold at Fort Mankato, Minnesota, on the day after Christmas, 1862.

Those Santees remaining in the state had little to hope for at the hands of Minnesotans. As the Civil War had provided a solution to the Indian question in the Indian Territory, the tragic events of 1862 served the same end in Minnesota. The state's representatives in Washington urged Congress to authorize the immediate expulsion of all Indians from Minnesota; not just the Santees, but also the Winnebagos whose fertile land in Blue Earth County white settlers coveted. Congress acquiesced. On February 21, 1863, it authorized the eviction of the Winnebagos. The Santee removal bill of March 3, 1863, revoked the earlier treaties with the tribe and by "right of conquest" extinguished title to their land in Minnesota. The government ordered the two tribes removed to a desolate tract of land at Crow Creek near Fort Randall on the Missouri River, in the Dakota Territory. There the army could keep them under scrutiny.

On May 4 and 5, 1863, 1,300 Santee Sioux, mainly women and children, boarded two steamboats that carried them into exile. While one of the vessels took on supplies at St. Paul, whites on shore, in a final act of reprisal, hurled rocks at the hated passengers. In addition to banishment, Washington suspended the tribe's annuity payments for four years and converted them to reimburse the damage claims of citizens of Minnesota. Well before this four-year period ended, crop failures at Crow Creek, coupled with a severe lack of essential supplies, reduced hundreds of Santees to starvation and death. Luckily for the Winnebagos, the Indian Bureau had relocated them from Crow Creek to the Omaha reserve in Nebraska in 1864.

As for Little Crow, his stature in the eyes of his followers diminished rapidly after his flight into the Dakotas, and his attempts to organize another attack on Minnesota from the land of the Teton Sioux failed. By July 1863, the discredited chief was back in Minnesota attempting to steal horses. On the afternoon of July 3, a farmer named Chauncey Lamson shot and killed Little Crow while the Santee was picking raspberries. The shooting took place to the south of Acton, where all the violence had begun the previous year. Little Crow's head was cut off and displayed at St. Paul. His body was disposed of in the refuse pit of a local slaughterhouse in Hutchinson. For his marksmanship, the state legislature awarded Lamson $500. Meanwhile, farther west, another severe struggle had erupted.

In 1858 gold was discovered in the Pike's Peak region of present-day Colorado, on the western edge of the Southern Cheyennes' country. As with all discoveries of precious metals in the West, the strike caused dramatic changes to the land and the Indian people near the strike. In 1859 a second find near Clear Creek sent even greater numbers of whites rushing to the area in the hope of making their fortunes. In that year alone over 100,000 people traveled to these fields along the new Smokey Hill Trail, which ran directly westward through the center of Cheyenne-Arapahoe territory as defined by treaty. A decade earlier, the Fort Laramie Treaty of 1851 had pledged the grasslands between the North Platte and Arkansas rivers to the Southern Cheyennes and Arapahoes. This trespassing was a source of irritation compounded by the multitude of Americans who actually spilled off the trail and squatted in the midst of Indian land, numbering over 34,000 by 1860. With the federal government's energies directed toward crushing the Confederacy, the United States again proved unresponsive to the needs of Indians and undependable regarding its treaty obligations.

In the years 1860 and 1861, white population and business enterprises increased dramatically in this region. "We have substantially taken possession of the country and deprived [the Indians] of their accustomed means of support," assessed Indian Commissioner Alfred B. Greenwood. In response to such rapid growth, the United States organized the Southern Cheyenne–Arapahoe lands into the Colorado Territory in preparation for statehood. Once again, the government wanted to secure further land cessions from the two tribes. By the terms of a new treaty concluded in 1861, the Treaty of Fort Wise, ten chiefs and delegates representing the Southern Cheyenne and Arapahoe relinquished all of their tribes' extensive landholdings except for a small, triangular tract along the Arkansas River in southeastern Colorado, designated the Sand Creek reservation. The civilization provision of the treaty called for the land at Sand Creek to be allotted in severalty to individual tribal members. With government assistance, the Southern Cheyennes and Arapahoes were expected to forsake the buffalo-and-horse culture and become self-supporting farmers. Most tribal members, however, had no interest in becoming farmers or abiding the new direction for them as outlined in the treaty. Instead, they preferred to continue raiding, hunting the buffalo, and moving about freely on their former lands.

The same elements that had produced calamity and death in Minnesota quickly emerged in the Colorado Territory: the clash of convictions within the tribes between forsaking or keeping the old ways, white demands for the Indians to stay off land ceded by treaty, and mounting food shortages among the Indians caused by the physical conditions of the reservation, in this case a sandy, barren, agriculturally sterile piece of land. The scarcity of food at Sand Creek during

1862 made it inevitable that more men would secure food by hunting outside its bounds, on their former ranges. There was even greater hunger in the following year. No buffalo, the staple of these people's diet, could be found within 200 miles of the reservation, reported their agent, Samuel G. Colley. Disease, brought in part by the lack of food, plagued the Southern Cheyenne and Arapahoe during that summer. Finally, out of desperation, the Indians reverted to raiding local farms and passing wagon trains, not necessarily to kill—the attacks resulted in remarkably few casualties—but to secure food. "Most of the depredations committed by them are from starvation," wrote agent Colley. "It is hard for them to understand that they have no right to take from them that have, when in a starving condition." William Gilpin, Colorado's first territorial governor and ex officio superintendent of Indian Affairs in the region, and his successor, John Evans, believed that the Indians must be forced to remain at Sand Creek and convinced to adopt the government's civilization measures before a more dangerous situation arose.

Then, in April 1864, a small, rather typical frontier incident turned into a disaster. It began with the arrival of a disturbing report at Camp Sanborn, Colorado. The report came from a rancher who charged that a party of Cheyenne had stolen horses and livestock from his land near Bijou Creek. Colonel John Chivington, Methodist minister, local politician, and militia commander of the District of Colorado, dispatched forty soldiers to disarm these Cheyenne and recover the allegedly stolen animals. North of Denver the militiamen encountered a group of Cheyenne herding horses and mules. The militia afforded them no opportunity to explain where they had obtained the animals, and a clash quickly erupted. The Cheyenne drove the soldiers off, then unleashed their anger with raids against ranches on the South Platte.

Outraged, Governor Evans, decided that a swift and concentrated display of force was necessary to protect Colorado settlers and to drive the Cheyenne to Sand Creek. He ordered a large force into the field under the command of Lieutenant George Eayre. Eayre's experience illustrates the difficulty plains commanders had in distinguishing peaceful from hostile Indians. In the spring of 1864 he assaulted a number of Cheyenne encampments in eastern Colorado and western Kansas, destroying clothing, food, weapons, and ammunition. Among Eayre's targets was the large camp of Black Kettle, situated along the banks of the Arkansas River. One of the leading chiefs of the Southern Cheyenne and a staunch advocate of peace and conciliation with the Americans (as were nearly all of the Cheyenne leaders at this time), Black Kettle had participated at the Fort Wise council in 1861 and, in March of 1863, had journeyed to Washington with a delegation of plains chiefs to meet President Lincoln. It was natural, therefore, that Black Kettle did not expect violence at the hands of the militiamen. The sight of soldiers approaching the camp caused little alarm. Lean Bear, a lesser chief, rode out of the camp with his son to greet the arrivals. On his chest Lean Bear proudly displayed a large medal, a token of the friendship of Lincoln. As he neared the soldiers, his hand raised in a sign of peace, he noticed too late that they had formed a skirmish line with artillery in position, facing the camp. When he was within twenty yards of the soldiers, Lieutenant Eayre gave the command to fire on him, his son, and the Cheyenne camp. The volley, immediately killing Lean Bear and his son, rocked the camp. Swiftly, swarms of Cheyenne warriors sprang to their horses and routed the aggressors. The militiamen retreated westward to Fort Larned, Kansas.

The immediate effect of Eayre's raids was to escalate the violence. Now Cheyenne and Arapahoe war parties launched devastating assaults against the major Colorado trails, the stagecoach lines from Fort Kearney in Nebraska Territory on the Oregon Trail to Denver, and the farms of settlers. They burned ranches, stole livestock, and took settlers as prisoners. In response, the alarmed Governor Evans issued a proclamation on August 11, 1864, authorizing each citizen in the Colorado Territory "to go in pursuit of all hostile Indians on the plains; [and] to kill and destroy as enemies of the country wherever they may be found, all such hostile Indians." Chivington concurred with the stern measures authorized by the governor. As Lieutenant Joseph Cramer evaluated his superior: "He [Chivington] believed it to be right and honorable to use any means under God's heaven to kill Indians . . . and 'damn any man that was in sympathy with Indians.'"

Once the Coloradans attacked them, the Cheyenne and Arapahoe reciprocated, escalating their attacks on settlers and cutting telegraph lines between Colorado and the East. By late August other plains tribes had joined in attacking whites. "It will be the largest Indian war this country ever had," Governor Evans predicted, "extending from Texas to [Canada] involving nearly all the wild tribes of the plains." An eyewitness described the volatile events to the *New York Times*, which published the account on September 8. The report alluded to the widespread but incorrect belief that agents of the Confederacy provoked these Indian attacks:

> Upon the overland route, devastation, terror, murder, has held a perfect carnival. From Denver to Fort Laramie to the Little Blue in Kansas, and to the Big Sandy in Nebraska, both within 150 miles of the Missouri, the Rebel Indians have swept like a hurricane. In a distance of four hundred miles along this great route they have captured at least 50 trains of merchandise or Government freight, driving stock, plundering and destroying to the value of a quarter of a million dollars. They have murdered two hundred white persons, among them many women and children. The stark bodies lie stripped and mutilated in the glaring sunlight, festering and rotting for want of burial, or half charred, are seen moldering amid the ruins of ranches, cabins, and stage-stations.

As hostilities increased and the death toll mounted, some level-headed Americans, such as the influential trader George Bent, attempted to reason with both sides, urging them to stop the warfare. Success seemed possible that fall at a council held at Camp Weld near Denver. There, Black Kettle, tired of raiding, ready to camp for the winter, and still an advocate of conciliation with whites, acted as spokesman for the other six Cheyenne and Arapahoe chiefs present. He declared that he, the other chiefs, and their people desired peace above all else. Governor Evans, Colonel Chivington, and the other assembled officials doubted the Indians' sincerity and therefore offered no formal peace arrangements. The council failed, but with an odd twist. Black Kettle and the other chiefs, having misunderstood their interpreter, left Camp Weld believing in the success of their initiatives and confident that conflict with the Coloradans had ended.

Unaware of the misunderstanding, Black Kettle led some 500 Cheyenne into winter camp on the Sand Creek reservation, where they thought they would be free from attack by the military. They knew nothing of the recent orders of Brigadier General Samuel R. Curtis, commander of the military Department of Kansas from Fort Leavenworth, to Chivington: "I want no peace until the Indians suffer more!" He was not alone.

In the early morning hours of November 29, 1864, Chivington, leading the First Colorado Volunteer Cavalry and one-hundred-day enlistees of the Third Colorado Cavalry, who carried with them four twelve-pound howitzers, attacked Black Kettle's sleeping encampment on the Sand Creek reservation without warning. It was virtually defenseless, filled with old men, women, and children. Most of the young men were miles away in Kansas that night hunting food to bring back for the winter. On a pole over Black Kettle's lodge floated both a white flag and a flag of the United States. Near dawn, the assault began. First the militia ran off all the Indian's horses, making escape from the coming assault all but impossible. Next a terrible volley of cannon and rifle shot ripped through the Cheyenne camp. Then the columns charged and encircled the camp, firing point-blank at its terrified occupants. Any surviving Cheyenne who had not fled were now subjected to the soldiers, who ravaged them with swords and knives. Men were castrated, and their organs, as some soldiers promised each other, were saved as souvenirs, to be used as tobacco pouches. Pregnant women's abdomens were sliced open, both mother and baby left to die. Children were dragged from their hiding places and murdered. Robert Bent, a local rancher who unwillingly accompanied Chivington, agonized, "There seemed to be indiscriminate slaughter of men, women and children." Some Cheyenne somehow managed to escape, Black Kettle being among the fortunate.

Sand Creek aroused few favorable responses among Americans. The most favorable was perhaps the ecstatic welcome of Chivington and his men upon their return to Denver. Cheyenne scalps were exhibited in the opera house, prompting wild enthusiasm. "All acquitted themselves well," proclaimed the *Rocky Mountain News*. "Colorado soldiers have again covered themselves with glory." Chivington's observation, "nits make lice," allowed some to feel justified about the slaughter of children. Outside of Colorado, much of the nation recoiled in horror. The Commissioner of Indian Affairs castigated the Colorado militia, referring to its attack at Sand Creek as a massacre in which Cheyenne were "butchered in cold blood by troops in the service of the United States." As public condemnation swelled, calls rang out for a governmental inquiry into what was already being called the "Sand Creek massacre." Two federal committees eventually issued reports. The Joint Committee on the Conduct of the [Civil] War, following its investigation, vilified the militia and the conduct of Chivington:

> Wearing the uniform of the United States, which should be the emblem of justice and humanity; holding the important position of commander of a military district, and therefore having the honor of the government to that extent in his keeping, [Chivington] deliberately planned and executed a foul and dastardly massacre which would have disgraced the [worst] savage among those who were the victims of his cruelty.

The joint congressional special committee agreed fully, concluding about Sand Creek: "The fact which gives such terrible force to the condemnation of the wholesale massacre of the Arapahoes and Cheyennes [was] that those Indians . . . believed themselves to be under the protection of our flag."

The Southern Cheyenne and Arapahoe kept on the move following the Sand Creek massacre. Some merely wandered the plains, avoiding all contact with whites. A number of them moved north into Sioux territory to reside with that tribe and their brethren, the Northern Cheyenne and Arapahoe. Still others, thirsting for revenge as word of Chivington's deed spread, organized huge war parties that scourged farms, trading posts, stagecoach stations, and wagon trains along the Platte River. Coloradans, anticipating that they had "adjusted" one problem at Sand Creek, ignited a far more deadly one for themselves and other whites on the plains. By the spring of 1865, hostilities burned themselves out for the moment, but they had cost "many valuable lives and $40,000,000," the commissioner of Indian Affairs concluded.

In October 1865, Southern Cheyenne and Arapahoe, joined by Comanche, Kiowa, and Kiowa-Apaches, met in council with federal emissaries at the mouth of the Little Arkansas River, where the United States offered all of them new treaties. The Little Arkansas Treaty required the Southern Cheyenne and Arapahoe to relinquish all claims to their Colorado lands, merely reiterating the Fort Wise Treaty of 1861. It also required that they forfeit the Sand Creek reserve and cede their cherished hunting grounds in western Kansas. In return the government promised the two tribes a new reserve south of the Arkansas along the Cimarron River. A minority of chiefs, including Black Kettle, signed the document. When other tribal members learned of their action, they expressed consternation and great condemnation. Within a week of finalizing the Cheyenne-Arapahoe accord, the federal government came to agreement with the Comanche, Kiowa, and Kiowa-Apaches, promising each of them reservations in the panhandle of northern Texas and the western part of the Indian Territory.

None of the tribes received the land pledged to them at the Little Arkansas; the United States Senate amended the treaties in such a way as to make the clauses granting the new reservations virtually meaningless.

The Civil War proved as much a turning point for the trans-Mississippi West and its Indian population as it did for the nation as a whole. Federal officials reduced the lands of the Five Civilized Tribes, while opening half of the Indian Territory for further implementation of the policy of placing the plains tribes on reservations. And westerners, with the federal authority's attention focused on the Civil War, used the opportunity to open more land in the trans-Mississippi West for white exploitation and settlement, expelling any tribe that stood in their way. But these actions heightened Indian hostility toward whites and galvanized among many the conviction to yield no further. Tribal leaders who still exhorted their people to follow the path of conciliation with whites found their arguments undermined by events of the Civil War years and their authority over younger warriors, who would not retreat from confrontation, waning. "Although wrongs have been done me I live in hopes [sic]," Black Kettle reflected. "But since they have come and cleaned out our lodges, horses, and everything else, it is hard for me to believe white men any more."

While in progress, the Civil War had been the center of Washington's concern. Indian affairs, of necessity, were pushed aside. But by the summer of 1865 the war had ended, and Washington quickly resumed, even stepped up, its efforts to solve the western Indian crisis. It had no choice. In the face of the turbulent atmosphere in the West and the hardened sentiments of embittered Indians and aggressive whites, federal offi-

Two Indians being sworn in to the Union Army.
Courtesy, State Historical Society of Wisconsin

cials could not delay. The Indians were described as "a set of miserable, dirty, lousy, blanketed, thieving, lying, sneaking, murdering, graceless, faithless, gut-eating skunks as the Lord ever permitted to inflict the earth," in the *Topeka Weekly Leader*, and "whose immediate and final extermination all men . . . should pray for." The Great Plains was a tinderbox, already ignited and about to explode into the bloody conflict known as the Plains Wars.

Suggested Reading

Annie Abel's trilogy is old, but still provides a useful understanding of the role of Indians in the Civil War era, especially her first two volumes: *The American Indian as Slaveholder and Secessionist* (Cleveland, 1915; reprinted 1999) and *The American Indian in the Civil War, 1862–1865* (Cleveland, 1919; reprinted 1999). Laurence M. Hauptman's *Between Two Fires: American Indians in the Civil War* (New York, 1996) details American Indian participation in the war between the United States and the Confederate States. Edmund J. Danzinger, Jr., *Indians and Bureaucrats: Administering the Reservation Policy during the Civil War* (Urbana, Ill., 1974) and David A. Nichols, *Lincoln and the Indians: Civil War Policy and Politics* (Columbia, Mo., 1978) are important works on these subjects. For biographies about the two important leaders in the intra-Cherokee struggle, consult Kenny A. Franks *Stand Watie and the Agony of the Cherokee Nation* (Memphis, Tenn., 1979) and Gary E. Moulton, *John Ross, Cherokee Chief* (Athens, Ga., 1978). Circumstances surrounding the Sioux are dealt with in Robert Huhn Jones, *The Civil War in the Northwest: Nebraska, Wisconsin, Iowa, Minnesota, and the Dakotas* (Norman, Okla., 1960), Kenneth Carley, *The Sioux Uprising of 1862* (St. Paul, Minn., 1961), and C. M. Oehler, *The Great Sioux Uprising* (New York, 1959). Stan Hoig's *The Sand Creek Massacre* (Norman, Okla., 1961) chronicles that great tragedy in the Colorado territory.

Chapter 6
Ambiguity and Misunderstanding

The Struggle between the U.S. Army and the Indians for the Great Plains

Thomas W. Dunlay

*A*nglo Americans and Plains Indians first came into serious conflict in Texas, where by the 1830s white settlement had penetrated the raiding range of the Comanches and Kiowas. The belligerence and mutual lack of understanding the Indian and white people displayed ensured future conflicts and the growth of a mutual hatred. Elsewhere the American settlement frontier remained east of the Great Plains, and through the 1840s only fur traders, trappers, and Santa Fe traders had any considerable contact with the Plains tribes. Nevertheless, the Plains people were certainly aware of the white presence in their homelands; whence came a variety of material goods on which they became increasingly dependent and diseases that devastated some tribes, especially the sedentary Missouri River folk. Though impressed by the tools and luxuries the whites dispensed, the Plains Indians remained ethnocentrically contemptuous of white behavior. In any case, at midcentury the Plains tribes had little conception of the vast number of whites or the power embodied in their technology and social organizations.

The westward expansion of the United States in the 1840s, followed by the California gold rush, changed this situation. Large numbers of whites began to cross the Plains by the Platte River route, while lesser numbers did so farther south. Comanche leaders promptly informed U.S. authorities that they did not object to whites crossing their territory, providing the travelers remained "orderly," a requirement that casts a curious light on the Comanches' fearsome reputation. Interestingly, they made a distinction between "Americans" and "Texans," not yet realizing the implications of the recent U.S. annexation of the Lone Star Republic.

Not until 1848 and 1849 did the U.S. Army first establish military posts beyond the eastern periphery of the Great Plains. In 1851, at Fort Laramie in present-day Wyoming, U.S. civil authorities held the first great council with the Northern Plains tribes, in which the former hoped to secure pledges of safe passage through the region for white travelers as well as intertribal peace among the Indian peoples themselves. The Plains tribes had for decades been accustomed to refer to the president as the *Great Father* or *Grandfather*, but they had no idea of the sort of authority the term implied for the "Great Father's" representatives. Nor could they imagine the sort of control the federal government expected ultimately to exercise over them, or the way they would be dispossessed of their lands once the same were coveted by whites.

In addition, they could not imagine that the white authorities regarded them as children, whose way of life deserved no respect and whose thoughts and wishes need be consulted only as a short-term expedient to further government policy. David Mitchell and Thomas Fitzpatrick, the experienced fur traders who negotiated the 1851 Fort Laramie treaty, must have realized that the Plains tribes considered themselves lords of the grasslands, tolerating a limited white presence in their territory only for their own convenience and economic advantage. Most whites, however, never grasped this viewpoint or regarded it as nothing more than foolish arrogance.

The Teton Sioux, by virtue of their numbers, had by midcentury acquired a dominant position on the Northern Plains, as far south as the Platte River valley. Together with their Cheyenne and Arapaho allies, the Sioux were asserting control over the Powder River country to the west and the Republican River valley to the south. Only in the 1850s did they begin to encounter a military power greater than theirs—that of the United States—and only gradually did they realize how great the disparity was or that their interests, as they perceived them, were incompatible with the purposes of the newcomers.

The first violent conflicts between the Sioux and Anglo-Americans were the product of misunderstanding and the irresponsibility or bad judgment of persons on both sides, a pattern that would repeat itself many times in the future. In the famous "Mormon cow" incident of 1854, the army attempted to follow a policy of punishing individual Indians for acts defined as offenses, in this case the shooting of an emigrant's cow near Fort Laramie. In theory this was preferable to punishing whole groups for individual acts; in practice it proved unworkable. Lieutenant Grattan's attempt to arrest the particular Sioux who killed the cow led to the deaths of himself, his whole detachment, and a number of Sioux, thanks apparently to a drunken interpreter, the inflexibility of Grattan, and the intransigence of the Sioux. The army then switched to massive retaliation, and the following year General William Harney attacked the first Sioux he could find at Blue Water Creek in Nebraska.

The next few decades would see many repetitions of the foregoing chain of events, with but minor variations. Neither side could see the other's viewpoint, and the actions of a few men on the spot often committed large numbers of people to increasing violence. The army repeatedly suffered a defeat when the bad judgment of one or two commanders placed a relatively small number of troops at the mercy of a greater number of Indians whose fighting prowess had been greatly underestimated. In turn, the Indians suffered defeat and serious losses, by their standards, when they allowed the soldiers, whose capabilities also were underestimated, to surprise their vulnerable camp. The Sioux often were "surprised" in camp because their leaders had assumed they were on good terms with the whites

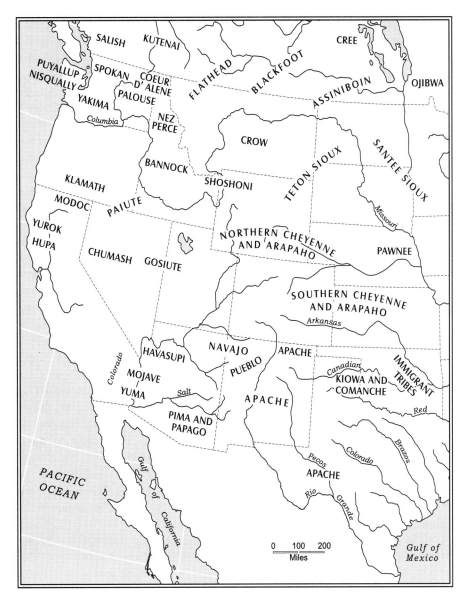

Major Western Tribes in the Mid-Nineteenth Century

or could settle any differences by talking to the leader of the approaching force. However, once the whites had defined a particular group or band of people as hostile, they attacked all those belonging to the said "enemy" tribe without considering whether the Indians concerned defined themselves as enemies of the whites. On both sides, therefore, persons innocent of any direct participation in violent acts suffered the vengeance of aroused fighters, phenomena frequently repeated across the Great Plains for the next generation.

In spite of such spectacular episodes, during the 1850s Indian-white conflict on the central and northern Plains remained desultory. White settlement did not really come within the range of the Sioux and the Cheyennes, and the army, for reasons of government policy and logistics, waged only a few intermittent campaigns against the Natives. On the southern Plains, on the other hand, the white settlement frontier confronted the Comanches and the Kiowas directly, and the army faced the problem of frontier defense hampered by its own shortage of troops, inferior mobility, and tactical methods ill-suited to the challenge. For several years the military tried to protect the settlers with a cordon of posts, staffed largely by infantry, and a small mounted force. This passive, linear defense proved inadequate since mounted Indian raiders could move freely between the posts and generally be on their way home with their booty—chiefly livestock and prisoners—by the time a pursuit was organized.

By the late 1850s, the regular army began to follow the example of the Texas Rangers, pursuing a more aggressive strategy, with an expanded cavalry force and members of the friendly tribes of the Texas frontier acting as both scouts and fighting auxiliaries. Troops and scouts pursued and attacked Comanches and Kiowas in Indian Territory and even farther north. This effective combination was unhinged when Texas forced the federal government to remove the friendly tribes—in the opinion of some officers the most effective defenders of the frontier—from Texas to the Indian Territory in 1859. Soon after, secession and civil war broke down all frontier defenses across the Plains.

It would be wrong, however, to imagine that Indian-white conflict on the Plains increased in the 1860s simply because the regular army was withdrawn to the East to fight another war. The real cause of "Indian trouble" always had been and still was white movement westward, and the Civil War did not stop or even greatly impede that phenomenon. Six new federal territories were organized during the war years, and major gold discoveries in the Rockies created new pockets of settlement whose lines of communication and supply ran across the Plains. The Santee Sioux outbreak in Minnesota in 1862 was the beginning of the bloodiest years of Indian-white confrontation in the region.

By 1864, Plains travel had become exceedingly hazardous for whites, whether traders, settlers, or would-be gold miners, and large numbers of Civil War volunteer troops were serving in the West, especially on the Platte River road. These volunteer organizations took an especially punitive approach to Indians they defined as hostile. There was a widespread belief that the mounting outbreaks throughout the Plains were the result of a Confederate conspiracy, which only aggravated the already existing racial and cultural prejudices against Indians among whites in the West. The most famous result of this attitude was the horrific massacre of Southern Cheyennes at Sand Creek, Colorado, put into effect by Colorado volunteer troops in 1864. As so often, the immediate result of such an assault was to aggravate dramatically the interracial hostility.

The end of the Civil War left a war-weary nation confronted with greatly intensified Indian-white conflict on the Plains and elsewhere. In 1865 and 1866

General William T. Sherman and commissioners in a treaty council with the Sioux at Fort Laramie, Wyoming, 1868. National Archives #NWDNS-111-SC-95986

the government made a concerted effort to negotiate treaties with the Plains peoples in hopes of avoiding further conflict and expense. These efforts failed because, as before, neither side could really understand what the other wanted or how the others viewed the situation. The Indians wanted to continue their accustomed way of life, one dependent on vast space and abundant game; certain of the white man's material goods appealed to them as an enhancement of this life, but there was no appeal in the white way of life as a whole.

The whites persisted in making treaties with Indian "main" chiefs, who could generally be induced to sign the documents in return for distribution of goods to their people, because no other way of dealing with semi-independent tribes was conceivable. But the intention was always to increase government control over entire tribes, until the time arrived when white authorities could make decisions without consulting the Indians' desires. The underlying philosophy was always that the whites knew what was best for the Indians—better than the Indians themselves did. Thus, even the most honorable white negotiator was in some sense engaged in deception—and in self-deception.

A dramatic example of such confusion lay in the treaty council at Fort Laramie with the Sioux in June 1866. There, the government representatives had promised to guarantee the Sioux extensive hunting grounds in the Dakotas, Montana, and Wyoming. But even as the council was in progress, troops passed through Laramie headed for the Powder River country to build forts to protect the Bozeman Trail, running directly through the hunting grounds being promised en route to the newly discovered Montana goldfields. Remembering the destruction of the natural environment along the Platte River road, the Sioux leaders could not look on this development calmly; a few chiefs signed the treaty, but others prepared to resist the establishment of Fort Phil Kearny and other posts. Apparently it had occurred to no one in authority that the newly proposed forts would be, to the Indians, directly incompatible with the promises of the treaty makers.

For the next decade the federal government would follow a carrot-and-stick policy toward the Plains tribes, alternating military operations and attempts at peacemaking in a pattern that confused the Indians and satisfied almost no whites. The end result, of course, was the confinement of the Plains people on reservations, deprived of their traditional way of life as well as the power of decision over their present lives. This, of course, had been the official goal all along. The overall tendency is clear, but any examination of details produces confusion, as it did for contemporaries.

The Plains tribes varied in their political organization, but none had the type of unitary state, able to compel the obedience of all, that whites considered normal and desirable. Much that seemed inconsistent or "treacherous" in their conduct stemmed from this fact and the related fact that the strongest, overriding loyalties were always to the most immediate group, dwindling as the group grew larger. Family, warrior society, band, division, then finally tribe, drew attachment and loyalty—virtually never "the Indians" as a whole.

One clear illustration of this point is the regular appearance of Indian scouts acting in alliance with the army. Often such scouts belonged to enemy tribes of the people the army was fighting. The Sioux, having acquired their dominant position on the Northern Plains at the expense of various weaker tribes, now found many among the Crows, Shoshonis, Arikaras, and Pawnees ready to provide needed expert assistance to the whites to defeat them. The Comanches on the Southern Plains found themselves in a similar situation. It was the dominant, stronger tribes who had the most to lose by submission to the whites; the weaker ones, seeing in the whites an ally against their immediate Native enemy, believed they had something to gain by joining the newcomers.

Other Indian allies of the white military, however, hailed from what whites considered the same tribe with which the army was engaged. Although whites might have been quick to label such individuals traitors, they found various reasons for undertaking to serve the army, generally without disloyalty to the group to which they actually owed their strongest allegiance. Economic benefits, expected advantages their band or family might gain from the whites as a result of their services, or the simple desire to get away from a reservation and engage in activities proper to warriors were among their motives. Some such scouts were bitterly disappointed in the end, while others of them later judged that they had made the best bargain they could under the circumstances. In any case, Indian scouts and fighting auxiliaries were present in most Plains campaigns, sometimes in small numbers, sometimes composing a substantial portion of the military force.

Significantly, their importance was out of proportion to their numbers, for they greatly extended the capabilities of white and black regular troops.

That the U.S. Army had to secure the services of Indians to fight Indians emphasizes some peculiar features of the Plains Wars. The United States, after all, had a population advantage over the Indians, as separate tribes or all together, that was ridiculously disproportionate. In technology, too, there was no comparison; the whites had railroads, telegraph systems, and mass production industry, while the Indians could not even make a steel knife. The result of any conflict between such disparate groups would seem a foregone conclusion, and in the long run, of course, it was. Nevertheless, considered as a whole, the Plains Wars proved to be the longest military engagement in American history, during which the army encountered innumerable frustrations and many tactical defeats. Both the abilities of the Plains Indians and the weaknesses of the U.S. Army made the conquest longer and rougher than might have been expected.

The country itself was commonly the Indians' ally and the army's enemy. Sheer distance imposed enormous logistical burdens on an army whose transport depended on animals and wagons. The coming of the railroad to the Plains made a significant difference, of course; Harney's army, campaigning against the Sioux in 1855, had had to carry its supplies by wagon all the way from Fort Leavenworth to western Nebraska and on to the Dakotas. After the Civil War, use of the railroad moved supply bases much nearer the campaigning areas. General William T. Sherman not unreasonably regarded the railroad as the answer to the "Indian Problem." Even so, supplies might have to be carried hundreds of miles from the nearest track into remote areas where the hostiles might be found.

For their part, the Indians never shared this disability; they lived off the land, and on the move, all their lives. Their "commissary" was the buffalo herds, the decline of which may have had as much to do with the defeat of the Plains tribes as any military activity. Nomadic peoples had no such difficulties in traveling rapidly across the country as did the soldiers, for their whole way of life and their material possessions were designed for mobility: Indian women and children with their household goods readily crossed streams that the army regarded as impassable.

White men generally did not admire the appearance of the Indian pony, but this scrubby beast had one great advantage over the big "American" horse used by the cavalry; it had lived on prairie grass all its life. The army horse was used to grain, without which its performance fell off rapidly. Army officers acknowledged that, with any sort of head start, the Indians could stay ahead of the cavalry in a straight chase indefinitely. Since each trooper had only one horse and most Plains warriors had several mounts, a "stern chase" generally was a losing proposition for the U.S. military. Some reckless attacks against Indians, such as Custer's at the Little Bighorn, were undertaken out of a fear that the hostiles might get away if the opportunity to strike was not seized, regardless of the apparent odds.

The Plains were not, strictly speaking, a desert, but parts of them, at certain times, were exceedingly dry. The Indians, of course, knew where to find potable water better than the army ever could hope to. In general, the Indians almost invariably knew the country much better than did their enemies, (unless the latter had an unusually well-qualified guide, white or Indian). Therefore the history of the Plains Wars is full of army columns being defeated as much by the country and its hardships as by the human enemy. In marching into the Powder River country in 1865 to campaign against the Sioux and Cheyennes, the commands of Colonels Nelson Cole and Samuel Walker lost most of their animals due to the hardships of the journey. They were forced, therefore, to burn most of their wagons and supplies and were near starvation—as well as under harrassment by the enemy, when rescued by other troops. Eleven years later General George Crook, far more knowledgeable about frontier logistics and Indian campaigning than either Cole or Walker, nonetheless found himself making what was called the "Horsemeat March"—so-called because his men had to slaughter their mounts as they broke down to avoid starvation—through the western Dakotas, scoring only one fight with the hostile Sioux.

The army found no complete answer to the Plains Indians' superior mobility. The troops used mule pack trains instead of wagons, and some commanders mounted their infantry on mules and captured Indian ponies, but they never could really hope to overtake a running enemy. The soldiers found that to force a fight out of the hostiles they had to catch them off guard; if the Indians themselves offered to do battle, it generally meant that they had the advantage or were assured of an escape route.

The sheer immensity of the country also made it hard for the army to locate the Indians. There was, of course, no aerial reconnaissance or electronic communications; the scouts of both sides rode horseback and carried their reports only as fast as their horses could traverse rugged terrain. No one could deny the Indians their superiority in scouting and trailing; such training started in boyhood, and few white scouts could match the Indians' abilities. Whites preferred to deem these "Indian" skills as inherent and hereditary, having nothing to do with intelligence or reasoning, rather than the result of long, intensive training. In any case, the army's best hope of finding hostile camps was the recruitment of Indian scouts.

In many ways Indian warfare was conducted as in preindustrial times, dependent as it was on the skills and stamina of men, not on the superiority of one side's technological complex. It was not altogether surprising, then, that preindustrial warriors, trained since boyhood for war, hunting, horsemanship, and endurance—and fighting in their own country—should enjoy certain immediate advantages over men more dependent on their industrial base and its products and first introduced to military training and Plains conditions as adults.

The disparity in numbers between whites and Indians was not immediately apparent in the conduct of these campaigns, since it was precisely at the points of contact on the frontier that the whites were thinnest. Many Indians persisted in believing that the few whites they saw in the West were all there were. Those Indians who traveled to the eastern cities were stunned by the number of whites they had seen. But they found it impossible to make their fellow tribesmen believe them. Besides, if the Indians could somehow suspend their worldview in order to believe the reports, the implications thereof were intolerable.

Away from the railroad and the telegraph line, the principal sign of the white man's allegedly superior civilization were his weapons; the point was emphasized by the Kiowa chief Satanta's famous remark that the only parts of the white man's road that appealed to him were guns and whiskey. Chief Washakie of the Shoshonis discouraged certain of his tribesmen who wanted to resist the whites by showing them a revolver and reminding them that, while the whites could make such a weapon, the Shoshonis could make only bows and arrows.

Indian fighting men frequently obtained firearms, either through trade or as prizes of war, but both the number and quality of these arms remain subjects of debate. Some army officers insisted that every hostile Indian by about 1870 had a Winchester rifle (a breech-loading repeating rifle far superior to the old muzzle-loading muskets) and an ample supply of ammunition, thoughtfully furnished by the Bureau of Indian Affairs. Some historians counter that the weapons most Indians carried were the old muzzle-loading smooth bores. The safest conclusion is that there must have been great variation over time and place. Beyond dispute is that the Plains Indians developed the technique of reloading metallic cartridges (which the newer rifles fired) before the whites realized this was possible. While this coup is a tribute to their ingenuity, it also points out both the ammunition supply problems facing the Indians as well as their early familiarity with this latest form of ammunition and the weapons that used it.

Therefore, to point out the preindustrial nature of Plains warfare, is not to say that it did not evolve or that the combatants did not adapt to technological innovations. Use of smoothbore musketry by Indian enemies in the early 1800s seems to have forced the Plains tribes to abandon the leather armor and massed charges they had developed with the introduction of the horse. They fought stripped to the breechcloth, not because they were "naked savages" but because a bullet could drive bits of clothing into a wound and increase the danger of infection. When Anglo Americans first encountered Plains warriors in Texas, they found that their long rifles were not well suited to fighting horsemen who could cover several hundred yards and fire twenty arrows in the time it took to reload an unwieldy muzzleloader. The Colt revolver, adopted by the Texas Rangers in the 1840s, made horseback combat possible and shifted the balance in the white man's favor. The revolver-wielding horseman could take on several Indians armed with muskets, bows, or lances, and so armed both Rangers and regular cavalry developed a certain conviction of superiority and a readiness to attack when opportunity offered. Indeed, a deep-seated conviction of cultural and racial superiority seemed confirmed, a tactical advantage that persisted more or less through the Civil War years.

The Civil War brought the first widespread battlefield use of new weapons developments, breech-loading and repeating rifles. The new rifles made previous notions of tactics obsolete, as witnessed by Civil War casualty lists. The breechloader accentuated the change by making it possible for a soldier to fire-

and reload-from a prone position, with nearly all of his body behind cover. The repeater only enhanced the possibilities.

Over the years after 1865, the Indians seem to have acquired increasing numbers of breech-loading firearms. There is no reason to doubt that they fully appreciated the advantage of a weapon that allowed them the maximum use of cover and which fired much faster than the familiar muzzle loader, and with far greater range and accuracy than the revolver. The repeaters were desirable, but the most useful feature of the new weaponry remained breech-loading, especially after the army gave up the repeating Spencer cavalry carbine in the early 1870s, adopting a single-shot breech-loading Springfield and putting troopers more or less on a par with the Indians.

Today we think of the Plains warrior as preeminently the "horse Indian," the "finest light cavalry in the world," in the opinion of some of their more admiring opponents. They could indeed fight well on horseback, generally better than the regular cavalry, and they took full advantage of the mobility the horse gave them, but they were by no means incapable of fighting on foot and very often did so, especially when on the defensive. In fact, some tribes showed considerable ability in building field fortifications or digging rifle pits. The Plains warrior was as much aware as any Civil War infantryman of the immense advantage held by a man in a hole or behind a rock over a man advancing toward him in the open.

There was a significant difference in military philosophy between the Plains tribes and the United States Army. We know that the Plains people placed a great value on courage and martial achievement; glory was the natural and legitimate desire of young men, a necessity for status. But this philosophy was perfectly compatible with the desire to live to enjoy one's triumph. There was nothing glorious about a high casualty list; war leaders who lost many men soon ceased to have followers, for their "medicine" was obviously deficient. The goal was to inflict the maximum damage on the enemy, perform brave deeds, and come home alive. Therefore, the underlying philosophy of Plains Indian warfare was to minimize loss of life and be ready to make an escape the moment things went badly.

To be sure, suicidal displays of bravery sometimes occurred when a man wanted to prove his courage, recover a wounded or dead comrade, or literally commit suicide. But the decision was that of the individual warrior, except in cases in which a village with its women and children was under attack. Ordinarily a war chief did not order his men to perform a maneuver likely to result in the loss of many of them. The idea that a leader would deliberately order men to attack knowing that heavy losses would occur in order to take some objective was unfathomable to the Indians.

White military men were ambivalent about this aspect of Plains culture. Their prime definition of courage was the unquestioned willingness to go when ordered into a high-risk situation. For some two hundred years the basis of tactics of conventional armies had been the close-order formation, armed with the smoothbore musket, trained to move shoulder to shoulder toward the enemy, taking losses without flinching. The musket was so inaccurate that the best results came from volley firing, not from individual marksmanship. The Civil War, fought with the more accurate rifle, demonstrated the obsolescence of such tactics, but it was hard to escape the philosophical heritage. Therefore, in the eyes of most white soldiers, the Indian warriors seemed deficient in courage.

The real difference was, however, apparent to a few army officers. The Indians were highly skilled individual fighting men, trained from boyhood, each relying to a great extent on his own judgment, alert to preserve his own life. By contrast, the U.S. soldier of the period was sketchily trained, required to rely on his leaders to think for him, and to act in unison with his fellows without considering his personal safety. But weapons technology had reached a point where the old military philosophy was no longer functional. Men had to disperse and make use of cover in order to avoid being slaughtered uselessly by more accurate, faster-firing weapons. An officer could no longer keep all his men within sound of his voice, dictating their every move.

Ironically, the military philosophy of the "primitive" Indian cultures was in some ways better adapted to take full advantage of the features the new weapons offered than was that of the armies representing "industrial" civilization. The Indians tried every expedient to avoid personal harm, let each man pick his own spot and dictate his own moves within loose or nonexistent battle plans, and never sacrificed lives to take ground, of which there was plenty on the Great Plains. The apparent flatness of the Plains is deceptive, and its native inhabitants knew well how to use every dip and rise to their advantage in military engagements. Concealment, ambush, and surprise were vital elements in their tactics, and they vastly preferred to have the odds on their side before committing to a particular fight: battling superior numbers might be glorious, but it was not practical. The chance to kill several of the enemy at little or no loss to one's own side was highly desirable.

That the difference between the respective combatants was inherent in their cultures and the country is suggested by the North West Rebellion of 1885, the Canadian Army's sole campaign against Plains Indians. In spite of their great difference in tradition and experience from that of the U.S. Army, the Canadian troops, using conventional European tactics against Indians and Métis, who fought much like Indians, encountered many of the same difficulties and frustrations, suffered several tactical defeats, and at least once landed near a disaster comparable to Custer's. Indeed, some of the Canadian commanders, judging from their own words and actions, were haunted by the possibility of a defeat like that at Little Bighorn.

The most experienced and perceptive U.S. Army officers came to appreciate these points. Increasingly in the years after 1865 the soldiers fought an enemy they seldom saw, except at a distance—even then little more than the puff of smoke from his rifle. Contempt for Indian "cowardice" was small compensation for the frustration of being unable to get close to the enemy and defeat him in a pitched battle, to say nothing of the occasional bloody defeat brought about by just such contempt and frustration.

Nothing said here should imply that the leaders of the frontier army were stupid or incapable of learning. Some, to be sure, proved incapable of adjusting from the mass battlefields of the Civil War to the elusive skirmishing on the Plains. But the real handicaps of the army were those inherent in its organization and doctrine and in the society it represented. An army organized on conventional, European lines that intended to fight similar enemies instead met foes with a talent for guerrilla warfare in country that gave them ample room to take full advantage of their mobility. And if this were not difficult enough, the frontier armies were expected to perform a wide range of police duties, tasks that often distracted them further from conducting Plains warfare.

A country facing little immediate foreign danger reduced its regular forces to some 25,000 men. Nevertheless, the traditional American reliance on wartime volunteers strangely did not apply in Indian wars. In conjunction with the overall tendency toward governmental centralization, the federal forces in the post–Civil War period largely assumed the role once shared by frontier riflemen, rangers, and other local volunteers and militiamen. Frontier whites frequently expressed contempt for the regulars and opined that the government could better protect frontier settlements by calling on the services of hardy westerners who knew how to use guns and loved to fight. There were at least a few such characters outside the pages of fiction, but after 1865 even the Texas Rangers had only a modest role in Indian-white conflicts. The backwoodsmen had given way to the bluecoat.

The postwar reduction of the army moved General Philip Sheridan to complain that no other nation would have tried to control the Plains, his area of command from 1868 to 1882, with an army of less than 50,000. Probably no general in history has ever had enough men, but Sheridan's point was this: Distance made concentration slow. Greater numbers of troops in the region might have made it possible to get enough men to a trouble spot quickly enough to contain or prevent hostilities simply by overawing the Indians. Sheridan, however, seems temporarily to have overlooked the difficulties experienced in supplying even the number of troops that he had in the field during campaigns.

The army never seems to have developed any official, formal doctrine on fighting Indians, nor in conducting relations with them. At any rate, there were no handbooks or textbooks on the subject. Randolph B. Marcy's *The Prairie Traveler,* published "by authority of the War Department" in 1859, was primarily a survival manual, useful for both military and civilian travelers on the Plains, although some space was devoted to a description of the Plains tribes and some six pages to Indian fighting. Marcy fully appreciated the importance of trailing and the value of Indian scouts; a few years later he did indeed give more detailed prescriptions for coping with the military problems of the Plains in his memoirs, rather than in an official publication. His suggestions were virtually the same as those actually followed by those commanding on the Plains, but no one was required to study his ideas

What Marcy had learned was also apparent to other experienced frontier soldiers who had open minds and were flexible. Lacking any formal doctrine, it was the judgment of these men that served as the basis of the army's military effort against the Plains tribes. The more sensible men realized that, regrettable as it might be, they would not win these wars in some great prairie Gettysburg. Soldiers had to increase their mobility as much as possible, but they must also acknowledge the enemy's superiority in this respect. They could not expect him to cooperate by fighting at a disadvantage. And while there was no way to avoid fighting in the enemy's country, commanders eventually decided that troops could campaign in the winter, when the Indian ponies were in their poorest condition and the hardships of flight and loss of property would fall the hardest on the women and children of a group. Above all, they might learn to turn against the enemy his own weapon of surprise.

In the East, Anglo Americans had generally fought sedentary Indians with permanent villages and fields. These Indians were fine guerrilla fighters, but should a white army manage to reach a particular village, it had little difficulty destroying the enemy's dwellings, crops, and household goods. In time, the devastated tribes had to acknowledge defeat and surrender their lands. In the West, however, those Native peoples who farmed were generally friendly or at least neutral; the hostiles were nomads with portable homes and no fields of crops to destroy. In this case, there was no geographical point to label as the "objective." Nevertheless, elusive as they were, white authorities finally insisted that the enemy villages themselves must be targeted.

It is often stated that the great weakness of the Plains tribes was their failure to post sentries. However, the hunting parties that were usually out from their camps often served the same purpose, and their great mobility gave those in camp an excellent chance of getting away, given the slightest warning. The army realized, therefore, that the villages had to be taken by surprise, and surprise meant a night attack.

The army's use of Indian scouts increased its chances of locating Indian camps without alerting them to the presence of soldiers. The scouts also guided columns of troops to strategic spots from which to attack, a task best accomplished under the cover of darkness. In addition, it often was the scouts who ran off the camps' pony herds, destroying the people's mobility.

The optimal time to attack a camp was just before dawn: this way the victims might be caught asleep and bewildered, but dawn's break would give the soldiers enough light to fight effectively in case of a counterattack. But even when truly surprised, the Plains warriors were likely to prove formidable in defense of their families, and some surprises proved disastrous for the soldiers. Writing of a march through the Big Horn Mountains by Colonel Ranald Mackenzie's command of 1,000 troopers and scouts in 1876 to attack the Cheyennes, Lieutenant

John G. Bourke commented that if the hostiles received any warning, in that rugged terrain, the army's casualties would only be limited by the amount of ammunition the Cheyennes had to expend. Even though Mackenzie did achieve surprise, the Cheyennes quickly retired to the rocks and turned the action into a stalemate, although they lost most of their household goods and horses. General John Gibbon surprised the Nez Perces in their camp at the Big Hole in Montana in 1877, having arrived with more fighting men than the Nez Perces had, chiefly infantrymen toting rifles of greater range and power than cavalry carbines. In spite of all such advantages, Gibbon's command was defeated and narrowly avoided a massacre.

An inescapable part of these attacks on Indians camps was that they put women and children in the line of fire, at least in the first minutes of the assault. Poor visibility and turmoil ensured that some women and children would be hit, even if the soldiers made a conscious effort to avoid this. Such a clear violation of nineteenth-century ideals of chivalry created moral problems, which the army never really resolved and which laid it open to attack by humanitarians. Few were willing to say outright that Indian women and children did not qualify as human beings, though some tried to imply it, for instance, by claiming that the "squaws" were foremost in the torture of captives. Generally speaking, "Indian warfare" was conceived as having different rules from "civilized" warfare, largely due to the fact that the enemy did not follow the rules as laid down by whites. General George Crook exposed the inconsistency of such thinking by pointing out that the killing of women and children in attacks on Indian camps was similar to what happened when besieged cities were bombarded with artillery. Crook concluded that the whites had not given the Indians many examples of the chivalry they were condemned for failing to emulate.

At any rate, the army had worked out a rough-and-ready strategy for coping with Plains Indian hostility. Converging columns, operating in winter if possible and with wagon transport minimized for increased mobility, entered the hunting grounds of the designated enemy. Indian scouts then sought out the hostile camps and guided a striking force for a dawn attack. In all such engagements, the army's "success" lay in the destruction of the victims' tepees and household goods, the loss of their supplies of dried meat, the loss of at least part of their pony herd, and, if possible, the taking of prisoners. Above all, the effect on the enemy's morale was of highest significance. And even if the targeted group managed to evade such an attack, constant harassment in bad weather might eventually bring them in to a fort or reservation to surrender.

The formula was not foolproof, as Custer's grand defeat and the other repeated frustrations the U.S. Army suffered on its Sioux campaign of 1876 demonstrated. In addition, winter campaigning on the Northern Plains proved more arduous than it had farther south, where the pattern was first worked out. On the high Plains, the distances involved prevented columns from really supporting each other and communication still depended on mounted couriers, often subject to considerable danger in traversing hostile territory. That the troops managed to function at all on the high Plains of Montana, Dakota, and Wyoming in the dead of winter is a tribute to their adaptability. It was when the army adopted a strategy that pushed the Indians into something approximating a war of attrition—a total war against the entire population and its resources—that the Indians realized that they could not win. They had neither the population nor the social organization to sustain such a conflict, and they regarded the loss of even a few men as a disaster. The army's adoption of total war forced proud warriors to consider the welfare of their families and chiefs to think of their bands, however crushing the blow to their personal pride.

Plains Indians waged what we might wish to call guerrilla warfare, enjoying a measure of success that this method often brings when employed against regular armies operating in difficult and generally unfamiliar terrain. But if their tactics were a classic example of guerrilla warfare, there was nothing of the ideological commitment, long-range goals, or centralized leadership we associate with twentieth-century guerrillas. Their goal was simply to be allowed to continue their accustomed way of life; they fought because that way of life was threatened, or for revenge, or because the whites attacked them in the first place—reasons for which people have fought throughout history. Considering the Indians' objective and the imbalance of the opposing forces, it is likely that no amount of centralization or elaborate ideology would have given the Indians what they would have considered a victory.

The whites' adoption of a policy of total war—not genocide in any strict sense of the term—might be considered an outgrowth of the Civil War. The same strategy of attacking Indian camps was practiced by General Harney against the Sioux in 1855 and probably owed much to the experience of Harney and other senior officers in the bitter Seminole War of 1835–1842, during which the army fought an elusive guerrilla enemy. Indian war had seldom been a matter of decisive battle between fighting men; it had commonly been necessary to attack the people and resources behind the warriors. Old frontier officers from the days before the fall of Fort Sumter and the start of the Civil War in 1861, like Randolph Marcy and George Crook, understood the military requirements of fighting Indians quite well; it was the men trained on the Civil War battlefields who had to adjust their thinking to the new situation.

In any case, the whole concept of "Indian resistance," on the Plains and elsewhere, is in some ways simply a white man's idea—not because Indians did not resist weapons in hand, but because the whites in a sense created the situation in which such "resistance" occurred. They persisted in categorizing and finding unity in the diverse peoples they encountered in the West, and especially so in "war." Since the approach of apprehending and punishing individual Indians for misdeeds proved unsatisfactory, even disastrous in such cases as the "Mormon cow incident," the concept of war against an enemy became mentally necessary. Since one could only be at war with some unified body of people, then the Sioux "nation" or Comanche "nation" had to be designated as the enemy. Some military men and civil officials were sophisticated enough to realize that this concept did not represent reality very well, but for those preferring an unambiguous situation, simple categories like "good" and "bad," "friendly" and "hostile," remained powerfully appealing.

Both the civil government and the army were burdened with two divergent concepts of their role in Indian-white relations. One was the concept of the federal government as the impartial mediator and regulator of contacts between whites and Indians, trying to prevent violence and injustice in the interests of both. The other was of the government, particularly its military arm, as the instrument for clearing the way for white expansion and settlement, "winning the West" in a campaign of conquest for the sole benefit of white people. Officially there was never any clear-cut decision for one concept over the other, but the latter obviously tended to prevail. Over the years, individual officials and army officers wavered as much as did the government, though some made unequivocal statements in support of one or the other view.

Symbolic of this internal struggle is a written exchange between Generals Crook and Sheridan in 1879. Reporting on the tragic consequences of the flight of the Northern Cheyennes from Indian Territory and the attempt to make them return there, Crook asserted that the soldiers involved, including himself, were only obeying orders, but that the government itself had been guilty of serious injustice. The Cheyennes had been forced to go to an unfamiliar, unhealthy reservation, had not received proper care thereafter, and therefore had no alternative but resistance. A number of this group had served as scouts for Crook earlier, and the general charged the government with ingratitude for forgetting their services. Sheridan, Crook's superior, responded that he could not pass Crooks report on to higher brass without comment. The "system," as applied to Indian affairs, was certainly faulty, but Sheridan saw no hope of changing it. Besides, he continued, the Cheyennes had committed atrocities against whites in their northward flight and were not deserving of sympathy. In any case, the soldiers could only obey orders.

Nevertheless, on other occasions Sheridan was ready to admit that Indians fought because of the pressure of white expansion. Many other soldiers acknowledged as much, and some even said that they would probably have done the same under like circumstances. Indeed most military men were quick to blame Indian-white violence on the civil government, the Bureau of Indian Affairs, Indian agents, and the division of authority between civil and military authorities, not to mention frontier civilians. There was much truth in such indictments, and in some cases there was even truth in the soldiers' assertion that they were the Indians' best friends. But ultimately the army was the arm of white society that necessarily enforced the will of that society on the Indians.

Although it seems redundant, it bears repeating that the two societies confronting each other on the Great Plains in the nineteenth century did not know or understand each other throughout their period of armed conflict. They knew neither each other's strengths nor weaknesses. The whites never imagined that Indian culture was not simply a lack of what white culture possessed—similar forms of law, religion, morality, among other things—that it had depth, complexity, and vitality, and that in clinging to it the Indians were not simply being obstinate, bloody-minded, or suicidal. Nor did whites realize that the unitary view of tribal society that they tried to impose on the Indians was hopelessly out of line with the facts, and so rendered their efforts to deal with such nonexistent tribal units failures from the start.

The Indians did not know that they were up against the modern state, with its ability to control the actions of great numbers of people and to call on the resources of a continent. They could understand territorial expansion, for the stronger tribes regularly engaged in it, but how could they ever have understood, or even imagined, the implacable purpose that demanded their total subjugation?

Suggested Reading

For an overview of the Plains Wars, see Ralph K. Andrist, *The Long Death: The Last Days of the Plains Indians* (New York, 1964). Indispensable military studies are Robert M. Utley's two works: *Frontiersmen in Blue: The United States Army and the Indian, 1848–1865* (New York, 1967) and *Frontier Regulars: The United States Army and the Indian, 1866–1890* (New York, 1973). Another view of the frontier army is Neil B. Thompson, *Crazy Horse Called Them Walk-a-Heaps* (St. Cloud, Minn., 1979). The background of Plains Indian tactics is found in Frank R. Secoy, *Changing Military Patterns on the Great Plains* (Seattle, 1953), showing the effects of horses and firearms on the early nineteenth century.

Among the various accounts of specific campaigns, perhaps the best are James L. Haley, *The Buffalo War: The History of the Red River Indian Uprising of 1874* (New York, 1976); William H. Leckie, *The Military Conquest of the Southern Plains* (Norman, Okla., 1963); Edgar I. Stewart, *Custer's Luck* (Norman, Okla., 1955); and John S. Gray, *Centennial Campaign: The Sioux War of 1876* (Fort Collins, Colo., 1976). For the Canadians' sole essay in Plains warfare, see Desmond Morton, *The Last War Drum* (Toronto, 1972). Stan Hoig, *The Sand Creek Massacre* (Norman, Okla., 1961) is the standard account of this notorious episode. For the background of U.S. Indian policy on the Plains, see Robert A. Trennert, *Alternative to Extinction: Federal Indian Policy and the Beginnings of the Reservation System, 1846–51*. For the beginnings of Indian-white conflict on the Plains, see Walter Prescott Webb, *The Texas Rangers* (Austin, Tex., 1965).

There are many fine tribal histories; see particularly George Bird Grinnell, *The Fighting Cheyennes* (Norman, Okla., 1956); T. R. Fehrenbach, *Comanches: The Destruction of a People* (New York, 1974); George E. Hyde, *Spotted Tail's Folk: A History of the Brule Sioux* (Norman, Okla., 1961); Donald J. Berthrong, *The Southern Cheyennes* (Norman, Okla., 1963); and Ernest Wallace and E. Adamson Hoebel, *The Comanches: Lords of the South Plains* (Norman, Okla.,

1952), an interesting blend of historical and anthropological technique. W. W. Newcombe, *The Indians of Texas* (Austin, Tex., 1961) studies the culture of each tribe and gives a good historical survey of the region.

Personal memoirs have their limitations but are indispensable all the same. One can sample a variety of viewpoints on Indians and analyses of the wars from a military standpoint by reading John G. Bourke, *On the Border With Crook* (New York, 1895); Robert G. Carter, *On the Border With Mackenzie* (Washington, 1935); Richard I. Dodge, *Our Wild Indians: Thirty-three Years Personal Experiences* (Hartford, Conn., 1883); Randolph B. Marcy, *Thirty Years of Army Life on the Border* (New York, 1866); and Marcy's *The Prairie Traveler* (New York, 1859).

Luther North, *Man of the Plains: Recollections of Luther H. North, 1856–1882,* Donald F. Danker, ed. (Lincoln, Nebr., 1961) is the leading source on the Pawnee scouts and their campaigns. George E. Hyde, *Life of George Bent* (Norman, Okla., 1967) is a remarkable account by a mixed-blood who chose to be a Cheyenne. George E. Schmitt, ed., *General George Crook: His Autobiography* (Norman, Okla., 1946) is worth reading for the general's pungent opinions, but he did not live to complete the account of his Plains campaigns. The only published study of the Indian scouts is Thomas W. Dunlay, *Wolves for the Blue Soldiers: Indian Scouts and Auxiliaries with the U.S. Army, 1860–90* (Lincoln, Nebr., 1982).

On the background of northern Plains warfare, see Richard White, "The Winning of the West: The Expansion of the Western Sioux in the Eighteenth and Nineteenth Centuries." *Journal of American History* 65 (September 1978): 319–343.

Several newer works published since the first edition of this book are valuable. D. McDermott, *A Guide to the Indian Wars of the West* (Lincoln, Nebr., 1998) is a very useful comprehensive work, explaining much of what I have said in detail. George Rollie Adams, *General William S. Harney: Prince of Dragoons* (Lincoln, Nebr., 2000) is a good biography of an important pre–Civil War figure. James R. Arnold, *Jeff Davis's Own: Cavalry, Comanches, and the Battle for the Texas Frontier* (New York, 2000) is a good study of one regiment and of Southern Plains warfare before the Civil War. Two works by William Y. Chalfant, *Cheyennes and Horse Soldiers: The 1857 Expedition and the Battle of Solomon's Fork* (Norman, Okla., 1989), and *Without Quarter: The Wichita Expedition and the Fight on Crooked Creek* (Norman, Okla., 1991), cover important early campaigns. Robert M. Utley, *The Indian Frontier of the American West, 1846–1890* (Albuquerque, N. Mex., 1984) is an important work that should have been cited originally. John S. Gray, *Custer's Last Campaign: Mitch Boyer and the Little Bighorn Reconsidered* (Lincoln, Nebr., 1991) is an important study of this famous episode.

Part II ❧
Visions of a New Order

Educational activities among Indian youth would reclaim the Indian population from barbarism, idolatry, and savage life. Savage and civilized life cannot live and prosper on the same ground. If the Indians are to be civilized and become a happy and prosperous people, which is certainly the object and intention of our Government . . . the few must yield to the many.

— Hiram Price, Commissioner of Indian Affairs

You said that you wanted to put us upon a reservation, to build us houses and make us medicine lodges. I do not want them. I was born upon the prairie where the wind blew free and there was nothing to break the light of the sun. I was born where there was no enclosures and where everything drew a free breath. I want to die there and not within walls.

— Ten Bears, Comanche

Chapter 7
The Bitter Years

Western Indian Reservation Life

Donald J. Berthrong

*I*n 1878 Washakie, a perceptive and eloquent Shoshoni chief; described the plight of his people. Within his lifetime Washakie remembered when Indians roamed free, enjoying abundant food provided by Mother Earth and her creatures. But the white man came with superior tools and terrible weapons better for war than bow and arrows, driving Indians from their vast hunting and gathering ranges on to confining reservations. The Shoshoni and other tribes, Washakie said, were only "sorry remnants once mighty, [who] are cornered in little spots of the earth all ours by right—cornered like guilty prisoners, and watched by men with guns, who are more than anxious to kill us off." United States government representatives promised the Shoshoni a "comfortable living" and protection from white intruders. Those promises were not honored. In Washakie's later life, he asked is it any wonder the Shoshoni, "nearly starved and . . . half naked . . . have fits of desperation" and think of revenge?

Numerous other Indian leaders could have echoed Washakie's remonstrance as the U.S. government, after the Civil War, implemented its reservation policy. The Comanches once ranged from north of the Arkansas River to south of the Rio Grande. Their population grew to about 14,000 people before warfare, disease, and reduced buffalo ranges began to diminish their numbers. In 1865 they still hunted over 30 million acres, although their population had declined to about 5,000 people. Two years later, the Comanches were forced to cede all but 3 million acres in southwestern Oklahoma, a reservation on which they would be made to live with the Kiowas and the Plains (Kiowa) Apaches. The confederated Cheyenne and Arapaho tribes shared the central Great Plains until the 1859 Pikes Peak gold rushers carved Colorado Territory out of much of the tribes' domain. After three treaties and a presidential executive order, the southern division of the two tribes was pushed aside to a 5 million-acre reservation in western Oklahoma. The southern Cheyennes and Arapahos were hardly settled on the new reservation when the U.S. government promptly lopped more than 300,000 acres off from it without the tribes' consent in order to provide lands for the recently removed Wichita and affiliated tribes. The Northern Cheyenne and Arapaho divisions were even less fortunate. The Northern Arapahos, rather than submit to Oglala Sioux dominance at the Pine Ridge agency, in 1878 joined the Shoshonis in the Wind

Shoshoni Indians at Fort Washakie, Wyoming, 1892. Some tribe members dance as soldiers watch. This is the last photograph of Chief Washakie, on the left, standing and pointing. National Archives #NWDNS-111-SC-87800

River Reservation. The Northern Cheyennes drifted between the Pine Ridge agency and the Tongue River country in Montana before they were finally settled in 1884 on a tract in eastern Montana, which was enlarged in 1900 to include some 440,000 acres of valley and mountain land.

After the Civil War, only the Navajo escaped the devastating land losses suffered by other western tribes. In 1868, after four miserable years at the untillable Bosque Redondo reservation on the Pecos River in eastern New Mexico, an estimated 8,000 Navajos were resettled on nearly 4 million acres in northwestern New Mexico and northeastern Arizona. Abandoning their practice of undertaking marauding raids on other tribes and white settlements, the Navajo resumed planting corn, beans, squash, and melons in arroyos and around natural springs, and they carefully tended the 15,000 sheep and goats purchased for them in 1869 by the federal government. By 1892 their flocks increased to 1.7 million animals, which became the key element in the Navajo economy. Rations paid for from treaty annuities fended off starvation when crops failed; only at last resort was the natural increase of sheep and goat flocks culled to feed families. Soon, the Navajos' hardy flocks required more dry, plateau land on which to graze. Beginning in 1878 and continuing into the 1930s, the U.S. government enlarged the Navajo domain by an additional 10.5 million acres. By 1900, while other tribal populations decreased, the Navajos' population increased to 22,000 people. Fortunately, too, the 1887 Dawes General Allotment Act, which formally marks the end of the U.S. government's reservation policy, was never used to dismantle the Navajo reservation, as it was to carve up the communal lands of scores of other Indian tribes.

In general, the objectives of the reservation policy are easily discernible. The government placed tribes on land reserves with fixed boundaries designated by treaties, statutes, or presidential executive orders. After 1871, when the U.S. Congress decided treaties were no longer an appropriate means of negotiating Indian land cessions, the will of Congress or an executive order determined a reservation's size and the conditions under which American Indians held land tenure. With complete power derived from the U.S. Constitution, Congress enacted laws that most frequently reduced the respective Indian groups' land base and intruded on their lives. Whenever tribal warriors refused to live as prescribed by the Indian Bureau, the U.S. Army soon maintained a garrison of soldiers to drive war parties back onto their designated reservation. From Forts Reno, Richardson, Sill, and Supply on the southern plains, Forts Ellis, Keogh, Randall, Robinson, and Stevenson on the northern plains, and Forts Bowie, Craig, Huachuca, McDowell, and Thomas in the Southwest, post commanders cooperated with Indian agents to keep warrior groups and their leaders within their reservations' boundaries.

The U.S. government hoped that once Indian tribes were effectively restricted to reservations, tribal customs and beliefs would dissolve and be replaced by the predominant Euro-American lifestyle. Every trait, skill, and belief deemed un-American would be suppressed by Indian service personnel and missionaries dispatched to reservations by American churches. The concept and acceptance of individual property would replace communal holdings, extended families would become nuclear families, traditional ceremonies and religion would be superseded by Christianity, and the power of chiefs and elders would be extinguished. The herbs and incantations of medicine men would give way to the prescriptions and scalpel of agency physicians. Males traditionally trained to war, hunt, and fish would now learn to be farmers, stockmen, and artisans, while females accustomed to life in camps and lodges would be taught domestic crafts used in white homes. Finally, through schooling, English would be substituted for tribal languages.

Reservations, whether one hundred-acre rancheros in California or reserves with millions of acres spanning western plains or mountains, became virtual open-air prisons from which Indians could not wander without a pass obtained from an Indian agent. Meanwhile units of U.S. Army cavalry and infantry, assisted by Indian scouts and agency police, poured forth from western forts to pursue, kill, capture, and imprison those who dared to flee the pestilence and hunger of a reservation. The daring, and ultimately tragic, flights of Chief Joseph and his band of Nez Perces, Standing Bear and his Ponca band, Morning Star (known as Dull Knife to whites) and his Northern Cheyennes, and Geronimo and the Chiricahua Apaches between 1877 and 1885 are evidence of the debilitating conditions on Indian reservations—as well as the determination with which the U.S. government sought to enforce its reservation policy.

Why, exactly, were western Indians penned on desolate, mountainous, and infertile reserves? The plain answer is because white farmers, ranchers, miners, lumbermen, railroad promoters, and land speculators coveted any land rich with any resources, whether or not such land belonged to Indians. Edward McCook, territorial governor of Colorado, eager to please his constituents, claimed: "God gave us the earth and the fullness thereof . . . I do not believe in donating to these indolent savages the best part of my territory, and I do not believe in placing Indians on an equality with the white man as landholder." Indians were deemed inferior to whites in social and economic organization. Indians' natural inclinations, whites asserted, led to continuous warfare, intensive slaughter of large game, and long periods of indolence. Most Americans, except a few such as Protestant Episcopal Bishop Henry B. Whipple or the novelist Helen H. Jackson, did not disagree with Lieutenant Colonel George A. Custer who viewed an Indian as a "savage in every sense of the word; not worse perhaps, than his white brother would be similarly born and bred, but one whose cruel and ferocious nature far exceeds that of any wild beast of the desert." Only after Indians were driven to reservations, stripped of arms, and rendered incapable of resistance would white farmers, ranchers, miners, and travelers be safe to carry out their civilized enterprises.

Commissioners of Indian Affairs echoed regional and national attitudes calling for alterations of Indian life and culture. In 1871, H. R. Clum, acting commissioner of Indian Affairs, called for Indians rapidly to assume "the relation of citizenship," educate their youths, undertake "industrial pursuits" through labor, develop a "sense of ownership in property, adapt to allotments in severalty and accept the benign and elevating influences of Christian teachings." Otherwise, 350,000 Indians in the United States and Natives of Alaska faced "utter extinction." Even if Indians managed to survive without change they would, in the opinion of Indian Commissioner Francis A. Walker in 1872, become "vagabonds in the midst of civilization . . . [and] festering sores on the communities near which they are located." Industrial instruction and manual labor, Walker believed, would counterbalance the "evil influences" of tribal life and the Indians "strong, animal appetites."

During the reservation era, governmental U.S. policymakers considered Indians "barbarous men" who must be taught to live in a "civilized way." It was therefore necessary for the federal government to provide funds "to carry the untaught barbarian through the period of his childhood into civilization." And as Indians were taught to live by manual labor, agency personnel, teachers, and missionaries would "reclaim them from a debasing paganism, and win them to a purer and more enabling faith." Governmental officials realized Indians' acceptance of a new way of life would be gradual at best. "There is little hope," Indian Commissioner E. A. Hayt concluded in 1877, "of the civilization of the older wild Indian, and the only question is how to control and govern him, so that his savage instincts shall be kept from violent outbreaks." Therefore, it was more feasible to focus governmental programs on "partial civilized" adult Indians, and especially on children. Government officials became convinced that educational and missionary efforts among Indian youth eventually would reclaim the Indian population from "barbarism, idolatry and savage life." Until the effect of Christianity and education was appreciable, the goals of reservation policy were not attainable. Traditional tribal organization meant "individual responsibility and welfare . . . [was] swallowed up in that of the whole, and the weaker, less aspiring, and more ignorant of the tribe will be the victims of the more designing, shrewd, selfish and ambitious headmen."

Over many centuries, American Indians had developed appropriate methods to correct or punish transgressors of tribal laws or customs. Behavioral codes were enforced by tribal opinion, religious beliefs, and among the Five Civilized Tribes by written statutes to maintain order and security. On the Plains, warrior societies carried out the decisions of the tribal or chiefs' councils. If possible, shedding of blood was avoided and horses and goods were presented to the offended individual or family to "cover up" a serious misdeed. A strong-willed and influential man could defy law enforcers, accept exile for a period of years, and return to the tribal camp circle without fear of additional punishment.

With reservation life, however, conflicts over tribal law enforcement procedures emerged as new legal procedures were imposed on Indians to bring them within American-style justice. Indian agents began to undercut the traditional authority of chief and warriors, trying to replace those who resisted government regulations and programs with more compliant leaders. Rations and annuity goods formerly distributed through chiefs and headmen in recognition of their positions within tribes now were issued to "ration bands" headed by men selected by Indian agents. On many reservations, Indian service personnel also attempted to break up large camps and place smaller groups on land where crops and vegetable gardens might flourish. When schools for Indian children became available, either on- or off-reservation, parents were expected to send their children to them under threats of withholding rations. Men were expected to abandon living with more than one wife, but the injunction was not universally enforced, especially among the older, well-established families. Despite laws prohibiting sale of liquor in "Indian Country," whiskey flooded onto reservations or was readily available in towns bordering Indian reserves. Maddened by liquor, Indian men and women alike brawled and committed acts of violence. As tribal legal and political institutions began to crumble, Indian agents realized the need for a police force to help them enforce existing laws and regulations and to maintain order and security on reservations.

John P. Clum, a young Indian agent, arrived in 1874 at the San Carlos Apache agency. Faced with turbulent conditions and dependent on army troops to maintain order, Clum recruited four trustworthy Indian men to act as police officers, and as the police force grew, the Indian agent appointed a white man as chief of police. In 1875 Disalin, a Tonto Apache chief, experiencing domestic problems with his wives that he blamed on Clum, strode into the agency office, drew a pistol, and shot without effect at a clerk and the police chief. Hearing the shots, the Indian policemen rushed to the agency office, and in preventing Disalin's escape, killed him. One of the policemen on hand was Chief Disalin's brother, who quietly related, "I have killed my own chief, my own brother; he tried to kill a white man, so we had to kill him."

To end the turbulence on the reservation, Clum's police, having been expanded to several companies, hunted down "renegade" Apaches, killing more than 150 persons in an effort to end Apache raiding in the Southwest. Soon agents on other reservations confronted with similar if less deadly conditions asked the Indian Office to authorize Indian police forces. In May 1878, Congress appropriated funds to pay small salaries for a total of 430 privates and 50 officers, allowing Indian agents to recruit men whom they trusted for sometimes dangerous duty in "maintaining order and prohibiting illegal traffic in liquor" on Indian reservations.

Indian police were usually warriors led by older men, whether fellow tribesmen or agency employees. As the Indian police proved loyal to the agent, white men were no longer needed as Indian police captains and were replaced by tribal men. Occasionally an Indian agent encountered resistance from chiefs who understood the new police would supplant warrior societies that carried out decisions of the chiefs' councils. At the Sioux agency in Pine Ridge, Dakota Territory, Red Cloud fought Agent V. T. McGillycuddy over establishing an agency police force. McGillycuddy and other Sioux agents prevailed by playing on intratribal factionalism to foil the chief's and other tribal leaders' opposition. In time, Indian police assumed roles other than that of law enforcer, as they slaughtered government-issue beefs, returned truants to boarding schools, carried messages for agents, took tribal censuses, and built roads and agency buildings. When young men began returning in the late 1880s from off-reservation boarding schools such as Carlisle and Haskell, they gradually were incorporated into agency police forces.

Five years after Indian police were organized, Secretary of the Interior Henry M. Teller decreed Courts of Indian Offenses. Except for some nine tribes or nations with recognized tribal governments, about two-thirds of all agencies possessed their own courts whose officers were deemed to be men of undoubted intelligence, honesty, and integrity. Inadequate congressional appropriations shackled the effectiveness of the courts, and agents dissolved courts of some jurisdictions because judges would not act against wrongdoers who belonged to their families or were influential tribal members or friends. Nevertheless, Secretary Teller, distressed by the persistence of polygamy and "heathenish dances" such as the sun dance "which perpetuated a war spirit and demoralized the young," believed the courts would reduce the influence of medicine men and adherence to tribalism. Assisted by Indian police, judges would help eliminate "heathenish customs" based on tribal practices "repugnant to common decency and morality." Indian judges were empowered to jail those found guilty of participating in traditional Indian ceremonies, of having more than one wife, and of gambling or drunkenness. An Indian who failed "to adopt the habits of industry, or to engage in civilized pursuits or employments but habitually spends his time in idleness and loafing" could be jailed or fined for the misdemeanor of vagrancy. While acting as Indian police and courts, tribesmen could mitigate Indian Office regulations by their understanding of tribal customs and practices. The next challenge to Indian law, however, stripped tribes of power to sit in judgment over certain crimes as specified by Congress.

In 1881, Spotted Tail, the astute Brule (Sioux) chief of the Rosebud agency, was murdered by a fellow tribesman, Crow Dog, who resented Spotted Tail's dominance over the agency, the chief's retention of rents collected from cattlemen for rangeland, and, perhaps, Spotted Tail's role in his dismissal as police chief. Knowing Spotted Tail's habits, Crow Dog waited for the chief on a road between his home and the agency offices and shot him dead. Crow Dog's family hastily assembled ponies and goods, which were given to Spotted Tail's family; by Sioux custom the matter was settled. Shocked by the perceived casualness of the settlement, the U.S. Attorney for Dakota Territory charged Crow Dog with murder. The Brule headman was convicted in the Deadwood territorial court and sentenced to hang for his crime. An appeal of Crow Dog's conviction in 1883 reached the U.S. Supreme Court; the trial court's judgment was reversed in *ex parte Crow Dog* on the ground that the 1868 Treaty of Fort Laramie preserved the right of Sioux to punish their tribal members for serious crimes. The Supreme Court ordered Crow Dog's immediate release from prison because the U.S. courts were without jurisdiction over crimes committed by Indians against Indians, including murder.

Now reformers demanded Congress enact a law bringing Indians under federal law for serious crimes. In March 1885, Congress enacted a major crimes statute that made seven crimes—murder, manslaughter, rape, assault with intent to kill, arson, burglary, and larceny—punishable in federal courts when committed on reservations by an Indian against another Indian, excluding members of the Five Civilized Tribes. The latter nations, which had their own written penal codes, an organized court system with provision for appeals of decisions to a federal district court in Arkansas, were considered capable of dealing with crimes committed within their lands. A year later, the Supreme Court in *United States* v. *Kagama* confirmed the major crimes statute in a murder case involving a Hoopa Valley reservation Indian. The law and its approval by the Supreme Court were the initial extension of federal jurisdiction into the internal control exercised by tribes over relations between tribal members. The passage of the major crimes law, "coupled with a new aggression attitude on the part of Indian agents . . . quickly eroded the social cement that tribal custom had provided to tribal societies."

Reservation policy was never an unchanging set of statutes and administrative regulations. And Indians modified their lifestyles and institutions to meet their new environment. When federal power began to challenge tribal cohesion, tribes maintained continuity through religious beliefs and ceremonies. Yet the reservation era, which continued far beyond the 1887 Dawes Allotment Act for many tribes, was a time of mounting governmental pressure on tribes to conform to Indian policy goals. When federal officials and Indian reformers found their objectives—conversion to Christianity, institutionalized education for youths, acceptance of manual labor for self-support, use of fixed tracts of land, accumulation of private property, rejection of medicine men, and a waning loyalty to chiefs' authority—were not advancing quickly enough, governmental pressure increased. Modification of material culture, religion, political systems, and social customs, a phenomenon known as *acculturation,* was slow and halting, especially on the more-isolated western reservations. Absorption into the dominant white population, known as *assimilation,* during this era was statistically insignificant among many western tribes. In short, Congress never appropriated sufficient funds to implement reservation policy effectively, and Indians clung tenaciously to their separate identity, never completely abandoning ancestral beliefs and customs. The failure of reservation policy becomes clearer as implementation of and Indian reaction to components of the federal programs are examined.

Until the last quarter of the nineteenth century, the western Indian population was virtually untouched by white education. Only mixed-blood and a handful of full-blood youth supported by philanthropists ever received education in a white schoolroom. Again, the Five Tribes of Oklahoma were an exception, as their leaders supported schools and academies from national funds and cooperated with missionary societies to educate their children. Yet full-blood children of the Five Tribes in eastern Oklahoma hill country infrequently attended schools, which were usually filled with offspring of tribal leaders, most of whom were fully acculturated. After the Indian wars ended, Indian policy planners decided education of children offered the greatest opportunity to implant white traits among tribal people. It was anticipated that Christian churches would also expand their educational activities on western reservations, but most of the cost of educating young Indians would be borne by congressional appropriations. Soon after reservation personnel were in place, money was made available to Indian agents to build boarding and day schools and to bring in teachers from eastern states. Initially, school capacities were limited to fifty pupils or less—meaning that not more than 5 percent of school-age youths were provided places in schoolrooms and dormitories. On a few remote reservations, into the twentieth century, as few as 10 percent of the children were able to attend reservation or missionary schools because of limited facilities. Educational statistics compiled by the government in the mid-1880s appeared more favorable than actual conditions warranted, for those reports indicate that accommodations existed for 48 percent of the total Indian school population. In any case, the quality of the education these children received was largely ignored.

Once at the new schools, girls and boys fresh from freedom and play of camp life were slowly taught to speak, read, and write the English language. One

Hopi man remembered he learned "little at school the first year except 'bright boy,' 'smart boy,' 'yes' and 'no,' 'nail,' and 'candy'." Basic arithmetic and vocational activities were added as the Indian pupils' learning skills increased. At first, Indian children knew no English and their teachers knew no tribal language. At boarding schools on reservations, teachers, many of limited competence, frequently quit because of isolation, meager amenities, and low salaries. Lonesome for parents and friends, bored by the rote lessons of the classroom, or frightened by threats of harsh discipline, pupils fled back to camps with such frequency that Indian policemen and school disciplinarians routinely searched out and returned them to the hard boards of school desks and ill-constructed dormitories. For years concerned parents from outlying settlements frequently camped near reservation boarding schools and expected to eat with their children in the schools' dining halls.

Late in the 1870s, two off-reservation boarding schools were added to the Indian educational system: Hampton Normal and Agricultural Institute in Virginia and Carlisle Indian Industrial School in Pennsylvania, both of which became models for later vocational training schools scattered throughout the West. Captain Richard H. Pratt, founder of Carlisle, assembled in 1879 young prisoners of war from southern Plains tribes and sons and daughters of Indian chiefs, headmen, and prominent warriors, hoping that they after returning to reservations his school's graduates would become a leavening influence among their tribes. As the Indian education system matured, Carlisle and other off-reservation schools restricted their enrollments to students who had completed six grades in reservation schools. Indian youths at Carlisle for as long as eight years were instructed in basic educational and vocational skills. Young males spent one-half of their school days learning to grow crops, care for farm stock, and become carpenters, printers, plumbers, wheelwrights, wagon makers, blacksmiths, painters, or tinsmiths. Female students were taught how to cook and preserve food, sew, and care for a home. Discipline throughout the Indian schools was harsh. Whippings or solitary confinement with a diet of bread and water were meted out for infractions of school regulations, which included speaking a tribal language. Military-style uniforms for boys and starched dresses for girls replaced comfortable camp clothing. The flowing hair of boys was closely cropped when they entered any Indian school. Teachers, disciplinarians, and school officials discouraged the practice of every kind of Indian custom and trait. Captain Pratt provided Carlisle students with a special experience by sending both boys and girls to live and work in white farm homes for periods up to three years. One former Cheyenne Carlisle student recalled that he received $1 per month and his room and board for his work as a farm laborer. Female students assisted the mistress of the home with kitchen and household chores. Pratt believed his "outing system" contributed to the acculturation of Carlisle students.

Undoubtedly, those who returned to the reservation were influenced by their institutional education. Designated as "school boys and girls" by tribal members throughout most of their lives, some of the graduates found employment in agency offices and schools. Nevertheless, their progress to positions of administrative responsibility was minimal. Young women from Carlisle, Hampton, or Haskell often became seamstresses, cooks, and matrons for dormitories and dining halls. Men worked as assistant agency farmers, school disciplinarians, interpreters for Indian agents, and, in a few instances, became Christian ministers or store clerks. Indian agents employed a number of the returned men as agency policemen but, failing to find uses for skills learned at off-reservation schools, scores of the former students enlisted in Indian scout companies garrisoned at army posts near their reservations. A few Carlisle, Hampton, and Haskell graduating classes easily filled available Indian service appointments for years. Therefore, rarely during the reservation era could a returned student expect to enjoy an agency or school appointment for more than a few years, so that more recently returned students might be so employed. In any case, most of the graduates simply returned to camp life, much to the displeasure of Indian agents and school officials. On many undeveloped western reservations, perhaps as many as nine of ten returned students found scant if any opportunity to use the knowledge and skills acquired in Indian schools.

Economically, Indians possessed only the right to use and occupy reservation land. They did not have fee simple, or permanent, titles to land as did white farmers, and even term or range stock issued by the government could not be sold without permission from the Indian Office. Reservation land was communal property, and as such was unavailable as a form of capital or security to finance individual enterprises. On the Plains, the government constructed two-story, wood-frame houses for leaders considered principal chiefs such as Quanah Parker of the Comanches, Red Cloud of the Oglala (Sioux), and Spotted Tail of the Brules. Otherwise, families lived in canvas tepees or poorly constructed log cabins. For decades after the reservation life began there were no farms to work, no houses to live in, no stoves on which to cook, and no sewing machines available to make white-style clothing. In the early twentieth century Rena Flying Coyote, a Cheyenne who attended Carlisle for six years and lived with white families on six "outings," claimed, with some exaggeration: "I have tried to show them [my people] that my kind of living (that is like a good citizen) is better than the old Indian way. I am the only full blood Cheyenne girl to return from Carlisle, who did not revert to the Indian custom." After returning to the Cheyenne and Arapaho agency, she married a non-Indian. The couple's resources at marriage were "just one horse and $40 with which we bought a stock of edibles and other necessary things to start housekeeping, and we [five years later] get praise on every side, we are said to have the best furnished house at Darlington." Among her six sons, several were college graduates, one was a lawyer, and another was a nationally known artist.

Categorizing the lives of the returned students is more complex than the testimony of Rena Flying Coyote might imply. Early graduates of reservation as well as off-reservation schools, especially full-blood young women, received pressure from families to marry noneducated tribal members. Indian agents adopted security measures at reservation boarding schools to prevent female students of marriageable age from being whisked off by suitors or family members intent on their marrying. Sometimes young women, while enjoying a vacation with relatives, yielded to family desires, married, and thereby ended their education. Nevertheless, the number of students who completed courses of study grew in the late 1880s and 1890s, and this, primarily, was the group of young men and women employed at agencies and reservation schools. No statistical summaries exist to give a comprehensive overview of the postschool lives of former Indian school students. Off-reservation school records and journals, however, provide some insight into the way they worked and lived. Mixed-blood and full-blood former students married their classmates generally at first from their own tribes but later from other tribes. These people frequently raised the next generation of off-reservation school students, and they worried when their children failed to complete courses of study in government schools. A small number of the original cache of graduates gained employment throughout off-reservation schools, others, after passage of the Dawes Act, farmed their allotment or became small ranchers and considered themselves at least nominal Christians. Less fortunate, most returned students after the reservation era were, as a group, the first to sell their allotments in order to buy consumer goods enjoyed by white neighbors. When their money was gone, they drifted about, living with older relatives who had held onto their land.

After tribes were confined to reservations, economic and social improvement was minimal because insufficient resources existed on reservations for tribes to develop new tribal economies. Tribes began reservation life with only their lodges, some weapons, camp equipment, clothing, pony herds, and inadequate supplies of food. By any reasonable standard, parents did not have enough food; their children, when first enrolled in schools, often arrived malnourished. Soon entire families became dependent on governement rations that infrequently lasted until the next issue day. Once on the reservation, tough beef and rancid bacon replaced the meat of buffalo and large game in the Native diet. Small amounts of flour, corn, coffee, sugar, and baking powder supplemented beef issues, and, as Congress reduced appropriations, food available for an adult varied from one-third to one-half that of a standard army ration. With large game becoming scarce, women were unable to dress and tan hides for sale to reservation-based traders to raise cash to buy food, cloth, and other necessaries. Hunger and privation became a familiar condition in lodges of formerly successful hunters.

Where agriculture was considered feasible, Indian agents distributed garden seeds and hand tools for Indian use. The beginning of all such agricultural pursuits were limited to small gardens and the odd acreage for field crops. Because reservation Indians rarely owned the work stock or breaking plows necessary to turn over tough prairie sod, agents contracted with local white men to break a few acres, the cost for such service eked out from surplus agency funds. With little success, Indian men and women equipped only with knives and axes tried to plant and cultivate "sod corn." Many reservations lay in regions of limited rainfall, and irrigation, because of cost, was not yet an option in the arid West. Agency personnel, usually hailing from the East or Middle West, tried unsuccessfully to replicate the planting, cultivating, and harvesting cycles that predictable climate and rainfall levels made possible. Patiently, therefore, Indians planted the seeds of various vegetables and grains in early spring as instructed. But before their crops matured, hot summer winds and droughts withered the young plants away to nothing. Indeed, if one growing season in five produced an appreciable harvest, an Indian farmer or gardener considered himself fortunate. Undaunted by crop failures, agents urged men to use scythes to cut wild hay and axes to cut firewood for winter use. Any expedient, however inefficient, was practiced to force Indians toward self-support by manual labor. After a decade of coaxing and threats by Indian agents, Cheyennes and Arapahos grew enough wheat, a crop well adapted to Oklahoma's climate, to warrant purchase of a steam-driven threshing machine. Their agent duly requested authorization to buy a thresher and other appliances at a cost of $800. The commissioner of Indian Affairs rejected the agent's proposal but added that estimates for flails (a hand-held thrashing instrument) would receive favorable consideration. Without assurance of reasonable returns from agricultural labor it is not surprising that throughout the reservation era, Indian men continued to resist farming, a type of work traditionally scorned by former warriors and hunters as woman's work.

Because agricultural production contributed little to tribal economies, Indian agents looked to other reservation resources to supplement congressional appropriations. Timber and particularly millions of acres of rangeland could possibly be leased at attractive prices to lumber corporations or ranching syndicates. Informally, chiefs like Quanah Parker of the Comanches and Spotted Tail of the Brules struck bargains with ranchers while Indian agents looked away. As a group, ranchers preferred to see reservations maintained as a source for inexpensive cattle ranges. Range rental agreements negotiated by Indian agents cost cattlemen less than did rangeland leased from white landowners after the vast public domain had been occupied. Therefore, syndicates of eastern and foreign investors together with western cattle barons obtained exclusive use of prime reservation rangeland. Indian agents planned to use rental or lease proceeds to buy food and foundation herbs to be tended by Indian men. But before the experiment could be fully tested, President Grover Cleveland intervened to dissolve the agreement—because of sporadic conflicts between cowboys and warriors and the ruling of his attorney general, which held that no statutory authority existed to lease land reserved for Indian use and occupancy in such a way that would grant property rights to the lessee (the ranching enterprises).

Thwarted again, Indians agents began to use Indians as freighters to bring agency supplies in from distant railroad depots. Transportation companies employed scores of Indian men who bought wagons and horses on credit in order to haul supplies from railroads to agency headquarters. Goods entrusted to Indian freighters arrived intact and undamaged despite weeks en route over deeply rutted roads and numerous river crossings. From wages the freighting men paid off their debts and earned enough money to support their families. Freighting jobs were avidly sought and circulated among male relatives. Whole families accompanied freighters, camping along roads, alleviating the tedium and stagnation of reservation life.

Nonetheless, expedients available to even the most resourceful Indian agents were insufficient to care for all the reservations' inhabitants. As early as 1875 Congress enacted a law requiring all able-bodied men to contribute by labor to self-support. Details of just how these essentially preindustrial societies were supposed to convert themselves into a rural, self-supporting population on the fringe of an increasingly industrializing national economy were never fully considered. On most reservations, employment was grossly inadequate for even the better-educated men and women; for the less skilled, the disabled, and the young, no alternative existed other than a reliance on government rations and annuity payments. The ration system, not terminated until the early twentieth century, was the only feasible way to prevent death by starvation. Toward the end of the reservation era, rations came to be viewed by Indian policy planners and reformers as a cause rather than a byproduct of the enervating environment of Indian reservations. In short, the hunting-and-gathering economies had been purposely destroyed, but no viable, economic system was erected to replace what nature had once provided to western Indians.

As mentioned, one way in which white Indian policy planners hoped to transform Indian society was by reducing the chiefs' power to lead their people. But as whites had done for centuries, contemporary white observers attributed more influence to chiefs than they actually possessed. Mistakenly, governmental officials believed chiefs were the fonts of authority rather than the spokesmen who reported a consensus arrived at in tribal councils. During times of crisis, chiefs among the Lakota (Sioux) deferred to the wishes of their tribe's warrior societies. When cattlemen controlled vast expanses of the Oklahoma Cheyenne and Arapaho reservations, these tribes' warrior societies led an effort to evict from reservation lands cowboys who harassed Indians in their camps. And warriors were hardly dissuaded from their objectives when shown rental or lease agreements signed by many of their chiefs. Nevertheless, Indian-office personnel and reformers clung to a notion that a "head chief" or a small group of chiefs could replace councils composed of band and warrior society leaders who were keenly attuned to tribal opinion and traditions. In some tribes, chiefs were intermediaries guided by elders, invested with religious prerogatives, who shaped tribal consensus. And the peoples' loyalty to band chiefs surged upward or ebbed away to immediate family once the chief's counsel proved inappropriate. Black Kettle of the Cheyennes, for instance, was pushed aside after the 1864 Sand Creek Massacre; Red Cloud of the Oglala Sioux maintained his role of agency spokesman only in definace of his tribal critics; and Manuelito of the Navajos, though revered as a fierce war leader, commanded less influence as his bouts with liquor became more frequent and his status among the people shriveled to little more than the agents' mouthpiece. If Indian service officials had understood the fluidity of political power within Indian society, perhaps they might have worried less about supporting a permanent group of chiefs or a head chief completely amenable to federal Indian policy.

But because the misunderstanding perpetuated, many reservations witnessed the evolution of three factions, although some of the factionalism was a residue of interband disagreements dating back to prereservation times. Typically, the smallest reservation faction centered about intermarried whites, their spouses' families, and returned students beholden to agents for jobs. When the Dawes Act was applied to reservations, this faction was manipulated and bribed by cession agreement commissioners to acquire "surplus land" (from their Indian neighbors) for white occupation. The second faction followed chiefs who early on had believed that further warfare against whites was futile. Essentially pragmatic, this faction was willing, however reluctantly, to travel the white man's road: send their children to school, plant gardens and field crops, listen to missionaries' preachings, abandon large camps for smaller settlements in which more-individualized labor was feasible, and if young, to take no more than one wife, wear "citizens dress," and heed the agents' advice. The third faction coalesced about leaders who deeply resented confinement on reservations and were fundamentally opposed to remaking the Indian into pseudo-whites. Red Moon of the Cheyennes in Oklahoma led his band as far away from agency headquarters as possible, even refusing to sign an 1890 cession agreement. Sitting Bull of the Hunkpapa Sioux after returning from Canada built his cabin forty miles from the Standing Rock headquarters. Lone Wolf of the Kiowas distanced himself from life at the agency, remaining aloof as much as possible from whites (although his son, Delos, graduated from Carlisle). In time, once the pragmatists found reservation policy did not lead to a suitable life they too became suspicious of and resistant to the white mans' policies.

Although their people might be divided by factions, the chiefs shared certain common characteristics. As young men they had earned redoubtable reputations as warriors and hunters. Many of their fathers, uncles, or grandfathers had been chiefs before them. As a chief's son or nephew matured, a young man and prospective chief was closely observed to see whether he possessed patience, wisdom, generosity toward less fortunate persons, and knowledge of tribal customs. During the reservation era, chances were a chief had never attended a white man's school and needed an interpreter to converse with an Indian agent or a commissioner sent to buy reservation land. He was expected, regardless of factionalism, to make wise decisions helpful to all of the tribe's people. If his judgments were contrary to Indian policy as construed by an Indian agent, the chief was moved aside and not invited to subsequent meetings and was not included among those chosen to visit the Great Father in Washington. Naturally, Indian agents preferred to deal with those chiefs willing to follow regulations flowing from Washington rather than with those who resisted government policies. Knowing they would be ignored or ridiculed, some resistant chiefs avoided meeting with agents unless it was vitally necessary. Throughout the West, however, chiefs who lived according to tribal customs maintained their roles as spokesmen and leaders during and beyond the reservation era despite governmental efforts to diminish their influence.

As mentioned, Indian policy planners hoped to use returned students from off-reservation schools to modify reservation politics. While the student population of those schools contained a cross section of tribal youths, a disproportionate percentage of the students were offspring of mixed-blood parents or of interracial unions. There were, of course, a sprinkling of students whose fathers were chiefs and former warrior leaders. Without regard to the students' parentage, Indian policy administrators wanted all returned students to become acculturated role models for their tribes. Noneducated persons, however, viewed the returnees with continuing suspicion, fearing that the young men and women had been too deeply influenced by white ideas. Furthermore, in the 1880s and 1890s, the male former students were far too young to be selected as chiefs, and those judged the most promising were employed at the agency and issue stations, where they were subordinate to Indian service employees. These employees were expected to live in houses, apart from the band camps in which older family members lived. Fairly fluent in English, many of these young men became interpreters whenever agents and land cession commissioners needed to explain policy and documents to chiefs. The chiefs, for their part, expected their young men to translate faithfully their speeches into English. Caught between cultures, the young interpreters' status was always inferior to that of white officials and their tribal leaders, and they were not expected to speak in their own behalf.

If western Indians did not put aside their leaders, neither did they discard traditional beliefs and ceremonies. However, the ceremonies and even the sacred tribal totems changed over time. New ceremonies were borrowed from neighboring tribes and became more complex or differed as priests incorporated their touches into older ceremonies. When woodland tribes took up life on the Plains, newly arisen culture heroes taught new religious ceremonies, reorganized tribal bands and warrior societies, and designated new political structures to govern tribes. The spirits of nature controlled life; people shared the world with spirits whose power for good and evil directly affected human life. Maheo, the All Father of Cheyennes, was part of all life. Through visions and dreams, supernatural spirits directed the actions and lives of humans. If a youth did not understand his vision a holy man explained its meaning and directed him in the use of his personal medicine bundle. The offerings and physical sacrifices to Maheo at a Sun Dance assured Cheyennes of health and well-being, as did proper veneration of the sacred medicine arrows and buffalo hat. Other than the Comanches, Plains tribes adopted the Sun Dance, varying the ceremony in length and detail to suit tribal needs and the teachings of their Sun Dance priests. The Sun Dance was a three- or four-day ceremony that tribal members believed, if performed properly, would assure tribal welfare. A tribal member vowed to sponsor a Sun Dance when some personal problem was solved or some misfortune had been avoided. During one day of the ceremony, male participants were suspended by thongs and skewers to the top of the Sun Dance pole and looked skyward until they tore themselves free from the skewers attached to their breasts or backs. White observers became so enamored with the spectacle of the Sun Dance that they failed to report the multitude of other tribal ceremonies and individual religious observances.

Toward the end of the reservation era, Christian teachings found acceptance among a minority of western Indians. Tribal members became ordained clergy and Native lay preachers who labored alongside white missionaries to convert people to Christianity. For many alleged converts, however, Christianity never dominated their religious beliefs. When death approached, men and women counted as Christian congregation members asked for the prayers of both Christian clergy and a holy man of their tribe. Uniquely, one former Plains warrior was ordained as a deacon in the Protestant Episcopal Church, preached for nearly forty years among his people, and was canonized as a saint about fifty years after his death. More usually, Indians simply accepted Christianity as another religious experience in addition to a Sun Dance or the night-long peyote ceremony.

The visions and teachings of the prophets Tavibo and Wovoka, Paiutes of Nevada, spread throughout the western Indians. For several centuries prophets had arisen whenever Indian peoples encountered the challenges of dealing with the Euro-American frontier population. Popé of the Pueblos, the Delaware Prophet, Handsome Lake of the Senecas, Tenskwatawa of the Shawnees, and Smohalla of the Columbia River Shahaptans had all led earlier revitalization movements among their people. Like the preceding prophets, Tavibo and Wovoka promised that if their teachings were properly observed, Indians would regain to control of their lives and lands. Tavibo, after vigils, received visions in 1870 foretelling destruction of the whites, but his teachings attracted followers only among neighboring tribes. Tavibo's son, Wovoka, known to whites as Jack Wilson, expanded his father's message into a comprehensive set of religious doctrines. From the plateaus, mountains, and finally the far-off Plains, tribal delegates visited Wovoka, carrying back to their tribes practices, ceremonies, and prayers guaranteed to assure peace and plenty following the cataclysmic destruction of the white oppressors.

Wovoka's doctrines forbade his followers to practice war and violence. Indeed, the prophet declared that all Indians of all tribes were to live peacefully as brothers and sisters. Indians should live simply, reject use of alcohol, purify themselves by ceremonial cleansing, and worship through meditation, prayers, songs, and dances. That done, the dead would rejoin the living, and all Indians would

Women performing the Ghost Dance, during the five day- and nightlong ceremonies, participants danced until they fell unconscious. National Anthropological Archives, Smithsonian Institution #55,297

start life anew in a world abounding in game, "free from misery, death and disease." During the five day and night long ceremonies, people danced until they fell unconscious; after reviving they reported having talked to deceased family members and friends—thus Wovoka's teaching became known as the Ghost Dance. Spreading more rapidly after 1889, the Ghost Dance rituals varied among different tribes. On the southern Plains the Kiowas, Comanches, and Cheyennes remained doubtful, while Wovoka's doctrines gained many adherents among the Arapahos and Wichitas. On the Northern Plains, acceptance of the Ghost Dance flourished as drought, starvation, and substantial land losses beset the western Sioux. The Sioux added to the ritual a Ghost Dance shirt which, when blessed, was said to protect a wearer from enemy bullets. Militancy and resistance, although antithetical to Wovoka's teaching, appealed to distraught Sioux warriors who gathered together in secrecy awaiting an opportunity to rise up against white oppression. But just how imminent a Sioux uprising was in 1890 depends on interpretation of contemporary reports written by Indian agents and army officers.

After Sitting Bull's return from Canada, agents at Standing Rock kept a wary eye on the Hunkpapa Leader. Sioux Indian agents, fearing the threats of hostility expressed by warriors and their leaders, banned the Ghost Dance, which only strengthened the participants' determination to continue and prevail. Agents sent requests for additional troops, one of whom claimed "Indians are dancing in the snow and are wild and crazy." James McLaughlin, agent at Standing Rock, ordered the arrest of Sitting Bull, considered the most likely leader of any concerted Sioux uprising. In a violent melee, Sitting Bull was killed, triggering a series of tragic blunders. Ghost dancers from the Sioux agencies fled to camps in the Black Hills, pursued by army units. Pinned down by troops, one group led by Big Foot, a Miniconjou from the Cheyenne River agency, surrendered at Wounded Knee Creek. On December 29, 1890, as the soldiers disarmed the band, a warrior overcome by tension seized his rifle, which discharged. Other men dropped their blankets and aimed their weapons at the surrounding troops. Simultaneously, Indians and soldiers opened fire, artillery shells raking Big Foot's people. Panic-stricken men, women, and children bolted from the camp only to be slaughtered by troopers of the Seventh Cavalry. Nearly 150 of Big Foot's band were killed; corpses, including those of women and children, were scattered out for three miles from where the fighting erupted. Perhaps another 100 Sioux died of wounds or froze to death. Dr. Charles A. Eastman, a Santee Sioux physician assigned to Pine Ridge agency near where the massacre occurred, worked frantically to save the wounded as they were carried into the agency. The army suffered fewer casualties: 25 dead and 39 wounded. When the Ghost Dance shirts did not protect Big Foot's people from army bullets and Wovoka's prophecies did not occur, the ceremony's adherents gradually abandoned the Ghost Dance, although some remained as believers into the twentieth century.

Another longer-lasting ritual filtered into the southern Plains as Tavibo received his first visions. Through Apaches, Comanches learned of peyote, the dried fruit of a cactus that when ingested produces hallucinations and euphoria. Rituals involving the use of peyote passed by the mid-1880s to the Kiowas, Cheyennes, and Arapahos went unnoticed by Indian agents. Indian agents visited camps infrequently and few enjoyed enough confidence among Indians to learn all that transpired in settlements remote from agency headquarters. Quanah Parker lent his powerful support to the new religious movement early, and, as young men returned from Carlisle, Delos Lone Wolf of the Kiowas, Leonard Tyler of the Cheyennes, and Cleaver Warden of the Arapahos became "road priests" of peyotism, spreading the rituals throughout the Plains, teaching peyote rites to former classmates. Persons who preferred to practice traditional ceremonies denounced the "Peyote Road" occasionally as "the half-breeds" religion. Combining Christian and Native concepts, the peyote ritual became a communion for adherents, who promised to remain truthful, devoted to family, abstain from alcohol, and generally lead an upright life. Peyote itself was believed to restore health, as its euphoric effects afforded at least temporary relief to many wracked by tuberculosis.

Even though condemned by federal officials, state legislatures, and missionaries, the peyote movement survived. Opponents of peyote urged its suppression, arguing the rite hindered conversion of Indians to Christianity and that consumption of peyote buttons was as dangerous as the use of opium. After a series of intertribal conferences, Oklahoma peyotists in 1918 received a state charter incorporating the movement as the Native American Church, which was amended twenty-six years later creating the Native American Church of the United States. The rites varied widely depending on the meetings' leaders, but accompanying the sacramental use of peyote were prayers, songs, meditation, drumming rites, and individual and group dedication to the Holy Spirit above, symbolized by a beautiful, brilliant-colored Peyote Bird. The peyote ritual was credited with bringing health to the sick and success and prosperity to individuals, family, and the larger Indian community. It was a response to the stagnation and despondency experienced by western Indians during the reservation and early agency era. Along with other older ceremonials, the Peyote Road helped maintain Indian spiritualism, which provided a cohesive force with tribal society. So pervasive was the Peyote Road that perhaps 50 percent of the Indian population by 1930 were participants in the Native American Church.

Substantial modifications of Indian culture occurred during the reservation era. Parents sent their children in increasing numbers to reservation and off-reservation schools in which they learned white people's ways. Older people received instruction in agriculture and stock raising, leading in some instances to self-support. Cabins and frame homes began slowly to replace lodges. The expanding white population in western states and territories increased social and economic relations between whites and Indians. More Indians began to wear white-style clothing, and they began to purchase wagons and buggies. There was less polygamy among Indians, and Anglicized names began to dot agency census roles, especially as students returned from schools. While far from reaching complete acculturation, Indian people were forced, cajoled, or persuaded to make some adjustments to their way of life. Nevertheless, Indians retained some control and were selective in their adaptations to white culture, mostly accepting those parts necessary to survive on reservations.

Much of tribal society and institutions remained intact despite intrusion of federal Indian policies into reservation life. Tribal councils still gathered to discuss issues affecting the lives and welfare of the people. Influential chiefs, headmen, and elders were still entrusted with placing the wishes of their people before Indian agents or the Great Father in Washington. Men and women principally chose their spouses outside their band or clan, and marriages occasioned feasts and exchanges of presents between families. Possessions, food, and shelter were shared generously with relatives, friends, and visitors. Herbs and incantations of medicine men were preferred to the pills and ministrations of agency physicians. Respectful deference was still accorded to holy men and keepers of tribal totems. Among the Cheyennes, for example, an unbroken succession of priests and keepers of the sacred arrows and buffalo hat taught their successors the ceremonies and prayers to supplicate Maheo, the All Father, and Mother Earth. Tribal languages predominated in camps and homes; English learned in schools was spoken only when dealing with whites. As with any human society, cultural and social change was not sudden. Abundant customs, beliefs, and rituals accompanied Indians into the twentieth century, providing tribal peoples with the means to maintain their separate identity.

Suggested Reading

For background information on Indian-white relations in the latter half of the nineteenth century, consult Robert M. Utley, *The Indian Frontier of the American West, 1846–1890* (Albuquerque, N. Mex., 1984). Excellent general studies containing information about the reservation era are Arrell Morgan Gibson, *The American Indian: Prehistory to the Present* (Lexington, Ky., 1980), chapters 14–19, and Francis Paul Prucha, *The Great Father: The United States Government and the American Indians* (Lincoln, Nebr., 1984), chapters 12–25. Robert A. Trennert, Jr., *Alternative to Extinction: Federal Indian Policy and the Reservation System, 1846–1851* (Philadelphia, 1975) examines the origins of the reservation policy and system. There are a number of informative studies detailing conditions for Indians during the reservation period and specific tribal responses: Donald J. Berthrong, *The Southern Cheyennes* (Norman, Okla., 1963) and *The Cheyenne and Arapaho Ordeal: Reservation and Agency Life in the Indian' Territory, 1875–1907* (Norman, Okla., 1976); Angie Debo, *Geronimo: The Man, His Time, His Place* (Norman, Okla., 1976); William T. Hagan, *United States–Comanche Relations: The Reservation Years* (New Haven, Conn., 1980, Reprint); George E. Hyde, *A Sioux Chronicle* (Norman, Okla., 1956); James C. Olson, *Red Cloud and the Sioux Problem* (Lincoln, Nebr., 1965); Ruth M. Underhill, *The Navajos* (Norman, Okla., 1956), especially chapters 9–16; and Donald E. Worcester, *The Apaches: Eagles of the Southwest* (Norman, Okla., 1979). Thomas Wildcat Alford, as told to Florence Drake, *Civilization* (Norman, Okla., 1936), Hagan, *Indian Police and Judges: Experiments in Acculturation and Control* (Lincoln, Nebr., 1980, Reprint), and David Humphreys Miller, *Ghost Dance* (New York, 1959) are also important in gaining a better understanding of this subject.

Chapter 8 ❧
Reformers' Images of the American Indians

The Late Nineteenth Century

William T. Hagan

*F*orty years after the founding of the Indian Rights Association, Herbert Welsh, a founder of the association and its guiding force during its first twenty years, characterized its members. "They are," stated Welsh proudly, "the elite of New England, New York, and Philadelphia, sober old society." The same could have been said of most of the members of the other organizations of reformers, or "friends of the Indians," as they liked to describe themselves. As a group they shared another quality: they were devout Christians, members of the Protestant denominations and the Friends (Quaker) societies. (Until very late in the nineteenth century, Roman Catholics, although quite active in Indian work, labored almost exclusively through the church's Bureau of Catholic Indian Missions, which was not a part of the coalition of reformers.)

The reformers discussed in this chapter belonged to the many organizations that sprang up in the twenty years following the Civil War. With one exception, the Board of Indian Commissioners, they were private organizations with no official status. In contrast, Congress authorized the Board of Indian Commissioners in 1869. However, its members were private citizens of a philanthropic bent who served without pay and shared their concern for, and views of, Indians and Indian policy.

The Indian Rights Association was merely the most prominent of the reformers' organizations that proliferated in the late 1870s and early 1880s— "proliferated" because the list is long, although most of the organizations on it had only an ephemeral existence. Besides the Indian Rights Association and the Board of Indian Commissioners, at least three other entities deserve mention. Two of them, the Women's National Indian Association and the Boston Indian Citizenship Committee, had their origins in 1879, the former in Philadelphia. The fifth group, the one least inclined to cooperate with the others, was the National Indian Defense Association. Although the NIDA did not appear until 1885, its founder, Dr. T. A. Bland, had been associated with A. B. Meacham who, in 1878, founded a monthly, *The Council Fire,* to publicize his views of the Indian cause.

While there were differences of opinion among the various groups of reformers, the degree to which they all agreed on the potential of the Indian to enter the mainstream and the policies that might best realize this potential is remarkable. Dr. Bland and his National Indian Defense Association were even less inclined than was Meacham, who died in 1882, to coerce the Indians to abandon their traditional lifeways. Nevertheless, they, too, agreed with the other groups that ultimately the Indian could and should assimilate into American society.

The reform groups' Indian policy consensus was principally reached at two annual meetings, the first of which was that of the Board of Indian Commissioners. Commencing for the first time in 1870, this meeting's attendees soon came to include representatives of missionary societies, and later expanded to include members of Indian rights associations. These were logical developments, for President Grant not only had sought the advice and counsel of the Board of Indian Commissioners, but he also brought the disparate Protestant churches into the federal Indian Service by permitting their leaders to nominate agency employees. Finally, the heads of boarding schools, such as General S. C. Armstrong and Captain Richard H. Pratt, as well as officials of the Indian Service began to attend this meeting, usually held in January. Journals of the January meetings, complete with speeches made and recommendations agreed upon, were included in the annual reports of the Board of Indian Commissioners. Thus not only did the meeting facilitate agreement among friends of the Indians who attended, the printed report enabled others to discover the "party line," the strategy for dealing with Indians and federal Indian policy as advocated by many reformers.

An even more celebrated forum for consensus was the Lake Mohonk Conferences, which began in 1883 and continued throughout the late nineteenth century. Although this event typically attracted more participants than did the January meeting hosted by the Board of Indian Commissioners, the Mohonk Conferences drew from among the same group. Every year several who had gathered in Washington in January for the first meeting would see one another again in late September or October at Lake Mohonk. The Lake Mohonk Conference also published an annual report, which helped to keep all interested parties abreast of current discussions and recommendations.

The images of the Indian held by the reformers naturally reflected the status of Indians in the United States. At the time the Board of Indian Commissioners was founded, and even later, when the churches were invited to participate in the administration of the Indian Service, the Plains tribes and the Apaches remained unconquered, and large areas of the West were still unorganized territories closed to white settlement. Within the next thirty years, the population of the United States nearly doubled, jumping from less than 40 million in 1870 to over 75 million in 1900. Consequently, the pressure on Indian land intensified, and new states and territories were organized; this helped account for the last wave of bloody Indian wars and the restriction of the tribesmen to the reservation.

Reformers were in general agreement that Indian civilization, as contrasted with that of the whites, was at a lower evolutionary stage, many generations behind. At the 1890 Mohonk Conference, the Reverend James McCosh, a former president of Princeton University, compared the Indians with the ancient Britons. The Britons, McCosh pointed out, also had painted their bodies, worn animal skins, and been pagan. However, as McCosh phrased it:

> From this race, or a like race, the great body of the people of that country have sprung, and most of those present at this convention.
>   I am sure that by the grace of God and the same means the Indians may be raised to a like belief and civilization.

Five years later, at Lake Mohonk, the Reverend M. E. Strieby of the Presbyterian missionary society made a similar comparison, this time with Highland Scots. Strieby declared that like the American Indians, the Highlanders, "before their sudden transformation into a civilized people," consisted of idle men and toiling women, the men's energies reserved for revenge, robbery, and murder. But like the ancient Britons, the Highlanders had passed rapidly from barbarism to civilization by breaking the power of the clan chiefs and introducing education and the church. Reverend Strieby was confident that the same pattern might hold true for the Indians.

Reverend Strieby's reference to "idle" men was a common criticism of Indian society by the reformers. *City and State,* the weekly newspaper of which Herbert Welsh was editor and publisher, explained it as "the indolence of barbarism lacking civilization's incentives to work." Even Dr. Bland portrayed the Indian as living a life of "careless indolence," as contrasted with the civilized life of "careful industry."

Dr. Bland, like other reformers, believed Indians must demonstrate proper industry by farming. He acknowledged that tribes like the Cherokees had been agriculturalists before the arrival of the whites, but, Bland said, they had "farmed in a very small way, and in a very primitive fashion." If most tribes had been agriculturalists in the fashion of white settlers, said the good doctor, the white man would not "have felt at liberty to kill them . . . and take their lands from them."

Welsh also viewed the conversion to farming as "in every instance . . . the first step which the Indian takes toward civilization." Raising cattle, in contrast, would not get the job done: "From its nomadic character," the life of a herdsman, said Welsh, " . . . is hostile to settled home life, while its loneliness and isolation are equally so."

But not only was the Indian economy in need of transformation, so too were Indians' social and political organization. Polygamy must be banned and as *Council Fire,* the organ of Meacham and Bland, put it: "Not until Indian women are recognized as women, and the men taught by precept and example to honor and respect womanhood, and that marriage is lawful and honorable, and to be honored, will the Indian race advance." The transitory quality of the marriage relationship in most Indian societies clearly, and understandably, shocked these Victorians.

Council Fire also advised the Native American, if he hoped to become civilized, to "abandon many of his old superstitions in religious matters." On that subject the 1895 Lake Mohonk platform likewise spoke for the reformers: "Our American civilization is founded upon Christianity. A pagan people can not be fitted for citizenship without learning the principles and acquiring something of the spirit of a Christian people."

Although religious people themselves, the reformers seemed incapable of comprehending the value to Indians of their traditional religions. Welsh dismissed a Navajo medicine dance he observed in 1885 as "neither a very interesting nor edifying performance." However, that was a relatively sophisticated reaction compared with a proposal he had made three years earlier on his first exposure to Indians. Visiting the Rosebud Sioux Reservation shortly after the annual Sun Dance, the most important ceremonial of the Plains Indian, Welsh suggested the government "turn this heathen festival into a Fourth of July Picnic. . . ." Nearly twenty years later he was still railing against "Indian dances which are the nursery and citadel of the superstitious and vicious elements of Indian life."

The reformers also were unanimous in viewing Indian communal ownership of property as incompatible with civilization. What was missing was the "selfishness" that drove whites, as two people as disparate in opinion as Dr. Bland and Senator H. L. Dawes of Massachusetts agreed. Senator Dawes was the embodiment of policies advocated by the Eastern friends of the Indian, while the friends considered Dr. Bland an impractical idealist. It was this Dawes-Bland consensus that ultimately led to the Dawes Land in Severalty Act of 1887 and a rash of special agreements negotiated in the 1890s to provide allotment in severalty for most of the large reservations.

The theory that apportioning reservation lands into individually held parcels would benefit Indians had developed a large following among government officials and private citizens well before the late nineteenth century. The Board of Indian Commissioners included it as one of its recommendations in its very first report in 1869 and every year reiterated the recommendation. The Mohonk Conferences and the joint meetings of the Board of Indian Commissioners and the representatives of the missionary societies also routinely endorsed it. The Indian Rights Association made severalty one of the recommendations of its first annual report. Furthermore, Mrs. Amelia Quinton, the leading light of the Women's National Indian Association, reminded an audience in 1896 that as early as 1881 her organization had petitioned the government to invoke severalty. Helen Hunt Jackson's celebrated *A Century of Dishonor* was devoted almost entirely to a scathing indictment of U.S. Indian policy; nonetheless, in the brief space she reserved for policy recommendation contained a firm an endorsement of severalty: "The utter absence of individual title to particular lands deprives every [Indian] . . . of the chief incentive to labor and exertion— the very mainspring on which the prosperity of a people depends."

Dr. Bland, although unwilling to push the Indian into it, believed that: "Land in severalty and citizenship must come and will come to the Indians. It is the ultimate solution to the Indian problem."

Welsh and the Indian Rights Association strongly favored allotment in severalty. Urging the passage of the Dawes Bill, Welsh said it was needed, "To break down the walls which separate the Indian today from our own world of thought and action. . . ." After its passage he defended it [the Dawes Act] as "the bridge over which the Indian may be led from barbarism to civilization. . . ." "The Indian," Welsh continued, "must become in all respects like ourselves, or else become extinct under the action of those unrestrainable forces of civilization which will not tolerate savage and tribal life."

The reformers recognized that the transition from "barbarism to civilization" would be a traumatic experience for the Indian. Again Welsh provides the illustration. After visiting the Omahas and Winnebagoes in 1892, he described them as being in

> the middle of that swift and treacherous stream which divides civilization from barbarism and which all Indians must cross. Doubtless its current will carry some away and its quicksands will engulf others, while those who succeed in getting safely over into the promised land will be both stronger and cleaner than they would have been were they not forced to cross it.

The reformers pointed with pride to those who had made the transition. And those good examples of what an Indian could become were invited to the annual meetings and were always singled out for praise when visited on their reservations. It also should be noted that the reformers, many of whom were also interested in the plight of American blacks, insisted there was a difference between all races. And when the comparison between Indians and African Americans was made, the Indian usually emerged the winner. One reformer, for example, attributed to them unspecified "noble traits" not shared by the blacks.

Captain Pratt, founder of Carlisle Institute, was adamant about not placing Indians in situations in which they would be lumped together with blacks for fear that the Indians would suffer from discrimination by association. Indeed, Pratt was reluctant even to send Indians out in groups because immediately, whether in churches or public schools, they would be segregated as a group and treated differently.

In general, the intermarriage of Indians and whites did not disturb reformers. There was some pointed criticism of the "squawman," the contemporary term for the white man who married an Indian woman, but this was based on the assumption that the man's motivation usually was to get at the property of the woman's tribe. What might have been expected to be the more sensitive subject of the marriage of Indian men to white women actually was approved, if the Indian were a representative of the progressive wing of his tribe. For example, the union of Elaine Goodale, a young white woman active in Indian work, and Dr. Charles Eastman, an educated Sioux, inspired no critical comment.

There was even one class of white man whom the reformers constantly compared unfavorably with Native Americans: this was what the Board of Indian Commissioners referred to in 1899 as "The fringe of lawless and dissolute men who too often hung about its borders, taught Indians the white man's vices and prevented true ideals of civilized Christian life from reaching the Indians." In the earlier years when reformers were on the defensive about Indian raids, they retaliated by blaming white frontiersmen for triggering the violence. William Nicholson, the Quaker presiding over the Central Superintendency in 1871, illustrates this tactic. (The Central Superintendancy was one of the administrative units of what was then known as the Office of Indian Affairs—later, the Bureau of Indian Affiars. That Superintendancy included states like Oklahoma, or what would become Oklahoma, and Kansas.) Kiowas under Nicholson's supervision were raiding into Texas. Nicholson's image of the Kiowas had them simply retaliating for having been "engaged in stockraising and doing well." The villains were white men, "worse than Indians" in Nicholson's phrase, who took Kiowa land in Texas and then invaded their reservation in Oklahoma to steal their horses. The "demoralizing influence of the class of white persons always found upon frontier settlements" was a major argument offered for the reservation system by the Board of Indian Commissioners in 1874.

This tendency to form an image of frontiersmen as worse than Indians is further illustrated by statements of Henry S. Pancoast and Philip C. Garrett. Pancoast was Welsh's companion on a trip to the Sioux reservations in 1882, each man's first real exposure to Indians. Pancoast described the Native Americans he met in glowing terms: "tall fine looking men, the faces of many showing great character and intelligence." The Indian women he found to have "generally pleasant and gentle faces." Contrast that with his comments on the western whites he encountered on the train that took him into Dakota Territory, whom he described as "the Falstaff's army of discontented, unsuccessful men—the gamblers, emigrants, and convicts—that go out as representatives of our dominant race to conquer the wilderness. . . ." Even an attractive young German girl who caught his attention was dismissed as having "meaningless blue eyes."

However, it was the gentle Philadelphia Quaker, Garrett, president for several years of the Indian Rights Association and a member of the Board of Indian Commissioners, the very embodiment of the reformer, who delivered the most damning indictment of frontier whites. He identified hate and avarice as the "two deadly foes to Indian civilization," both of them embodied by white men:

> The more than savage, the satanic, hate of the fiends in human shape, whose thirst for adventure and blood allures them to the wild life on the border, and the equally satanic avarice, whose selfish clutch tolerates no bar of humanity nor morality between it and the gratification of its cupidity.

Although reformers generally agreed on the Indians' potential and how to best move them toward civilization, some dissent was extant. Meacham and Bland, as already noted, were inclined to see the Indian as less desperately in need of civilization. George Bird Grinnell, an ethnologist and author of some excellent studies on Plains Indians, opposed premature allotment of tribes such as the Pawnee and Cheyenne whom he did not believe were ready for it. But, it was another ethnologist and reformer, Alice Fletcher, who made the best defense of the Native American and his way of life.

In a magazine article in 1883, Fletcher presented an image of the Native American far removed from that of the savage sorely in need of civilization, to which most reformers clung. She dismissed the idea of Indian anarchy by sketching a closely knit tribal society based on clans and phratries, with tribes united in some instances in confederacies. Fletcher also defended the Indian against the charge of indolence and sloth, heard so often at Lake Mohonk and elsewhere, stressing the "grave responsibility" of the hunter in a society "dependent upon the precariousness of game." After giving him high marks for honesty and faithfulness, she still concluded the Indian would have to change because the "peculiar environment" that had shaped him no longer existed. Fletcher was that unusual reformer who turned her energies to the practical problems. She served as an allotting agent for the government, bringing the severalty, in which she so firmly believed, to the Omahas and other tribes.

What kept Alice Fletcher in the good graces of the reformers was her wholehearted support of the thesis that the tribes people must abandon their traditional lifestyle, regardless of how appropriate it once may have been. Reformers

Alice Fletcher (at left) oversees land allotment to Nez Perces, Idaho, ca. 1890. Courtesy, Denver Public Library, Western History Department #X-30996

mostly suspected other ethnologists, however, of opposing integration. At Lake Mohonk in 1886, Garrett first deplored the romanticization of the Indian, criticizing "pandering, on the part of historians, to the popular craving for the picturesque." But he saved his heaviest fire for the ethnologists—specifically exempting Fletcher, whose philanthropy "swallowed up her anthropology." Other ethnologists, he feared, desired "to preserve these utensils for the study of his specialty." As Garrett acknowledged:

> Every tribe converted to civilized ways removes one more living illustration of ethnology, and remands to the past crystallization of written records and museum collections all search into those customs and manners and implements so much easily read in the living tribe.

In June 1893, John Wesley Powell, the director of the Smithsonian's Bureau of Ethnology, made a request of the commissioner of Indian Affairs that illustrates why the reformers disapproved of ethnologists. Powell asked the commissioner to permit the holding of the Kiowa Medicine Dance, which had been prohibited by the Kiowa agent, as "it seems probable that the approaching date for the Medicine Dance will afford one of the last opportunities for studying the ceremonial." This was essential, claimed Powell, because observation of such ceremonials "give exceptional facilities for the study of legendary lore from which the prehistoric origin and development of customs and beliefs may sometimes be ascertained." Welsh denounced this sort of thing as:

> the natural conflict between a spirit that would use these Indians for ethnological purposes and, therefore seeks to keep them much as they are, and the Christian spirit which would seek to develop them into a higher manhood and womanhood.

Although they had their differences, Welsh and Captain Pratt saw eye-to-eye on the baneful influence of ethnologists. Pratt accused Powell of "a deep fear that our work would destroy the Indian in the Indian before the Science of Ethnology had developed all the hidden and conjectural history of the Indians." Captain Pratt was not a member of the reformers. However, he depended on them for support, attended their meetings in Washington and Lake Mohonk, and espoused their view that the salvation of the Indian lay in their full integration into American society.

Where Pratt could be distinguished from the reformers was in the way he would implement the change. Pratt was a radical, and he advocated extreme measures. He had no patience with the reservation system for preparing the Indian for civilization and assimilation, condemning reservations as "prisons." Pratt believed the Indian had to be "individualized." "Christ's mission was to save individuals," he said, "and our efforts must take the same direction else they fail."

He opposed granting the Indians allotments in severalty because those very allotments "anchored" them to the reservation, forcing them to remain in a "mass of ignorance." By 1900 Captain Pratt found himself increasingly isolated as a result of his abrasive comments on the reformers.

Although he could not agree with most of Pratt's radical program, Senator Dawes did share with Pratt a growing contempt for the reformers. Like Pratt, Senator Dawes frequently attended the reformers' meetings in Washington and at Lake Mohonk, and he welcomed their support when their views coincided with his own. Like Pratt, however, the senator was generally inclined to dismiss the reformers as visionaries. To his wife, who had attended the 1888 Lake Mohonk Conference without him, Dawes confided his dismay at the conferences' "airing and endorsement of the impracticable schemes of theorists." When Harvard Law School Professor James Bradley Thayer, a member of both the Boston Indian Citizenship Committee and the Indian Rights Association, proposed legislation designed to bring law to the reservation, Dawes was particularly annoyed. Sometime later, describing Thayer to Pratt as one of the Boston "doctrinaires," the senator deprecated the professor's proposal as a bill drafted in a library by a man who had never "seen an Indian on a reservation." Dawes even disagreed with the reformers about the implementation of the severalty law that carried his name, arguing that they were urging it on Indians not ready for it. "Severalty must follow, not precede the transition from a wild blanket Indian to one having some aspirations for a better life," he stated.

Between 1865 and 1900 reformers images of the Indian had changed very little. The easy optimism of the 1880s, after the Plains Wars had ended and the reservation programs had begun, had disappeared. By the 1890s the reformers were disputing with each other the details of the civilization policies. Were rations and annuities pauperizing the Indian, and therefore counterproductive? Should Indian landholdings be further reduced to provide them capital to develop the land they retained? Were day schools or boarding schools best, and should the students be supplied government rations and have their tuition paid from tribal funds? Should the funds themselves be distributed per capita to eliminate another crutch for tribalism?

But never indispute among reformers was the basic image they held of the Native American throughout this period. He was their fellow human being and child of God, endowed with the potential to take his place in American society as a full-fledged citizen. And in this they never wavered. Today, cultural pluralism has achieved an acceptance that causes hypersensitivity to the reformers' ethnocentrism. One flinches at their casual talk of savages and barbarism. But, placed in the context of their times, the reformers' evaluation of the Indian and their willingness to work for his acceptance as a full-fledged fellow citizen deserve recognition and commendation.

Suggested Reading

There is a substantial literature on the reformers. Henry E. Fritz, *The Movement for Indian Assimilation, 1860–1890* (Philadelphia, 1963) and Robert Lewis Merdock, *The Reformers and the American Indian* (Columbia, Mo., 1971) are pioneering studies. Larry E. Burgess, *The Lake Mohonk Conferences on the Indian, 1883–1916* (Ann Arbor, Mich., 1979) traces their history. Two other useful studies of organizations of friends of the Indian are Helen M. Wanken, *"Women's Sphere" and Indian Reform: The Women's National Indian Association, 1879–1901* (Ann Arbor, Mich., 1968), and William T. Hagan, *The Indian Rights Association* (Tucson, Ariz., 1985). Frederick E. Hoxie, *A Final Promise: The Campaign to Assimilate the Indians, 1880–1920* (Lincoln, Nebr., 1984) carries the story of the reformers up to the 1920s. For an indispensable survey of Indian affairs in the entire period, consult Francis Paul Prucha, *The Great Father*, 2 vols. (Lincoln, Nebr., 1984).

Chapter 9 ૐ
From Bullets to Boarding Schools

The Educational Assault on American Indians

David Wallace Adams

*E*ven after the last of the military battles had been fought and the Indian peoples were at last confined within the boundaries of the reservation, their subjugation still was not complete. The process merely shifted to new ground, where a subtle but no less fateful chapter in the history of Indian-white relations was about to unfold. If "civilization" was to defeat "savagism"—and this was how white people defined the confrontation between the two races—then civilization must ultimately win a victory over the Indian that was both psychological and intellectual. In the end, it required that Indians come to accept the idea that defeat at the hands of whites was not only in the interests of a higher good—civilization—but in their own best interests. It was a matter of common sense to policymakers that the best hope for accomplishing their assimilative aims was to concentrate their efforts on the younger generation of Indians, those not fully confirmed in the old tribal ways of their ancestors. In short, an aggressive educational program was required. The next campaign against the Indian, then, was to be waged in the classroom. The issue at hand was no longer the dispossession of the Indians' land, but rather the possession of their minds, hearts, and souls. It was to be a gentle war, but a war just the same.

To understand this next phase of federal Indian policy, it is necessary to understand the mind frame from which policymakers operated. The program they came to erect followed naturally from a series of beliefs they held regarding the Indians' past and future and the power of education as a social and elevating force. The first of these beliefs related to the idea of civilization and its opposite, savagism. The concept that some peoples on the globe were more civilized than others was often portrayed as a ladder, with the upper rung representing civilization and the lower rung representing savagism. It was believed that some societies such as the nations of Europe and the United States had climbed the ladder of civilization to its highest rung, while other, less-fortunate peoples were still positioned near the bottom. Per this model, American Indians were still largely savages. The reasons underlying this classification were several: their paganism; their lack of appreciation for the values of hard work and private property; their disdain for sedentary farming; their entanglement in a web-like network of clans, kinship systems, and religious societies; their casual, even hostile, attitude toward monogamous marriage; and, finally, their blind loyalty to hereditary tribal chiefs. It was a long list. And while those who spoke about such matters often possessed little accurate information on the actual nature of Indian lifeways, this never stopped them from speaking confidently on the matter—or from passing judgment. Whites were civilized; Indians were savages. It was that simple.

A second belief of policymakers stemmed from their view of history as one vast moral tale infused with symbolic meaning. History, in short, was the story of man's progressive advancement from savagism to civilization. Indeed, because civilization was morally superior to savagism, it was virtually an immutable law of history that the former would triumph over the latter. All of this had profound implications for the Indian. For as relics of an earlier, more primitive social order, Indians could no longer continue to exist as Indians—that is to say, as savages. To survive, they must choose the path of civilized progress; to reject that path was to invite a well-deserved extinction. The price of the Indians' survival, then, was their cultural suicide. As Henry Price, commissioner of Indian Affairs, expressed it in 1881:

> There is no one who has been a close observer of Indian history and the effect of contact of Indians with civilizations, who is not well satisfied that one of two things must eventually take place, to wit, either civilization or extermination of the Indian. Savage and civilized life cannot live and prosper on the same ground. One of the two must die. If the Indians are to be civilized and become happy and prosperous people, which is certainly the object and intention of our government, they must learn our language and adopt our modes of life. We are fifty millions of people, and they are only one-fourth of one million. The few must yield to the many.

It was when policymakers addressed the question of just how to effect the Indians' assimilation that the discussion turned to education. Whereas under normal circumstances it might take the Indian several hundred years to climb to the upper rungs on the ladder of civilization, reformers believed that an aggressive educational campaign could accomplish the feat in a single generation. The power of education, then, was that it could speed up the historical advancement process. The trick was to gain access to the Indian's mind while it was still malleable, still open to the civilized teachings of whites. If this could be accomplished, if Indian youth could be taught the skills and ideas of white civilization, then the rising generation of Indians might obtain the necessary means to survive in the white world. If after all this Indians still chose to reject the ways of civilization, then they must face the consequence—extinction. And if this should come to pass, then, policymakers told themselves, at least they could find comfort in the thought that they had fulfilled their responsibility toward the nation's aboriginal wards. Nonetheless, reformers remained optimistic that the Indian could indeed be "saved." The answer lay in education. The Indians needed schools.

The subsequent rise of the Indian school system represents a dramatic shift in late-nineteenth-century federal Indian policy. One need only look at the increase in annual congressional appropriations to appreciate the change. In 1877, Congress appropriated $20,000 for Indian education; by 1880, $75,000; by 1885, $992,800; and by 1890, $1,364,368. Similarly, as the number of schools multiplied during this same period, Indian school attendance tripled from a mere 3,598 in 1877 to 12,232 in 1890. While these figures are impressive, they belie the fact that the growth of the Indian school service was frequently a fitful and chaotic story. For behind the consensus on the power of education as an instrument of assimilation, there was deep disagreement over the most efficacious means of carrying out the educational campaign. More specifically, policymakers differed as to which type of school might best accomplish their aims: the reservation day school, the reservation boarding school, or the off-reservation boarding school.

Some favored the reservation day school. The day school usually took the form of the familiar one-room schoolhouse, but in this case it was often attached to a modest residence for the teacher and perhaps a small kitchen for preparation of the pupils' noontime meals. On larger reservations, there were often several such schools scattered across the landscape, built conveniently near Indian villages. The day school had several advantages. A significant argument in its favor was that it engendered the least amount of resistance from parents. Another advantage was that it held out the possibility of enabling teachers to influence Indian parents through their children, the children, in a sense, becoming instruments of civilization. Finally, of the three types of schools it was the least expensive to operate. Nevertheless, the day school did suffer from one major defect: as an instrument designed to assimilate Indians into the mainstream culture it was simply ineffective. While it might introduce the Indian child to the mysteries of reading, writing, and arithmetic, it was ill-prepared to accomplish the task at hand: to turn Indian children into white Americans.

The rise of the second type of school—the reservation boarding school— resulted from two weaknesses in the day-school approach. First, since many Indians still lived a seminomadic lifestyle, even within reservations, the day school simply failed to reach large numbers of children. Second, the day school's influence over the child was limited to only those hours of school attendance. Teachers often complained that their efforts to teach children the ways of the dominant society were undermined by the omnipresent realities of camp life, to which the child returned at night and on weekends. What was needed, it was argued, was to place the child in a totally civilized environment, an environment so controlled that the child's every act could be observed, monitored, and altered. The reservation boarding school promised to do just this.

By the 1870s most Indian reservations could claim a boarding school. In what would become an annual fall ritual, Indian children were rounded up by the agency police force, often at gunpoint, and carted off to school. Once in school students not only received instruction in academic subjects but in the manual trades as well, with most attention being given to teaching the Indian child how to farm. Some schools even had some cattle and a few sheep so students might try their hand at raising stock. But just as important as the boarding school's program in the practical arts was the fact that now, under the continuing watchful eye of school officials, the Indian student could be taught to walk, eat, sleep, pray, dress, and think like whites. While "deluded" old Indians might harbor thoughts of teaching tribal youth the old ways of life and belief, all this would be more difficult once Indian youth were sequestered behind the school's barbed-wire fence for nine months out of the year, with their entire range of experiences limited to the world of the boarding school.

But as school and government officials soon learned, the reservation boarding school was not without its problems. While it was indeed more effective than was the day school, in its own way it suffered from the same old problem. Put simply, by being located on the reservation, it was still too close to the source of savagism. While students were prevented from having daily contact with their parents, school life was still affected by the pulse of reservation affairs just beyond the school gate. Even while institutionalized, students could intuitively sense when their relatives were moving out for the fall hunt; they might still steal a glimpse of family members as they gathered at the agency for the semimonthly distribution of annuity goods; and they could still hear, or at least imagined that they could, the echo of ceremonial drums in the surrounding hills. Then too, there was the familiar problem of relapse, although now it took on an altogether different form. Whereas before it happened on a daily basis, now it took the more dramatic form of students shedding almost completely in the summer months their newly acquired civilized habits for the old ways of camp life. As one agent observed: "How soon they seem to forget all they have been taught, after they return to camp."

The solution to this problem seemed couched in the third type of institution, the off-reservation boarding school. The rise of the off-reservation boarding school can largely be credited to the remarkable and controversial figure of U.S. Army Lieutenant Richard Henry Pratt. To impress upon the southern Plains' tribes the government's impatience with Indian harassment of white settlers, the army decided in 1875 to transport seventy-two Arapaho, Cheyenne, Kiowa, and Comanche warriors from Fort Sill, Oklahoma, to St. Augustine, Florida, where they were to be incarcerated for an indefinite period in the city's old Spanish fortress. As an old Indian fighter, Pratt was assigned the task of overseeing the whole venture. But once Pratt had his prisoners under lock and key, he inaugurated an experiment that clearly went beyond his designated orders.

For years Pratt had privately been formulating his own views as to what was needed to solve the Indian problem. Now he had an opportunity to put his plan into operation. Step by step, he turned this Florida prison into a school for civilization. First, the prisoners were issued uniforms and put through a rigorous program of marching and drilling. Then he turned the prison's chapel into a class-

The Carlisle Indian School, founded in 1879, was the prototype for government off-reservation boarding schools. These Kiowa boys were photographed in their school uniforms in March 1880.
Courtesy, R. B. Hayes Presidential Center, Fremont, Ohio

room where, aided by a few retired school teachers, he taught his prisoners some English and arithmetic. Next, he involved his Indians in a number of projects, such as performing odd jobs in the community and making Indian curios for local shopowners. All this began to have a profound effect on his Indian pupils. Within a year's time, prisoners could be seen on the streets of St. Augustine speaking a little English and purchasing store items with money they had earned from their own labor. Meanwhile, Pratt's experiment was attracting considerable public attention. Influential visitors began to visit the prison and all were unanimous in their belief that Pratt had made remarkable progress in transforming hardened warriors into civilized red men.

Pratt, meanwhile, was convinced that he had discovered the solution to the Indian problem. When the prisoners were released in 1879, a group of younger Indians expressed their desire to learn more of "the white man's road." Pratt was then allowed to follow seventeen of this group to Hampton Institute, a prominent institution in Virginia hitherto devoted exclusively to the education of blacks. Remaining at Hampton nearly a year, Pratt soon began lobbying with Washington for his own school where his Indian work might be carried on in a grander scale. Finally, he was given some unused military barracks in Carlisle, Pennsylvania, and detailed to carry on his experiment. Pratt was soon roaming across the Dakotas collecting students for his new school. In October 1879, Carlisle Indian School opened its doors with 136 students.

Carlisle Indian School offered students an expanded version of Pratt's Florida prison program, a combination of academic study and industrial training in a highly regimented environment. If students could be subjected to such a program for five years, thoroughly isolated from reservation influences, Pratt argued, then the problem of how to civilize the Indian would be solved. Again, visitors flocked to Carlisle to see Pratt's school in operation, and, they were impressed with what they saw. Within a few year's time Congress had authorized the construction of several more off-reservation schools in the Far West. A third model for Indian education—the off-reservation boarding school—had come into existence.

In the last two decades of the nineteenth century, a major effort was made to create a true "system" of Indian education. By 1892 Congress had passed a compulsory attendance law for Indian children. The day school, the reservation boarding school, and the off-reservation boarding school were all to play a part in the emerging system. Indian children, it was determined, should begin their education at the day school, move on to the reservation boarding school, and then complete their education in a Carlisle-type institution. But this was the "ideal" method of sorting. The fact of the matter is that for years countless numbers of Indian children were taken directly from their villages and thrown into the nearest boarding school. But regardless of where children entered the system, government officials were adamant in their belief that the boarding school experience, whether on or off the reservation, was crucial to accomplishing the Indian's assimilation. And therein the assault on traditional Indian identity was waged most fiercely.

As soon as the Indian child entered boarding school the war for his mind, heart, and soul began. For those children unfamiliar with whites, the first few days at school were particularly harrowing. Almost immediately the new arrival was subjected to a series of ordeals which, taken together, were designed to strip him of all outward signs of his cultural heritage. After a thorough scrubbing, during which he was introduced to the "gospel of soap," the child discovered that his camp clothes and moccasins had been taken away and replaced by the standard wool uniform and a pair of stiff-soled shoes. Next, if his family had not already been assigned an English-speaking last name at the agency, the new recruit received one at school. This was done partly because the teacher was often simply unable to pronounce the child's name in his native language. But the name change also was motivated by the fact that traditional Indian-naming practices did not provide for surnames. In the eyes of school officials, this was simply further evidence of the Indians' primitive cultural ways; it revealed how little Indian societies valued lines of inheritance and their disdain for private property. From this perspective, giving the Indian child a new name was a significant step in the civilization process.

The next assault on the new arrival came in the form of a haircut. While cutting the Indian boy's long hair may have appeared to school officials as a modest alteration on behalf of civilization, to the child it signified much more. How much more is suggested by this description of what transpired in the late 1880s when school officials attempted to give haircuts to some Sioux boys at Pine Ridge Boarding School. As J. C. McGillycuddy described the scene in the *McGillycuddy, Agent:*

> In each bathroom a teacher armed with shears was prepared to begin operations. Curious peepers stood close to the windows on the ground floor, deeply regretful of the drawn shades that barred their observation of the activities carried on behind them. There the matron scaled a small boy and taking a lousy braid in one hand, raised the shears hanging by a chain from her waist. A single clip and the filthy braid would be severed. But unfortunately, at that moment a breeze blew back the shade from the window. The previously baffled effort of a youngster plastered against the casing on the outside of the window was now rewarded by a fleeing glimpse of his playmate seated in the chair and a tall lean woman with a pair of shears in her hand prepared to divest the boy of his hair—a Delilah bringing calamity upon an embryo Samson.
>
> Like a war whoop rang out the cry: *"Pahin Kaksa, Pahin Kaksa!"* The enclosure rang with alarm, it invaded every room in the building and floated out on the prairie. No warning of fire or flood or tornado or hurricane, not even the approach of an enemy could have more effectively emptied the building as well as the grounds of the new school as did the ominous cry. "They were cutting the hair!" Through doors and windows the children flew, down the steps, through the gates and over fences in a mad flight toward the Indian villages, followed by a mob of bucks and squaws as though a bad spirit pursued all. They had been suspicious of the school from the beginning; now they knew it was intended to bring disgrace upon them.

Once the student had been stripped of the outward signs of his tribal past, he did his best to adjust to the realities of school life. He soon found that every minute of the day was regulated and scheduled, from the bugle call that roused him from slumber each dawn until the order for "lights out" came at day's end. In the interim, when not attending class or performing chores, the student was kept marching and drilling in military fashion. For those who went through the experience, some of their most vivid memories of boarding school were of the military atmosphere that pervaded its day-to-day routine. Remembers one Hopi: "When I entered school it was just like entering the school for Army or soldiering. Every morning we were rolled out of bed and the biggest part of the time we would have to line up and put guns in our hands. . . . When a man gave a command we had to stand at attention, another command grab our guns, and then march off at another command." All of this was intended to instill in the student what presumably was lacking in his native upbringing—self-discipline, habits of orderliness, and a respect for punctuality. The school now took it upon itself to impose from without what the child lacked from within.

Students were expected to respond to the regimentation of boarding-school life with absolute obedience. As one school reminded its students: "The moment a student is instructed to do a certain thing, no matter how small or how great, immediate action on his part is a duty and should be a pleasure. . . . Obedience means marching right on whether you feel like it or not." Should students resist the institutional demands for complete compliance, school officials had at their disposal a host of methods for whipping the noncompliant back into line. While the Indian office officially announced in 1895 that corporal punishment was no longer to be used in Indian schools, the fact of the matter is that it was resorted to for many years to come. "Sometimes I would see the teacher or principal whip a boy with a good-sized willow," recalls one Klamath man. "Sometimes they would make the boy take off his shirt and then the boy would never get over it." One of the most commonly reported methods was to have the guilty party run the gauntlet between two lines of students armed with straps. But there were many other forms of punishment in the school superintendent's arsenal, most of which appear to have been designed to induce psychological pain in the student. Realizing that Indian youth dreaded public humiliation even more than physical punishment, school officials readily employed such measures as shaving heads, forcing the guilty to wear signs on their backs, or sentencing boys to the awful fate of wearing a dress. At one school a student recalls that the superintendent utilized an especially cruel method of shaming students who wet the bed, the punishment being to carry the urine-soaked mattress on his back around the school grounds. As one Kiowa woman would remember of her boarding school experience in Oklahoma: "You get punished. Everything you do you get punished."

Regimentation and stiff discipline alone would not transform the Indian child. In the last analysis, the Indian child had to learn all the knowledge and values associated with civilized living. Furthermore, he must be taught the manual skills that would enable him to support himself without government assistance. These notions translated into a standardized instructional program wherein students divided their time between academic subjects and the "practical arts." Most educators agreed with the boarding-school superintendent who had worked among the Sioux that "a string of textbooks piled up in the storehouse high enough to surround a reservation if laid side by side will never educate a being with centuries of laziness instilled in his race." It was commonly agreed, then, that the Indian must be taught to think in the white man's way, but he must also be taught to work.

The first years of academic instruction were given over to teaching the Indian child the basic skills associated with reading, writing, and arithmetic. English, not surprisingly, assumed a position of immense importance in the first few years of the child's education. The reason for this was as much political as pedagogical. If the Indian was to be thoroughly absorbed into the mainstream of American life, it was deemed a matter of common sense that he should acquire the national language. "This language, which is good enough for a white man and a black man," the commissioner of Indian Affairs explained in 1887, "ought to be good enough for the red man." It followed that the rule "English only" was rigidly enforced both in and out of the classroom and that its violation was sure to meet with stiff punishment. Many students found the process of learning the white's language a painful and frustrating ordeal. Charles Eastman, a Sioux who became a physician, would never forget the first time the teacher called on the class to recite. "For a whole week, we youthful warriors were held up and harassed with words of three letters," he recalls. "Like raspberry bushes in the path, they tore, bled, and sweated us those little words rat, eat, and so forth—until not a semblance of our native dignity and self-respect was left."

Once the words began to come, the student was introduced to other subjects. Two subjects that assumed particular importance were U.S. history and geography. The study of the nation's history promised to engender patriotic sympathies, develop an appreciation for the duties and rights of citizenship, and, perhaps most important of all, convince the child that his dependent status was both inevitable and justified. This latter lesson was to be reinforced in geography class where teachers not only taught the physical features of the Earth but also carried on a comparative evaluation of the cultural contributions made by the different races. It was here that the Indian student first encountered directly the ladder of civilization concept. It was here that he could come to accept his own degradation as an objective fact, a necessary step, it was argued, if he was to begin to climb the ladder. Operating from this perspective, one school chose to publish some examinations marked 'excellent" in geography class. Among those published was this one:

Question: To what race do we all belong?
Answer: The Human race

Question: How many classes belong to this race?
Answer: There are five large classes belonging to the Human race.

Question: Which are the first?
Answer: The white people are the strongest.

Question: Which are the next?
Answer: The Mongolians or yellows

Question: The next?
Answer: The Ethiopians or blacks

Question: Next?
Answer: The Americans or reds

Question: Tell me something of the white people.
Answer: The Caucasian is away ahead of all of the other races—he thought more than any other race, he thought that somebody must made the earth, and if the white people did not find that out, nobody would never know it— it is God who made the world.

In this class the students appeared to be learning their lessons well. On another paper one student commented: "The red people they big savages; they don't know anything."

Given the content of their academic subjects, many students no doubt welcomed the fact that half of the school day was devoted to manual and industrial training. At reservation boarding schools this meant that Indian boys spent a good deal of the day working with saws and hammers and hoeing in the school garden. For girls the emphasis was on cooking, cleaning, and sewing. The off-reservation school offered a more varied and advanced curriculum, with boys having the opportunity to master a specific trade such as masonry, harness making, or tailoring and girls getting a chance to pursue coursework in secretarial training. For the most part, however, the thrust of the curriculum was to turn the sons of warriors into productive farmers and the daughters of "squaws" into nineteenth-century Victorian housewives. The transformation sought was thought to be not only consistent with the dictates of civilization, but, once accomplished, it would relieve the government of its moral responsibility to feed and clothe a people once proud and independent but now reduced to indolence and dependency.

While industrial training unquestionably taught students many valuable skills, all too often the effectiveness of such programs was undermined by institutional realities at odds with stated educational aims. The problem was that boarding-school officials were under great pressure from Washington to make their institution as self-sufficient and efficient as possible. Consequently, students were expected to grow much of their own food, make their own uniforms and dresses, clean the school buildings and grounds, and build new additions to the school complex. This push for self-sufficiency, carried out in an environment where the concern for orderliness took on paranoiac proportions, had the effect of transforming a potentially meaningful industrial training program into a prison-like labor camp. The aim of students acquiring new skills frequently gave way to concerns with student productivity. In 1890, for instance, the superintendent at Albuquerque pointed with pride to the fact that sixteen girls in the sewing department had turned out in a single year 238 aprons, 33 bedspreads, 73 chemises, 170 dresses, 261 pairs of trousers, 194 pillow cases, 224 sheets, 107 skirts, and 85 towels. The sacrifice of educational aims to institutional efficiency is also reflected in the manner in which chores were assigned. Students often found themselves consigned for several months at a time to such jobs as laundering, scrubbing floors, or cleaning the school stable. As one Winnebago complained: "I worked two years in turning a washing machine in a government school to reduce the running expenses of the institution." If this was the white man's idea of education, many students concluded, they wanted nothing of it.

But as school officials saw it, this very attitude was part of the Indian's problem. The Indian not only needed to be taught how to work, he needed to be taught to want to work. This was in turn linked to the problem that the Indian child came from a culture that placed little value on individual competition in the form of property accumulation. In short, the Indian lacked in his approach to life a firm appreciation for the most important ideal in the entire American belief system—rugged individualism. It followed that the student should be bombarded throughout the school day with references to the virtues of work, competition, and individual accomplishment. This message was in fact transmitted in the workplace, classroom primers, sermons, and school assemblies. And in the following instance the theme even received poetic expression in the school newspaper under the title "The Man Who Wins."

> The man who wins is the man who works
> The man who toils while the next man shirks . . .
> And the man who wins is the man who hears
> The curse of the envious in his ears
> But who goes his way with head held high
> And passes the wrecks of the failures by—
> For he is the man who wins.

To students who came from cultures in which individual status was attained through cooperative sharing, often ritualized in the form of elaborate gift-giving ceremonies, the message seemed strangely self-serving.

In many ways the most pronounced assault on the Indian's identity came from the school's effort to convert him to Christianity. For many educators, the Indian's "heathenish superstition" lay at the very heart of his backwardness. As one government official observed, it was quite impossible to construct a "superstructure of enlightened civilization" on a "foundation of savage superstition." Operating under this assumption it made sense that the missionary spirit should pervade every aspect of the child's education. And so it did. In the dining hall and the classroom, at Sunday church services and periodic prayer meetings, the message remained the same: the gods, rituals, and ceremonies of the Indian, while often picturesque, must be sacrificed upon the altar of the white man's more civilized religion.

For those students who had been instructed to the sacred ways of their grandfathers or who had experienced firsthand the great religious ceremonies of their people, the message was a disquieting one to say the least. Many students, before leaving for school, had been warned by their elders about this very subject.

Thomas Wildcat Alford, a Shawnee, would always remember clearly the instructions that he and others had received from village chiefs on the eve of their departure. The young braves were to learn all that the white teachers tried to teach them, it was explained, with one exception.

> Very solemnly the chiefs spoke to us. They reminded us of the responsibility we had assumed for our people when we consented to undertake the mission. We were not to go as individuals, but as representatives of the Shawnee tribe. The honor, the dignity, and the integrity of the tribe was placed in our hands. They told us of their desire that we should learn the white man's wisdom. . . . We should learn all this in order that when we came back we would be able to direct the affairs of our tribe and to assume the duties and position of chiefs at the death of the present chiefs. . . . But there was a proviso attached to the promise that we would be chiefs—*a positive demand that we should not accept the white man's religion; we must remain true to the Shawnee faith.*

"But as time passed," Alford goes on to explain, "and the interests of my teachers became stronger, their pleas more insistent, I could not ignore the subject." In the end he would come to know "deep in my soul that Jesus Christ was my Savior." Other students would make other choices.

All of this leads us to the question: how did the Indian student respond to the boarding school experience? Many students simply resisted the whole educational process. The reasons are not difficult to discern. Many perceived the efforts of school officials as little more than a self-serving attempt to dispossess the Indian of his last possession—his culture and identity. Viewing the experience from this cultural, even political perspective, these students viewed the classroom and drill field as but another setting for the historic confrontation between whites and Indians. But there were other reasons as well, some of which younger children may have scarcely been able to articulate. These reasons had not so much to do with the content of the school curriculum as with the manner in which it was transmitted. The school's heavy reliance on corporal punishment and public shaming techniques, as well as the teacher's total insensitivity to the child's cultural background, clearly fall into this category. And then, too, there was the pain and loneliness that came with being separated from parents and relatives. All in all, it is little wonder that the Indian child, especially if he or she was taken directly from the Indian camp, should experience a full range of emotions, beginning with fright and confusion and culminating in resentment and frequently rejection. This attitude was all the more likely if the reservation police had taken him or her against the wishes of the parents. Imagine, for example, how receptive the Mescalero Apache children rounded up for school in the fall of 1887 would be to the whites' school. As the agent described it, when the police appeared on the scene on the morning of the roundup, the parents "hurried their children off to the mountains or hid them away in camp, and the police had to chase and capture them like so many wild rabbits." When it was all over, we are told, "the men were sullen and muttering, the women loud in their lamentations, and the children almost out of their wits with fright." It is difficult to imagine that these children, once in school, would easily be converted to the ways of whites.

The response of resistance took several forms. Some students chose the path of escape and simply ran away. While the distant location of the off reservation school often ruled out this option, the reservation boarding school was a different matter. To some superintendents it seemed to make little difference how many bars they placed on the dormitory windows, how closely students were watched, or how stiff the punishment for running away might be; the discontented still seemed to find a way to slip beyond the school fence. Sometimes as individuals, sometimes in small groups, they set out on foot for the open prairie, picked their way along wooded river banks, and ran like the wind across desolate mesas in search of a friendly campfire. Neither the threat of a sudden desert storm, a prairie blizzard, or the inevitability that a policeman would soon be on their tracks was sufficient to dissuade the determined runaways. As one superintendent in Sioux country complained: "An Indian child will runaway whenever the roving disposition seizes it." This official, like many others, had come to the conclusion that only "a wall surrounding the school, with iron gates, sentinels posted, could prevent escape."

A more dramatic form of resistance was to burn down the school. It is difficult to judge how many students actually turned to arson as a form of protest. What is clear is that the school reports sent back to Washington made frequent reference to the outbreak of unexplained fires. "The burning of the boarding school and laundry buildings the past spring was a serious loss to the reservation," one superintendent reported. "It still is a mystery how the fire originated in the school room proper." Some of these fires can of course be explained away by the all too shabby construction of some school structures and the outright negligence on the part of employees, but it is also evident from the tone of many of these reports that student conspiracy was strongly suspected. A simple scolding, a public thrashing, or a denied request to visit relatives might be enough to provoke an embittered student to plot the school's destruction. But many no doubt acted out of a much deeper dissatisfaction with boarding-school life and thought out carefully the beneficial consequences that would flow from an arson plot successfully executed. Thus, many Winnebago students got what they wanted when a "mysterious" fire swept away the school in 1891. The agent was forced to announce: "The children were all sent home." Whatever their motivation, to the consternation of government officials, students continued to express their displeasure with the whites' schools by setting them ablaze. By the first decade of the twentieth century, the problem had grown to epidemic proportions. As commissioner of Indian Affairs Francis E. Leupp would later recall: "Explanations of the perils as well as the wickedness of such actions, and even the ordinary penalties which lay within the power of the teachers to impose, were alike powerless to break up this wanton fancy for the firebrand as a panacea."

A third manner of opposition took the form of passive resistance. When teachers came west to raise up the "savage," most assumed that they would find their new pupils eager to learn the teachings of civilization. To their unpleasant surprise, what they frequently encountered were suspicious captives consciously determined to maintain their cultural identity, regardless of the teacher's remonstrances to the contrary. Most frustrating from the teacher standpoint was the uncanny ability of the Indian student dutifully to go through the motions of boarding-school routine, outwardly compliant with all its rules and regulations but inwardly resistant to the substance of the school's teachings. In the classroom this attitude manifested itself in the form of the student responding to the teacher's lesson with a numbing silence. Needless to say, most teachers found this attitude both ungrateful and unnerving, and it may go a long way toward explaining why teacher turnover posed such a problem for the Indian school service. In any case, teachers could only wonder day in and day out what thoughts were running through the minds that lay behind the expressionless eyes that stared back at them. The answer to this question may be provided in part by a poem written by a group of Navajo students in the 1930s titled "My Thinking":

> If I do not believe you
> The things you say,
> Maybe I will not tell you
> That is my way.
>
> Maybe you think I believe you
> That thing you say,
> But always my thoughts stay with me
> My own way.

If many students resisted the boarding school, many others cooperated with it. Again, the question is "why?" The answer is especially difficult to formulate for the simple reason that students left behind only the sketchiest of testimony as to the reasons for their compliance. While there is some evidence of this sort, a more profitable approach might be to analyze what tribal leaders said about the school issue. This discussion must in turn be prefaced by the understanding that Indian communities were deeply divided on how to respond to their status as subjugated wards of the nation. While some chose to resist all efforts of the government to teach them the "new way," others came to the conclusion that Indians must seek to accommodate themselves to the new realities of their present situation. For those adopting the latter position, the value of learning the white man's way took on a different light.

That some tribal leaders looked favorably on the boarding school there is little doubt. When one old Sioux chief visited some of his people's children away at boarding school, he compared their presence there to putting "seeds in the ground." "If I don't see them growing after a time I feel uneasy," he explained. "Then I look again, and if I see them sprouting, I feel glad. So I feel about our children. I see that seed is growing here now, and by and by it will do good among my people." Occasionally, Indian parents, with the aid of an interpreter and the reservation agent, wrote letters to their offspring in school urging them to be diligent scholars. Thus, one Sioux father wrote his son: "I am glad that you are trying to learn. Don't run away from school. It will be your own good if you learn ... learn to talk English; don't be ashamed to talk it." Similarly, an Indian mother wrote to her child: "I am sorry you are not coming home next summer, dear child, but if you like to learn something it is a good place for you. Learn all you can; it will be for your own benefit."

While responses such as these do not appear to have represented the sentiments of most Indian parents, they still raise the question of why even small tribal factions should favor cooperation with an institution whose major purpose was to assimilate Indian children forcibly to the ways of whites. One reason for this response is that some Indian parents as well as students came to accept and internalize white people's definition of the basis of Indian-white conflict. As previously shown, school officials went to great lengths to convince students that the

Young girls in a sewing class at Albuquerque Indian School. Courtesy, NARA's Rocky Mountain Region #NRG-75-AISP-14

historic conflict between Indians and whites was in fact one great cultural tale, that it could only be understood if viewed in the deeper context of savagism versus civilization. It appears that some Indian elders, in the wake of their race's near destruction at the hands of whites, and confronted with the immense technological power and material wealth of their conquerors, were beginning to accept as truth white pronouncements on the limited worth of Native cultures. Thus, when a group of Navajo headmen, long opposed to white schooling, returned from a government-sponsored visit to the World Columbian Exposition held in Chicago in 1893, one description of what the group had witnessed sounded strangely similar to the doctrine of civilized progress. It all started with Christopher Columbus.

> The boats were there like which men had when they discovered this country. White man said there might be more land. That ship went back across the ocean and told the people more land here, and more came across. Mexicans at first came over. 'Way back the ships used to go by sail and wind; now they go by steam. We saw lots of white people's guns. 'Way back they did not have good guns; now they have good ones. Light used to be from lard or grease, and then oil; now it's electric lights. We saw different kinds of hoes and plows and shovels—all things to work with. To know how to read and write does good, for they can think more; they can see more; they see better with eyes.

The speaker ended his account with the line: "It is time to let up now." The meaning to the assembled Navajos was eminently clear. They should turn their children over to the agent for education.

Further evidence that changing parental attitudes on the comparative worth of Indian and white ways could affect attitudes on the education question is illustrated by a letter written by a Sioux father, Brave Bull, to his daughter at Carlisle:

> Ever since you told me I have worked hard, and put up a good house, and am trying to be civilized like the whites, so you will never hear anything bad from me. When Captain Pratt was here he came to my house, and asked me to let you go to school. I want you to be a good girl and study. I have dropped all the Indian ways, and am getting like a white man, and don't do anything but what the agent tells me. I listen to him. I have always loved you, and it makes me very happy to know that you are learning.

The letter ends with Brave Bull's answer to a request from his daughter: "Why do you ask for moccasins? I sent you there to be like a white girl, and wear shoes." Needless to say, while the denial of the desired moccasins was surely a disappointment, her father's conversion to white ways must have considerably lessened any guilt the girl might have felt in abandoning the ways of her people.

A second reason for cooperating with the school program sprang from a very different motivation: the desire to survive as a people. It will be remembered that policymakers in Washington constantly stressed the point that the only alternative to the Indians' civilization was extinction. Indeed, the entire Indian school system had been created out of the philanthropic desire to acculturate the Indian child to the ways of whites, thereby saving them from the tragic fate that awaited the unassimilated. As Indians reflected on their current status and past fortunes, there was considerable evidence to justify the conclusion that the choice they faced the was exactly as policymakers had framed it: civilization or extinction. Thus, it appears that a major reason why some Indian leaders cooperated with government efforts to educate their children was not out of the belief that white ways were necessarily superior to Indian ways, but out of the conclusion that education was the only road to survival as a people. Perhaps this underlay Geronimo's remarks to Carlisle students in 1904. "You are here to study, to learn the ways of the white man. Do it well." Then, in reference to Pratt, the old warrior added, "Your father is here. Do as he tells you. Obey him as you would your own father. . . . Obey all orders. Do as you are told all the time and you won't get hungry."

And this leads to still another aspect of the cooperative response, and one markedly similar to the earlier discussion of passive resistance. In this case the student demonstrated outward compliance, listened to what his white teachers taught him, accepted some things, rejected others, integrated some teachings into his own system of beliefs, but in all cases retained a sense of who he was—be it Navajo, Sioux, or Hopi. Under this form of cooperation, then, students consciously, or perhaps even unconsciously, sorted out and accepted knowledge essential to individual and tribal survival and discarded that which threatened their cultural identity. Some students may have, for instance, regarded it as a matter of tribal self-defense that they should learn to read and write the whites' language but out of the same motivation concluded that they should spurn the words of the white preacher. Hopi anthropologist Emory Sekaquaptewa has termed this response *compartmentalization*. "The nature of compartmentalization," he writes, "argues that one need not reject his cultural values to make an adjustment to an alien situation." Sekaquaptewa suggests that Hopi children over the past century have become very adept at this. This suggests, then, that boarding schools were a place where Indian students began to learn ways of reaching an accommodation with the larger white world, but not at the price of surrendering their distinctive Indian identity.

But the process whereby students attempted to define the terms on which they would reach an accommodation with the white world extended beyond the years spent at boarding school, which leads to the question: what happened to students when they returned home? The answer was immensely important to the Indian Bureau. The rationale for the boarding school had always been that it provided the ultimate solution to the problem of how to assimilate the Indian. Boarding school graduates, it was argued, would return to their reservations as emissaries of "Civilization," dedicated to uplift and transform their people. This was the plan. But as it turned out, the Indian Bureau was soon confronted with what it chose to call "the returned student problem." Numerous reports observed that many returned students who appeared to have been thoroughly made over by their school experience, once back on the reservation almost immediately began to "backslide" down the ladder of civilization, in some cases slipping all the way to their "original lowly position"—savagism. Boarding-school officials countered these pessimistic reports with studies of their own, suggesting that the vast majority of students did indeed live up to school expectations. As to which assessment was correct, it is difficult to say. It does appear, however, that a significant number of boarding-school graduates, when confronted with the option of returning to the lifeways of their ancestors, willingly abandoned many of their white teachings.

Typical was the case of Don Talayesva. Talayesva, a Hopi, had attended both a reservation and an off-reservation boarding school before returning to his village in 1909. Freed from the restraints of institutional life, he spent the first night home sleeping on the roof of a pueblo dwelling where he gazed at the star-speckled Arizona sky and contemplated the meaning of his boarding-school experience. He recalled this moment in his autobiography, *Sun Chief:*

> As I lay on my blanket I thought about my school days and all that I had learned. I could talk like a gentleman, read, write, and cipher. I could name all the states in the Union with their capitals, repeat the names of all the books in the Bible, quote a hundred verses of Scripture, sing more than two dozen Christian hymns and patriotic songs, debate, shout football yells, swing my partners in square dances, bake bread, sew well enough to make a pair of trousers, and tell "dirty" Dutchman stories by the hour.

But as for the future, Talayesva "wanted to become a real Hopi again, to sing the good old Katcina songs, and to feel free to make love without fear of sin or rawhide [whip]."

If the case of Talayesva had been an isolated story of a returned student having gone astray, it would have been of little concern to policymakers. But such was not the case. Federal officials were increasingly learning what teachers and missionaries over the past two and a half centuries had come to realize before them, namely, that the process of turning Indians into whites was not an easy business.

By the 1920s, a new generation of reformers was calling for a wholesale revampment of Indian education. Their views soon found forceful expression in a government-sponsored but independent investigation of the nation's entire Indian policy. Carried out under the direction of Lewis Meriam, this landmark study resulted in a series of findings and recommendations published in 1928 under the title *The Problem of Indian Administration*. The so-called Meriam report offered a blistering indictment of boarding school conditions, arguing that instead of educators attempting to eradicate all vestiges of Indian culture, they ought to attempt "to develop it and build on it rather than crush out all that is Indian." And while both the reservation and off-reservation boarding school were to remain permanent fixtures in the Indian school system, the Meriam report set in motion a gradual decline in their numbers, with the reservation day school and the local public school assuming an increased importance in the structure of Indian schooling. But the most important legacy of the Meriam report was that it prompted a long overdue reexamination of those fundamental principles that had historically governed the nation's Indian policy. Policymakers were now asked to consider the possibility that Indian ways were not necessarily savage ways, that education was not synonymous with civilization. Indian education would never again be quite the same.

Suggested Reading

For an overview of the issues surrounding federal Indian educational policy during the period treated in this chapter, see Henry E. Fritz, *The Movement for Indian Assimilation, 1860–1890* (Philadelphia, 1963); Loring Benson Priest, *Uncle Sam's Stepchildren: The Reformation of United States Policy, 1865–1887* (New Brunswick, N.J., 1942); Francis Paul Prucha, *American Indian Policy in Crisis: Christian Reformers and the Indian, 1865–1900* (Norman, Okla., 1976); Prucha, *The Churches and the Indian Schools, 1888–1912* (Lincoln, Nebr., 1979); Brian W. Dippie, *The Vanishing American: White Attitudes and U.S. Indian Policy* (Middletown, Conn., 1982); Frederick E. Hoxie, *A Final Promise: The Campaign to Assimilate the Indians, 1880–1920* (Lincoln, Nebr., 1984); Wilbert H. Ahern, "Assimilationist Racism: The Case of the 'Friends of the Indian,'" *Journal of Ethnic Studies* 4 (Summer 1976): 23–32; and Irving G. Hendrick, "The Federal Campaign for the Admission of Indian Children into Public Schools, 1890–1934," *American Indian Culture and Research Journal* 5 (1981): 13–32.

For the role of Pratt and the Carlisle Indian School in the history of Indian education, see Richard Henry Pratt, *Battlefield and Classroom*, edited by Robert M. Utley (New Haven, Conn., 1964); Elaine Goodale Eastman, *Pratt, the Red Man's Moses* (Norman, Okla., 1935); and Jacqueline Fear-Segal, "Nineteenth-Century Indian Education: Universalism Versus Evolutionism," *Journal of American Studies* 22 (August 1999): 323–41.

For selected aspects of the boarding-school story, see David Wallace Adams, *Education for Extinction: American Indians and the Boarding School Experience: 1875–1928* (Lawrence, Kans., 1995); Brenda J. Child, *Boarding School Seasons: American Indian Families, 1900–1940* (Lincoln: Nebr., 1998); Micheal C. Coleman, *American Indian Children at School, 1850–1930* (Jackson: Miss., 1993); Clyde Ellis, *To Change Them Forever: Indian Education at the Rainy Mountain Boarding School,*

1893–1920 (Norman: Okla., 1996); K. Tsianina Lomawaima, *They Called It Prairie Light: The Story of Chilocco Indian School* (Lincoln: Nebr., 1994); and Robert A. Trennert, *The Phoenix Indian School: Forced Assimilation in Arizona, 1891–1935* (Norman, Okla., 1988). Several American Indian autobiographical accounts include descriptions of boarding-school life. Notable among these are *Luther Standing Bear, My People, the Sioux* (Boston, 1928); *Standing Bear, Land of the Spotted Eagle* (Boston, 1933); Leo W. Simmons, ed., *Sun Chief: The Autobiography of a Hopi Indian* (New Haven, Conn., 1942); Jim Whitewolf, *The Life of a Kiowa Indian,* edited by Charles S. Brant (New York, 1969); Louise Udall, *Me and Mine: The Life Story of Helen Sekaquaptewa* (Tucson, Ariz., 1969); and Charlotte J. Frisbie and David P. McAllester, eds., *Navajo Blessing Singer: The Autobiography of Frank Mitchell, 1881–1967* (Tucson, Ariz., 1978).

Chapter 10 🙠
The Divided Heart

The Indian New Deal

Graham D. Taylor

*I*n the summer of 1928, the Brookings Institute for Government Research released a report of more than eight hundred pages entitled *The Problem of Indian Administration*. Based on a two-year investigation by a team of social scientists under the direction of Lewis Meriam, the report was objective and moderate in tone, in striking contrast to the polemics that characterized much of the debate over the conditions of Native Americans. Nevertheless, the Meriam study's conclusions were bleak and pessimistic: provisions for welfare, health, and education of the people on the reservations were "grossly inadequate," and the administration of allotment had "resulted in much loss of land . . . without a compensating advance in the economic ability of the Indians." As a result, American Indians were among the most impoverished people in the United States. Less than 2 percent of Native Americans had incomes of more than $500 a year, and more than half had incomes well below $200 a year, derived primarily from leasing or selling of their inadequate parcels of lands to neighboring white farmers or ranchers. Furthermore, the long-standing policy of assimilation, deliberately intended to "crush out all that is Indian" had demoralized these people, destroying their family and community life, producing a mixture of mistrust and indifference toward even genuine efforts to improve their conditions.

The understatement typical of the Meriam report made it all the more devastating an indictment of government policies dating back to the Dawes Act of 1887. For forty years these policies had been imposed virtually without opposition. Now they were demonstrably and categorically judged to have failed. Through its quiet but unqualified condemnation of the results of allotment, and its proposals for reform, the Meriam report represented a watershed in the history of government relations with Native Americans.

The Meriam report, however, also marked the culmination of a movement for reform that had begun earlier in the 1920s. Initially, that reform movement had focused on the perennial problems of corruption and mismanagement within the Bureau of Indian Affairs. Soon, criticism expanded to encompass a wide-ranging attack not simply on the administration of the governement's Indian policy but on the premises of policies underlying them. This challenge to the fundamental principle of assimilation was ultimately incorporated in the programs of the Indian New Deal in the 1930s. At the same time, it created divisions between the "old" missionary-based reformers, who remained committed to assimilation, and the "new" reformers of the 1920s. These divisions extended into Indian communities and ultimately would undermine the achievements of the New Deal era.

By 1920 the full impact of the allotment policy was becoming apparent on the western reservations. Under the Dawes Act, allotments were to be held in trust by the government for a minimum of twenty-five years, but by World War I the trust period was coming to an end for many American Indians. The Burke Act of 1906 accelerated the process of transferring land titles to allotments to those deemed "competent" to manage their own affairs. Commissioners of Indian Affairs between 1909 and 1928, including Charles Burke himself, sponsor of the 1906 act, sought to extend the trust period as they witnessed the results of the policy (Many Indians who received titles sold, lost, or were tricked out of their land.) But western congressional representatives in Congress pushed effectively for rapid implementation of allotment to achieve the ultimate goals of the Dawes Act—the establishment of the Native American as individual property owner and U.S. citizen. In 1924 the Indian Citizenship Act, which finally granted U.S. citizenship to Indian peoples, was passed to hasten this process, and legislators looked forward to the day when the Bureau of Indian Affairs could be terminated completely. In fact, the combined legislation resulted in the rapid dispossession of much of what remained of Native Americans' lands, as the newly entitled proprietors were forced to sell their meager estates to pay local taxes or simply to survive! By the 1930s, the land base of Natives had diminished to less than 50 million acres, one-third its size in 1887.

The devastating results of allotment were most dramatic in Oklahoma, where the Five Civilized Tribes (previously subjected to measures similar to those of the Dawes Act in the 1890s) had lost 40 percent of their lands, and in the Plains and Great Lakes regions, where the Sioux had alienated (lost title to) one-third of their allotted acreage. Some groups such as the Chippewa of Minnesota and the Winnebago of Wisconsin had lost more than 80 percent of their lands. Their reservations were characterized by a "checkerboarding" of allotted and alienated lands, which provided an insurmountable obstacle to later efforts to consolidate Native resources to promote economic development in the communities.

Ironically, however, the new reform movement of the 1920s initially directed its attention toward the problems of Native communities in the Southwest who had escaped the full implementation of allotment and resisted pressures for assimilation. Indeed, the Pueblos of New Mexico became the focal point for a revival of public concern over the government's Indian policies. At the same time, the various controversies surrounding the Pueblos revealed the fissures that ultimately would separate the traditional reformers from the Indians' new allies.

The Pueblos confronted challenges from two directions in 1921. The first involved their traditional lands. Although the Pueblo lands had not been allotted, about 10 percent of their grants had been alienated between 1848 and 1912, including valuable irrigated acreage. The question of title to these lands was a subject of considerable historical controversy and was further confused by a 1913 Supreme Court decision that, as wards of the U.S. government, implied that the Pueblos did not have the authority to alienate their lands. At the instigation of Interior Secretary Albert Fall, in 1921 Senator Holm Bursum of New Mexico introduced a bill that would confirm the transfer of title to the disputed claims out of the hands of the Pueblos, who now took the position that the land continued to be theirs, although they disputed the Supreme Court ruling that they lacked the competence to dispose of their resources as they saw fit.

The Indian Rights Association, a Philadelphia-based organization that represented the traditional white reform movement, opposed the Bursum bill. In this stance the Indian Rights Association was joined by two new groups, the Eastern Association of Indian Affairs, led by anthropologists interested in preserving Pueblo society and culture, and the New Mexico Association on Indian Affairs, comprising white artists and intellectuals living around Taos, New Mexico. The New Mexico group was most active in generating national interest in the Pueblo land issue, promoting an All-Pueblo Council among the villages, and using their contacts in the media to publicize the plight of these people. Their efforts were enhanced by the sudden resignation of Secretary Fall amidst emerging scandals in the Interior Department in 1923. In short order, the Bursum bill was defeated, and, after considerable legislative maneuvering, a Pueblo Lands Act was passed in 1924 that established procedures for an equitable settlement of the disputed claims.

The alliance of old and new reformers to block the Bursum bill dissolved, however, over a concurrent issue, the proclamations of Indian Commissioner Burke in 1921 and 1923 that prohibited or limited traditional ceremonies such as the Sun Dance among the Pueblos and other tribes. This "Dance Order" had been an objective of the Indian Rights Association and missionary reformers for many years. In contrast, the Taos-based group, which had broadened into a national organization known as the American Indian Defense Association, opposed the Dance Order, regarding it a blatant attempt to suppress Native culture and an attack on religious freedom. They encouraged the Pueblos to openly defy the Bureau of Indian Affairs and vigorously lobbied to repeal the order. By 1926 the Indian Defense Association had stymied the Dance Order and blocked passage of a bill that would have enabled Burke to prosecute Indians in federal courts or before reservation tribunals that had no due-process procedures.

Throughout the remainder of the decade, the reform groups expanded their activities to address the broad range of problems of Natives. The Indian Rights Association and Indian Defense Association worked in tandem to resist successfully another of Fall's schemes that would have opened up some of the reservations to mining and oil drilling without compensating the Indian communities residing on them. But the underlying divisions among the reformers that had emerged in the Dance Order debate remained just beneath the surface. While

Commissioner of Indian Affairs John Collier addresses the crowd at the Tohono O'odham Rodeo, 1940. Standing next to him is Tohono O'odham leader Pete Blaine. Courtesy, Arizona Historical Society, Tucson, AHS #8508

both groups agreed that American Indian communities needed protection from despoliation by white landowners and business interests and that the Bureau of Indian Affairs was underfunded and inefficient, their differences became apparent in regard to the question of changing basic government policies toward the Indians.

At the center of this debate was John Collier. The emerging leader of the Indian Defense Association, Collier was the virtual embodiment of the new reform movement, a vigorous lobbyist, organizer, and publicist, and a man of strong, abrasive views and overwhelming energy. To a certain extent, Collier's ideas about Native Americans were uniquely personal, but they reflected as well a general shift in intellectual attitudes toward race, culture, and material achievement as a measure of social value.

John Collier brought to the problems of Native Americans in the 1920s an unconventional and wide-ranging intellectual background. A "reform Darwinist and self-made sociologist," Collier admired the ideas of critics of industrial society such as nineteenth-century thinkers Peter Kropotkin and William Morris. He devoted much of his life to preserving traditional communities against what he perceived as the onslaught of Western industrialization, with its emphasis on individual self-interest and unlimited technological change.

Throughout his career, Collier alternated periods of energetic reform activity with periods of withdrawal into wilderness solitude. During the World War I era, Collier was drawn into the community-organization movement among immigrant groups in New York City. Following the demise of the community-organization movement at war's end and a brief, frustrating experience as director of adult education in California, Collier retreated to Taos, New Mexico, where he encountered the Pueblos. Here, he believed, he had at last found a genuinely cohesive culture group that had successfully resisted the encroachments of white civilization and all its attendant social ills. He quickly embraced the Pueblos' cause as his own.

Collier was attracted to Native communities in the Southwest precisely because they so clearly rejected assimilation. To him, the pressures to assimilate represented a far more insidious and fundamental threat to American Indians than did the crass and open exploitation denounced by traditional white reformers. Collier's ideas on this subject reflected his own basic rejection of the values of industrial society. At the same time, his respect for Native cultures was shared by a growing number of intellectuals and social scientists. In the 1920s, novelists and poets such as Oliver La Farge, Mary Austin, and John Nichardt began to undermine the literary stereotypes of American Indians, while anthropologists such as Franz Boas, Robert Lowie, and Ruth Benedict argued that cultural differences among groups did not demonstrate their relative position on a single evolutionary scale (the old civilization as ladder model) but that each culture must be viewed on its own terms. By the mid-1920s these radical views had emerged to challenge the conventional evolutionist arguments that had long been used to justify the coerced assimilation of Native Americans.

Total rejection of assimilation, however, remained a minority view even among supporters of Collier's Indian Defense Association. Even the Meriam report, commissioned by Interior Secretary Hubert Work in 1926 after the reformers rejected an in-house investigation of the Bureau of Indian Affairs, circled gingerly around this subject. While documenting the results of existing policies and deploring them, the Brookings Institute study concluded that the "fundamental requirement" of government programs should be "the social and economic advancement of the Indians so that they may be absorbed into the prevailing civilization or be fitted to live in the presence of that civilization at least in accordance with a minimum standard of health and decency."

The Hoover administration endorsed the findings of the Meriam report, and in 1929 Charles Rhoads, a former president of the Indian Rights Association, was appointed Indian commissioner by Interior Secretary Ray L. Wilbur, also a supporter of the Philadelphia-based reform group. Rhoads moved quickly to introduce improvements in the Bureau along the lines proposed by the Meriam study. W. Carson Ryan, director of Indian education under Rhoads, began closing down the unpopular boarding schools and replacing them with day schools located near the reservations, established a placement service and student-loan program, and generally upgraded the quality of teaching. Health services were also improved, through enlargement of medical and nursing facilities and staff and an emphasis on preventive medicine. Rhoads even joined with Collier in 1929 in drafting proposals for legislation to encourage tribal councils, establish a special federal court to review treaty claims, and settle outstanding debts incurred by Natives under a misconceived loan program set up during World War I to expand tribal livestock herds.

Nevertheless, Rhoads remained committed to the ultimate goal of assimilation and refused to halt the allotment process. The Meriam report had suggested that the Bureau permit the consolidation of allotted lands under tribal management on a trial basis on several reservations, but Rhoads and Wilbur declined to undertake even this limited experiment. Consequently, by 1930 Collier and the anti-assimilationist reformers had parted ways with Rhoads. Collier lobbied with the Senate Indian Affairs Committee, which had initiated its own study of the problems of Native Americans in 1928, urging it to repudiate the new commissioner's policies. The committee, dominated by western Democrats such as Senator Burton Wheeler of Montana and Senator Elmer Thomas of Oklahoma, supported Collier's position, partly in order to discredit the current Republican administration.

By 1932 the Rhoads reform program was in shambles, assaulted by Collier and congressmen, and undermined by the Great Depression, the effects of which reduced appropriations to the Bureau of Indian Affairs to a point where Indians, badly off at the best of times, were reduced to desperate circumstances. Rhoads's failure to improve conditions for Indians by relying on moderate and conventional reform measures set the stage for a more far-reaching change in policy following the election of Franklin Delano Roosevelt as president.

President Roosevelt's appointment of Collier as commissioner of Indian Affairs in 1933, after considerable political maneuvering by interested parties, came as a shock to the old reformers, but even the Indian Rights Association gamely offered "support and cooperation," noting that Collier, "an outstanding critic," was "being told in effect, 'Show us how it should be done.'" While moving quickly to acquire relief funds for Indians through the various emergency programs set up by the Roosevelt administration, Collier began to work on a major policy initiative, with the assurance of support from Interior Secretary Harold Ickes, who had been one of the founding members of the Indian Defense Association.

In keeping with the spirit of reconciliation that temporarily prevailed among reform groups, Collier solicited advice on policy changes from a wide variety of sources. In January 1934 a conference of reform groups chaired by Meriam met at the Cosmos Club in Washington, D.C. The conference recommended an end to allotment, the settlement of all treaty claims, the establishment of tribal organizations that would gradually take over the administrative powers of the Bureau of Indian Affairs and assume control of tribal resources (including allotted lands, which should be consolidated into economically viable units) and the establishment of a substantial loan fund to promote economic development. Collier also circulated questionnaires to anthropologists and reservation superintendents, and subsequently presented his proposals to a series of assemblies of Native Americans around the country. Although some critics charged that these meetings were little more than "window dressing" intended to present the appearance of widespread support for Collier's program, the process of consultation was unusual, reflecting the new commissioner's conviction that policies should not be unilaterally imposed by the government, as had long been the case, as well as his desire to preempt potential opposition to the proposed reforms.

The bill drafted by Collier and two Interior Department lawyers, Nathan Margold and Felix Cohen, was introduced in Congress by Senator Wheeler and Representative Edgar Howard of Nebraska in February 1934. It was a long and extremely complex piece of legislation, encompassing virtually the entire range of policies affecting Native Americans. In addition to the proposals of the Cosmos Club conference, the bill included provisions for the establishment of a special federal court for Indian affairs and measures that would not only expand educational opportunities for Native Americans but "promote the study of Indian civilization and preserve and develop the special cultural contributions and achievements of such civilization, including Indian arts, crafts, and traditions." Various loan funds were proposed to encourage tribal organization, improve health and educational facilities, and contribute to the consolidation and development of tribal economic resources.

The unity among reform groups eroded quickly, however, following the introduction of the Wheeler-Howard bill. By the end of March 1934, the Indian Rights Association began openly criticizing the provisions for an Indian court and tribal organization, charging that these measures would perpetuate the segregation of Native communities from the mainstream of American society and retard progress toward the ultimate goal of assimilation. Harsher critics argued that tribal organization and land consolidation would make the program a "communist experiment," a claim that extremist groups among the Natives, such as Joseph Bruner's American Indian Federation, would later resurrect. Meanwhile, white special interests in the West and their representatives in Congress were suspicious of the provisions relating to consolidation of reservation resources— not because this step would transfer ownership of allotments to tribes, but because, in practice, it would extend the control of the federal government over these resources by giving the Interior secretary ultimate power over the classification, leasing, sale, or development of tribal lands, timber, and subsurface minerals. Indian leaders also noted the ambiguity of these provisions. Those who held allotments in trust (without title) feared the loss of their property to community control, while tribes that already had councils, such as the Navajos in the

Southwest and the Iroquois in New York, believed that the program would dilute the authority they now possessed and undermine their historic claims to sovereignty.

Collier was inclined to dismiss the arguments of white westerners as self-serving, but he was troubled by the measure of opposition from Native groups and still wanted to accommodate the views of the assimilationist reformers, particularly since Senator Wheeler began to share their doubts about the bill, proclaiming that his aim was to help Indians "adopt the white man's ways and laws." In April 1934, Collier proposed a series of amendments to the bill that would ensure that individual property not be arbitrarily transferred to tribal ownership and allow tribes to decide by referenda whether to come under the provisions of the bill—a crucial concession.

Even these concessions were not satisfactory to critics of the plan, and in May 1934 the House Committee on Indian Affairs redrafted the entire bill, eliminating the proposal for a federal Indian court, substantially limiting the powers of tribal organizations over economic resources, and requiring a series of tribal plebiscites to determine whether Native American communities would come under the act, organize tribal governments, and establish tribal corporations to manage the use and sale of natural resources. Those groups that rejected any or all of these steps would remain under the existing regulations of the Bureau of Indian Affairs.

Collier would later maintain that the changes in the bill were "a major disaster to the Indians," and other historians of the Indian New Deal have concurred that the final measure, signed into law as the Indian Reorganization Act on June 18, 1934, "bore little resemblance to Collier's original proposal." The point is well taken, although the act did bring an end to allotment, established the legal groundwork for protecting Native American culture, and initiated local self-government in place of the bureaucratic absolutism that had prevailed over most of these communities in the preceding fifty years. The limitations imposed by Congress on the original proposal, however, reflected the divisions and uncertainties that characterized not only the reform movement but also Native American communities at the time. Despite the bad effects of earlier policies, allotment and assimilation had produced changes that could not be reversed or ignored. Some Indians actively favored assimilation. Others, tempered by experience with wildly fluctuating government policies in the past, simply wanted to hang on to what little property they still possessed. Still others, reflecting traditions of independence or motivated by less admirable aims of personal aggrandizement or enrichment, simply rejected any measures that left American Indians under the control of a government agency.

White reformers, too, were divided over the purpose of the act, disagreements that extended beyond, or, more accurately, intermeshed with differences over the desirability of assimilation. In testimony before Congress on the Wheeler-Howard bill, Collier himself offered ambiguous views on the subject of assimilation. At one point he flatly stated that the bill was not intended to reverse that trend or to substitute "collective" for "individual enterprise." Later, he predicted that the transition from the present condition of trusteeship to full self-determination would be a matter of generations at least. At yet another point he suggested that the Mexican communal village would provide a model for Native American tribal organizations. Some critics have cynically concluded that "Collier gave every faction . . . what it wanted, stood firm on nothing but the need to pass the bill, and was purposely vague throughout."

Yet Collier and those who shared his aspirations faced dilemmas that they believed required a tempering of their commitment to full self-determination for Native Americans and their rejection of assimilation. They recognized that Native American groups varied widely in terms of cultural cohesion and economic circumstances, and they wanted a program that would be flexible enough to accommodate assimilated groups while protecting others, like the Pueblos, from future attempts to force assimilation upon them. The reformers also feared that too rapid a devolution of government control over tribal resources to Native communities would result in the permanent loss of these resources, duplicating the experience of individual allottees under the Dawes Act. During the drafting of the original Wheeler-Howard bill, Allan Harper and La Farge, two of Collier's closest allies in the reform movement, warned that "if we advance too fast or fail to safeguard the exercise of [tribal self government] in a manner that ensures that . . . they will be really educational and beneficial to the Indians . . . the result will be only a reaction which will set back the whole process of freedom among our Indians."

Neither assimilation as an end nor paternalism as a means to improve Native American economic conditions was completely abandoned, despite Collier's own predilections. These ambiguities—on the question of assimilation as opposed to preservation of culturally unique groups and on the question of limited guardianship as opposed to full self-determination—lay at the heart of the Indian New Deal. The inability of Collier and his administration to resolve these ambiguities to the satisfaction of the reform groups and the Indians themselves would ultimately weaken and limit the effects of a program that by any standard represented the most enlightened approach ever attempted in the grim history of relations between the U.S government and the Native people of this continent.

Despite his disappointment over the Wheeler-Howard Act (Indian Reorganization Act), Collier set about implementing the new policies with his customary vigor. Making a virtue of necessity, the reformers in the Bureau announced that "the principle of self government" would be "carried to a new phase" through the referenda required under the act. During 1934 and 1935, 263 American Indian tribes and communities participated in the referenda, with 172 agreeing to come under the act and 63 rejecting it. Although the summary statistics of tribal voting on the Indian Reorganization Act are a matter of some controversy, the best estimate is that 70 percent of the 258 groups that held referenda between 1934 and 1935 agreed to accept it, comprising about 60 percent of the Native American population of the United States, excluding that of Oklahoma and Alaska.

To Collier's dismay, some of the largest and most prominent tribes were among those who rejected the act. The Iroquois of New York, who had sought unsuccessfully to be excluded from the act during the debates in Congress, vigorously opposed it, maintaining that it impinge on their claims to sovereignty. The Klamaths of Oregon, who also had a strong tribal organization, rejected the act by a large margin. Perhaps the biggest disappointment to the Bureau was the rejection of the act by the Navajos of Arizona and New Mexico, the most populous American Indian community in the country, by a close vote in a heavily attended referendum in June 1935. Furthermore, many of the tribes that did vote favorably in the initial referenda moved slowly or not at all toward the subsequent phases of tribal council organization and establishment of tribal corporations. Between 1936 and 1945, only about half of the Native groups that had accepted the act set up tribal governments, and only 40 percent had reached the point of setting up business enterprises, thus qualifying for loans from a $2 million revolving credit fund provided for in the Wheeler-Howard Act.

Meanwhile, however, Collier continued to work for additional legislation to extend the Reorganization program. During the debates over the Wheeler-Howard bill, Senator Thomas of Oklahoma had intervened to exclude American Indians in his state from the key provisions of the proposal, including those relating to organization of tribal corporations. This effectively blocked the Oklahoma tribes' access to the revolving credit fund. During October 1934, Thomas and Collier met with assemblies of Oklahoma tribes. Following these sessions, Collier drafted a bill that would protect Native Americans in that state from the kind of swindling that had already deprived many of them of their lands and mineral claims while permitting those individuals deemed "competent" to manage their property to assume full ownership and rights thereof. The bill also provided a mechanism for establishment of tribal corporations that could acquire land and borrow from a special federal fund.

This bill also encountered much resistance when introduced by Thomas and Representative Will Rogers of Oklahoma in Congress in April 1935, and a number of objectionable features were removed, although the provisions for tribal incorporation and establishment of a loan fund were retained. A number of American Indian groups in the western part of Oklahoma organized tribal governments under the act and made good use of their loans, but only a small part of the Five Civilized Tribes was able to take full advantage of the measures as their land base already had been diminished beyond hope of recovery. Nevertheless, Collier encouraged resurrection of local governments among these groups and provided loans to them through credit associations.

Native people in Alaska also had been excluded from the Wheeler-Howard Act through an oversight in drafting the revised bill, so in 1936 Congress enacted the Alaskan Reorganization Act to enable them to draw on the revolving credit fund. A number of villages proceeded to tap these funds to develop fishing and canning industries. Meanwhile, the Interior Department attempted to establish six Alaskan reservations in order to secure the Native people's title to these lands. But in this endeavor the Department encountered resistance from white commercial groups, whose arguments that the government did not have the authority to transfer title claims to the lands was upheld by the U.S. Supreme Court in 1949.

One of the problems that Collier recognized from the outset of his tenure as commissioner was that most Bureau personnel were not well informed about the varying cultural traditions of disparate Native American groups, the result, in part, of past commitment of the Bureau to assimilation, aggravated by the practice of shifting officials from one reservation to another. Furthermore, as the tribal organization process got underway, it became apparent that many Native American groups were equally unfamiliar with the legal intricacies involved in drafting constitutions and charters, and the "models" drafted by the Interior Department lawyers were not always appropriate to particular situations. To bridge the communications gap, in 1934 Collier established an applied anthropology unit to provide information on traditional tribal organization. This experiment was not entirely successful, although some anthropologists such as La Farge and Morris Opler contributed effectively to organizational efforts among tribes in the Southwest. Collier later concluded that anthropologists were not well-equipped to carry out the kind of specific program-related studies that he needed, while some anthropologists believed that their attempts to provide objective analysis had been undermined by resistance from administrators both at the reservation level and Collier's own staff, each having equally doctrinaire views about American Indian culture. In any event, the applied anthropology unit was disbanded in 1938, and despite this discouraging experience, Collier continued to seek a role for anthropology in government policy, encouraging an "Indian Administration Research Project" sponsored by the University of Chicago in 1941–1945. Furthermore, his general attitude toward the value of social science in administration represented a significant break with past practice in the Bureau of Indian Affairs.

Collier had an equally wide-ranging and ambitious view of the value of economic planning of Native American resources and encouraged cooperative efforts between the Bureau and other New Deal agencies such as the Civilian Conservation Corps and the Resettlement Administration, culminating in the establishment of the Technical Cooperation–Bureau of Indian Affairs (TC–BIA) project with the Soil Conservation Service in 1936. Under the auspices of this project, the two agencies carried out joint surveys of a number of western reservations and drafted plans to conserve and improve physical resources without disrupting the cultural and social patterns of the Indian communities on them. Although most of these recommendations were pigeonholed after 1941, when funding for Indian Affairs was sharply curtailed, the surveys did provide valuable information on resource needs, particularly in the Southwest, and reflected Collier's commitment to end the isolation of the Bureau and overcome administrators' preoccupation with day-to-day routines at the expense of long-range development.

Collier's desire to promote cooperative relations with other government agencies was shaped in part by his need to find additional funds to carry out his reform program. While Congress passed the Wheeler-Howard Act and other related measures, opponents of the program in Congress managed to delay appropriations for several months while seeking to impose limits on funding for controversial elements such as tribal organization and land consolidation. Throughout his term as commissioner, Collier had to fend off sniping attacks on his program from hostile Congressmen, including Senator Wheeler, who in 1937 introduced a bill to repeal the act bearing his name. Although the process was time consuming and did little to improve Collier's image as an abrasive and dogmatic spokesman, his appearances before various Indian Affairs committees were effective in turning back these direct challenges, and he was supported in these endeavors by other reformers, including the old-line Indian Rights Association. More insidious was the battle of the budget, as both the Bureau of the Budget and Congress chipped away at appropriations for the Bureau of Indian Affairs. Indeed, the Bureau's regular operating expenditures increased by a modest 25 percent between 1935 and 1940. Collier was able to augment funding for his programs by tapping other New Deal agencies, but after 1941 these sources faced cutbacks—at the same time that appropriations for the Bureau of Indian Affairs were being slashed. Consequently, funds for specific programs such as tribal organization and promotion of traditional crafts were virtually eliminated.

Collier and his supporters were inclined to blame congressional parsimony for the limitations and weaknesses of the Indian New Deal, but there were some serious internal problems as well. While reform groups such as the Indian Rights Association supported Collier against frontal attacks on the Reorganization Act, they were far from uncritical of the program. In 1939 when a second effort to repeal the Wheeler-Howard Act was mounted, the Indian Rights Association supported an alternative proposal that would exempt certain tribes from the organizational provisions of the act while ensuring them access to educational benefits and other financial aid. Throughout the 1930s that association persistently criticized those aspects of the Indian New Deal that they believed would permanently segregate Native Americans and retard progress toward assimilation.

And these views had a receptive audience among the reservation administrators within the Bureau of Indian Affairs. Many of the veterans of the pre-Collier era had trouble adjusting to the new approach to policy and, as one observer noted, "screened the instructions they got from Washington and their appraisal of the local situation" to fit these preconceptions, in which assimilation and paternalism continued as the most important elements. A number of Bureau officials had loudly opposed the Wheeler-Howard bill in 1934, leading Ickes to impose on them a controversial "gag order." Some continued to covertly undermine the program, but even the majority who loyally sought to carry out the reforms did not accept or even clearly comprehend the underlying philosophy. This breakdown of communication was particularly notable in the implementation of tribal organization, as reservation officials were reluctant to encourage any serious participation by Indians. One superintendent, for example, proposed to handpick a committee of "levelheaded men" who "are not too anxious for too much authority" to draft a tribal constitution, and keep out "reactionary Indians who are incompetent." Most reservation officials were less blunt, but there were few who exhibited much interest in encouraging tribal councils to assume a substantial role in the administration of social and economic programs on the reservations.

Collier's most serious problems of communication, however, were with the Native Americans themselves. Convinced of the value of direct, face-to-face contact, Collier devoted much of his time to meeting with delegations and assemblies of Indians to explain his programs and address complaints and misconceptions. Nevertheless, many of his listeners remained unconvinced or were perplexed by the intricacies of the array of laws and regulations introduced in the Indian New Deal. In 1934, for example, Collier presented the Bureau draft of the Reorganization bill to various Native groups, many of whom never appreciated the differences between this draft and the final Wheeler-Howard Act. Consequently, a number of Indians opposed tribal organization because they feared that as a result they would lose title to their allotments even though the act specified that consolidation of allotments, under tribal control could only be carried out voluntarily. During a later phase of the process, some tribal councils introduced measures that the Bureau determined exceeded their authority under the act, contributing to widespread suspicion that the Bureau's call for tribal self-government was little more than a sham.

A few Indian leaders chose to exploit this confusion and mistrust to advance their own political or financial interests. The American Indian Federation, an Oklahoma-based organization established in 1936 by Bruner and O. K. Chandler, started a campaign to repeal the Wheeler-Howard Act and provided a rich source of hostile witnesses for congressional committees seeking to discredit Collier's program. Collier, in turn, charged that this group's major aim was to swindle Native Americans and that it was associated with Nazi organizations such as the Silver Shirts and the German-American Bund. His vigorous arguments, however, helped to stem growing legislative hostility toward the Indian New Deal on the eve of World War II.

But not all the Native American critics of the Collier program could be dismissed as cranks or schemers. There were some who sincerely believed that the Indian New Deal, by retarding assimilation, would condemn their people to perpetual poverty and subjection. Among these were adherents to the views of

Carlos Montezuma, who before his death in 1923 had maintained that the only solution to the problems of his people was the abolition of the Bureau of Indian Affairs and that "reform only meant the strengthening, not the diminishing of bureaucratic control in the lives of American Indians." During the New Deal era, Montezuma's ideas were expounded by critics such as the Iroquois Alice Lee Jemison, and various "Montezumist" groups emerged on reservations in the Southwest.

And, in practice, tribal organization under the Wheeler-Howard Act contributed to discontent among Indians by exacerbating existing factional rivalries on the reservations, particularly in the Plains region, where younger mixed-blood tribespeople educated in white schools were able to acquire control over some of the tribal councils, arousing fears that they would use their positions to deprive full-bloods of their allotments and claims. Even in the Southwest, where the divisions produced elsewhere by allotment and assimilation were absent, factionalism emerged, as for example, among the Pueblos, whose traditional religious leaders confronted followers of the "Peyote Church."

Indeed, the frustrations and internal divisions that helped to undermine the Indian New Deal can be traced in microcosm through the experience of the Navajos of New Mexico and Arizona during the Collier era. The political, social, and economic problems that shaped the Navajo response to the New Deal were complex though by no means unique among Native Americans. The Navajo reservation had not been allotted, but the prospect of oil discoveries there had led the Bureau in 1922 to set up a tribal council to represent the Navajos in leasing drilling rights, required under the 1868 treaty. As was to be the case with tribal organizations in the New Deal period, the formation of the council in 1922 promptly led to the outbreak of factional disputes between the communities in the southern section of the reservation, led by Chee Dodge, a wealthy rancher, and those in the northern section, headed by Jacob Morgan, a strong proponent of assimilation who had support from local white Protestant missionary groups. And throughout the remainder of the 1920s, the factions disputed issues involving the disposition of contemplated oil leasing revenues.

When he had first arrived in New Mexico, Collier had endorsed the creation of the Navajo council as an example of the kind of reform he hoped would extend to all Native communities. By the end of the 1920s, however, he had reversed his position, denouncing the council as a puppet government that endorsed the schemes of certain Bureau officials and local white business interests and unrepresentative of the Navajo people. By the time Collier became commissioner of Indian Affairs, the problems of the Navajos had become more complicated. Most of them depended on herding livestock—principally sheep—for their livelihood, but by 1930 the Bureau had determined that the Navajo range was overgrazed and that the Navajo herds would have to be reduced. The situation worsened over the next two years, as the Navajos were unable to sell their stock and the range continued to deteriorate.

Despite his hostility toward the tribal council, Collier concluded that he had to depend on it to carry out a program of herd reduction and conservation of the Navajo range. When he unveiled these plans to the Navajos in 1933, proposing to supplement diminished earnings as a result of herd reduction with emergency relief funds, the council agreed to endorse the program over the objections of some Navajos. But the larger herders successfully lobbied for an across-the-board, rather than a pro-rated, reduction in livestock, enabling them to cull their herds of less-productive animals while poorer Navajos lost most of their traditional source of income. Furthermore, the stock-reduction program was inadequate, and further cuts were mandated in 1934. Finally, Collier's hopes to alleviate the problem by extending the Navajo reservation proved futile when Congress failed to enact a proposed boundary extension bill.

At this inopportune moment, the Indian Reorganization Act was presented to the Navajos for ratification. Although the Bureau tried to ensure the frustrated Navajos that the second herd-reduction effort had been carried out more equitably than the first one, the large herders continued to resist, and the general mismanagement of the program left a residue of enduring bitterness among the Navajos toward Collier. Morgan's faction, opposed to the Reorganization Act because of what he considered its anti-assimilationist bias, exploited this dissatisfaction, and the tribe rejected the program in June 1934. The writer Oliver La Farge, who was on the reservation during the ratification campaign, noted that there was "complete confusion in the Indian mind due to treating soil erosion, stock reduction, the boundary bills and the reorganization bills all together," and that "this was a vote of non-confidence in the present administration." Collier did not improve matters by announcing to the Navajos that their rejection of the Wheeler-Howard Act would not have any effect on the stock-reduction program.

Subsequently, Collier endeavored to introduce improvements in Navajo economic conditions and to reorganize the council to make it more representative. But many Navajos remained embittered over herd reduction and what they perceived as the commissioner's high-handed methods of administration. In 1938 Morgan's faction took control of the tribal council, and, although unable to alter Collier's programs, Morgan used his position to turn council meetings into forums for criticizing the Indian New Deal and demanding Collier's resignation.

The problems of the Navajos were extraordinarily difficult and convoluted, and the failure of the Indian New Deal to take hold among them was due as much to fortuitous circumstances as to misjudgments on the part of Collier and his staff. Nevertheless, the Navajo situation highlighted some of the inherent weaknesses of the Indian New Deal. Tribal organization on many of the reservations succumbed to factionalism that undermined the effectiveness of the councils. Distrustful of tribal governments that seemed unrepresentative and ineffective, many Indians refused to support New Deal programs. Those with allotments, except on a few reservations, declined to exchange them for shares in tribal corporations, severely limiting the process of land consolidation essential to the success of the program of economic development. The absence of indigenous support for tribal organization opened the way for critics such as Morgan and Jemison and their allies among the missionary organizations and assimilationist reformers who charged that the Indian New Deal perpetuated bureaucratic control of Native Americans behind a façade of self-government and threatened to leave their people stranded indefinitely in poverty and backwardness, isolated from American society. Collier's hopes to revive Native American communities as self-sufficient and autonomous entities were thwarted by the crushing and complex economic problems of the reservations, the growing hostility of Congress and traditional white reform groups toward his program, and the legacy of bitterness, mistrust, and division that shaped the response of Native Americans toward New Deal programs.

Nevertheless, the Indian New Deal was by no means a complete failure. Even though the funds allocated by Congress to Collier's programs were inadequate to meet the needs of Native Americans in the depression years, there were some significant improvements in conditions for many tribes, particularly in the Plains region where cooperatives were able to draw on the revolving loan fund to build up their livestock herds and conserve their lands. Even among the Navajos, Collier was able to bring in additional income through emergency work-relief programs of the New Deal and reduce the kind of petty graft in the Bureau that in the past had siphoned government money away from the Indian communities for whom it was intended. The renewed emphasis on Native traditions in education and promotion of Indian arts and crafts had a lasting effect: these measures probably represent the major achievements of the Collier era. Even the tribal organization program, for all its defects, encouraged a degree of political activism on the reservations unprecedented before 1934, culminating with the establishment of the National Congress of American Indians in 1944, which lobbied successfully over the next two years for an Indian Claims Commission, a significant measure that had been blocked in Congress when it was first introduced in the Indian Reorganization bill.

Despite these achievements, Collier's vision of Native communities as autonomous, self-sufficient, and self-governing entities remained unrealized when in 1945 he resigned as commissioner, worn down by the continuing battles over appropriations with Congress and increasingly interested in promoting a Pan-Indian movement throughout the Americas. The limited impact of the New Deal on American Indians weakened their resistance to a renewed drive for assimilation in the aftermath of World War II, which took the form of proposals to "terminate" the role of the federal government in Indian affairs and "relocate" natives off the reservations so that they might become part of America's industrial workforce. In the long run, Collier's efforts to stimulate a renewed self-consciousness among Native Americans laid the foundation for a reversal of these disastrous policies in the 1960s. But the tribal organizations of the New Deal represented at best a first step toward the goal of the reformers of the 1920s to create a genuinely democratic, economically self-sufficient, and culturally independent system for Native Americans within the United States.

Suggested Reading

The historiography of the Native American in the twentieth century and particularly of the Indian New Deal has experienced explosive growth in the past decade and should continue to expand our knowledge as more specialized works are published. The interested reader might want to consult periodicals such as *The Western Historical Review, Journal of the West, Pacific Historical Review, Ethnohistory, The Indian Historian,* and *The Journal of American History* as well as the various books mentioned here. Included here are only some of the major works in the field.

The effects of the Dawes Act summarized in the Meriam report cited in this essay have also received substantial analysis in three other books. Delos S. Otis, *The Dawes Act and the Allotment of Indian Lands* (Norman, Okla., 1973), edited by Francis P. Prucha, is a republication of a study made in 1933 for Congress, with Collier's support, to document his argument for repeal of allotment. Leonard A. Carlson, *Indians, Bureaucrats and Land: The Dawes Act and the Decline of Indian Farming* (Westport, Conn., 1981) is a work by an economist. The background to the Dawes Act is traced by Wilcomb Washburn, *The Assault on Indian Tribalism: The General Allotment Law (Dawes Act) of 1887* (Philadelphia, 1975).

John Collier's own account of his career and the Indian New Deal is in *From Every Zenith: A Memoir* (Denver, 1963) and in an earlier version, *Indians of the Americas* (New York, 1947). D'Arcy McNickle, who worked with Collier in the Bureau of Indian Affairs, provides a sympathetic account in McNickle and Harold E. Fey, *Indians and Other Americans: Two Ways of Life Meet* (New York, 1959 and 1970). The most comprehensive study of Collier and the Indian New Deal in general is Kenneth R. Philp, *John Collier's Crusade for Indian Reform, 1920–1954* (Tucson, Ariz., 1977). The first of a two-volume study of Collier is Lawrence C. Kelly's *The Assault on Assimilation: John Collier and the Origins of Indian Policy Reform* (Albuquerque, N. Mex., 1983), which focuses on the reform movement of the 1920s. Graham D. Taylor, *The New Deal and American Indian Tribalism: The Administration of the Indian Reorganization Act 1934–1945* (Lincoln, Nebr., 1980) examines tribal organization in the Indian New Deal. Margaret Szasz, *Education and the American Indian: The Road to Self-Determination 1928–1973* (Albuquerque, N. Mex., 1974) reviews educational reforms under Rhoads and Collier. There are some useful unpublished Ph.D. theses in the field, including John L. Freeman, "The New Deal for the Indians: A Study of Bureau-Committee Relations in American Government," (Princeton University, 1952), which traces disputes over the Wheeler-Howard Act in Congress, and Donald L. Parman, "The Indian and the Civilian Conservation Corps," (University of Oklahoma, 1967).

Studies of the impact of the New Deal on particular native American communities are also increasing. The Navajos have been the subject of a number of valuable works, most notably Kelly, *The Navajo Indian and Federal Indian Policy, 1900–1935* (Tucson, Ariz., 1968); Parman, *The Navajos and the New Deal* (New Haven, Conn., 1976); and Peter Iverson, *The Navajo Nation* (Westport, Conn., 1981). Laurence M. Hauptman, *The Iroquois and the New Deal* (Syracuse, N.Y., 1981) analyzes opposition to the Collier policies among the Six Nations. Thomas Biolsi, *Organizing the Lakota: The Political Economy of the New Deal on the Pine Ridge and Rosebud Reservations* (Tucson, Ariz.,1998) addresses the Sioux. Another valuable study of native Americans that reviews their reactions to the Indian New Deal is Hazel W. Hertzberg, *The Search for an American Indian Identity: Modern Pan-Indian Movements* (Syracuse, N.Y., 1971). An interesting aspect of this period is found in Robert Fay Schrader, *The Indian Arts and Crafts Board: An Aspect of New Deal Indian Policy* (Albuquerque, N. Mex., 1983).

No study of modern native American history would be complete without reference to Felix Cohen's *Handbook of Federal Indian Law* (Washington, D.C., 1941), which brought together a wide range of sources on the subject. Cohen's analysis has been challenged on the subject of tribal sovereignty by Russell L. Barsh and James Y. Henderson in *The Road: Indian Tribes and Political Liberty* (Berkeley, Calif., 1980). Washburn, ed., *The American Indian and the United States: A Documentary History* (New York, 1973) assembles numerous government materials on native Americans, including reports of the commissioners of Indian Affairs, Congressional debates on the Wheeler-Howard Act and other laws, and various court decisions and related legal materials.

Chapter 11 ❧
Dislocated

The Federal Policy of Termination and Relocation, 1945–1960

Donald L. Fixico

*W*orld War II brought about many changes to the world, the United States, and the American Indians. A myriad of sociocultural experiences emerged among Indian Americans after approximately 25,000 of them voluntarily served in the U.S. armed services and an estimated 40,000 to 50,000 Native men and women worked in ammunition plants, airplane factories, and other war industries.[1] Their devoted patriotism was impressive, convincing federal officials and the American public that Indians were, at long last, ready to be assimilated into the mainstream society. Within several years, the federal government enacted a twofold federal Indian policy of termination and relocation in order to sever its paternalistic, protective "trust" relationship with the tribal groups and to relocate Indians to urban areas.

Termination and relocation were not new concepts conceived during the years following the war. Ever since the American founding fathers established the U.S. government in 1776, federal policy had frequently attempted to "assimilate" Native Americans into the dominant society by terminating the unique legal rights of Indian people and their properties, despite the fact that the Constitution recognized the legal status of the tribes (Article 1, Section 8). Treaties between the United States and tribal groups authorized relocating the people to reservations, especially those concluded during the nineteenth century. The Dawes Land Allotment Act of 1887 sought to individualize and civilize Indians during the turn of the twentieth century, until Commissioner of Indian Affairs John Collier implemented "New Deal" programs to restructure tribal governments and preserve Indian cultures. The interruption of World War II and increasing anti-Collier sentiment spawned a change between 1945 and 1960 in federal In-

---

1 Of the estimated 25,000 Indian men who served in the armed forces, 22,000 enlisted in the United States Army, 2,000 in the Navy, 120 in the Coast Guard, and 730 in the Marines. Their performances in the war netted 71 Air Medals, 51 Silver Stars, 47 Bronze Stars, and 2 Congressional Medals of Honor (Lieutenant Ernest Childers, an Oklahoma Creek, and Lieutenant Jack Montgomery, an Oklahoma Cherokee). An estimated 200 to 300 Indian women joined the nurses' corps, military auxiliaries, Red Cross, and the American Women's Voluntary Service. See William Coffer, *Phoenix Decline and Rebirth of the Indian People* (New York, 1979).

dian policy commonly known as "termination and relocation," billed by bureaucrats as a sincere policy to alleviate the native Americans' poor living conditions.

Assimilation was the fundamental objective of this Indian policy, and understanding its underlying ideology is prerequisite for comprehending the twentieth-century policy of termination and relocation. Presumably, Indian people would benefit from assimilation and enjoy living as "modern citizens." Reservations could no longer support the people, argued the bureaucrats, and relocating them to urban areas seemed logical, since they might find jobs and better housing there. In short, integration into urban society would liberate Indians from the bonds of unemployment, poor housing, malnutrition, and discontentment. Furthermore, federal Indian experts interpreted Native American participation in World War II as an important step in desegregating rural Indian communities. To government officials, integrating Indians into mainstream society was raison d'être for abrogating federal Indian "trust" relations that virtually held the people captives on reservations.

The newly emergent view that American Indians were ready to become members of society was reinforced by two federal reform measures that played major roles in effecting a revision of Indian policy. First, the Hoover Task Force Commission Report in 1947 advised limiting governmental involvement in Indian affairs. The Task Force's positive confirmation of Indian progress resulted in a recommendation for reducing the superfluous bureaucracy of the Bureau of Indian Affairs. Offices would be consolidated to provide efficient, streamlined services, and selected Indian hospitals and schools would be closed. Decentralizing the Indian Service in Washington, D.C., was the chief recommendation of the Hoover Report, which included an outline of actions for discontinuing most Indian Service programs. This, in turn, was the basis for the second relevant measure—the Zimmerman Plan (named for the Assistant Commissioner of Indian Affairs). The Bureau of Indian Affairs categorized tribes—based on their relative economies—into three groups: those ready for immediate independence by liquidating the trust relationships; an intermediate group requiring some assistance before withdrawal of all federal responsibilities; and a large, third group needing continued assistance.

The second major reform offered individual tribes millions of dollars as compensation for the past violations of their treaties, if authorized by a review commission. In 1946 Congress passed the Indian Claims Commission Act, establishing a commission "to hear and determine the following claims against the United States on behalf of any Indian tribe, band, or other identifiable group of American Indians of the United States or Alaska." In effect, once and for all, the federal government attempted to settle its debts with the tribes; once payments were made, past federal injustices committed against Indian people would be considered redeemed. By the end of the 1950s, the Indian Claims Commission had reviewed some 125 cases and authorized an estimated $42 million to particular tribes for past violations. Within several years, the number of claims filed increased faster than the commission could render its decisions. Twice, the Claims Commission asked for and was granted two additional five-year periods to complete its work, but not all of the filed claims were presented. A total of $669 million had been awarded to the tribes by September 1978 when Congress dissolved the commission, leaving 133 of 617 dockets unresolved. These were transferred to the U.S. Court of Claims.

Indian participation in World War II had nurtured the seeds of termination, which grew into a reform policy when Congress took action under advisement from the Bureau of Indian Affairs. Bureaucrats erroneously interpreted Indian participation in the war as readiness for integration into the mainstream society. In actuality, after the war Indian veterans and those who served in the industrial factories experienced social upheavals. In reporting to service, many had left reservations and rural allotments for the first time. In the months spent away from their traditional home environments, they practiced the lifeways of the dominant culture. Out of their native element, they compromised their traditional values in order to cope with life in the outside world, to which they could not help but compare their Native lifestyle.

Furthermore, the people waiting for them to return said the spirits of the dead enemy soldiers had contaminated them. (Purification ceremonies were customarily held to decontaminate the veterans.) Living again on reservations and rural allotments proved difficult for the returned warriors, whose personalities and Native perspectives had changed, causing the psychological disharmony of their spiritual balance. While they had changed, life on the reservations and allotted homelands had remained relatively the same.

Sadly accounts of maladjustment among Indian veterans were all too frequent. N. Scott Momaday captured this traumatic experience in his Pulitzer Prize–winning novel, *House Made of Dawn,* as did Leslie Silko in a similar account, *Ceremony,* a story about Indian veterans returning to the reservation after fighting in the Pacific theater. These vivid literary works narrate and interpret the drastic social and psychological changes in Indian lifestyles. The Pima war hero Ira Hayes, a private first-class Marine who helped raise the American flag at Iwo Jima, became one of the most celebrated Indians of World War II. Unfortunately, as a veteran he experienced a series of personal problems. In trying to piece his life back together after returning to the Pima Reservation in Arizona, the war hero found interacting socially with his people difficult, yet he could not successfully cope with the mainstream society. Feeling alienated from his Pima brethren as well as from other Americans, Hayes turned to alcohol. During a cold night in the mountains of Arizona in January 1955, Hayes, a broken man, died of exposure.

The immediate postwar years were extremely difficult for Native Americans. Scarce jobs on the reservations and in rural communities and an overburdened land base could not support the overgrowing Indian population. To make

Woody J. Cochran (Cherokee) holds a Japanese flag in New Guinea. Lieutenant Cochran earned the Silver Star, Purple Heart, Distinguished Flying Cross, and Air Medal. National Archives #NWDNS-75-N-FIVE-148

matters worse, a severe blizzard struck the Southwest during the winter of 1947–1948; the Navajos were devastated, some to the point of starvation. The media reported their destitution, thereby arousing national concern for the hapless Indians. In an effort to help the Navajos and their Hopi neighbors, Secretary of the Interior Julius Krug, at President Truman's request, proposed a ten-year program to provide both tribes vocational training and develop the resources of their reservations. In early December 1947, President Truman summarized federal efforts in uplifting American Indians. "Our basic purpose is to assist the Navajos—and other Indians—to become healthy, enlightened, and self-supporting citizens, able to enjoy the full fruits of our democracy and to contribute their share to the prosperity of our country."

More than two years passed before Congress approved the Navajo-Hopi bill (in 1950), which funded a program to improve the two tribes' livelihoods. Per this plan, the government assisted Navajos by relocating them to Los Angeles, Salt Lake City, and Denver, and helping them to find jobs. During midsummer 1951, the Bureau of Indian Affairs began assigning relocation workers to Oklahoma, New Mexico, California, Arizona, Utah, and Colorado with the intention of expanding the program. The next year the Bureau officially extended the Relocation Program to all Indians and added more cities that offered employment and housing. In early February 1952, the first relocatees arrived in Chicago. During 1955, relocation workers processed 442 Native Americans for direct employment in Los Angeles, Denver, and Chicago, at an average cost per person of $450, which increased to $750 five years later. To help place the increasing number of applicants in cities, the Bureau of Indian Affairs opened additional offices in Dallas, Cleveland, Minneapolis, Oklahoma City, Seattle, Tulsa, and the San Francisco Bay Area. In the next several months, offices were established as well in St. Louis and San Jose. By late 1954, 6,200 Native Americans out of an estimated reservation population of 245,000 had been resettled in cities. Approximately 54 percent of the relocatees came from three northern areas—Aberdeen, South Dakota, Billings, Montana, and Minneapolis, Minnesota. The remaining 46 percent hailed from southern areas—Gallup, New Mexico, Phoenix, Arizona, and Anadarko and Muskogee, Oklahoma. Indians were relocated to twenty different states, with Los Angeles and Chicago being the leading urban relocation centers.

Curiosity and the attraction of city life influenced many Indians to apply for relocation. Veterans, relatives, and friends made reservation Indians envious when they talked about adventurous good times in the cities. Typically, an inquiry made at the Indian agency on a reservation or at a regional office started the paperwork. Both young and old could apply, but all applicants had to be at least 18 years old and in reasonably good health. Officials checked the applicant's job skills and employment records, then contacted the relocation office in his or her city of choice. Relocatees arrived in the designated city, usually via bus or train, where a relocation worker met them. Next, the relocation office issued a check to the relocatee to purchase toiletries, cookware, groceries, bedding, clothes, and an alarm clock to ensure punctual arrival for work. Normally the Bureau of Indian Affairs paid the relocatee's first month's expenses, including rent, travel expenses to work, clothing, and groceries. After that, the relocatee and his or her family were on their own financially. Relocation officers provided counseling and assistance in job placement and monitored the urban Indian's progress up to nine years. And periodically a neighborhood clergyman stopped by to visit them.

The majority of applicants were young males. Frequently men left families on reservations, intending to send for them once they found a job and housing in the city. Generally, those relocatees with higher education moved farther from tribal homelands, and they proved more successful in making the transition from reservation to urban lifestyle.

Government officials assumed the assimilation process would become easier as more Indians entered the metropolitan mainstream. Maintaining quotas for processing relocatees and the false impression of successful Indian urbanization later inspired federal cutbacks of Indian programs. One frugal congressman, who asserted that Indian programs strained the federal budget, emphatically stated that the government's expensive supervision of Indian affairs for the next fifty years would cost between $500 million and $2 billion. *"They do not need a Federal guardian NOW, nor will they need one for the next 50 years!"*

Truman's "Fair Deal" programs provided social services to all needy citizens, including American Indians and other minorities. The president viewed all segments of society as having the same rights. He even supported desegregation at the risk of losing his popularity. He advocated that equal rights and educational opportunity should not be denied to any citizen. During a conversation, Truman philosophically stated that he looked on all Americans as one nation, "White, black, red, the working man [and] the banker."

Truman's philosophy on desegregation of Indian communities was implemented through the Bureau of Indian Affairs when he appointed Dillon S. Myer, a Republican from Ohio, as the new commissioner of Indian Affairs. Indians qualified for the commissioner's position were passed over, provoking Indian groups and pro-Indian supporters to criticize Myer's appointment, especially since presiding Indian Commissioner John Nichols had not been notified that he was being replaced. Myer shared President Truman's ideas on Indian affairs and was regarded as a hard-line assimilationist. Also a headstrong advocate of dissolving "needless" Indian programs, Myer worked to terminate trust relationships in order to assimilate Indians into the mainstream. Myer had served as the director of the War Relocation Authority, a program that had forcibly moved Japanese Americans from the West Coast to inland concentration camps during World War II. At fifty-nine years of age, Myer continued to operate in his customary military fashion. His stern and forceful personality demanded immediate action in terminating trust relationships and the expedient reduction of federal Indian services.

Myer's actions upset citizens critical of the Bureau of Indian Affairs for abruptly dissolving its responsibilities to American Indians. Pro-Indian supporters charged the commissioner with misusing his authority and of expediting the termination of federal trust relations with certain tribes before they were ready to support themselves fully. Myer was derogatorily referred to as "Stalin" and "Mussolini" rolled into one, and labeled a "tin-headed dictator." Calls for Myer's removal quickly followed the election of Republican Dwight D. Eisenhower as president in 1952.

"Ike" followed the tradition of other incoming presidents by appointing new personnel to top federal positions. He selected Glenn L. Emmons, a banker from Gallup, New Mexico, as his commissioner of Indian Affairs. Again, qualified Indians such as Choctaw Harry F. W. Belvin of Oklahoma and New Mexico's Indian Council representative, Alva Adams Smith, were passed over for the position. Frustrated over the matter, Senator William Langer of North Dakota objected to Emmons's appointment, charging that one commissioner after another came from New Mexico (referring to William Brophy and John Nichols). The senator had the support of the National Congress of American Indians and rumor had the two collaborating to overturn Emmons's appointment.

Like Myer, Emmons advocated termination of federal Indian trust relations, although he enjoyed a friendly relationship with Indian people in the Southwest. Having spent much of his life in New Mexico, he was familiar with their cultures and had learned about their ways. And as a banker, he personally knew many Indians and sometimes arranged loans for those who were poor financial risks. Emmons sincerely believed that termination was best for Indian Americans, if in the long run they were to improve their livelihoods. Gradual withdrawal of federal trust responsibilities, he believed, would give Indians an opportunity to exercise economic independence without the hindrance of federal restrictions. Unlike Commissioner Myer and Senator Arthur Watkins, who publicly opposed Indians frequently, Emmons was a liberal terminationist who possessed a humanitarian sensitivity for his constituents. He particularly worked to prevent exploitation of Indian groups and provide relocation services to support them.

The change from a Democratic to a Republican administration during the early 1950s enabled relocation to gain momentum as a moving force behind the termination policy. Throughout the Eisenhower years, increasing migration from reservations and allotments to cities, plus termination of trust relations, complemented the Eisenhower ideology of conforming all Americans, including ethnic groups, into one society. Eisenhowerism promoted a nationalistic attempt to involve everyone in building a patriotic, strong, but conservative society to protect American principles for a free democracy. And, in general, Americans experienced an improved standard of living through their own achievements.

Astronomically high debts left from the war made the Eisenhower administration conscious of excessive spending, urging retrenchment in federal budgeting. An acute difference in philosophies of the Truman and Eisenhower administrations on federal Indian spending is noteworthy. Under the Truman administration, the Indian Claims Commission authorized large settlements to pay off Indian groups, and the Hoover Task Force surveyed Indian conditions, resulting in large expenditures and additional bureaucratic paperwork. Although the Truman administration laid the groundwork for termination, the Eisenhower administration actively prepared tribal groups for the end of government trusteeship and services. Under Eisenhower, retrenchment of the national budget ominously warned the tribes of dangerous realities that lay ahead; expensive federal programs like theirs would likely be cut.

During this period, terminationists such as Senator Patrick McCarran of Nevada, Senator Arthur Watkins of Utah, and Representative Henry M. Jackson of Washington were the leading policymakers for federal Indian affairs in Congress. They wanted to end the trust relationship and federal Indian programs for two important reasons. They deemed Native Americans as capable of supporting themselves without governmental assistance and funding Indian programs too costly.

Economy-minded administrators and insensitive actions worried Native Americans, who operated on a different system of ingrained cultural values that terminationists failed to understand. Powerful political figures who controlled congressional Indian affairs such as Senator Watkins were convinced that Indians had life too easy, and they wanted Indians placed on a competitive basis with everyone else. To compound the situation, racial prejudice and discrimination hindered Indian progress, thereby preventing Indians from obtaining well-paying professional jobs and attaining respectable social status in the "white man's world."

Another influential group in Congress consisted of sincere protectionists such as Senators Reva Beck Bosone of Utah, Richard Neuberger of Oregon, and James Murray of Montana. Familiar with Indian people and reservation conditions, they only introduced legislation to end trust status at the requests of tribal groups. (Certain tribes and individuals were quite capable of running their own business affairs without trust restrictions, although this number was small.) Some congressional representatives, such as Senator George Smathers of Florida, originally advocated dissolving federal/Indian relations but, after learning more about American Indian conditions, they joined the anti-termination ranks. On the other side of the termination issue, the number of pro-terminationists swelled, especially when uninformed and neutral congresspersons were easily convinced to vote for termination legislation.

Termination reached its peak in 1953 and 1954 during the Eighty-third congressional session. In all, Congress entertained 288 public bills and resolutions affecting Indians, 46 of which it enacted into law. The Bureau of Indian Affairs submitted 162 reports to the Senate and House of Representatives as part of the legislative studies on Indians. Finally, in early June, Congress sealed the fate of Indian people when it approved a general resolution that established the termination policy affecting all tribal groups. Senator Jackson introduced House Concurrent Resolution 108 in the Senate and Representative William Harrison of Wyoming sponsored the legislation in the House of Representatives. The essence of this landmark resolution reads as follows.

> Whereas it is the policy of Congress, as rapidly as possible, to make the Indians within the territorial limits of the United States subject to the same laws and entitled to the same privileges and responsibilities as are applicable to other citizens of the United States, to end their status as wards of the United States and to grant them all of the rights and prerogatives, pertaining to American citizenship; and
>
> Whereas the Indians within the territorial limits of the United States should assume their full responsibilities as American citizens.

Within several weeks, H.C.R. 108 had initiated other legislative efforts to liquidate applications implemented under the Indian Reorganization Act of 1934. This largely involved dissolving tribal corporations based on the act. More important, H.C.R. 108 singled out thirteen tribes for withdrawal of trust status, and Congress started immediate termination procedures for six other groups. Pro-termination bureaucrats in Washington remained convinced that tribalism and federal trust paternalism hindered Indians from improving their livelihoods. The following year, Congress approved termination legislation for the six designated groups—the Menominee of Wisconsin, the Klamath of Oregon, certain Indian groups of Oregon, the Alabama-Coushatta of Texas, the Ouray and Ute of Utah, and the mixed-blood Paiute of Nevada. The move to end federal-Indian relations caused tense feelings among the tribes as the momentum for termination increased. One Indian Bureau official asserted that the Indian Service knew well that H.C.R. 108 would shock Indians across the nation, and he hoped Congress would not consider any similar legislation until it studied the effects of termination on the six groups.

Reports to Congress described the members of these tribes as fairly educated, economically self-sufficient, and already assimilated into nearby towns composed mainly of whites. The Eighty-third Congress terminated the federal trust relationship with the Menominees, who were to serve as a role model for other groups. Considered as one of the largest and wealthiest tribes, the Menominees numbered 3,059 members who owned 233,902 acres of bountiful timberland. The Menominees seemed ready for termination, but a disagreement occurred between some tribal members and federal officials over the terms negotiated for dissolving the tribe's trust relationship. A pending per capita payment of $1,500 was partially to blame when Assistant Secretary of the Interior Orme Lewis opposed the payment. He claimed the tribal members were already economically independent and had no need for such payment. Approximately two-thirds of the Menominees held jobs in the tribal timberlands or at the sawmill, and the remaining one-third worked in nearby communities. Besides the per capita issue, a faction of Menominees vehemently protested the elimination of the government trust relationship. In fact, Gordon Keshena charged the Bureau of Indian Affairs with meddlesome paternalism, stating it had been in business 125 years and had controlled everything his tribe did. "Everything we wanted to do, we had to go to the Bureau and ask them," said Keshena, "Can we do this? Can we do that? You cannot ask the people to go on their own and govern themselves now, when for all those years they have not been permitted to do anything for themselves."

Without delay, the Bureau of Indian Affairs carried out the provisions of termination legislation for the Menominee and began procedures to withdraw trust relations from other tribes. On June 30, 1953, the Muskogee Area Office announced its plans to commence programs for the Five Civilized Tribes, certain Indians of the Quapaw Agency, and the Mississippi Choctaws. In addition, withdrawal programs for the Coushatta and Chitmacha groups in Louisiana, Cherokees on the Kenwood Reservation, and the Thlothlocco Creek Tribal Town were under consideration. On the same day, the Interior Department reported that the Prairie Island Band of Minnesota had approved a proposal to abolish federal supervision over half of their affairs. Meanwhile, the Bureau initiated programs to prepare the Osages of Oklahoma and the Flatheads of Montana for termination. The Bureau closed three hospitals, and local public school authorities took over operations of sixteen Bureau day schools and assumed the academic work at three boarding schools, affecting 1,100 Indian students.

The movement to free Indians from federal trust restrictions continued during the rest of the decade. From 1954 to 1960, Congress terminated the trust relationships of fifty-four tribes, Indian groups, communities, and allotments. Although this figure is high, some persons owning allotted lands desired abolition of their trust status. These self-confident abolitionists had sufficient education and adequate business experience to succeed without governmental trust protection. Unfortunately, the Bureau of Indian Affairs had convinced Congress that most Native Americans could supervise their own affairs. The truth, however, was that the majority of Indian Americans needed more time before they could achieve satisfactory livelihoods.

Emmons and his administration soon realized possible dangers of terminating tribes too quickly, especially the Native groups who claimed they were ready. This caused federal Indian affairs to focus on economic progress as a means of "preparation" for terminating tribes. Unlike the earlier years of the decade when congressional action concentrated on passing termination legislation, the remainder of the 1950s witnessed an emphasis on preparing tribal groups economically for the ultimate end of federal trust supervision. The Bureau made loans to tribes, enabling them to invest in enterprises, develop programs, and arrange loans to its members. In addition, it began educational programs designed to make Indians self-sufficient and to convince them that they no longer required federal assistance.

Some tribes were pressured into accepting final termination deadlines; others experienced reduction of federal services. In practice, whether or not tribes were ready for full independence was largely irrelevant to federal officials intent on fulfilling quotas to meet termination deadlines on schedule. Unfortunately, over the years the tribes had become too dependent on federal assistance, and only a few appeared ready for total independence. But the fact is those few, like the Menominees and the Klamaths, who owned rich timberlands and possessed large deposits of natural resources on their reservations, proved unable to manage their business affairs effectively for competing as corporations in the business world.

After approving H.C.R. 108, Congress entertained another important measure, House Resolution 1063, in an attempt to reduce federal involvement in Indian affairs. This resolution proposed to extend state jurisdiction over Indian reservations in Wisconsin, Nebraska, California, Oregon (except Warm Springs Reservation), and Minnesota (except Red Lake Reservation). President Eisenhower approved the resolution as Public Law 280 without consulting the tribes or obtaining their consent for authorizing state jurisdiction over their reservations. Public Law 280 expedited decentralization of the Indian Service in Washington, D.C., and shifted government responsibilities to the states. In addition to assuming civil and criminal jurisdiction over Indian country, the states contracted with the federal government for providing services to Native Americans. State officials criticized P.L. 280 for the increased responsibilities that it transferred to state governments, claiming the services for Indian citizens strained state budgets.

Indian health service was another responsibility that the federal government wished to relinquish. Congressional approval of P.L. 568 authorized transferring Indian health facilities and services to another federal department, Public Health Service. Commissioner Emmons and Minnesota Senator Hubert

Humphrey claimed the move would provide better health care to Native Americans. Many Indians felt uncomfortable applying for health services with non-Indian citizens. Red tape and excessive paperwork compounded their uneasiness. Therefore, Indians commonly turned to traditional Native cures as an alternative or did without treatment completely. Still, statistics for the next ten years indicated a dire need for professional health care. Indeed, disease and fatality rates were extraordinarily high among the Native population. Indians were three times more likely than were whites to die of pneumonia and influenza. Indians contracted hepatitis at eight times the rate of any other ethnic group, and rates of Indian infant mortality, tuberculosis, and alcoholism were the highest in the nation. Overall, Native Americans had a life expectancy of forty-four years, as compared to seventy years for white Americans.

Federal policymakers hypothesized that by dissolving Indian health services, Indians would start relying on public services such as the Public Health Service or even private health care centers. In actuality, most Indians simply avoided public health services. Many Indians believed that they were socially unacceptable to the mainstream population, for even among financially independent Indians, many individuals experienced social maladjustment, feelings of discomfort living in non-Indian neighborhoods, and uneasiness working with strangers. The cities were so different, with their tall buildings, strange noises, and crowds of people, that a large number of relocatees elected to return to their quiet, less crowded reservations to escape the tension and anxiety of urban adjustment.

Commissioner of Indian Affairs Glenn L. Emmons (center) represents President Eisenhower at a meeting with the Michasukie Seminole Nation, December 19, 1954. At issue was returning land and rights to the Indian nation. © Bettmann/CORBIS

In spite of the foreign environment of metropolitan areas, an increasing number of Indians applied for relocation to leave impoverished reservations and rural allotments behind to try to start a new life in the cities. In an effort to meet the needs of the increasing number of relocatees, Congress passed P.L. 959 in August 1956. The act provided vocational training for adult Indians, services that soon became part of the Relocation Program. These general services took three forms. First, on-the-job training provided on or near reservations offered twenty-four-month apprenticeships. Prospective relocatees needed work experience and job skills, both of which increased their chances for better employment once in urban areas. Second, the adult-training program focused on adults only, particularly those with families. Training was available in specific occupational areas such as carpentry and plumbing, stressing manual skills. Applicants had to be between the ages of eighteen and thirty-five, although older persons showing good aptitude were accepted. The third vocational service provided job information and helped Indians find work near reservations. To improve the general situation, the Bureau of Indian Affairs urged industries to locate near reservations, and program officers negotiated with employers in urban areas to hire relocatees.

During 1957, the Bureau's relocation services assisted 7,000 Indians at a cost of $3.5 million, more than twice the sum appropriated for the previous year. Overall, Indian progress seemed to be on the upswing. An estimated 132,000 Indian children attended schools of all types throughout the country. Financially, the total income for oil, gas, and other minerals leased on reservation lands nearly doubled, from $41 million in 1956 to more than $75 million in 1957.

Relocation offered a fresh start for Indians who wanted to begin new lives. Bureau officials encouraged urban relocation on a voluntary basis, although some people reported having been cajoled into relocating. Brochures and pamphlets circulated throughout reservations and communities tried to convince Indians that a better life awaited them in cities. Pictures of white executives dressed in white shirts wearing ties and sitting behind desks insinuated that relocatees could obtain similar positions. Photographs of suburban homes with white picket fences were included to entice women to think that relocation was best for their families. Still, these propagandized efforts were not enough if federal policy was to succeed in relocating the masses of reservation and rural Indian population. Continual pressure was applied on nonurban Indians as long as a significant portion of Natives remained on reservations and allotments.

Nevertheless, promises of successful livelihoods in urban areas never materialized in most cases; rather, relocation disillusioned the relocatees, especially those who never before had left reservations or traveled long distances. The reality confronting them was a dramatic cultural shock. Even getting off the bus in a strange, large city for the first time was traumatic for most relocatees. The newcomers knew very little about modern gadgets and street life. Stoplights, traffic, sirens, clocks, elevators, telephones, and other mechanical contrivances were alien to Indians fresh off the reservations. Confused, they became frustrated with their ignorance of modernization. Learning to live in the "white man's world" was a difficult challenge and often overwhelmed the neophytes. One individual was "lost" in his hotel room for twenty-four hours: having misplaced the Bureau of Indian Affairs' address, he was perplexed and did not know what to do; although he had the Bureau of Indian Affairs' telephone number, he was ashamed to ask anyone how to dial the phone.

Psychological self-doubt typically afflicted urban Indians who had foregone Native traditions to learn the ways of the dominant culture. Relocatees, once a people proud of their heritage, lost confidence and felt they had no control over their lives. Loneliness engulfed them, while thoughts of relatives back home occupied their minds. Even more damaging, loss of traditional family roles occurred when fathers could not support their loved ones and left, thereby creating an absence of the traditional father-figure and extra burdens for mothers who were forced to raise their children alone. Lacking sufficient training and education to find decent jobs, Indian single mothers were at a loss. Marital problems and broken families fostered delinquency among children who were frequently absent from school or dropped out altogether. All too often relocatees turned to alcoholism to escape the harsh reality of urbanization. Demoralized and not knowing what to do, they lived a "drifting" existence in the cities' ghettos. Need for food and shelter sometimes compelled them to commit petty crimes—others contemplated self-destruction, a frequent occurrence that contradicted many tribes' traditional values.

In response to the pressures of forced assimilation into metropolitan areas, Indian youths expressed their dissatisfaction with federal policy and the Bureau of Indian Affairs. The newly founded National Indian Youth Council became the Indian voice of unhappiness, and the National Congress of American Indians, founded in 1944, also criticized the Bureau of Indian Affairs. Instead of solving Indian problems through termination and relocation, the National Congress of American Indians claimed that the government had created more problems for Indians. Now they had to contend with the Bureau's bureaucracy, "withdrawal of trust" policy, and urbanization.

In addition to rising Indian protest, organizations led by non-Indians and former Bureau officials spoke out against the Eisenhower administration's supervision of Indian affairs. Oliver La Farge, president of the Association on American Indian Affairs in New York, blasted the Bureau of Indian Affairs, alleging that the federal government broke its trust relations and did not act in the best interests of Indians. In one instance, La Farge stated that desire for oil and other minerals lying under Paiute land was the real motive for terminating the trust with the Paiutes. Former Commissioner John Collier pointed out that 177 full-blooded Paiutes, who possessed 45,000 acres of land in Utah, would lose land precisely because it was believed to overlay abundant subsurface minerals. Shrewd opportunists, Collier claimed, would manipulate the Indians out of their lands shortly after termination. He concurred with La Farge that greed was the real motive behind termination and charged that Commissioner Myer had acted "to atomize and suffocate the group life of the tribes—that group life which is their vitality, motivism, and hope."

Meanwhile, rumors circulated that Commissioner Emmons and other government officials harassed tribal leaders into ending federal trust relations. Emmons became the focus of an attack when critics accused him of being a tool of "big business" that would exploit Indians to control their natural resources. During a meeting with a delegation of Standing Rock Sioux, the commissioner rose to his own defense, insisting that "We have to face the day when the Government is going to get out of the Indian business." The concerned commissioner asserted that he had "a solemn obligation to raise the standards of the Indian people so when that times does come they will have such a level of income that they can afford to be relieved of the Government restrictions." Emmons said it plainly, "darn it I will fight to the last ditch to see that doesn't come over night, of course."

Undoubtedly Emmons strove to assist Native Americans, and along with other government officials he worked for Indian independence, but harming Indian people in the process was unavoidable. The varying degrees of Indian socioeconomic progress toward assimilation created a paradox for the government. Frequently, federal officials were led to believe that Indian residents of a particular area were socially and economically ready for termination, when this was not truly the case. This resulted in confusion and opposition from tribal members as well as criticism from concerned persons. Nevertheless, Emmons planned to give all American Indians, ready or not, full rights of citizenship as well as freedom from discriminatory restrictions by July 4, 1976—the celebration of America's bicentennial.

Concerned citizens wrote President Eisenhower about the government's inept termination policy and the destructive effects of relocation on Indian Americans. The president explained that the central aim of federal policy was working constructively and cooperatively with Indians on programs to prepare them for full independence. He clarified the government's position by assuring the public that both the secretary of the Interior and the commissioner of Indian Affairs explicitly opposed "wholesale" or "overnight" termination of federal trust responsibilities in Indian affairs.

In spite of additional legislation and efforts of the Indian Service to help Indian people, attacks on the federal government persisted. Unfortunately, the inability of bureaucrats to understand the complex socioeconomic conditions of Indian maladjustment to urbanization fueled the criticism. Undoubtedly, Secretary of Interior Douglas McKay and Commissioner Emmons wanted what was best for Indians, but, like most bureaucrats, they lacked perception of the social and psychological consequences that termination and relocation programs caused. It was imperative to understand that American Indians had surrendered much of their Native identity as they strove to fulfill their potentials as middle-class citizens. In short, American Indians were deIndianized and forced to assume roles as non-Indians in a foreign environment—something many lacked the ability to do.

Following World War II, the decade of the 1950s was an embroiled period of drastic change in federal-Indian relations. During the latter half of the 1950s, Congress was committed to protecting Indian rights, whereas the Eighty-third Congress in the earlier years had stressed termination of trust responsibilities. The shortsightedness of members in the Eighty-third Congress on Indian affairs is evident with the optimistic approval of H.C.R. 108, which had been blindly promoted without sufficient discussion or consideration of possible negative repercussions on the Indian population. Incredibly, a small body of federal officials exercised tremendous power over Indian affairs, while congressional attention focused mainly on foreign relations in Indochina (Vietnam), McCarthyism, and civil rights. Moreover, Indian affairs seemed far less important after the nation slipped into an economic slump during the fall of 1957 and early 1958.

While the nation suffered financially, increased monies were appropriated for Indian programs, which contradicted the retrenchment guidelines of the early 1950s. The Eighty-fifth Congress, for instance, appropriated a record $109,410,000 for Indian programs, and Bureau of Indian Affairs' operations in 1957 amounted to 25 percent, or $21 million, more than the previous year. Improving the overall economy of Native groups forced the cost of administering Indian affairs to spiral upwards. Meanwhile, developing tribal programs became a distinguishing characteristic of federal Indian policy in the late 1950s. Emmons's leadership exemplified a more patient and humanitarian attitude toward Indian affairs than that of preceding administrations in the Indian Service. In contrast to the tough "get out of the Indian business" approach of the Eighty-third Congress, the later congresses exhibited a concerned "prepare the Indians" policy. This change in federal attitude toward Indian affairs predominated throughout the remaining years of the second Eisenhower administration. During this term, fewer new tribes were named for termination, and the essence of federal-Indian relations focused on seeking solutions to federal "trust withdrawal" problems. A prime example is the Klamath controversy over the procedure to sell timberlands. With the final withdrawal of trust status set for 1961, 250 to 275 members would receive $43,000 each in per capita payments from the timberland sales. When the termination deadline arrived, 78 percent of the Klamaths voted to receive revenue from the sales. Thus, the government distributed $68 million to the tribe.

The end of the 1950s did not represent the end to termination and relocation. Throughout the early and mid-1960s, tribes and allotments were still being terminated of trust status. In fact, between World War II and the origin of the Indian self-determination policy in the late 1960s, the government processed 109 cases of termination, affecting 1,369 acres of Indian land and an estimated 12,000 Native Americans. Relocation of reservation and rural Indian populations to cities continued, and a noticeable demographic trend emerged, indicating that an increasing number of American Indians were urbanized. (Today, just over one-half of the total Indian population resides in urban areas.) As the United States entered the 1960s, the federal government's attitude toward Indian affairs changed to a commitment to preserving indigenous American cultures and supporting Indian self-determination. Relocated Indians became accustomed to new urban lifestyles. And out of the terminated tribal communities and urban ghettos sprang forth a new generation of American Indians.

Suggested Reading

There are few major studies on termination. They are Larry W. Burt, *Tribalism and Crisis, Federal Indian Policy, 1953–1961* (Albuquerque, N. Mex., 1982) and Donald L. Fixico, *Termination and Relocation: Federal Indian Policy, 1945–1960* (Albuquerque, N. Mex., 1986).

Earlier studies include Gary Orfield, *A Study of the Termination Policy* (Denver, 1964); Oliver La Farge, "Termination of Federal Supervision: Disintegration and the American Indians," *Annals of the American Academy of Political and Social Science* 311 (May 1957): 41–46; and Arthur V. Watkins, "Termination of Federal Supervision: The Removal of Restrictions over Indian Property and Person," *Annals of the American Academy of Political and Social Science* 311 (May 1957): 47–55.

Overviews of termination include Charles F. Wilkinson and Eric R. Briggs, "The Evolution of the Termination Policy," *American Indian Law Review* 5 (1977): 139–184 and Frederick J. Stefon, "The Irony of Termination, 1943–1958," *Indian Historian* 11 (September 1978): 3 –14. See also Debra R. Boender, "Termination and the Administration of Glenn L. Emmons as Commissioner of Indian Affairs, 1953–1961," *New Mexico Historical Review* 54 (October 1979): 287–304. Other studies are S. Lyman Tyler, *Indian Affairs: A Work Paper on Termination, with an Attempt to Show Its Antecedents* (Provo, Utah, 1964) and Larry Hasse, "Termination and Assimilation: Federal Indian Policy, 1943–1961" (Ph.D. diss., Washington State University, 1974). See also Kenneth R. Philip's book, *Termination Revisited: American Indians on the Trail of Self-Determination, 1933-1953* (Lincoln, Nebr., 1999).

The first terminated tribe, Menominee, is the focus of Stephen H. Herzberg, "The Menominee Indians: From Treaty to Termination," *Wisconsin Magazine of History* 60 (1977): 266–329 and "The Menominee Indians: Termination to Restoration," *American Indian Law Review* 6 (1978): 143–204. Refer also to Nancy O. Lurie, "Menominee Termination: From Reservation to Colony," *Human Organization* 31 (Fall 1972): 257–270. The most thorough study is Nicholas Peroff, *Menominee Drums, Tribal Termination and Restoration, 1954–1974* (Norman, Okla., 1982).

Literature on other tribal groups are Susan Hood, "Termination of the Klamath Indian Tribe of Oregon," *Ethnohistory* 19 (Fall 1972): 379–392; Angie Debo, "Termination of the Oklahoma Indians," *American Indian* 7 (Spring 1955):

17–23; Stanley Underdal, "On the Road Toward Termination: The Pyramid Lake Paiutes and the Indian Attorney Controversy of the 1950s" (Ph.D. diss., Columbia University, 1977); and Faun Dixon, "Native American Property Rights: The Pyramid Lake Reservation Land Controversy" (Ph.D. diss., University of Nevada, 1980). Retribalism after termination is in William T. Hagan, "Tribalism Rejuvenated: The Native American Since the Era of Termination," *Western History Quarterly* 12 (1981): 4–16.

The Relocation Program and Indians in urban areas is covered in James Gundlach, "Native American Indian Migration and Relocation: Success or Failure," *Pacific Sociological Review* 21 (January 1978): 117–127. See also Lawrence Clinton, Bruce A. Chadwick, and Howard Bahr, "Urban Relocation Reconsidered: Antecedents of Employment Among Indian Males," *Rural Sociology* 40 (1975): 117–133. A major study is Elaine Neils, *The Urbanization of the American Indian and the Federal Program of Relocation and Assistance* (Chicago, 1971).

Relocation to certain cities are in Theodore Graves and Minor Van Arsdale, "Values, Expectations and Relocation: The Navajo Migrant to Denver," *Human Organization* 25 (Winter 1966): 300–307; and Joan Ablon, "Relocated American Indians in the San Francisco Bay Area: Social Interaction and Indian Identity," *Human Organization* 23 (Winter 1964): 296–304, "America Indian Relocation Problems of Dependency and Management in the City," *Phylon* 66 (Winter 1965): 362–371, and "Relocated American Indians in the San Francisco Bay Area: Concepts of Acculturation, Success, and Identity in the City" (Ph.D. diss., University of Chicago, 1963).

On urban Indians, see: Joan Weibel-Orlando, *Indian Country, L.A.: Maintaining Ethnic Community in Complex Society* (Urbana and Chicago, 1991), Terry Straus and Grant P. Arndt, eds., *Native Chicago* (Chicago, 1998), Susan Lobo and Kurt Peters, eds., *American Indians and the Urban Experience* (Walnut Creek, Calif., 2001), Edmund Danziger Jr., *Survival and Regeneration: Detroit's American Indian Community* (Detroit, 1991) , and Donald L. Fixico, *The Urban Indian Experience in America* (Albuquerque, N. Mex., 2000).

Chapter 12 ❧
Finally Acknowledging Native Peoples

American Indian Policies since the Nixon Administration

Laurence M. Hauptman

For over three-quarters of a century after the massacre of Wounded Knee in 1890, American Indians remained largely invisible to the public at large. Although the 1930s witnessed a flurry of federal programs to aid Indians under the New Deal, throughout most of the twentieth century, most Americans focused on other matters, largely unconcerned with the consequences of a three-hundred-year frontier process. Indeed, according to Alvin M. Josephy, Jr., until the 1960s the *Time-Life* Corporation maintained the editorial policy of its founder and publisher Henry Luce not to publish any articles on American Indians. Much of this historical amnesia was to change in the Nixon-Ford presidential years from 1969 to 1977, as the American public began to take notice of the historic problems and disastrous policies long suffered by American Indians.

In November 1969, a small cadre of idealistic American Indians, working with the leadership of the Oakland–San Francisco Bay council, seized Alcatraz Island and proclaimed it for "Indians of All Nations." Organized by Adam Fortunate Eagle Nordwall, an Ojibwa artist and businessman, this event immediately drew worldwide attention. The media focused on the occupation of this notorious, deserted, maximum-security federal penitentiary. The Indians skillfully equated the event with their own tribesmen's "imprisonment" in terrible poverty and federal neglect on reservations and in urban areas. Much of the early news attention focused on a young, charismatic Mohawk, Richard Oakes, who became the spokesman for the Indians on the island. However, off the island, Nordwall continued to conduct much of the negotiations with federal officials who demanded the removal of the Indians and threatened to invade the island with federal marshals and military personnel. The newspapers presented the confrontation as an Indian war, but this time some of the writers as well as the public saw the Indians as the "good guys," the tired but persistent film and TV image of Indians as "hostiles" and "renegades" now reversed. The takeover of Alcatraz predated the more radical direction of Indian politics, most visible later in the rise of the American Indian Movement. By the summer of 1970, less committed

Indians and hangers-on began to outnumber the original occupiers, yet, the United States Coast Guard did not retake Alcatraz until June 11, 1971.

This dramatic and long-lived event had a direct influence on the next three decades. Those on the island, "veterans" of the takeover, later became prominent in the Indian world, including Wilma Mankiller, Cherokee tribal chair, and Gerald L. Hill, former chief attorney of the Oneida Nation of Indians of Wisconsin and former head of the American Indian Trial Lawyers Association. In the midst of the Vietnam War and social upheavals throughout the United States, these Indians attempted to focus Americans' attention on issues related to America's forgotten peoples, their poverty and their dissatisfaction with federal and state policies.

Background

The occupation of Alcatraz was the manifestation of frustration that had been building up for years, feelings traceable well back into American Indian history. In the quarter century after V-J Day and the end of World War II, the federal government's policies were especially destructive to American Indians. Although policymakers used varied terms to describe postwar federal Indian policy, including "emancipation," "federal withdrawal," or "readjustment," the most frequently employed, and perhaps the most descriptive word to characterize the new direction, was "termination." In actuality the policy of termination was both a philosophy and specific federal legislation applied to Indians. As a philosophy, the movement encouraged assimilation of Indians as individuals into the mainstream of American society while concurrently advocating the end of the federal government's responsibility for Indian affairs. To accomplish these objectives, Congress passed termination legislation that falls into four general categories: first, the end of federal treaty relationships and trust responsibilities to certain specified Indian nations; second, the repeal of federal laws that set Indians apart from other American citizens; third, the removal of restrictions of federal guardianship and supervision over certain individual Indians; and fourth, the transfer of services provided by the Bureau of Indian Affairs (BIA) to other federal, state, or local governmental agencies or to Indian nations themselves.

The "termination laws" of the Truman and Eisenhower administrations during the late 1940s and 1950s ended federally recognized status for 109 Indian groups. They also removed restrictions on Indian trust lands, easing their lease or sale; shifted responsibility for Indian health care from the BIA to the Department of Health, Education, and Welfare; and established relocation programs to encourage Indian out-migrations from reservations to urban areas. Even the creation of the Indian Claims Commission in 1946 became part and parcel of congressional efforts at "getting the United States out of the Indian business." Although the actions of the Indian Claims Commission were noteworthy in providing the bases of later Indian litigation, the commission was mandated by congressional action to pay monetary damages for Indian land and resource losses and did not allow for any return of lands to the Indians.

Exploiting the tensions and fears emanating from the Cold War, members of Congress during the 1950s and early 1960s justified the pork-barrel funding of massive hydroelectric projects that undermined Indian communities in the East and the West. Both Republican President Eisenhower and Democrat President Kennedy advocated and carried out these initiatives, major flood-control programs advocated by an iron triangle of interlocking interests—state and federal politicos, the United States Army Corps of Engineers, and hydroelectric power companies. The projects upset and affected a great many Indians including the Senecas in New York and Pennsylvania, the Pueblos in New Mexico, and the Lakotas in North Dakota. Thus, according to the American Indian Policy Review Commission, the federal government purchased only 595,157 acres of land for tribal use from 1934 to 1974 under provisions of the Indian Reorganization Act; in the same forty-year period, federal agencies condemned 1,811,010 acres of Indian lands! Besides land loss, massive projects such as the Bonneville Dam, the Grand Coulee Dam, and the Dalles Dam destroyed traditional fishing sites of Indians in the Northwest. While the federal government provided a settlement to various Indian nations for the "damages," moneys from Washington could not replace the social, cultural, and religious significance of these permanently altered areas.

Although urban migration of American Indians did not begin with the federal relocation programs of the 1950s, Washington-initiated policies during that decade did indeed encourage the urbanization of Native Americans. In 1951, Commissioner of Indian Affairs Dillon S. Myer established the Branch of Placement and Relocation. This branch, through offices in Chicago, Cleveland, Dallas, Denver, Los Angeles, Salt Lake City, and later in other cities, funneled Indian relocatees from reservations. Through the placement offices, the BIA deliberately sent Indians to urban areas far from home—a policy echoing the early federal boarding school mandates—as a way to acculturate them swiftly to white mainstream values. As a component of the overall termination policy, federal officials sought to end the reservation system, which effectively supported separate cultural enclaves that worked against assimilation. While many American Indians, much like earlier European immigrants, saw a move to the city as a way to provide for their families and shake off the shackles of poverty and colonialism, federal officials did little to improve reservation economies, thus speeding up the process of urbanization. This resulted in increasingly larger urban Indian communities, from Los Angeles to New York City. And the poor conditions that these new arrivals typically faced spawned Red Power activism, the first explosion of which came at Alcatraz in San Francisco harbor, immediately after a fire that destroyed the American Indian center in the Bay Area. Although neither Nordwall nor Oakes was a federal relocatee, the group that took Alcatraz included a significant number of Southwestern and Plains Indians who had "taken advantage" of the program.

On the state level, American Indians faced restrictions on their civil rights. In the post–World War II era, Congress awarded state jurisdiction over criminal and civil matters to five states, including Wisconsin and New York. And various states continued to restrict Indian fishing and hunting rights under the auspices of federal treaties. Even after World War II, some state constitutions, especially those of the western states with large Indian populations, prevented Indians from voting. Nevertheless, some points of light suggested change in the future.

Harrison v. *Laveen,* one of the more important cases in American Indian legal history, came before the Arizona Supreme Court in 1948. Frank Harrison and Harry Austin—one a veteran of World War II and both members of the Mohave-Apache Indian tribe residing on the Fort McDowell Indian Reservation—sought to register to vote in Scottsdale, Maricopa County, Arizona. Roger G. Laveen, the county recorder, refused to permit the Indians to register. What followed was a major test case brought on behalf of Indian voting rights, largely orchestrated by legal scholar Felix S. Cohen, the National Congress of American Indians, and the American Civil Liberties Union. The plaintiffs and their attorneys argued that the Indians attempting to register possessed all of the qualifications for suffrage set forth in the constitution and laws of the state of Arizona, and insisted that their rights as citizens, as guaranteed under the Arizona and United States constitutions, had been violated. The Arizona Supreme Court held for the plaintiffs. The court interpreted the phrase "person under guardianship" in the state constitution as having no application to Indians "or to the Federal status of Indians in Arizona as a class." Yet, even after the case was decided, certain other western states continued to restrict Indian voting rights for another decade.

Nixon's Presidency

The presidency of Richard Nixon was the turning point in the contemporary history of American Indians. Because of his intiatives affecting Native American lives and welfare in the post–World War II period, he today is still regarded by many Indians as the greatest president.

On July 8, 1970, in a most important presidential message to Congress, Nixon enunciated a clear shift in federal Indian policy. Calling the American Indians the "most deprived and most isolated minority group in our nation," the president acknowledged that from first contact, "American Indians have been oppressed and brutalized, deprived of their ancestral lands and denied the opportunity to control their own destiny." He next acknowledged the failures of past responses of the United States government: "Even the federal programs which are intended to meet their needs have frequently proven to be ineffective and demeaning."

Nixon then rejected "forced termination" and turned attention to ending that federal policy. To him, the federal government had not a charitable responsibility to American Indians but a legal obligation. He stressed that through "written treaties and formal and informal agreements," Indians had ceded "claims to vast tracts of land and have accepted life on government reservations" in exchange for American commitments to provide them a "standard of living comparable to that of other Americans." Thus, terminating "this relationship would be no more appropriate than to terminate the citizenship rights of any other American." Besides, Nixon continued, the termination policies of the past decade and a half had failed, and they had clearly proven harmful to Indians. President Nixon maintained that the threat of termination also generated Indians' fears and distrust of all federal programs, which weakened their effectiveness. Moreover, termination had increased dependence on the federal bureaucracy rather than fostering independence from it. "Of the Department of the Interior's programs directly serving Indians," the president stressed, "only 1.5 percent are presently under Indian control. Only 2.4 percent of HEW's Indian health programs are run by Indians."

Realizing that he was taking a historic step in reversing policies, Nixon emphasized: "In place of policies which oscillate between the deadly extremes of forced termination and constant paternalism, we suggest a policy in which the federal government and the Indian community play complementary roles." The president brilliantly concluded: "The Indians of America need federal assistance— this much has long been clear. What has not always been clear, however, is that the federal government needs Indian energies and Indian leadership if its assistance is to be effective in improving the conditions of Indian life. It is a new and balanced relationship between the United States government and the first Americans that is at the heart of our approach to Indian problems. And that is why we now approach these problems with new confidence that they will successfully be overcome."

Two events in 1972 and 1973 had a direct bearing on the reevaluation of federal Indian policies: the takeovers of both the Bureau of Indian Affairs building in Washington, D.C., in late October of 1972 and of Wounded Knee in February 1973. President Nixon, who had done so much already to change the direction of federal Indian policies during his first term, now responded much like he did during the Watergate crisis. He ordered political surveillance, illegal wiretaps, and IRS audits of Indian activists and reacted with massive federal force at Wounded Knee. The takeover of the BIA occurred after the "Trail of Broken Treaties" caravan reached Washington, D.C., just before the American presidential election in the fall of 1972. Led by Hank Adams, a major advocate of Indian fishing rights in the Pacific Northwest, the caravan had traveled across the country bringing Indian treaty rights concerns to the American public's attention. Although the protest was intended to be a peaceful one, some of the activists, prior to ending their occupation, sacked the building and carried off vital files needed by Indian nations for their litigation. Three months later, members of the American Indian Movement (AIM), led by Russell Means and Dennis Banks, took over the hamlet of Wounded Knee, the site of the massacre of Sioux Indians in 1890, on the Pine Ridge Reservation in South Dakota. For over two months, these Indians were in a face-to-face showdown with federal marshals, the FBI

Indian activists that took over the Bureau of Indian Affairs in Washington, DC, armed themselves with makeshift weapons and vowed not to leave without a fight, November 3, 1972.
© Bettmann/CORBIS

and American military personnel, and, as a result, the occupation received worldwide media attention. Before the takeover ended, several Indians and non-Indians were killed and wounded in this armed confrontation.

On October 22, 1970, Nixon signed Public Law 91-489 returning Ozette, Washington, to the Makah Indians, over the strong opposition of environmentalist groups, including the Olympic Park Association. Two months later, he signed federal legislation returning Blue Lake and 48,000 acres to the Taos Pueblos. These sacred tribal lands had been "acquired" by the federal government in 1906 and included in the national forest system in an executive order issued by Theodore Roosevelt, a move which aimed to protect the area from logging operations. Later, in 1972, President Nixon supported and signed federal legislation returning 21,000 acres of the Gifford Pinchot National Forest to the Yakama Indians of Washington.

Other improvements came with the restoration of federal trust status to terminated Indians and in federal hiring practices. In late December 1973, Congress, with the support of the Nixon administration, restored to federal status the Menominees of Wisconsin, an Indian nation that had been terminated in 1961. As a result, other previously terminated Indian nations, such as the Klamath of Oregon and the numerous Indian Rancherias of California, were later restored to federal status. Thus they became eligible for federal programs and moneys as well as access to federal courts to protect themselves from state actions. On June 20, 1972, in the immediate aftermath of the Watergate burglary, Commissioner of Indian Affairs Louis R. Bruce, Jr., extended Indian preference in employment to all positions within the Bureau of Indian Affairs. Previously, favor only in original hirings had been the agency's rules since 1934. Later, in 1974, the United States Supreme Court upheld the Nixon administration's actions.

Nixon's positive legacy also included Indian education. In 1969, the United States Special Subcommittee on Indian Education had issued a report that labeled the federal government's Indian education policies "a failure of major proportions" and a "national tragedy." Over the next decade, Congress, with the support of Presidents Nixon, Ford, and Carter, substantially increased funding for Indian schools, encouraged the building and establishment of reservation day schools, and began the process of closing the much criticized Indian boarding schools. The first of two major pieces of Indian education legislation was passed during the Nixon years: the Indian Education Act of 1972, which provided funding for urban, rural non-reservation, and terminated or nonfederally recognized Indians. The second, the Indian Self-Determination and Education Assistance Act of 1975, became law during the presidency of Gerald Ford. This was the most important piece of federal legislation dealing with Indian education since the New Deal; among other things, the 1975 act allowed Indian nations to contract to run education and health programs themselves, a revolutionary principle

A member of AIM (left) offers a peace pipe to Kent Frizzell (right), assistant U.S. attorney general, at Wounded Knee, SD, during a ceremony ending the bloody standoff between AIM and federal authorities, April 5, 1973. Beside Wallace Black Elk (kneeling), are AIM leaders (from right) Russell Means, Dennis Banks (headband), and Carter Camp (vest). AP Photo/Jim Mone

after 150 years of BIA's colonial administration. Three years later, building on these two remarkable pieces of legislation, President Jimmy Carter signed P.L. 95-561, which increased funding for Indian children in the public schools while promoting greater Indian parental involvement. As is true of most federal legislation, the success of laws depends on continued funding by Congress, and in this regard, there have been periodic shortfalls in this area since the late 1970s.

Despite his sincere efforts, Nixon's support of legislation affecting Native Americans did not always resolve long-standing concerns, and, in some cases, required further federal action to correct the wrong course once taken. One such example is the Navajo-Hopi Land Settlement Act of 1974, supported by President Nixon, which hoped to resolve the ninety-year dispute over the Joint Use Area. The so-called Joint Use Area was a reservation of nearly 2.5 million acres in New Mexico, established for the Hopis in 1882 by executive order of President Chester A. Arthur, to resolve that tribe's complaints about Navajo encroachment on their lands. Over subsequent decades, thousands of Navajos, with federal acquiescence and much to the distress of the Hopis, steadily occupied land within the 1882 reservation boundaries, with the two tribes bickering steadily thereafter. The 1974 law called for the removal and relocation of the Navajos in the disputed region and elevated tribal tensions to the point that the *New York Times* reported that "Rival Tribes Threaten War over Million Acres." The dispute continued disastrously until federal court-ordered mediation in 1992.

Perhaps more significant was the Alaska Native Claims Settlement Act (ANCSA). Under the act, Alaska Natives obtained 44 million acres of land and nearly a billion dollars in compensation. Alaska was divided into a dozen geographic regions and twelve different regional corporations were established to manage these lands and promote economic development. The act had overwhelming congressional bipartisan support, including the strong endorsement of Senator Edward Kennedy of Massachusetts. Nearly a decade and a half later, President Ronald Reagan signed amendments to the Alaska Native Claims Settlement Act that improved, but did not completely solve, problems caused by the original 1971 legislation. The status of Alaskan Natives and their lands increasingly has received more attention over the past three decades. In 1997, the United States Supreme Court in *Alaska* v. *Native Village of Venetie Tribal Government* made a landmark decision. The court unanimously decided that Alaska Indian lands were "Indian Country," not subject to state jurisdiction despite the passage of ANCSA in 1971 and its amendments in 1987.

After Nixon

By the time President Nixon resigned his office in August 1974, many more Indians were officeholders in Washington, D.C., and past policies were under extreme attack. By 1977, the position of commissioner of Indian affairs was elevated to the level of assistant secretary of the Interior for Indian affairs, a move advocated by every major Indian organization in the country since the takeover of

Alcatraz. Washington officials seemed more responsive to Indians, especially to their criticisms of the colonial nature of the administration of Indian affairs. In the wake of this new visibility, Congress established the American Indian Policy Review Commission in January 1975 and called for a thorough investigation of the historical and legal status of American Indians. Five of the eleven Commission members were of Indian ancestry, while six others were congresspersons. With some understanding of the diversity of the Native American world, Congress, in creating this commission, named three members from federally recognized Indian communities, one from an urban community, and one from a nonfederally recognized community. The group set up nine task forces, which would make separate reports and recommendations on issues ranging from health care and economic development to acknowledgment of unrecognized (federally) or previously terminated Indian communities.

Indeed, much of the modern impetus for federal recognition came from the American Indian Policy Review Commission, although the movement could be traced further back, to the American Indian Chicago Conference of June 1961. This earlier convocation, organized by Sol Tax of the University of Chicago, was designed to provide a forum for all Native American communities, East and West, federally and nonfederally recognized, concerning a wide variety of issues—treaty rights, land loss in federal dam projects, poverty, and many others.

As of January 3, 2001, the United States government recognizes 561 Indian tribal governments. On that date, the Interior Department recognized its trust responsibilities to two Alaska communities—the King Salmon Tribe, and the Shoonaq Tribe of Kodiak—and restored federal recognition to the Chinook Indian Nation of Washington and the Lower Lake Rancheria of California, the latter having been terminated in the 1950s. A week earlier, President William Clinton signed the Omnibus Indian Advancement Act, restoring federal recognition to the Graton Rancheria of California, which also had been terminated in the 1950s; the act also extended federal status to the Loyal Shawnee Tribe of Oklahoma.

Today, federal recognition of an American Indian Tribe can be achieved in three ways: first, a tribe may take action in court to force the United States to recognize its trust responsibilities to it; second, a tribe may be deemed a federally recognized tribe by congressional legislation; or third, a tribe may follow a bureaucratic and often convoluted process established by the Department of the Interior's Branch of Federal Acknowledgment in the Bureau of Indian Affairs. To long-neglected Indian communities, attaining federally recognized status fosters community pride and allows them to gain a more equal footing in the Native American world. In most cases, it also provides them with access to federal Indian programs and allows them, as newly recognized Indian nations the right to sue for land in federal court as well as to seek other federal protections against the willful actions of states. In more recent times, federally recognized status often, but not in all cases, allows Indian nations, to put purchased lands into trust, with the secretary of the interior's approval, giving special tax advantages to them. This strategy has been used effectively in recent years by Indian nations intent on entrepreneurial activities such as gaming.

The petition route through the Department of the Interior, the third option, was established in 1978 and modified in 1994. This proceeds through the Bureau of Indian Affairs' Branch of Federal Acknowledgment, which requires historical and genealogical evidence in its evaluation. In the East as well as in the West, many Native American communities have not yet been able to secure federal recognition because it is a time-consuming, expensive, politically charged, sometimes even a demeaning, process. Congressional politics and budget cutting, BIA stonewalling, and racist perceptions all stand as possible roadblocks on the route to federal recognition. Moreover, certain Native American leaders themselves do not want Washington to recognize more Indian communities, such as the populous but nonfederally recognized Lumbee of North Carolina, since they fear the further shrinking of the federal pie to Indian communities.

Much of the success that American Indians have achieved since 1970 has been the result of the expansion of legal opportunities for Native Americans. Attorneys—warriors with attaché cases—have helped the federal courts rewrite numerous wrongs over the past three decades and have worked with the Senate Indian Affairs Committee to draft corrective legislation in numerous areas. It is not surprising that this legal redirection began in the Nixon-Ford years, 1969 to 1977. The founding of the Native American Rights Fund (NARF) has dramatically affected Indians and Indian policies. Not only has the organization revolutionized the case law affecting Native Americans in this country, but NARF has also been the training ground for young, aspiring attorneys, both Indian and non-Indian, seeking to specialize in Native American legal issues.

NARF was established after an eighteen-month pilot project of California Indian Legal Services. The Ford Foundation, hoping to create a national legal program for Indians, built on the success of the ongoing California program and became its major financial supporter for its first three years. NARF eventually separated from the California Indian Legal Services in 1971, soon growing from a three-attorney pilot project to a major law firm of eighteen attorneys. NARF moved its headquarters from California to Boulder, Colorado, and later opened a Washington, D.C., office, which primarily focuses on national legislation affecting Native Americans as well as eastern Indian legal matters. With the help of a grant from the Carnegie Corporation, NARF established the National Indian Law Library in Washington, D.C., which serves as the major legal clearinghouse for tribal and legal-services attorneys working on behalf of Native Americans. In 1984, NARF opened an Anchorage office to serve the legal needs of Native Alaskans. Today, NARF's thirteen-member Board of Directors, composed entirely of Native Americans, has five major priorities: (1) the preservation of tribal existence; (2) the protection of tribal natural resources; (3) the promotion of human rights; (4) the accountability of governments to Native Americans; and (5) the development of Indian law.

From the start, NARF attorneys achieved notable successes in carrying out these priorities. From 1971 through 1973, they lobbied to restore the Menominee of Wisconsin to federal tribal status, and much of the success in achieving federal recognition or in restoring federal status to other Indian nations belongs to the hardworking men and women of NARF. Whether working for New England Indian nations or for Alaska villages seeking protection from state jurisdiction, this organization took advantage of the changing climate from the Nixon-Ford years onward to advance the interests of Native Americans nationwide.

In 1976, in *Fisher* v. *Montana,* NARF attorneys won a United States Supreme Court decision that recognized that tribal courts had exclusive jurisdiction in Indian adoption proceedings in which all parties were tribal members. Significantly, two years later, in a move supported by NARF, the United States Congress passed the Indian Child Welfare Act, thus setting minimum standards for the removal of Indian children from their families and establishing standards for adoptive and foster-care placement. Since 1978, especially in the United States Supreme Court case *Mississippi Band of Choctaw Indians* v. *Holyfield* (1989), NARF attorneys have given priority to this concern, becoming advocates in promoting the stability of Indian families and, at the same time, allowing tribal courts self-determination on this important issue.

NARF achieved one of its most heralded victories in 1980. Largely as a result of the efforts of Tom Tureen, a non-Indian working for NARF, Maine Indians—the Penobscot, Passamaquoddy, and Houlton Band of Maliseet—received a settlement award of $27 million and additional moneys totaling $54.5 million to purchase back 300,000 acres of their traditional lands in Maine.

In March 1985, NARF attorney Arlinda Locklear, in the Oneida land claims case, won a 5 to 4 decision in favor of the Indians before the United States Supreme Court. Earlier, in January 1974, the Oneidas, in a landmark case before the United States Supreme Court, had won the right to enter federal courts to sue for their lands based on state violations of the federal Trade and Intercourse Acts of 1790 and 1793. This case, *Oneida Nation* v. *Oneida and Madison Counties, New York,* opened up land claims suits for federally recognized Indian nations in the original thirteen states. The 1985 test case involved fewer than nine hundred acres of the extensive Oneida tribal land claim. The United States Supreme Court held that Oneida and Madison counties, New York, were liable for damages—fair rental value for two years, 1968 and 1969—for unlawful seizure of Indian ancestral lands. Associate Justice Lewis F. Powell, Jr., who wrote the majority opinion, insisted that the Indians' common-law right to sue was firmly established and that Congress did not intend to impose a deadline on the filing of such suits, effectively nullifying the counties' contention that the Indians had not made a timely effort to sue and thus had forfeited their legal rights. The decision neatly erased the main argument against the Indians and opened the door for further

Oneida litigation involving their lost lands. The high court also suggested that, because of the tremendous economic implications of the case, Congress should help settle the New York Indian land claims, as it had done in Connecticut, Maine, and Rhode Island. In 1993, in one of the more important cases, NARF attorneys helped push for a congressional land claims settlement involving the Catawba Indians and the state of South Carolina. The Catawbas were also restored to federal status and provided federal moneys (along with state compensation) to repurchase approximately 15,000 acres of former tribal lands in York County.

Hard-fought NARF victories have also been achieved in the area of human rights, especially concerning the sanctity of Indian remains and the repatriation of burial goods.[1] Many thousands of Native American peoples had been dug up from their graves in the United States and were now held in the nation's universities, museums, state and federal agencies, and tourist attractions. In 1868, the United States Surgeon General ordered the procurement of Indian crania for the Army Medical Museum; over four thousand heads were subsequently taken from Indian graves, burial scaffolds, morgues, hospitals, and POW camps in the name of "scientific research." Through the leadership of NARF attorneys, this issue has been a major focus of the organization's legal efforts.

Indeed, NARF took up this issue long before the public outcry of the late 1980s. In the 1982 United States Supreme Court case, *Charrier* v. *Bell,* NARF attorneys argued successfully that artifacts dug from graves in an ancient Tunica-Biloxi Indian burial ground in Louisiana belonged to that Native American community. With the growing concern over this issue, the organization pushed for legislative remedies throughout the 1980s. Largely as a result of their efforts, in 1989 the Nebraska State Legislature passed the Unmarked Human Burial Sites and Skeletal Remains Protection Act, expressly intended to "assure that all human burials are accorded equal treatment and respect for human dignity without reference to ethnic origins, cultural backgrounds, or religious affiliations." This precedent-setting law required the return of tribally identifiable human remains and associated grave offerings held by public entities in the state, as well as the protection of unmarked burials throughout the state. Momentously, over thirty other states have followed the Nebraska example in passing laws to protect Indian graves. Moreover, in November 1990, President Bush signed into law the Native American Graves Protection and Repatriation Act (NAGPRA). The new federal law increased protections for Indian graves located on federal and tribal lands and provides for native control over cultural items obtained from such lands in the future; outlawed commercial traffic in human remains; required all federal agencies and federally funded museums (including universities) to inventory their collections of dead Native Americans and associated funerary objects and repatriate them to culturally affiliated tribes or descendants on request; and mandated that all federal agencies and federally funded museums repatriate Native American

1 The issues surrounding the repatriation of Indian burial remains and objects are discussed in Chapter 16 by James Riding In.

sacred objects and cultural patrimony under procedures and standards specified in the act.

A major sign of cultural resurgence on the part of American Indian nations has been the establishment of numerous tribal museums over the past three decades, including the largest project of all, the Mashantucket Pequot Museum and Research Center in Connecticut which opened in 1998. Tribal museums have become a very noticeable part of Indian life, promoting learning from early childhood to adult education, countering stereotypes, and attracting tourists to Indian country. This movement has been stimulated by reactions to some museums and their policies that allowed for the displays of human remains, served as permanent custodians of Indian bones, and/or offended contemporary Indians by insensitively exhibiting medicine bundles, false face masks, and other sacred items. Indians nationwide also accused museums of unfairly, and sometimes illegally, obtaining Indian artifacts that they demanded should be returned to them.

This backlash against the "cultural colonialism" of certain museums led also to the passage of several important pieces of federal legislation: the National Museum of the American Indian Act of November 28, 1989, as well as the previously mentioned NAGPRA. The first act committed the United States government to build a major Indian museum on the Mall in Washington, D.C., as part of the Smithsonian Institution. The act also allowed for the Smithsonian to acquire the private collection of the Museum of the American Indian and create a satellite museum—the National Museum of the American Indian—in New York City. Importantly, the Smithsonian was ordered to consult and cooperate with traditional Indian religious leaders and tribal government officials to create an inventory of all Indian human remains and funerary objects held by the museum, identify tribal origins of these materials, and expeditiously return such remains and associated funerary objects to descendants or to the tribe. Tribal officials themselves could also initiate the process if they could identify and bring evidence to prove their case before the Secretary of the Smithsonian.

One of the greatest changes in Indian Country since the late 1970s has been the proliferation of Indian gaming. What began as limited bingo operations along with cigarette sales to provide Indian nations such as the Seminoles of Florida with quick revenues to deal with immediate economic and social needs since has grown into a multibillion-dollar industry, with diverse Indian communities owning and operating more than two hundred casinos nationwide. From small side-of-the-road operations in the Southwest to the Mashantucket Pequot's Foxwoods, the largest casino operation in the Americas, gaming has grown into a significant industry in Indian communities. Gaming operations expanded greatly during the Reagan-Bush era, the administrations having viewed them as a good substitute for federal government subsidies of Indian welfare and other social services.

On February 23, 1987, in the case *California v. Cabazon Band of Mission Indians,* the United States Supreme Court held that federal and tribal interests preempt state law in regulating or prohibiting bingo games run by Indian nations. The next year, the United States Congress passed the Indian Gaming Regulatory Act, which set the parameters on Indian-run bingo operations and allowed for the expansion of tribally licensed gaming and the establishment of tribal casinos to fulfill the "principal goal of federal Indian policy," namely "to promote tribal self-sufficiency and strong government." It recognized that "Indian tribes have the exclusive right to regulate gaming activity on Indian lands if the gaming activity is not specifically prohibited by federal law and is conducted within a state which does not, as a matter of criminal law and public policy, prohibit such gaming activity." The act created the National Indian Gaming Commission, a regulatory body within the Department of the Interior, and required tribal-state compact agreements on gaming activities on Indian lands, which need the approval of the secretary of the interior. While some Indian nations have taken this path toward economic self-sufficiency, others view this road as one of surrendering tribal sovereignty by making compacts with the various states, with the enemy.

Hence, over the past three decades, there has been a remarkable makeover of Indian policy and for the first time an acknowledgment that American Indians have a distinct status in the American polity. No longer willing to be administered in a colonial relationship, American Indians have asserted their rights—both as Indians and as American citizens. On April 29, 1994, President Clinton addressed 322 leaders of federally recognized Indian nations at the White House, issuing a major policy statement, the most important one since President Nixon's of 1970. Clinton committed his administration to a government-to-government relationship with Native American tribal governments, applying it to each executive department and agency of the United States. The memorandum was issued to ensure that the rights of sovereign tribal governments were fully known and respected by federal agency heads and their staffs, who would henceforth work to build "a more effective day-to-day working relationship reflecting respect for the rights of self-government due the sovereign tribal governments."

Today, American Indians still face racial discrimination, desperate poverty (although lessened in certain cases by gaming), and state intransigence on taxation, jurisdiction issues, and in other areas. And American Indian leaders still look warily on Washington, well remembering the broken promises of the past. They understand that even today the president, Congress, and the United States Supreme Court have the power to reverse the gains of the last three decades. Nevertheless, Indian leaders also realize that in the years since Alcatraz, "Indian wars" have lessened and that their concerns, while not completely resolved to their satisfaction, finally have been acknowledged.

Suggested Reading

The best brief survey of twentieth-century American Indian policies is Peter Iverson, *"We Are Still Here": American Indians in the Twentieth Century* (Wheeling, Ill., 1998). Most of the major congressional acts, executive orders and presi-

State and Federally Recognized U.S. Indian Reservations*

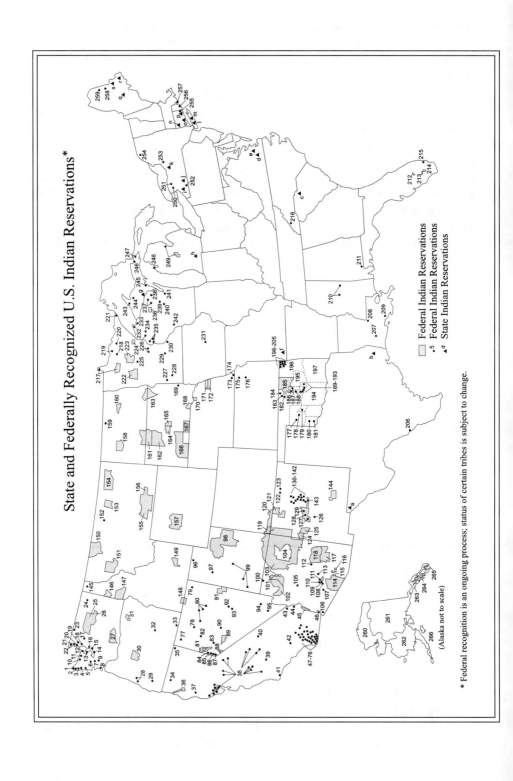

☐ Federal Indian Reservations
•5 Federal Indian Reservations
▲d State Indian Reservations

(Alaska not to scale)

* Federal recognition is an ongoing process; status of certain tribes is subject to change.

Washington
1 Makah
2 Ozette
3 Quileute
4 Hoh
5 Quinault
6 Skokomish
7 Squaxin Island
8 Shoalwater
9 Chehalis
10 Lower Elwha
11 Jamestown Klallam
12 Port Gamble
13 Port Madison
14 Nisqually
15 Puyallup
16 Muckleshoot
17 Sauk Suiattle
18 Tulalip
19 Stillaquamish
20 Upper Skagit
21 Swinomish
22 Lummi
23 Nooksack
24 Kalispel
25 Colville
26 Spokane
27 Yakama

Oregon
28 Siletz
29 Cow Creek Band of Umpqua
30 Warm Springs
31 Umatilla
32 Burns Paiute
33 Fort McDermitt

California
34 Karok
35 Fort Bidwell
36 Hoopa Valley
37 Round Valley
38 Small rancherias
39 Tule River
40 Fort Independence

41 Santa Ynez
42 San Manuel
43 Fort Mohave
44 Chemehuevi
45 Colorado River
46 Quechan
47 Palm Springs
48 Morongo
49 Soboba
50 Santa Rosa
51 Ramona
52 Cahuilla
53 Pechanga
54 Pala
55 Pauma
56 Rincon
57 San Pasqual
58 Mesa Grande
59 Viejas
60 Jamul
61 Sycuan
62 La Posta
63 Campo
64 Manzanita
65 Cuyapaipe
66 Capitan Grande
67 Inaha-Cosmit
68 Santa Ysabel
69 La Jolla

70 Los Coyotes
71 Torres-Martinez
72 Augustine
73 Cabazon
74 Twenty-Nine Palms
75 Barona
76 rancheria

Nevada
77 Summit Lake
78 Winnemucca
79 Elko
80 Te-Moak
81 Pyramid Lake
82 Lovelock
83 Fallon
84 Reno Sparks

85 Yerington
86 Carson
87 Dresslerville
88 Washoe
89 Walker River
90 Yomba
91 Goshute
92 Ely
93 Duckwater
94 Moapa
95 Las Vegas

Utah
96 NW Shoshone
97 Skull Valley
98 Uintah & Ouray
99 Paiute

Arizona
100 Kaibab
101 Havasupai
102 Hualapai
103 Navajo
104 Hopi
105 Yavapai
106 Cocopah
107 Gila Bend
108 Maricopa
109 Gila River
110 Camp Verde
111 Salt River
112 Payson
113 Fort McDowell
114 Tohono O'odham
115 Pascua Yaqui
116 San Xavier
117 San Carlos
118 Fort Apache

Colorado
119 Ute Mountain
120 Southern Ute

New Mexico
121 Jicarilla Apache
122 Taos
123 Picuris
124 Zuni
125 Ramah Navajo
126 Alamo Navajo
127 Acoma
128 Laguna
129 Canoncito
130 Jemez
131 San Juan
132 Zia
133 Santa Clara
134 San Ildefonso
135 Pojoaque
136 Nambe
137 Tesuque
138 San Felipe
139 Cochiti
140 Santa Ana
141 Santo Domingo
142 Sandia
143 Isleta
144 Mescalero

Idaho
145 Kootenai
146 Coeur d'Alene
147 Nez Perce
148 Duck Valley
149 Fort Hall

Montana
150 Blackfeet
151 Flathead
152 Rocky Boys
153 Fort Belknap
154 Fort Peck
155 Crow
156 N. Cheyenne

Wyoming
157 Wind River

North Dakota
158 Fort Berthold
159 Turtle Mountain
160 Spirit Lake

South Dakota
161 Standing Rock
162 Cheyenne River
163 Sisseton
164 Lower Brule
165 Crow Creek
166 Pine Ridge
167 Rosebud
168 Yankton
169 Flandreau

Nebraska
170 Santee Sioux
171 Ho-Chunk
172 Omaha
173 Sac and Fox
174 Iowa

Kansas
175 Kickapoo
176 Potawatomi

Oklahoma
177 Cheyenne
178 Arapaho
179 Wichita
180 Caddo
181 Kiowa
182 Ponca
183 Tonkawa
184 Kaw
185 Osage
186 Otoe
187 Pawnee
188 Iowa
189 Kickapoo
190 Sac and Fox
191 Potawatomi
192 Shawnee
193 Seminole
194 Chickasaw

195 Muscogee
196 Cherokee
197 Choctaw
198 Peoria
199 Shawnee
200 Quapaw
201 Ottawa
202 Wyandot
203 Seneca Cayuga
204 Miami
205 Modoc

Texas
206 Kickapoo
a Tigua
b Alabama-Coushatta

Louisiana
207 Coushatta
208 Tunica-Biloxi
209 Chitimacha

Mississippi
210 Mississippi Choctaw

Alabama
211 Poarch Creek

Florida
212 Brighton Seminole
213 Big Cypress Seminole
214 Miccosukee
215 Dania

South Carolina
c Catawaba

North Carolina
216 Cherokee

Virginia
d Pamunkey
e Mattaponi

Minnesota
217 Red Lake
218 Deer Creek
219 Bois Forte
220 Vermillion Lake
221 Grand Portage
222 White Earth
223 Leech Lake
224 Fond du Lac
225 Sandy Lake
226 Mille Lacs
227 Upper Sioux
228 Lower Sioux
229 Shakopee
230 Prairie Island

Iowa
231 Sac and Fox

Missouri
f E. Shawnee

Wisconsin
232 Red Cliff
233 Bad River
234 Lac Courte Oreilles
235 St. Croix
236 Lac du Flambeau
237 Sokaogan Chippewa
238 Potawatomi
239 Menominee
240 Stockbridge-Munsee
241 Oneida
242 Ho-Chunk

Michigan
243 Ontonagon
244 L'Anse
245 Hannahville
246 Bay Mills
247 Sault Ste Marie
248 Grand Traverse
249 Isabella
g Lac Vieux Desert
h Potawatomi

New York
250 Tuscarora
251 Tonawanda
252 Allegheny
253 Oneida
254 St. Regis
i Cattaraugus
j Oil Springs
k Onondaga
l Poosepatuck
m Shinnecock

Connecticut
255 Mashantucket Pequot
n Shagticoke
o Paugusett
p Paucatuck Pequot

Rhode Island
256 Narragansett

Massachusetts
257 Wampanoag

Maine
258 Houlton Maliseet
259 Micmac
q Penobscot
r Pleasant Point
s Indian Township

Alaska
260 Inupiat
261 Athapaskan communities
262 Yup'ik, Alutiiq
263 Tlingit
264 Haida
265 Annette Island
266 Unangan

dential speeches, and United States Supreme Court decisions in the post–World War II period to the year 1999 can be found in Francis Paul Prucha, Ed., *Documents of United States Indian Policy*, 3rd edition (Lincoln, Nebr., 2000). Two distinct interpretations of the federal government's termination policies are: Donald L. Fixico, *Termination and Relocation: Federal Indian Policy, 1945–1960* (Albuquerque, N. Mex., 1986); and Kenneth R. Philp, *Termination Revisited: American Indians on the Trail to Self-Determination, 1933–1953* (Austin, Tex., 1999). For one Indian nation's efforts to overcome termination and federal withdrawal, see Nicholas Peroff, *Menominee Drums: Tribal Termination and Restoration, 1954–1974* (Norman, Okla., 1982). For one federal agency's important relationship with various Indian nations throughout the United States, see Robert H. Keller and Michael Turek, *American Indians and National Parks* (Tucson, Ariz., 1998). For energy policies and their impact on American Indian communities, see Marjanne Ambler, *Breaking the Iron Bonds: Indian Control of Energy Development* (Lawrence, Kans., 1990); and Donald L. Fixico, *The Invasion of Indian Country in the Twentieth Century* (Niwot, Colo., 1998).

The best studies of the struggle of American Indians to win recognition for their fishing rights on the Great Lakes and in Michigan, Wisconsin, and Minnesota are the excellent works by Ronald Satz, *Chippewa Treaty Rights: The Reserve Rights of Wisconsin's Chippewa Indians in Historical Perspective* (Madison, Wisc., 1991); and Robert Doherty, *Disputed Waters: Native Americans and the Great Lakes Fishery* (Lexington, Ky., 1990). For the issue in Washington state, see Fay G. Cohen, *Treaties on Trial: The Continuing Controversy Over Northwest Indian Fishing Rights* (Seattle, 1986). The struggle in the American West involves protection of American Indian water rights. For this key issue, see Lloyd Burton, *American Indian Water Rights and the Limits of the Law* (Lawrence, Kans., 1991). For a carefully study of a disastrous federal effort to solve a major intertribal controversy, see David Brugge, *The Navajo-Hopi Land Dispute: An American Tragedy* (Albuquerque, N. Mex., 1994). The shifts in federal Indian education policies are effectively presented in Margaret Szasz, *Education and the American Indian: The Road to Self-Determination Since 1928*, 3rd edition (Albuquerque, N. Mex., 1999). For two Indian nations' struggle, one successful and one not, to attain federal recognition, see Laurence M. Hauptman and James Wherry, Eds., *The Pequots in Southern New England: The Fall and Rise of an American Indian Nation* (Norman, Okla., 1990); and Jack Campisi, *Mashpee: Tribe on Trial* (Syracuse, N.Y., 1991).

For the origins of Indian gaming, see Hauptman, *The Pequots in Southern New England* cited above, as well as Harry Kersey, Jr., *An Assumption of Sovereignty: Social and Political Transformation Among the Florida Seminoles* (Lincoln, Nebr., 1995), which provides an excellent analysis of tribal chairman Howard Tommie's role. A good starting point on American Indians' urban experience is Edmund Danziger, Jr., *Survival and Regeneration: Detroit's American Indian Community* (Detroit, Mich., 1992). There is a need for policy studies on individual states and American Indians. For New York State policies, see Laurence M.

Hauptman, *The Iroquois Struggle for Survival: World War II to Red Power* (Syracuse, N.Y., 1986); and Hauptman, *Formulating American Indian Policy in New York State, 1970–1986* (Albany, N.Y., 1988). For background works documenting eastern Indian land claims, see George Shattuck, *The Oneida Indian Land Claims: A Legal History* (Syracuse, N.Y., 1991); and Hauptman, *Conspiracy of Interests: Iroquois Dispossession and the Rise of New York State* (Syracuse, N.Y., 1999). The brilliant attorney Rennard Strickland has recently written another insightful work, a collection of essays on contemporary Native Americans: *Tonto's Revenge: Reflections on American Indian Culture and Policy* (Albuquerque, N. Mex., 1997). The best work on the Indian experiences in Vietnam and after is Tom Holm, *Strong Hearts, Wounded Souls: Native American Veterans of the Vietnam War* (Austin, Tex., 1996).

Four autobiographies are essential to understanding Native Americans in the second half of the twentieth century: Wilma Mankiller and Michael Wallis, *Mankiller: A Chief and Her People* (New York, 1993); Frank Mitchell, *Navajo Blessingway Singer: The Autobiography of Frank Mitchell, 1881–1967,* Charlotte Frisbie and David McAllester, Eds. (Tucson, Ariz., 1978); Clinton Rickard, *Fighting Tuscarora: The Autobiography of Chief Clinton Rickard,* Barbara Graymont, Ed. (Syracuse, N.Y., 1973); and, for the most accurate account of the Alcatraz takeover, Adam Fortunate Eagle Nordwall, *Heart of the Rock* (Norman, Okla., 2001).

Part III ❧
The Night is Far Gone,
The Day is Near

On most Indian reservations the land resources are insufficient either in quantity or quality to support the present population. Population is increasing much faster than the national rate, industrial development is negligible, and a large portion of the inhabitants face the alternative of remaining wholly or partially unemployed or of leaving home to seek employment. . . . To attain a fully adequate standard of living comparable to that of the national average, it is probable that more than half of all Indians would have to seek their livelihood off reservation.

— Dillon S. Myer, Commissioner of Indian Affairs

To say that there has been an American Indian cultural renaissance over the last thirty years is a pale statement of the obvious. American Indians, young and old, are reinvesting their tribal cultures with a commitment and energy that is inspiring. Young people are flocking to cultural activities of all sorts, clamoring to participate, while in previous years older generations had despaired of being able to preserve certain traditions. Now, there is no need to worry about the future of Indian cultures.

— JoAllyn Archambault, Standing Rock Sioux

Grand Entry at the American Indian Center's 46th Annual Powwow. © 2001 by Warren
Perlstein, All Rights Reserved

Chapter 13

Bury My Heart in Smog

Urban Indians

Blue Clark

*T*heir lives were a circle.

The American Indian husband and wife were born on a reservation or in a rural Indian community. Indian grandparents helped raise them as youngsters, and Indian aunts and uncles assisted their transition from childhood to adulthood. Once married, the Indian couple moved to a town to obtain money. There they had and brought up their own children.

The curve of their circle began with frequent visits to their reservation kinfolk to maintain cultural ties. The circle was completed when the couple retired with a little money to live out their lives back in the land of their ancestors' birth. The big city provided hardly more than a street with a house number. Home was not their urban residence. Home was where traditions were rooted.

History

Before the turn of the twentieth century, official U.S. government policy encouraged the placement of boarding-school Indian youth in white Americans' homes during the summers and holidays. Called the outing system, the policy aimed to foster assimilation and prevent the Indian student from returning to "the blanket" on the reservation. Many such "outing-system" Indians did indeed join an urbanizing America and remain in or near a city after finishing school. Using their newly acquired training and skills, they found jobs that allowed them to send some extra money back to their reservation family.[1]

An 1884 Supreme Court decision underscored the dilemma for the Indian. A Sioux Indian named Elk moved from his reservation to Omaha, Nebraska. He ended his tribal membership when he entered the city. However, he was denied the right to vote in a municipal election, which the Supreme Court upheld. The decision left Elk without his tribal membership as well as without normal citizen-

---

1 Although the term *urban Indians* is widely used, and the practice is continued in the present chapter because of the ease of the phrase, it is wrong. A more correct phrasing is Indians in an urban setting. Indians are not really urban; they reside in cities, then return to their reservation or rural homes. Many Indians do not display the characteristics of an urban resident, as for instance, aggressiveness, materialism, and white and middle-class values.

ship rights. The decree pointed out the irony of the assimilation policy because once Elk left his tribe, he became a stateless person.

To discourage the alleged idleness of the dole, the Indian Service in 1903 began make-work projects on Indian reservations to replace the practice of merely dispersing government rations. Officials hoped that in the process of turning hunters into laborers, the government would, in time, spend far less money on Indians. Two years later, Charles E. Dagenett of the Bureau of Indian Affairs (BIA) opened a small office to help find off-reservation employment for Indians in the Southwest. Dagenett, a Peoria Indian, provided Indian gang labor to railroads, seasonal agricultural workers, and outing employment for Indian girls to work as domestics in towns.

The Dagenett plan grew modestly but steadily. The idea spread slowly from the Denver office into the northern Plains region and into southern California. Dagenett contacted potential employers who had a railroad project or irrigation channel, made arrangements for Indian workers, persuaded the area superintendent of Indians to deliver the laborers, and then encouraged the Indians in the nearest agency to go to work. Congress appropriated small sums of money in 1907 and 1911 to increase on-reservation economic development as well as off-reservation employment. Dagenett's efforts assisted the urban transition of the first generation of city Indians in recent history. These few city workers and their families became the nucleus of the large numbers of urban Indians in the United States today.

The Indian railroad workers and farm day-laborers lived on the outskirts of cities in squatter camps. In the 1920s, the Meriam report survey staff discovered deplorable conditions in the migrants' settlements. There, in tents or crude shacks, Indians lived without running water and sanitary facilities. Still, these workers made more money than their reservation relatives did. Towns and cities near concentrations of Indian reservations and rural communities naturally received the largest numbers of Indian migrants from the 1920s onward.

Meanwhile, U.S. foreign involvement offered other avenues for employment experience: over 10,000 American Indian men served in the U.S. armed forces during World War I, while some Indian women held factory jobs to replace men in the service. In addition, whole families of Indians moved under government sponsorship to work in defense-related industries. For some of the nation's Indians, the wartime exposure to the nonreservation world served as a bridge between cultures. The agent for the Southern Cheyenne reported with obvious satisfaction after the war:

> One Cheyenne, typical, no account, reservation Indian with long hair went to France, was wounded, gassed, and shell shocked. Was returned, honorably discharged. He reported to the agency office square shouldered, level eyed, courteous, self-reliant, and talked intelligently. A wonderful transformation, and caused by contact with the outside world. He is at work.

The skills that many Indians learned in the employment sector or overseas benefited them once they took up residence in the nation's cities. However, their numbers paled in comparison to the vast majority of Indians who continued to live on reservations and in other rural enclaves. Between the two world wars, Indians traveled to Oklahoma cities in the largest numbers, as the trend in urbanization of Indians increased.

The Great Depression brought further urbanization pressures to bear on Indians. When Indians faced starvation during the earliest years of the Depression, they received a small share of the federal funds of the New Deal. With part of the funds, the BIA expanded its off-reservation employment program. The plan, established in 1930, focused on finding jobs for boarding-school graduates, who had skills and the important sponsorship of their school and agency superintendents. The Bureau opened ten such employment services near reservations in the Southwest in the hope of locating urban employment for Native workers. In addition, the Indian Division of the New Deal's Civilian Conservation Corps employed some 20,000 Indians each year from 1933 to 1943. Unfortunately, as the Depression worsened, so did the placement record of the revitalized Guidance and Placement Division of the Indian Service. Job opportunities dried up for Indians and non-Indians alike. In 1940 the Bureau finally closed its employment services sector.

The United States' entry into World War II provided another boost to Indian urbanization. Between 1941 and 1945, an estimated 150,000 Indians participated directly in the agricultural, industrial, and armed services aspects of the nation's war effort. For the first time, large numbers of Indians left reservations bound for cities, where they found gainful employment in defense-related factories. With that push, New York City, followed closely by Chicago, took the lead in 1940 for Indian urban population. Among the Navajo, located in the Southwest, over 3,600 persons saw direct military service, while over 15,000 Navajos moved into urban defense-industry jobs.

Navajo and other GIs and urban workers who returned to Indian reservations after the war faced hard times that grew harsher still as the years passed. The New Deal programs were gone. They were no longer as welcome in urban factories. And knowledge learned in the Pacific theater campaigns or in defense-industry factories had no outlet on the reservation. Even veterans trained for civilian careers could find no jobs. When nearby towns failed to offer employment opportunities, idleness turned to restlessness in the postwar recession.

Building on a special program for placing selected Navajo youth in off-reservation jobs, the federal government opened job-placement offices in Denver, Salt Lake City, and Los Angeles in 1948. Congress responded with a labor recruitment and relief measure (Public Law 390) and then with the Navajo-Hopi rehabilitation act in 1950 (Public Law 474) to encourage on-reservation relief and development and additional off-reservation employment. While shrouded in concern, here was yet another removal effort. The object of the new legislation partly was to move the overcrowded Indian reservation population to cities. In this case, instead of a "Long Walk," the Navajos took a long ride on a bus. The following year one of the most famous Indians of the era, Ira Hayes, arrived in Chicago aboard a bus. He did not like the city and resented the coercion used to gain his transfer from his loving Pima family in Arizona to the lonely streets of Chicago. His was a complaint heard over and over from other relocated Indians.

In 1954 the BIA changed the name of the relocation policy to the Voluntary Relocation Program to sweeten the image of the operation as well as to mute the sting of what opponents termed "pressured relocation."

The cold-blooded image of the relocation program had grown in part from the application of the controversial federal policy of termination. Termination meant an end of the federal trust protection over Indian lands and the "transfer of Bureau functions to the Indians themselves or to appropriate agencies of local, State, or Federal government." Just as in the earlier allotment policy, the role of relocation was to terminate the Indians' relationship with the land and sever their relationship with the federal government. The government would "get out of the Indian business" even if the cost was the loss of Indian lives and lands. The chief of the relocation division of the BIA stated at the inception of the program that, "The sooner we can get out, the better it will be. . . ."

Indian urbanization changed in both pace and direction. From 1930 to 1960, Indian urban population increased fourfold, and a demographic movement evolved from east to west, from Oklahoma to California. During these years, Indians moved outward, in a circular pattern at times, from their reservation or rural homes to nearby towns and then to more distant cities. Indians of all groups demonstrated the greatest and most rapid increases in urban population in the United States for that period. Most Indians who headed east landed in New York City. In the Midwest, Chicago most often served as journey's end.

Since 1960, Indians in growing numbers have moved farther away from their reservations. The trend continues. Nearly one-fourth of all Indians moving to another state move to California, the favorite destination for most western Indians who decide to leave home. The great majority of these persons settle in urban centers.

New forces and individuals gathered in cities to confront Indian policymakers in the 1960s. Some of the Indian youth by the early years of the decade had attended urban colleges. Though they were more articulate and more aggressive than their elders were, they retained a strong link to their reservations. The more educated Indian youth had seen the problems their people faced in the cities and felt the anguish of governmental neglect of Native lives. They had also been exposed to the materialism of towns and to the organizational activities of the civil rights and antiwar groups that were beginning to stir on campuses.

American Indians in various communities also began to air their concerns in conferences and public hearings. Indians had attended the first national Indian conference to consider off-reservation problems in Seattle in early 1968. The President's National Council on Indian Opportunity held public hearings in 1968 and 1969 throughout the West. LaDonna Harris, the Comanche Indian wife of a U.S. senator from Oklahoma, chaired the Committee on Urban Indians. Committee members were appalled to hear testimony about chronic problems in an unceasing stream. To point out only one example, in Dallas, Texas, with an estimated 8,000 Indians in the poorer sections of the city in need of municipal recognition and the attendant services thereof, the director of the community action projects was not even aware that there were Indians in his city. In other urban centers, Indians were invisible to municipal agencies and remained the most underserved of all minority groups.

The Council study concluded that "one-half of the Indian population in the United States is located in urban areas. Yet none of the programs of the Federal government are aimed" at urban Indians. The study requested that Congress move some funding to urban regions, that Indians be empowered to make decisions affecting Indians, and that Indians be free to choose the life that they wanted to live without government dictation but with some government funding. Finally, the Council called for the opening of urban legal-aid offices to inform urban Natives of their rights and to jar municipal officials into recognizing Indian rights.

In his historic message to Congress on American Indians the same year, President Richard Nixon recognized "the severe problems faced by urban Indians." He added, "the time has come to break decisively with the past and to create conditions for a new era in which the Indian future is determined by Indian acts and Indian decisions." Responding to the request of Indian people in the hearings, the president officially halted the policy of termination of tribes. He turned the emphasis of relocation from removal to self-help. President Nixon's special message on Indians also specifically underlined the Bureau's obligation to reservation people to the exclusion of urban Natives.

Amid the agitation of activism, the press of public hearings, and the relentless drift of Indians into urban areas, the Bureau determined to change relocation policy. New offices for employment assistance for Indians opened in 1970, and more services to help Indians adjust to off-reservation life were provided. Successful job placement intensified. Even so, vocal opposition continued to mount steadily as more Indians discussed relocation and employment in public forums. Most of those who expressed an opinion supported job training and counseling while at the same time wished an end to the imposition of a move to the city upon an individual unprepared to contend with the bustle of town life.

In 1972, the BIA allowed relocation to end, although it still maintained many of the program's positive features and continued to offer urban Indians counseling, instruction, and employment assistance training. Government money henceforth was channeled into reservation economic development schemes and industrial plants.

In retrospect, what effect did relocation have? Many Indians were strongly coerced into an urban life; many would have chosen such a life eventually, but at their own, less costly pace. In other words, the government hastily transferred the reservation crisis from one area to another. The attention given to relocation took desperately needed resources away from reservations, the government abrogating many responsibilities to Indians in the process. Finally, the migration hardly brought economic well-being to the people relocated. Neither the reservation population nor the relocatees benefited much.

Government relocation as a policy actually brought only one-third of the Indians to cities. Most Indians in urban centers had arrived there without government assistance. Some came to the city to visit relatives, remained there after leaving military service, sought a brother or sister who knew of a job, or arrived there seeking economic gain. First Americans stayed in cities in the hopes of earning more money than they could on their reservation. Those who moved suffered physical and psychological cultural shock. Some suffered trauma so severe they dropped out of any future efforts to better their lot in life. The government attempt to force assimilation on the Indian failed in the city, just as it had failed in the allotment era in an earlier epoch.

Foster care placement of Indian children in non-Indian homes combined with the movement of large numbers of American Indians into cities posed a threat to the very survival of Indian cultural heritage. For the first time, Indian children were born in cities and grew up cut off from their tribal languages and totems. To Indian activists, it appeared that the circle of Indian life was taking a final turn. Congress in 1978 responded and enacted the Indian Child Welfare Act (Public Law 608), designed to protect the "best interests of Indian children." Thereafter, tribal cultural heritage and tribal interests were to be taken into consideration when Indian placements arose.

Governmental leaders' hope that the Indian would disappear into the larger population in the cities did in part take place, as Indians in cities married non-Indian spouses more frequently than did reservation dwellers. Fullblood distinctiveness diluted in urban centers, and most urban Indian women married non-Indian men. But in spite of the thinning of bloodlines, the American Indian had not assimilated into the U.S. urban population. The Native had not melted into the general American populace. None of the historic policies that forced, pressured, and exploited Indians succeeded in ending the separateness of Indians. The Native spirit, the tribal distinction, the yearning for the past, the bitterness of the present, continued. Their spiritual heritage, their ethnic roots, and their tribe remained outside the city for many Indians: urban centers were places in which one earned a living, not places in which one lived a complete life.

Cultural Conflict

In the face of Indians' ability to maintain their separateness, federal government policy hardened during the 1950s. Dillon Myer, Commissioner of Indian Affairs 1950–53, hoped that Indians would melt into the urban populace and cease to be a drain on the federal treasury. Indeed, men like Myer and other termination advocates in the 1950s looked with satisfaction toward the day when Indians lived in cities without any Bureau of Indian Affairs' expenditures of time or money.

Obviously, early expectations were falsely high. Government officials planned for relocation to improve the economic well-being of Native peoples. At the agency office, Indians looked at brochures featuring photographs of suburban, ranch-style houses with picket fences, aimed at enticing wives to town. Similar pictures in pamphlets circulated in reservations also showed women posing next to an electric refrigerator or television set. Such images, with alluring views of city success, stood in stark contrast to the squalor and desperation of daily life on the reservation or in rural communities. Nevertheless, what the relocated Indians actually experienced, whether with Bureau sponsorship or on their own, was quite different from the government-sponsored propaganda.

American Indians have been the most rural group of any in the U.S. population. In many aspects, the city was the polar opposite of the rural Indians' milieu. The rude transition the relocatee faced was analagous to a resident of the United States being swiftly transported to China and then expected to fend for him- or herself. The Indian person new to the city was bewildered, alone, and frightened. He was far from familiar people and things including tribal language, respected elders, longed for valleys, and the coyote, bear, and turtle. City noise contrasted with the solitude and expanse of the reservation. The congestion of town was alien to a person from an extended family in a rural area where one rarely encounters a stranger. The coldness of the average city dweller offended the Indian long accustomed to the camaraderie of relatives. Indeed, the aggressiveness and materialism of city residents appeared rude and crass to a person accustomed to propriety and poverty. Loneliness screamed out in a person once safe in communal quarters at home. Among Indians, outspoken individuality and acquisitiveness stood in glaring contrast to identification with the group. Strict punctuality as opposed to a good-natured and tolerant sense of time confused many Natives.

Some Indians never bridged the great chasm of language. Non-Indians characterized the Indian's polite silence as sullenness. In reality, when the Indian did not respond readily in conversation, he or she may have been giving careful attention to the well-meaning banter the non-Indian person produced in a seemingly endless sociable stream.

In the urban classroom, the silent Indian child did not receive the help he or she needed because the pupil was afraid to speak up or ask the teacher for assistance. One Indian mother reported her frustration in a statement regarding her children who attended a public school, "I hear a lot of things I get sore about, but then I don't do anything about it because of my poor English and all that."

The Indian woman who needed prenatal care did not receive it because she had no telephone and more than likely no automobile in which to travel to a physician. She even may have lacked the bus fare.

Housing customs in cities did not allow large Indian families to dwell under one roof, and municipal ordinances forced extended families to splinter; children no longer obtained the cultural reinforcement from grandparents forced to return to the reservation or to move in with other relatives.

Once in the city for job training, the Indian person typically received instruction in a low-skill job, such as automobile fender repair. The Bureau spent only a short time finding a job for the relocated trainee once instruction was completed. The BIA permitted one job change at the start. A standard joke of the time was that the Indian trainee got a choice of a great variety of occupations in the city, as long as it was as either a welder or a beautician.

Once on the job, though, the worker faced more than the usual adjustment problems. The American Indian from the reservation had not grown up in a home in which the father got up every weekday morning to report to work in order to bring in a weekly paycheck. Indeed, the whole concept of wage labor was not a long-standing ancestral trait. Worse, the laborer might well have to endure the usual round of rude jibes about his "squaw" and derogatory nicknames such as "chief" and "buck." He also likely encountered disparaging albeit corny jokes about the rain: too much rain and the worker was dancing too much; too little, and he needed to do some more.

As the individual Indian worker struggled through the workweek, he realized that grasping at the dream of success could never assure the reality of success. The almost desperate hope of the migrant seemed out of reach. By every measurement, American Indians ranked on the lowest economic and social levels in cities.

Indian people concentrated in service work, domestic, and laborer categories—the lower end of the occupational scale. Urban Indians resided in the most substandard housing, had the least satisfactory sanitary facilities, had the highest rate of illiteracy, commanded the highest rate of diseases per capita, were more often unemployed, and when employed were more often underemployed and received lower wages than did members of any other group in the city. In short, the urban Indian was among the poorest of poor urban dwellers. The Indian in the city was only slightly better off economically than were his or her reservation relatives.

Not surprisingly, some urban Indian family members fell into an all too familiar pattern of frustration, despair, alienation, apathy, and suicidal behavior. City vices may have been easier to pick up than city virtues. Many Indians found temporary companionship in the neighborhood tavern. Because most of the Indians who imbibed did so out of doors or in a bars generally known for their rowdy clientele, the image of the "drunken Indian" quickly emerged. Some Indians entered the revolving door of alcoholism with its arrests, hospitalization, and release back onto skid row. Most American Indian arrests were alcohol-related. Rising absenteeism on the job soon resulted in the layoff of the drinking Indian worker, chalking up one more on the relocation "failure" statistics.

With so many barriers, both brought with them and first encountered in the city, it is a wonder that any relocatees remained in cities. In frustration, desperation, and anxiety, most of the relocated Indians abandoned their tiny apartments, along with any such dreams of making a new and successful life in the city. The data vary widely, but it is believed that between 40 to 70 percent of the relocatees abandoned the city. Some Indians left after as little as three months. The director of social services for the Minneapolis Native American Center, Dennis His Gun, a Sioux, summed up the defeat repeated time and time again:

> But I think everybody who comes to the city has a dream—a dream of making it, a dream about improving their lives. But then prejudice slaps them right in the face and they're worse off. Call it culture shock. When your bubble is burst, there's nothing left but to go back home and start dreaming again.

Nevertheless, some Indians stuck it out, determined to remain in the city to strive for the betterment of their families. Others hesitatingly returned to the city for another try. In all cases, however, the BIA offered no assistance after the time limit for adjustment ended for those who qualified.

Urban Indians therefore sought assistance from other groups. At first, only a few such avenues were open. The forlorn, lost, and confused city dweller could turn to travelers' aid for limited material assistance, but for cultural reinforcement and support the weary Indian family turned most often to relatives, if there were any living nearby. If not, then the migrants sought assistance from other American Indians whom they might encounter in the city.

Another source of support might be an Indian church located in the poorer section of town. Some American Indian churches fostered American Indian centers. In Chicago, St. Augustine's, and in Sioux City, St. Paul's Episcopal Church, provided the nucleus around which developed an American Indian center to aid other needy Indians. In Los Angeles, the American Friends Service Committee provided monetary and clerical assistance for the fledgling American Indian operation, which began as an Indian social club and expanded into an organization providing social services.

The urban Indian center served as a focal point for the complex network of intertribal organizations that had informally begun in the city. As relocation pressures continued, the resources of the centers were stretched to the breaking point. Even the BIA had to expand its services to Indian clients as the volume of need rose. In Chicago, the current and relocated Indians from across the country banded together to form the first Urban Indian Center in the United States. Today, it is recognized by the Smithsonian Institute, National Museum of American Indians

American Indian Center, Chicago. © 2001 by Warren Perlstein, All Rights Reserved

as the oldest urban Indian center in the United States. Gradually, more Indians became involved, as new skills were learned and Indian cultural values were successfully used in assisting Indians in cities.

To break the barrier of adjustment to the city, some urban migrants clustered in a particular district or neighborhood, creating a cultural enclave wherein Native language and Native customs would predominate, lessening the blow of culture shock for the individual inhabitants.

In time, a myriad of clubs, guilds, societies, and other organizations sprang into existence in the Indian areas of cities. During the week a Saturday night Indian dance club might host practice sessions for Native drummers, as well as meetings in which the young and elderly might gather for conversation about the week's activities. An Indian powwow club might meet regularly to perform dances and ceremonies as a link to the past. Sometimes talented members might perform for pay for other civic groups, but most often those in the club carried on cherished traditions for the cultural enrichment of its own members.

Help in adjusting also came from the cyclical movement of Indian families back to the reservation, purposely done to maintain kinship ties, attend important ceremonies, and share in some tribal experiences. Many Indians traveled the summer circuit of reservation powwows and ceremonials: Navajo families commuted from Albuquerque to the Navajo Reservation, while Sioux families journeyed from the workplace in Denver to the Rosebud Reservation; and Mohawks working in the steel industry returned to their reservations for social gatherings. One Onondaga ironworker apprentice offered the following explanation of the circular traveling he did yearly. Fortunately, his employer understood and allowed his absences:

> I missed five or six days of school to go home for Midwinters, for the Ceremonies. We have the longest Midwinters at Onondaga, lasts 18 to 21 days, it's our New Year, it's like Thanksgiving for different things, with a separate day for each. I'm one of the younger singers, that sings the spiritual songs as well as the social songs . . . it's more important to me right now that I went home for the Ceremonies than to continue in school.

Natives carried strong cultural ties into the cities, too. Indian community center socials, the all-night "49" or Indian sing that may have used a car hood as an impromptu drum, and the spread of the powwow by the urban phenomenon among Indians continued Indian traditions. Indian culture had not died out in the cities, as was the ardent hope when relocation began. Even Christian Indian churches retained much of the flavor and essence of Indian traditions. The music at the Fifth Sunday Sing at an Indian Christian church incorporated reservation vocales, melodies, and musical style. Other singers in the urban region blended Indian and mainstream American music. Paul Ortega entertained audiences with a folk style, while Floyd Westerman utilized country and western arrangements, and Larry Emerson inspired Indian youth with Christian evangelism. The band XIT as well as Billy Thundercloud, Redbone, and Jim Pepper offered American Indian rock music.

A strong Plains Indian stream flowed through modern Indian ceremonial patterns, centered on the powwow and Indian art. The city gallery featured western Indian art of the Plains and Southwest. The dual role of Indian and urbanite was reinforced through adoption of intertribal art forms and ceremonial costuming. One Indian artist might have painted a scene of another's tribe, while color mixtures representing clan membership may have been mingled into another tribal artist's work on canvas. On the powwow field, a dancer of one tribe might have borrowed the beadwork design or featherwork of his neighbor from another tribe. An Indian woman from the Pacific Northwest might participate in a Plains-style powwow, even though such was not her home tradition.

The mixing of styles and traits is called Pan-Indianism. The movement formed a bridge between tribes and brought marginal mixed-bloods back into full-blood ceremonies. All of the participants shared in the cultural spirituality that set Indians apart from their non-Indian neighbors. What may have appeared to an outsider as a self-indulgent social gathering done to the hypnotic repetition of a drum, was in reality a vehicle to build an ethnic identity, break social isolation, pass on traditions to youth, and reaffirm religious bonds. In Indian associations, many sought refuge from the terrible loss of identity that marked modern urban existence. In the Pacific Northwest, some workers commuted to an Indian Shaker Church service. On the Plains, the Indian individual could have attended a peyote ceremony of the Native American Church. The services blended traditional ritual with Christian symbolism, rural with urban worshippers, and Native languages with English.

Conclusion

The sociological and anthropological literature that examined urban Natives of North America found that women weathered the acculturation of cities better than men did. Traditional couples survived, especially those with previous job experience, better than did individuals. All, however, underwent profound shock when they entered the alien world of urban centers. Those who had successful experiences in towns bordering reservations generally fared better than did those who came directly from reservations or rural communities and who lacked communication and work skills.

Native peoples have not vanished down concrete sidewalks. Recent policies did not drastically change Native attachment to a separate identity. American Indians maintained their customs and lifeways in cities for a very long time. Mission Indians within the San Antonio, Texas, church compounds stubbornly clung to their heritage in spite of Spanish efforts to assimilate them. Indian people of Long Island and Massachusetts continued their links with the past in the face of European American assimilation. American Indians have been a vital part of urban life in the Americas since the first settlements of Europeans. Natives will continue to play an important role in cities in the United States as part of an enduring legacy.

Suggested Reading

Literary works offer a glimpse into the lives of urban Indians. Byrd Baylor's *Yes Is Better Than No* (New York, 1977) is a delightful tragicomic novel; Dan Cushman penned an uproarious account of the escapades of an Indian GI on the reservation who commutes to the city, leading his mother often to exclaim *Stay Away, Joe* (New York, 1953); while Clair Huffaker detailed the antics of a fictitious reservation Indian on the outskirts of Phoenix in *Nobody Loves a Drunken Indian* (New York, 1967). Well-known Indian novelist and poet James Welch in *The Death of Jim Loney* (New York, 1979) and *The Indian Lawyer* (New York, 1990) offered a dark, somber account of mixed-blood alienation from white and Indian society. Chippewa writer Gerald Vizenor through many works, especially *Dead Voices* (Norman, Okla., 1994), cast light on the struggles of contemporary Indians. The Indian Child Welfare Act forms the ever-present background in Barbara Kingsolver's *Pigs in Heaven* (New York, 1993). Indian author Janet Campbell Hale in her autobiographical *Bloodlines* (New York, 1993) described urban life, while in her novel *The Jailing of Cecilia Capture* (New York, 1985) depicted the troubled experjences of an Indian female law student in the San Francisco Bay Area. The mixed-blood characters that populate Louis Owens's, Sherman Alexie's, and Louise Erdrich's novels, Albertine Strong's *Deluge* (New York, 1997), Ignatia Broker's *Night Flying Woman* (St. Paul, Minn., 1983), and Darryl Wilson's *Morning the Sun Went Down* (Berkeley, Calif., 1998), chronicle in literary form urban Indians' tribulations. *Grand Avenue* (New York, 1995) by Greg Sarris became an acclaimed HBO film (1996). The paradox of the Indian in the city is the subject of W. S. Penn's *The Absence of Angels* (Norman, Okla., 1995), as well as *When Nickels Were Indians* (Washington, D.C., 1997) by his sister Patricia Penn Hilden. *Survivor's Medicine* (Norman, Okla., 1998) by E. Donald Two-Rivers and Hanay Geiogamah's *New Native American Drama* (Norman, Okla., 1980) are gritty portrayals of urban Indian themes. Betty Louise Bell's *Faces in the Moon* (Norman, Okla., 1994) and *Grass Dancer* (New York, 1994) by Susan Power stress the return to Indian roots. Acoma writer Simon Ortiz, "Woman Singing," in John R. Milton, ed., *The American Indian Speaks* (Vermillion, S. Dak., 1969): 34–44, provided one of the finest literary treatments of the cultural "pull" of the reservation and kinfolk.

Scholarly literature abounds on the urban Indian. Among the more useful are the collected papers in Jack Waddell and Michael Watson, eds., *The American Indian in Urban Society* (Boston, 1971); the government report, *Urban and Rural Non-Reservation Indians* (Washington, D.C., 1977) by the American Indian Policy Review Commission; the focused study of Edmund Danziger, *Survival and Regeneration: Detroit's American Indian Community* (Detroit, 1991); the revised *Indian Country, L.A.* (Champaign, Ill., 1999) by Joan Weibel-Orlando; *The Urban Indian Experience in America* by Donald L. Fixico (Albuquerque, N. Mex., 2000); and the collection of Susan Lobo and Kurt Peters, eds., *American Indians and the Urban Experience* (Walnut Creek, Calif., 2001). Personal Indian insights are supplemented by: Mark Momoe's *An Indian in White America*, edited by Carolyn Reyer (Philadelphia, 1995); the tragic *Chief: Life History of Eugene Delorme, Imprisoned Santee Sioux* edited by Inez Cardozo-Freeman (Lincoln, Nebr., 1993); and Emily Benedek's *Beyond the Four Corners of the World* (New York, 1995) on the odyssey of Ella Bedonie's Navajo family.

Chapter 14 ❧
Native Sovereignty

Then and Now in California and the Northwest

Clifford E. Trafzer

Native sovereignty is a term used a great deal by contemporary Native Americans, a defining and significant term in English that indicates that all power rests with Native people and their chosen representatives. American Indians view sovereignty in a unique way, one based on tribal experience and memory. Native sovereignty is not a power derived from the United States, Canada, or any other foreign nation. Native sovereignty is a gift of creation received when holy forces first established "laws" by which American Indians should live. Thus, Native American sovereignty in California, the Northwest, and elsewhere emerged at the beginning of time, during the creative era of American Indian history when animal and plant people interacted with spiritual forces and elements of the natural environment to put the world into motion. Native sovereignty is a tribal construct that continues to operate within tribal societies in California and the Northwest to this day.

According to history of the Maidu Indians of northern California, water once covered every part of the Earth. Although there was no land, life existed. At this time, Earth Maker and Coyote floated on a raft in an endless sea, each day peering off across the water wondering where the sea met the sky. One day Earth Maker told Coyote that he had a vision of solid land, a place where there would be sun, moon, clouds, mountains, valleys, lakes, rivers, rain, deserts, forests, fog, plants, animals, and other elements of the natural environment. Earth Maker conceived of such a place, the Earth, and put his vision into focus by singing about creation. He sang until Robin, fluttering above a nest floating in the sea, sang back to him. Together they sang until Earth Maker proclaimed that he would create Earth from Robin's nest by extending ropes in different directions and placing mud from the bottom of the Ocean onto the ropes. Earth Maker created the Earth and all its natural features before creating plants and animals—and ultimately the people.

Earth Maker gave all the people laws by which to live. He determined that there would be life and death, sunlight and darkness, males and females. He instructed the people in sexual relations and forbade them to marry closely related partners. Earth Maker told the people to care for their children and teach them the dances, songs, stories, and ceremonies of the people. Earth Maker gave the people their lands and empowered them with sovereignty so that Maidus could make choices for themselves in accordance with traditional laws.

In similar fashion, Coyote was both a creative and destructive force in Northwestern Indian history. Among the *Nimipu* or Nez Perce, Coyote feared for his life when a great monster set about to eat everything that he could swallow. Before the monster reached him, Coyote tied himself to the earth, but the great monster managed to swallow him anyway. But wise Coyote had prepared for this ordeal and faced it bravely and confidently. Inside the monster's stomach, Coyote used five stone knives that he previously had hidden on his body to cut away at the insides of the monster, finally penetrating its heart and killing it. Afterward, Coyote cut the monster to pieces, throwing the body parts in different directions and thusly creating the many diverse tribes. According to the Nez Perce, Coyote used the blood of the monster to create the greatest of people, the Nimipu.

After creating the Nez Perce people, Coyote created fruits, vegetables, plants, and animals. He told the people how, where, and when to hunt and gather, establishing the laws for all living things. One of the laws maintained that no one should ever stop the natural flow of the Columbia River. Nevertheless, five giant women called the *Tah Tah Kleah* built a dam on the river to prevent the salmon from traveling upstream. That way, the monster women could harvest all the fish, but in doing so they deprived the people upriver from eating the river's fish in accordance with the law. When the people met in council to discuss their course of action, only Coyote volunteered to break the fish dam and reestablish the old law allowing the river to run freely. Brave Coyote outsmarted the five giant women, broke the fish dam, and became a salmon chief, leading the fish into the inland Northwest to spawn. Coyote empowered the people to take their just share of fish but not to exploit the salmon. Coyote gave the people sovereignty at the time of creation, and as long as the people followed Native laws, they could freely determine their village, tribal, and inter-tribal organizations and personal activities.

For thousands of years, American Indian families, villages, and "tribes" enjoyed their Native sovereignty, fending off threats from various enemies but generally secure in their own dominion. To be sure, no utopia existed prior to the European invasion of California or the Northwest, as Indians fought other Indians, conquered lands, and forced the diaspora of others. However, within families, villages, and tribes, people largely maintained their right to determine their own course of actions and enjoyed a great deal of autonomy. They adhered to tribal laws, including kinship, marriage, religious, civil, and criminal law—all set down at the time of creation and used by people for generations before the arrival of foreigners. Natives chose their leaders, whom they replaced when necessary. They decided when and where to hunt, fish, farm, and gather. In short, the people assumed sovereignty as a natural right until the arrival of non-Natives.

During the sixteenth and seventeenth centuries, European adventurers traveled along the Pacific Coast, stopping briefly in present-day Alta California, Oregon, Washington, Alaska, and British Columbia. Most textbooks present these expeditions as harbingers of progress, civilization, trade, enlightenment, and advanced settlement. But the arrival of Spanish, Russian, British, and, finally, American explorers represent the onset of far more negative things to Native Americans. Although First Nations people did not know it at the time, the European and American newcomers laid claim to their lands and all of their resources, assuming a "right of discovery." Native Americans living along the Pacific Coast believed themselves superior to the foreigners, just as the Americans and European explorers believed themselves superior to Native Americans. The difference was that Europeans and Americans would eventually act on their assumption of superiority, subjugating American Indians and spreading their hegemony over Native peoples. While these foreigners did indeed challenge Native sovereignty, particularly after they established permanent settlements on Native lands, Native Americans argue that at no time did Native people relinquish their rights to determine their own destinies: never did they surrender their Native or cultural sovereignty.

In 1741, Vitus Bering claimed the Aleutian Islands, and later all of Alaska, for Tsarist Russia. Soon thereafter, Russian traders exploited Native men, women, and children in the far Northwest, forcing the people into slavery in order to hunt the numerous fur-bearing animals of the region and collect their pelts. The Aleuts and Inuits resisted the Europeans' designs, so between 1762 and 1765, Russians launched a campaign of near-extermination, reducing the Aleut population from roughly 25,000 to 2,500 persons. Russian traders, merchants, and missionaries eventually established trading centers and towns in southeast Alaska. In 1812, Russians resettled on Pomo and Coastal Miwok lands at Fort Ross, where they raised crops to support the Russian colonies to the north. By this time, the Spanish were firmly established in California, where they had planted presidios, missions, and pueblos among American Indians. Like the arrival of Russians in the Aleutians and Alaska, the settlement of Spaniards in California threatened the sovereignty of regional Indians.

In 1769, the Franciscan priest Junípero Serra led the Sacred Expedition into Alta California as part of a larger effort to resettle Native lands, introduce Catholicism, and establish Spanish rule. Leading the military wing of the expedition was Captain Gaspar de Portola, while Juan Perez navigated supply ships northward from Acapulco. Many diverse bands of Kumeyaay Indians lived in the area, occupying several autonomous villages, including Cosoy, near the present-day Old Town district of San Diego. There the Spanish established a fledgling presidio and mission and immediately challenged the Kumeyaay for control of the region. While some Kumeyaay willingly worked for the Spanish, helping them build the mission and fort, others the Spanish impressed into their service as laborers, the foreigners deeming the Kumeyaay subjects of the Spanish crown

The California Missions

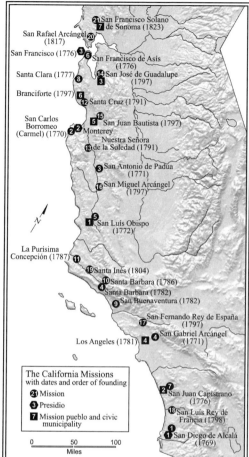

San Rafael Arcángel ㉒ (1817)

San Francisco (1776) ❸❻ San Francisco de Asís (1776)

㉑ San Francisco Solano ❼ de Sonoma (1823)

Santa Clara (1777) ❽ ⑭ San José de Guadalupe ❸ (1797)

Branciforte (1797) ❻ ⑫ Santa Cruz (1791)

San Carlos Borromeo (Carmel) (1770) ㉒ ⑮ ❺ San Juan Bautista (1797) Monterey

Nuestra Señora ⑬ de la Soledad (1791)

❸ San Antonio de Padua (1771)

⑯ San Miguel Arcángel (1797)

❺ ❶ San Luis Obispo (1772)

La Purísima Concepción (1787) ⑪

⑲ Santa Inés (1804) ⑩ Santa Bárbara (1786) ❹ Santa Barbara (1782) ❾ San Buenaventura (1782)

San Fernando Rey de España (1797) ⑰ ❹ San Gabriel Arcángel Los Angeles (1781) ❹ (1771)

The California Missions
with dates and order of founding
㉑ Mission
❸ Presidio
❼ Mission pueblo and civic municipality

0   50   100
Miles

㉗ San Juan Capistrano (1776)
⑱ San Luis Rey de Francia (1798)
❶ San Diego de Alcalá (1769)

and thereby under Spanish authority. While the Kumeyaay at Cosoy and other villages understood that the newcomers acted with impunity and superiority, the Native people acted and reacted in the best manner open to them to ensure their safety and well-being. Some Kumeyaay worked with the newcomers while others fled to isolated villages where they continued their lives in a "traditional" manner. In both cases, the Kumeyaay did not surrender their right of self-determination: they simply had to adjust to a new and dangerous situation.

So whether they outwardly cooperated with the newcomers or avoided them entirely, the Kumeyaay retained Native sovereignty and resisted Spanish rule. Cahuilla scholar Edward Castillo has stated that "permanent colonization almost from the beginning raised native suspicions and ultimately led to violence." When presidio soldiers raped Kumeyaay women, abused children, and threatened Native men for protecting their family members, Father Luis Jayme asked Father Serra to move Mission San Diego de Acala farther up the San Diego River. In 1775, Serra consented to the request, and Father Jayme moved the mission six miles up the river to the Kumeyaay village of Nipaquay—the present site of San Diego Mission. Some Indians helped build the new mission, while others fled the mission to live with friends and relatives further in the interior. Tensions between the Spanish and Indians continued, however. Indians resented forced labor, separation of the young people from their parents, poor food, and foreign law (both civic and Church law). In 1775, the Kumeyaay rose in rebellion against the Spanish, killing Father Jayme and setting aside Spanish law to regain control of their lives. The revolt lasted only briefly before Spanish soldiers retook the mission site and much of the surrounding area. Nevertheless, the rekindled Native sovereignty was never again extinguished. Some Kumeyaay re-

mained with their relatives away from the mission, while others returned voluntarily or forcibly back into the mission system. The Kumeyaay may have had to
bend to foreign powers in order to survive under new circumstances, but they
never gave up their belief that they should and would decide their own course of
action.

The same is true of the Quechan of southeastern California, a Hokan-speak-
ing people often called the Yuma Indians. For many generations the Quechans
had lived successfully in the Colorado Desert, near the junction of the Colorado
and Gila rivers. There they developed a culture based on agriculture, farming the
bottomlands of both rivers and supplementing their crop harvests by hunting
and gathering. The Quechans first met the Spanish in 1540, when Hernando de
Alarcón and Melchior Díaz visited their lands as arms of the famous expedition
of Francisco Vasquez de Coronado. Although neither of the men remained in the
region, the Quechans were soon to meet other Spaniards, the most influential of
whom was Father Francisco Tomas Garcés. He first visited their homelands in
1771, while on an expedition down the Gila in search of an improved land route
to Alta California. Quechans already had knowledge of the Spanish in California,
indicating as much through hand signs and drawings of the ocean's waves. Garcés
left Quechan territory and explored along the present border of Mexico and California, determining that if one were to cross the mountains to the west, one could
reach the Pacific Coast.

Of course, Garcés was correct, but instead of continuing to the coast he
returned to San Xavier del Bac before traveling south to the presidio of Tubac,
where he related his theory to Captain Juan Bautista de Anza. Anza eagerly planned
an expedition to open the land route from Sonora to California, but fighting with
Apaches intervened, forcing him to delay his expedition until 1774. With a few
Spanish soldiers, and accompanied by Father Garcés, Captain Anza led the first
European overland expedition along the present-day international border, then
an ancient Indian trail that the Spanish called *El Camino del Diablo* (the Devil's
Highway). The route took them through a remote but beautiful desert landscape
where there is little water. Still, the expedition arrived safely into the welcoming
ministrations of several Quechans. Anza and Garcés found a particularly kind
friend in a man they called Salvador Palma, one of many local headmen and one
who originally championed the Spanish. Palma and other Quechans treated the
Spanish as foreign dignitaries, honoring them, feeding them, and ferrying them
across the Colorado River. Now the expedition proceeded across the Colorado
Desert and the coastal range, arriving safely at Mission San Gabriel and thus
becoming the first Spaniards to use a land route from Sonora to California.

Past historians have argued that Anza's expedition of 1774 was a watershed
in the history of the Spanish borderlands because it opened a new emigrant trail
to Alta California. This is correct, but the expedition also signaled a new era of
tragedy and change for the Quechans, particularly Palma, who did not understand the full implications of the Spanish expeditions through his homeland.

Perhaps some Quechan leaders warned of future problems, but if so, the cautions went unheeded, as Palma maintained his friendship with Anza, Garcés, and the other Spaniards. In fact, Spanish documents suggest that Palma encouraged the Spaniards to return to the Quechan homelands (along the Colorado River near present-day Yuma, Arizona; Winterhaven, California; and Algodones, Mexico), which both Anza and Garcés did in 1775. This time, however, the Spanish arrived with 240 emigrants on their way to resettle lands already claimed by California's First Nations. If we are to believe Spanish documents, the Quechans asked the Spanish to remain with them in their homelands, but Anza explained that the Spanish immigrants were on their way to California. Ultimately, this group of people settled near the shores of a great bay they found and named San Francisco. Their presence would forever alter the lives of the people already living there—the Ohlone Indians of the Bay Area.

In 1776, Spanish settlers claimed the area surrounding San Francisco as their own, taking over Native lands and asserting their civil, military, and religious laws. The Ohlones had their own laws and had lived without European interference for generations, but the arrival of Spanish settlers, soldiers, and missionaries changed all of this, as the Spanish asserted their dominance over Native people. Spaniards systematically stole Indian lands and allowed their cattle, horses, burros, and mules to graze on Native crops. The newcomers instituted Spanish laws and punished Ohlones for asserting their indigenous rights. Some Ohlones became part of the mission system, while others fled into the interior to remain apart from the Spanish. Here, again, the basic pattern of what happened to Native Americans everywhere when confronted with European settlement played itself out, but in no way does this suggest that the people relinquished their Native sovereignty. In fact, Indian agency in the face of Spanish domination was so marked that most Native people refused to succumb to Spanish power and demands.

This was clearly the case among the Quechans when the Spanish returned again to Yuma Crossing in 1781 to establish a civil, military, and missionary presence at places the Spanish described as San Pablo y San Pedro de Bicuñer and La Purisima de la Concepcíon. That same year the Spanish crown established two civil settlements, two missions, and one presidio among the Quechans. Father Garcés led four missionaries in building two distinct missions about fifteen miles apart to minister to two large Quechan populations. While the priests impressed Indians into service to construct the missions, civil authorities claimed Native lands and forced Indians to clear trees and brush for homes and gardens. Some Quechans joined in the colonizing effort, while others protested. Palma led the pro-Spanish faction until the Spanish whipped one of his sons along with others, stole Quechan lands, impressed Indians into forced labor, and allowed horses and cattle to graze on Native foods growing along the river. Then Palma disappeared from the scene, working quietly with other leaders to unify Quechans against his former friends. Garcés worried that the Quechans were planning an attack, but

Captain Fernando Rivera y Moncada did not heed the Father's concerns, believing that the Indians would never rebel in the July heat. Rivera was wrong.

On July 17, 1781, Quechans asserted their sovereignty and superiority, launching a well-planned, three-prong attack that caught the Spanish by surprise. One group of Quechan warriors destroyed the small detachment of soldiers living on the south bank of the river, in present-day Yuma, Arizona, while two other groups attacked the settlement and church at both Bicuner and Concepcíon. Quechan warriors concentrated on killing the men, but they likely also killed a few women and children during the revolution. The warriors killed the two priests at Bicuner, but they originally spared Fathers Garcés and Juan Barrenache, who gathered the survivors at Concepcíon and led them south to the rocky knoll later called Pilot Knob. They lived there a few days praying for help, but one morning a group of Indians surrounded the survivors and ordered the priests to come out to talk. According to Quechan elders Lee Emerson and Henry DeCourse, disenchanted Tohono o'Odham people killed the priests or pushed the Quechans into attacking the two Franciscans. During the 1970s, the two Quechan elders stated that Odham warriors used war clubs to kill the two priests, and they maintained that when the Catholics fell to the ground, the Indians watched their souls leave their bodies and ascend into the sky. Historians may never know for certain who killed Fathers Garcés and Barrenache, but it is known that in the aftermath of the uprising, Spanish soldiers rescued the captives and rarely used the Quechan crossing on the Colorado River again. For the most part, the Quechans ruled their homelands uncontested until the 1840s, when the people of a new nation, the United States of America, appeared to threaten their security.

The arrival of whites meant something even more devastating to Indians than their depopulation resulting from communicable diseases such as smallpox, cholera, malaria, measles, and influenza, to which they had not been previously exposed. The Indians were unaware that Europeans and then the Americans claimed their homelands by right of discovery, arbitrarily laying claim to vast regions of the Pacific Northwest. During the late eighteenth and early nineteenth century, British, American, Russian, Spanish, and other naval expeditions plied the waters of the Pacific Coast, visiting and trading with Native Americans from California to Alaska. It is doubtful that many Indians worried greatly about the arrival of new men in their lands, because the people had a great sense of security and superiority, at least until the newcomers' diseases spread among them. Some prophets had warned of the coming of new men, and Indians in the interior of present-day Washington and Oregon had prepared for the coming of strangers by singing special songs in honor of the newcomers.

Most Native Americans along the Pacific Coast enjoyed a positive trading relationship with the foreigners, and although the traders thought they received the best end of the trade, Native Americans believed they benefited far more by receiving numerous manufactured goods such as cloth, needles, nails, hatchets, knives, iron, pots, and beads. Natives could either use these goods themselves or trade them with other Indians, receiving much in exchange. Northwestern Indians traded more with the British than with any other foreign nation, but the arrival of Meriwether Lewis and William Clark in the Northwest significantly bolstered the American trade and claim to the region.

In 1805 the Lewis and Clark Corps of Discovery, having pushed up the Missouri River as far as the Mandan villages in North Dakota, turned west and traveled across present-day Montana with the help of the Shoshoni woman Sacajewea, and her husband, the French trader Charboneau. After crossing the lands of the Lemhi Shoshonis of the Rocky Mountains, the American explorers entered the Bitterroot Valley, where they met Flatheads who helped them find the Lolo Trail through the Bitterroot Mountains. On the western edge of the Bitterroots, the Americans met the Nimipu or Nez Perce. Half-starved and half-lost, the rag-tag group was no threat to the Nez Perce, and portions of this nation helped the Americans build canoes and travel down the Clearwater River to the Snake River, and from the Snake to the Columbia. At the confluence of the Snake and Columbia rivers, Yakama and others sang prophecy songs one evening to the Americans all night long. Native prophets had predicted change, but few people believed that these newcomers would inaugurate so much change. Lewis and Clark continued down the Columbia to the Pacific, spending the winter of 1805–1806 among the Clatsop of Oregon. In the spring, Lewis and Clark began the long journey back to St. Louis and from there to spread the word about the bountiful resources of the West.

Long an important trade commodity among many peoples of the world (including American Indians), furs brought fabulous earnings when sold to Asian merchants. Sea-going fur traders had operated along the Pacific Coast for years, but after the Lewis and Clark Expedition, the North West Company, Hudson's Bay Company, and American Fur Company avidly competed for pelts in the Northwest. The expeditions of American and British fur companies to the Northwest brought changes to Native people, most of which were limited to the introduction of new trade items, diseases, and forms of labor. Some Indians worked for the fur companies, but all of them felt the influence of trade items and diseases. Still, few traders challenged Native sovereignty or tried to claim vast regions of the Native Earth. Few traders had any desire to alter Native religions, spiritual practices, or ceremonies. However, a spark of interest in the white people's god led Hudson's Bay traders to send a few Native boys east to study Christianity. When a separate small delegation of Native men traveled to St. Louis in 1831 to seek spiritual knowledge, Protestant churches—and later the Catholic Church—dispatched the first missionaries to the Northwest.

Marcus and Narcissa Whitman established a Presbyterian mission among the Cayuses, while Henry and Eliza Spalding built their mission among the Nez Perce. Both tribes had shown an interest in Christianity, but after the planting of missions in their homelands, some Indians began to question the worthiness of the white people's religion. Over the years several denominations proselytized to the Indians, arguing among themselves about who had the "right" theology. The sectarianism that characterized the nineteenth century has never ended, and neither has the denigration of Native religions by some Christians who dismiss Native religious practice as barbaric, heathenistic, animalistic, and even Satanistic. Missionaries and government agents challenged Native spiritual sovereignty, but they could not destroy Native religions in the region or their spiritual sovereignty. Protestant efforts in the Northwest to Christianize Indians, like the Catholic missions in California, split Native communities and caused internal difficulties that still reverberate among Native people today. But resilient Native groups, particularly those who rejected Christianity, maintained and revitalized their Native religions, ensuring their survival. Although the spiritual component of Native sovereignty has too long been ignored by scholars, it always was and still remains a significant element of Native survival.

After the 1830s, Protestant and Catholic missions were much a part of Northwestern Indian history. However, in Spanish and then Mexican California, Catholicism prevailed well into the 1840s. In 1833, the Mexican government in California secularized the missions, which opened mission lands to private ownership. Some Indians remained at the missions after secularization, but many more took their skills as *vaqueros* and *vaqueras* (cowboys and cowgirls) to work on the many ranchos of California. Indeed, many vaqueros in California were Indians, not *Californios* as generally assumed, who worked for little or no wages. But whether they remained on the missions or lived with their families in native communities attached to the ranches, Indians chose their own course of livelihood. Many other Indians in California lived in communities apart from non-Natives, continuing their age-old subsistence patterns of trading, hunting, gathering with some selective agriculture. Nevertheless, the lives of a great many Indians changed radically after 1846, when the United States fought a war with Mexico to secure a border along the Rio Grande and to take the "Mexican Cession," a vast region that encompassed most of present-day California, Arizona, Nevada, Utah, New Mexico, and Colorado.

By the middle of the nineteenth century, Indians throughout the West , including those in California and the Northwest, were keenly aware that the United States claimed their homelands. After their victory in the war against Mexico, Americans poured into the Pacific West and quickly claimed dominance over the Indians, but Native Americans did not surrender their sovereignty. Indians tried to learn how to deal with the United States and its people, listening to oral stories shared among the people about what others had heard and had learned from personal experience. It was difficult for Native leaders to decide what to do in the face of a new and overwhelming national presence, but they did their best to represent the best interests of their people through words and actions. The many diverse Native cultures reacted to the new situations brought on by American occupation in different ways. Some Indians sought accommodation with the "New Men," agreeing to treaties to pacify the persistent newcomers and then merely going about their business as they always had. Others attacked the whites in an attempt to drive them away, while still others moved away from emigrant trails and non-Native towns. Indians acted and reacted to the new circumstances placed before them as best as they could, drawing on their past experiences to determine their future courses.

Matters worsened after January 1848, however, when Indians working for James Marshall found gold at the Maidu village of Koloma. In one way or another, the Gold Rush that followed influenced the lives of every California Indian and those beyond the future state's borders. Initially, Californios took their Native ranch hands to the gold fields to pan placer deposits, and by 1850, about half of the gold miners were California Indians. While some Indian miners were independent, most of them worked for Californios. In either case, they generally made their own decision about when and where to work, at least until non-Native miners from Oregon began murdering California Indian miners. After 1850, white miners killed Indians indiscriminately, hunting down men, women, and children to kill or enslave. White Indian hunters murdered thousands of Indians, whether or not their victims were miners. Indeed, California became a killing field where ruthless outlaws murdered, raped, and kidnapped California's First Nations people.

The killings significantly reduced the Native population. In 1800, the Native population in California stood between 200,000 and 250,000 persons; on the eve of the Gold Rush, approximately 100,000 California Indians existed. However, between the 1850s to the 1860s, the California Indian population declined to approximately 30,000 persons, and the population continued to decline until 1900, when it slowly began to recover. Most of the killings occurred in northern California, where, of course, miners found the largest gold deposits. However, southern California was not exempt from interracial violence. Emigrants flooded across the Gila Trail, working their way west from Yuma Crossing, across the Colorado Desert, and into the inland mountains of southern California. The Quechans, Cahuillas, Cupenos, Luisenos, Serranos, and Kumeyaay of the region dealt with American emigrants on a regular basis, particularly the Cahuillas and Cupenos occupying the desert and pass regions along the emigrant trail. Some Indians tolerated the white settlers but others chose to end the invasion and control of the region by the United States. Many of California's Native people retaliated, killing whites whenever possible. They too killed men, women, and children, but in comparison with whites, they killed far fewer people.

Antonio Garra, a man of mixed Cahuilla and Cupeno ancestry (and possibly Quechan), organized a confederacy and advocated the defeat of the Americans. His revolt was short-lived and confined to a small area, but it represented the feelings of many Native Americans who understood that the coming of Americans to California presented a permanent and dangerous situation. Juan Antonio, a powerful Cahuilla leader, chose to eliminate Garra and hand him over to the Americans. Perhaps, Juan Antonio recognized an internal threat to his own power base among the Cahuilla, or perhaps he believed that it was in the best interest of his people to cooperate with the Americans. Contemporary Cahuilla elders like Katherine Saubel are not clear about Antonio's motives, but they all understand that his action led officials of the United States and San Diego County to try and execute Garra. The Americans used the execution as a warning to other Indians not to oppose American hegemony in the region. Native Americans in southern California continued to resist American theft of lands and governmental actions, but few of them rose in an outright rebellion against the United States.

Although Juan Antonio had handed over Antonio Garra, he never surrendered his sovereignty or that of his people. This was also the case among the Quechans who rose in a war against emigrants, traders, and ferry operators along the lower Colorado River. Their actions led Major Samuel Peter Heintzelman to lead a multiprong attack on Quechan villages and people during the early 1850s. Quechan warriors fought well during the various frays, but near Picacho Peak along the Colorado River, Chief Huttamines concluded a peace agreement with Heintzelman. The Quechans agreed to allow the U.S. military to occupy Fort Yuma, and they agreed to permit emigrants to pass unmolested along the Gila Trail through the Yuma Crossing and into the Colorado Desert. However, their negotiations with Heintzelman never included the surrender of tribal, personal, spiritual, or cultural sovereignty. For a time, Quechan leaders believed they held the upper hand in the region, but that condition rapidly deteriorated as a result of disease, malnutrition, and political changes brought by the Office of Indian Affairs and the United States Army.

During the early 1850s, the United States sent commissioners to negotiate treaties with California's First Nations. American Indians met with the commissioners up and down the state in 1851–1852, and they signed eighteen agreements creating eighteen large reservations. The tribes would have secured for themselves 7,488,000 acres, or a mere 7.5 percent of California, had the treaties been ratified. The commissioners sent the documents off to the United States Senate for ratification, but in a secret session, the Senate refused to ratify any of the agreements, the senators determining that allowing California Indians to keep even a fraction of their former homelands was unacceptable. The decline of Quechan power, however, is not synonymous to the surrender of sovereignty, and none of the Native people of southern California surrendered their sovereignty, even when they agreed to sign treaties with the United States.

Non-Native Californians wanted all of the land and resources in the Golden State and set out to steal it "legally" by not ratifying the treaties. Government officials in California failed to inform the Indians that they had no legal land base or relationship with the Untied States, and the national government repeatedly failed to protect Indian rights, laws, and lands. In fact, the United States Army and civil officials turned a blind eye when state, county, and local officials—particularly local judges and sheriffs—championed the theft of Indian lands by white settlers. When Indians conducted their seasonal rounds, traveling into the mountains and valleys to hunt, gather, and visit, whites moved onto Indian lands and told returning Natives to find somewhere else to live. Local government officials repeatedly condoned such nefarious actions, making the Indians "strangers in a stolen land."

In California, white settlers wanted Native lands and Native labor, often hiring Indians to work on their ranches because Indians had superior skills as cowboys and ranch hands. In order to acquire labor cheaply, city and county sheriffs often incarcerated Indians for vagrancy, sentencing them to jail because they had no money to pay their fines. Usually non-Indians paid the prisoners' fines, and in return received a court-sanctioned order for the Indians to pay off their debts to society by working for a specified amount of time on a particular ranch. Non-Natives also acquired Native labor by claiming Indian children. Under California Statute 133, a series of laws dubbed "An Act for the Government and Protection of Indians" but in reality a wholesale exploitation of California Indians, whites could become guardians of Indian children. As a result, some whites acquired labor by taking Indian children into their homes, claiming that they did so in the best interest of the children. In fact, some whites abused Native children, forced them to work as slaves, and even sold their charges' sexual favors to others. In the worst cases, outlaws murdered Indian parents and placed the orphaned children under their own custody, subsequently using or selling them at will. Native communities worked desperately to protect their people, particularly the children, but many children nonetheless suffered because government lawmakers and non-Native individuals had their way.

Edward Fitzgerald Beal, a famous explorer, who was selected as California's first superintendent of the Office of Indian Affairs, also exploited Native labor through the reservation system. Through Beal's leadership, the government established five reservations in California, the best known of which was at Fort Tejon in southern California. In 1853, Beal established this Indian reservation in the foothills north of Los Angeles, on which he gathered numerous Native people from a variety of tribes and bands. The stated objective of the reservation was to "civilize" Indians by "training" them to work on ranches and farms—occupations that some Indians had performed in their own communities for years. With government funding, Beal used Native labor to graze a large herd of cattle and raise a variety of crops near the southern end of the Central Valley. Although some officials genuinely desired to assimilate California's First peoples into American society, others wanted to exploit their labor to benefit themselves through the purchase, management, and sale of livestock and crops. Although the first reservations in California failed, the reservation model became a key component of national Indian policies in the western United States. Treaties and reservations became the enlightened method of "solving the Indian problem," as government agents negotiated with the tribes to limit their lands to reservations and congregate as many native peoples onto these lands as possible. The liquidation of Native land title was far more important to U.S. officials and citizens than the civilization of Indians, and this was certainly foremost in the minds of Isaac Stevens and Joel Palmer in 1854–1855 when they met with several tribes in the Washington and Oregon territories.

In 1853, the United States had split the Oregon Territory in half, fashioning the new Washington Territory. The borders of both territories included lands from the Pacific to the Dakotas, a huge area and the home of numerous Native Americans. President Franklin Pierce appointed Isaac Stevens governor and superintendent of Indian affairs of Washington Territory, and in 1854, Stevens arranged a series of treaty councils with Indians living along the Pacific Coast, Puget Sound, and the Columbia River Basin. Oregon Superintendent of Indian Affairs Joel Palmer conducted negotiations with the Indians in Oregon Territory, while Stevens concentrated on Washington Territory. Having no experience in Indian affairs, Stevens had his secretaries compose treaties based on the recently concluded Otoe-Missouri Treaty. With these "cookie-cutter" treaties, Stevens negotiated with the various tribes, sometimes coercing, lying, and cajoling them into signing the documents. On the Medicine Creek Treaty concluded near Olympia, Washington, Stevens actually forged the names of Nisqually Chief Leschi and his brothers onto the treaty. Even though Stevens employed interpreters who spoke most of the major Native languages, he conducted all of his negotiations west of the Cascade Mountains in the Chinook Jargon, a trade language unsuited for treaty councils. Some tribes refused to negotiate, while others acquiesced reluctantly, feeling that they had little choice but to do so. Although some agreed to limit their land base and live with government agents amongst them, not one Indian announced in the oral tradition that he or she had given up their people's Native sovereignty. This was as unthinkable to the people historically as it is today.

In 1855, Stevens met the Nez Perce, Yakama, Cayuse, Umatilla, and others at the Walla Walla Council, establishing three treaties and reservations in present-day Washington, Oregon, and Idaho. The Indians felt pressured into accepting the treaties, signing them only reluctantly. Kamiakin, leader of one band of Yakama-Palouse people, opposed the treaties but ultimately signed as an act of peace and friendship—not as a means to surrender his lands. Neither he nor Owhi, Teias, Old Looking Glass, Lawyer, Five Crows, nor any other leader ever agreed to cede their Native sovereignty. They endorsed the treaties by touching the pens, but this hardly equated to the relinquishing of tribal sovereignty. Furthermore, Native leaders made an agreement in their way, through the oral tradition, since few of them could speak, read, or understand English. Their spoken words had much more meaning to them than those written on treaties—documents Native people did not create. To assert their sovereignty, some Native nations prepared to comply with the treaties, but others prepared for war. Kamiakin, Qualchin, and other leaders retaliated against miners crossing their lands on their way to the new diggings at Colville in northeastern Washington. Some of the miners had stolen horses and goods, some had raped Native women, and some of these men Qualchin executed.

A full-scale war erupted after a few Yakamas killed Indian Agent Andrew Jackson Bolon in 1855, and the war continued intermittently until 1858, when Colonel George Wright defeated the people in the Battles of Four Lakes and Spokane Plains. After Wright hanged several leaders, including Qualchin, and shot others, including Owhi, he took women and children hostage and threatened to kill every Indian on the Columbia Plateau if they ever rose again in war. Throughout the events leading to the conflict and the war itself, each Native person, band, and nation maintained its sovereignty, choosing whether or not to fight or surrender. Kamiakin fought the United States Army and, rather than surrender, fled to Canada and then into Montana, where he lived with Flatheads until the era of the American Civil War, when he returned to his father's country in the heart of the Palouse Hills. Until his death in 1877, Kamiakin refused to live on the reservation or accept goods from the Office of Indian Affairs. On occasion, Kamiakin reminded agents and others that he had never surrendered his lands or his right to decide the direction of his life or that of his people. After his death, his family lived on and off Northwestern reservations, choosing their own course of action and asserting their personal sovereignty.

Kamiakin died a year after the Lakota, Cheyenne, and Arapaho victory at the Little Big Horn, an event that ushered in a new era of Native American history, one in which the United States demanded that all non-reservation Indians move onto a reservation. The Nez Perce had negotiated a treaty and reservation in 1855 at Camp Stevens, Washington Territory, but after whites discovered gold on their Lapwai reservation, the government engineered the "Thief Treaty" of 1863 to steal tribal lands so recently promised them in perpetuity. Only Chief Lawyer and fifty-one of his followers signed the new treaty, which reduced the reservation to one-tenth its original size, ceding 6,932,270 acres for 8 cents an acre. In doing so, Lawyer surrendered lands that he did not control and made a decision that was not his to make. He made these decisions in violation of tribal law, an infraction well noted today by Nez Perce people. As a result, those Nez Perce people affected by the sham treaty refused to abide by it, continuing their residence on their traditional lands. In 1876, General Oliver O. Howard, who commanded the Department of the Columbia, was given responsibility to enforce the government's order that the non-reservation Nez Perce move onto the reservation, and in 1877 he threatened them with violence unless they relocated.

After receiving threats by Howard at the Fort Lapwai Council in 1877, all the non-treaty and non-reservation Nez Perce leaders (and two Palouse chiefs) agreed to move onto the reservation in Idaho, except the venerated Toohool-hoolzote. However, before the Nez Perce and Palouse arrived on the reservation, a few young men murdered belligerent white men, and soon the people were embroiled in

Famous Nez Perce leader Chief Joseph. Edward S. Curtis Collection, the Library of Congress.

war. Several hundred Nez Perce and Palouse, including the famous Nez Perce leader, Chief Joseph, crossed the Bitterroot and Rocky Mountains in an incredible effort to escape the army, fought gallantly during the war of 1877 as they moved through Idaho, Wyoming, and into Montana. The Nez Perce and Palouse finally surrendered at the Bear Paw Mountain in October 1877. The Indians agreed to a conditional surrender with the understanding that they would be permitted to return to the Idaho reservation, but General of the Army William Tecumseh Sherman exiled the people to Fort Leavenworth, Kansas, and to the Indian Territory. From 1877 to 1885, the Nez Perce and Palouse languished in Eekish Pah, the Hot Place, but when the government finally permitted them to return home, U.S. officials split the people, sending some to the Nez Perce Reservation in Idaho and others to the Colville Reservation in Washington. The government forced Chief Joseph, the leader of the Wallowa Band, to the Colville Reservation, where many of his descendants, and those of the Palouse leadership, live today. But whether they returned to the Colville or Nez Perce reservation, the people lived out their days under the watchful eye of agents. However, they, too, never surrendered their sovereignty or their right to self-determination.

During the late nineteenth and early twentieth century, most Indians living off the reservations, as the Nez Perce and Palouse had, moved onto them. Some Indians took up homesteads under the Indian Homestead Act, but all of them lost these homesteads over time. But in spite of the fact that the people lost most of their lands through treaties, conquests, and taxes, they retained their ability to act and react to situations in ways consistent with their cultures, families, and people. Decisions involving the best course of action to take created factions among Native peoples. Some people became Christians and acculturated into white society by taking wage-earning jobs; others continued to hunt, fish, and gather while practicing their traditional religions. Still others worked for wages while supplementing their incomes by fishing, hunting, and gathering. Some Indians became Christians but continued to pray, sing, and celebrate through First Food Ceremonies, the old Washat faith, the Waptashi Religion, and Indian Shaker Church. Many Native Americans relocated onto reservations, while others formed their own communities off the reservations, often intermarrying with non-Natives who became part of these unique Native communities.

Native identities were fluid among the various communities until the government and reservation communities began categorizing Indians, often in reaction to the General Allotment Act of 1887, which created individual land allotments on former reservation lands. Government agents (and later anthropologists) began determining the "real" Indians and recording the amount of Indian blood they determined each person could claim, realigning native identities in accordance with white hermeneutics. Several Indians in Washington, Oregon, Idaho, and California defied categorization. Often the most conservative Native Americans, they frequently lived on the margins of white and Native societies, near their traditional lands, the graves of their loved ones, and sacred places, far from the reservations where they could live free from government agents and other non-Native influences. They became the targets of others who determined that since they did not live in reservation communities, they could no longer be considered Indians. Thus, although these Indians considered themselves Native Americans, outsiders—particularly government agents, white settlers, and academics—determined that they were no longer Indians.

The issue of Indian identity is often linked to one's tie with a reservation, but many Indians, especially those in California and urban areas in the Northwest, had no reservation. Once the California delegation in the U.S. Senate engineered the non-ratification of the eighteen original treaties, only a few tribes in California secured for themselves a minute portion of their former lands. Between the 1850s and 1890s, non-Natives in California stole most of the prime lands, particularly those near the Pacific Coast. Many reservations in the Pacific West resulted from presidential Executive Orders without the treaty-making process, but far too many Native communities were not included in these presidential designations and therefore have no land base held in trust by the federal government. While some of these tribes have since been recognized by state governments, many others still have no state or federal standing as "official" Indian tribes. For many years such tribes have applied to the Bureau of Indian Affairs for federal recognition. However, successive Democratic and Republican administrations have stonewalled these recognition efforts, thereby exempting the federal government from having to provide these Indians with health services, educational opportunities, loans, and other benefits. Nevertheless, most of these non-recognized tribes still consider certain lands as their tribal homelands, even if they do not own these lands that are not presently part of a recognized reservation. This is the case for several tribes in the Pacific West.

During the late nineteenth century, many tribes in southern California did not have reservations or lands clearly delineated as their own. The United States had created some reservations in California during the last three decades of the nineteenth century, but many non-reservation Indians lived in southern California during the 1890s. This situation came to the attention of Albert A. Smiley, who sat on the Board of American Indian Commissioners. Smiley spent his summer months in New York and wintered in Redlands, California, near a number of Native communities that had existed for generations but were not formally recognized by the government as legal reservations. In 1891, Smiley recommended that the United States create several small reservations in southern California. President Harrison agreed and ordered Smiley to lead a commission to recommend where to place the reservations and how much land to include. In order to blunt any criticism that he was "giving America back to the Indians," Smiley recommended that the government reduce the number of acres on reservations already in existence and add new trust lands for those Indians without lands. Therefore, some reservations lost lands in the transaction as new ones arose.

The Smiley Commission suggested that the Twenty-Nine Palms Band of Mission Indians (Chemehuevis and Serranos) secure 160 acres in the Twenty-Nine Palms area, and by Executive Order of 1895, the United States created the reservation. Unfortunately, the government failed to recognize the traditional lands of the Chemehuevis and Serranos on the oasis—lands previously and quietly claimed by the state in 1875 and sold to the Southern Pacific Railroad. Instead, the United States established the Twenty-Nine Palms Reservation south of the oasis on a waterless desert landscape at the base of a rocky mountain. The Indians refused to move to this barren spot and remained on the oasis until 1909–1910, when the government forced the people to move southeast to the Cabazon Reservation near Indio, California. Then the government added a section of land to the Cabazon Reservation to be held jointly by the original Cahuilla people at Cabazon and the Chemehuevis. According to Chemehuevi elder and former Cabazon chairman Joe Benitez, the government never asked the Cahuillas at Cabazon if they wished to host the Chemehuevis, so when the newcomers arrived, they received a chilly reception. Over the years, Susie Mike led the only Chemehuevi family to remain on the Cabazon Reservation, but her son, Joe Benitez, and his children have tribal membership at Cabazon while maintaining a relationship with members of the Twenty-Nine Palms Band and other Chemehuevis living on the Colorado River.

In spite of the fact that the government of the United States dictated policies to the Twenty-Nine Palms Band, the Cabazon Band, and many other Indian tribes, the Native peoples never abandoned their Native sovereignty. And when the federal government forced the tribes to take up land allotment or assignments during the late nineteenth and early twentieth century, again the people refused to relinquish their sovereignty.[1] During the early twentieth century, most tribes

1 During the 1920s and 1930s, several different tribes in Southern California organized into the Mission Indian Federation to demand the destruction of the Office of Indian Affairs so that tribes could exercise full tribal sovereignty by choosing for themselves how to spend yearly appropriations from the Congress without white bureaucrats dictating Indian policies. Even when tribes agreed to join the Indian New Deal during the 1930s under the Indian Reorganization Act (IRA),

became more active in their own affairs, organizing collectively for the good of all people on their reservations. This was particularly true of confederated tribes of the Pacific West, including the Warm Springs Confederated Tribes of Oregon, and the Colville Confederated Tribes and the Confederated Tribes of the Yakama Nation, both in Washington. Several different tribes lived on these northwestern reservations, speaking a variety of languages, including Sahaptin, Chinook, Salish, and Paiute. In spite of the linguistic and cultural differences between the people, members of the confederated tribes created governments to represent all of them —sometimes with the help of government agents and sometimes in spite of them. In this way, the people united politically, asserting their collective Native sovereignty and extending it to new governmental forms that suited them best. Although the federal government sanctioned some tribal governments, it did not give the tribes the right to organize politically or to assert their tribal sovereignty in this manner. Instead, the right to form a body politic emerged out of their traditional narratives, the histories and experiences of the people that emerged at the beginning of time and put Native people into motion.

In 1946, numerous tribes used their innate sovereign powers to organize the National Congress of American Indians, the first national group created by Native people for Native people. The Congress was a natural outgrowth of the New Deal era and World War II, when more than 24,000 Native Americans joined the armed forces and fought for the Allied Powers. (The Indian population numbered slightly more than 345,000 in 1940.) Many Native peoples gave their lives defending the lands they loved, the lands of their ancestors and the land that held the bones of their loved ones. Others helped win the war by working in defense plants, making ammunition, weapons, airplanes, ships, tanks, uniforms, and a host of other war materials. They had purchased war bonds to help the government buy ships, planted victory gardens, and conserved rubber, tin, and paper. Like other Americans, Native Americans had sacrificed to win the war, and when the conflict ended, they returned home demanding a greater say in their own affairs. This was not the first time Indians had asserted their sovereignty, but the war proved a watershed in Native American history.

 Partially in reaction to the political organization of Native Americans, some federal officials decided to terminate their relationship with selective Indian tribes, including some in the Pacific West. Government officials tried desperately to terminate the Colville Confederated Tribe in Washington, for example, but tribal leader Lucy Covington almost single-handedly prevented her tribe from agreeing to terminate, insisting that the people stand solidly against any attempt to

they did not give up their traditional sovereignty. Many tribes throughout the Pacific West agreed to reorganize during the Great Depression, establishing formal tribal governments with constitutions and working with the Office of Indian Affairs on a government-to-government relationship. Some tribes joined in this process, while others ignored the proposals of Commissioner of Indian Affairs John Collier to become IRA tribes.

destroy the tribe. Covington prevailed but other tribes lacked her kind of leadership and foresight. Of all the people of the Pacific West, the Klamath people of Oregon perhaps provide the best example of the confusion and hardships caused by the misguided and mean-spirited federal policy of termination. Without fully understanding the terms of termination and believing they had little choice but to acquiese, the Klamath collectively voted to severe their relationship with the United States for a cash settlement. By the time the people realized they had made a mistake, the government had agreed to termination and refused renewed recognition of the Klamath people, who fought for the restoration of federal recognition until 1978, when the government once again deemed the Klamath a federally recognized tribe. The Klamath people had used their sovereignty to destroy their relationship with the United States, and they had used their sovereignty to reestablish their government-to-government relationship. The federal government terminated other tribes in the Pacific West, but not all of them were as successful in reestablishing their formal relationship with the United States, although they still seek to do so.

Whether or not a particular tribe terminated its relationship with the federal government, it still asserted its sovereign rights. Throughout most of the Pacific West, many tribes championed their sovereign rights to fish, hunt, and gather on and off the reservations, just as their ancestors had done before them. Long before California, Oregon, Washington, and Idaho became states and began regulating fishing, hunting, and gathering through state laws, Native Americans took the bounty of nature in accordance with their own traditional laws. In the Northwest, several tribes shared a sacred story of creation which included an explanation of Salmon's origins and the right of the Salmon People to travel up the rivers flowing into the Pacific so that the Salmon could spawn to replenish themselves while at the same time giving sustenance to many species, including humans. Native Americans were to take a sufficient number of salmon for their own use and trade, but they were not to take too many salmon or jeopardize future salmon runs. According to Palouse elder Andrew George, there was a time when humans took too many salmon, so Salmon Chief asked Rattlesnake for some of his power since humans avoided Rattlesnake. Reluctantly, Rattlesnake gave Salmon some of his power, enabling the fish to bite and infect humans. The ability of the salmon to bite humans was a reminder to Indians not to overfish these sacred animals.

The Indians have never violated their sacred laws forbidding overfishing or blocking the flow of the rivers, but the United States Corps of Engineers, the Bonneville Power Authority, and other private and public corporations within various states have violated the First laws by building dams. The Indians had a natural right to fish as long as they did not threaten the salmon run. Some contemporary observers have suggested that Indians have depleted the salmon by overfishing, but these same critics have exhibited selective memory about non-Native fishermen. This includes the commercial fishing enterprises owned by Washington state's former Senator Slade Gorton's family that contributed to the destruction of the catch. Commercial and sports fishing have done far more damage than all the Indian fishers put together. Many Native nations have asserted their sovereignty to protect their fishing rights, but they have also chosen to work with non-Native fishermen, governments, and private industries to preserve the salmon, species that have been key components of their cultures and religions since the beginning of time.

The fight for fishing rights brought many Native Americans and non-Native peoples together, as has the fight to reclaim Native lands. Recognized and unrecognized tribes and peoples rallied together to assert their sovereign rights from the 1950s through the 1990s, and fishing rights will remain an important issue among Native Americans for generations to come. In the same way, Indians have fought for their lands. Indeed, the assertion of sovereign rights led several young Native Americans to reclaim Indian lands during the 1960s and 1970s (a process that continues more quietly today). In 1969, a group of Native Americans landed on Alcatraz Island in the San Francisco Bay. The island had once been the sole domain of Ohlone Indians, but the federal government claimed it in the nineteenth century and operated a penitentiary on the island in the twentieth century. When the government abandoned the island and closed the prison, no longer using the land, some Native Americans believed it should be returned to Indian people. The occupation of the island by Indian activists that began on November 20, 1969 emerged in part to reclaim Alcatraz as Indian country. Cahuilla scholar Edward Castillo was one of the first activists onto the island. He envisioned the island's takeover as a tremendous protest against the federal government and a significant public relations statement for Indian people. A'Ani scholar George Horse Capture remembered that seeing the Indians on Alcatraz Island reminded him of a Marine invasion that would change the world forever. Something dramatic happened when the young Native people took over Alcatraz.

Although the Indian occupation of Alcatraz Island ended on June 11, 1971, the event accelerated the Indian movement to assert actively and openly Native American sovereignty. Alcatraz was not the first time Indians had applied their sovereignty to a situation, but the historical event galvanized a generation's demand for a greater voice in every aspect of their lives. Afterward, Native American leaders became more involved in issues involving their people's health, education, economic development, political organization, and a host of others. American Indians used their sovereignty to voice their concern over the desecration of Native American holy places, archaeological sites, and burials. They organized collectively to pass the Native American Religious Freedom Act of 1978 and the legislation that created the National Museum of the American Indian. Equally important, Native Americans supported the passage of the Native American Graves Protection Act of 1990, legislation designed to force government agencies and institutions of all kinds that received federal funding to repatriate Native American remains and patrimony (grave goods and sacred objects).

Many archaeologists working and teaching in the Pacific West fought the legislation and its implementation, arguing that the return of Native American human remains and patrimony was contrary to scientific discovery and academic freedom. Lakota scholar Vine Deloria countered that the return of Native remains and sacred objects was a matter of humanity, and Pomo Executive Secretary of the Native American Heritage Commission Larry Myers has argued that many anthropologists, archaeologists, and government officials simply have failed to understand or appreciate the basic indecency of the matter. In California, the Native American Heritage Commission worked vigorously to protect remains and sacred sites. Cahuilla elder Katherine Saubel, Paiute-White Mountain Apache Bill Mungary, Paiute-Shoshoni Dorothy Joseph, Wyandot Clifford Trafzer, Cahuilla William Calloway, and other commissioners have worked on behalf of the entire Native population of California to preserve and protect cultural resources that link the past to the present. More than any other state, California has led the way to repatriate human remains and patrimony while mitigating the impact of tremendous growth within the state. This has been an endeavor championed by dedicated Native leaders throughout the Pacific West, and many have watched with great interest the unfolding controversy over remains in contention in Washington state. The most sensational such case revolves around the so-called Kennewick Man, fossilized human remains found by an archaeologist contracted by the Army Corps of Engineers. The Corps designated the Umatilla Tribe as the most likely descendent of Kennewick Man, and the tribe desired to rebury the remains. However, a number of archaeologists challenged the ruling, some claiming that the ancient remains resembled those of Europeans, not Indians. After years of conflict, court challenges, and administrative wrangling, the government asked the Umatillas to rebury the remains. Further challenges have postponed reburial.

During the late twentieth century, Native American tribes attempted to stimulate their economies by creating small business, attracting light manufacturing, farming, ranching, lumber industries, fishing, hunting, tourism, the film industry, art galleries, jewelry stores, hotels, restaurants, gasoline stations, smoke shops, bingo halls, and other commercial concerns. Throughout the twentieth century, tribes attempted numerous economic strategies to help their people, but gaming emerged as the most viable one. At the turn of the twenty-first century, Native Americans again asserted their sovereignty by establishing gaming on their reservations, first through bingo halls and then through Las Vegas–style table games, slot machines, and other video games. Gaming is nothing new to American Indians, who have gambled since the beginning of time. Many traditional stories exist among a diversity of Native peoples living in the Pacific West that deal with gambling. These include moccasin games that determined that there should be day and night, races between the two legged and the four legged creatures to determine who would eat the other, wrestling matches to decide life or death, ball games to determine the greatest athletes, and canoe races to decide if one group or the other would reside in a particular area.

Drawing on the strength of traditional beliefs, some tribes in California, Oregon, Washington, and Idaho have built casinos to find an economic security that has eluded Native people since the invasion of non-Natives into their lives. In California, the Cabazon Band of Cahuilla Indians established Fantasy Springs Casino, initiating the gambling business among the First Nations of California. Many of their neighbors have followed suit, including the Agua Caliente Band of Cahuillas, Twenty-Nine Palms Band of Mission Indians, Soboba Band of Mission Indians, Morongo Band of Cahuilla Indians, and San Manuel Band of Mission Indians. In the Northwest, the Lummis, Colvilles, Umatillas, Warm Springs, and Nez Perce have found success in gaming, and there are others. Gaming has changed life on reservations in many positive ways, providing funding for health care, homes, food, roads, police, education, and other needed goods and services. Gaming has provided jobs and economic opportunities for tribal members as well as non-Native peoples and stimulated the economies of non-reservation communities surrounding reservations offering gaming. On the negative side, gaming has also increased traffic, pollution, and rates of crime on reservations, bringing some of the ills of the non-Native world to the reservation.

Nevertheless, gaming has also helped revitalized Native American culture, providing funding for tribal historic preservation offices, libraries, archives, special collections, and oral history projects. Some tribes have established museums and cultural centers that stimulate interest and new research through exhibits, films, books, articles, and other public programming. With gaming revenue, tribes have hired linguists to help them preserve and perpetuate Native languages, and they have helped public schools finance cultural and linguistic programs that enhance the education of all children. Each year, the San Manuel Band of Mission Indians near San Bernardino, California, offer classes for students and teachers to learn about California Indian history, culture, language, arts, music, dance, and foods. Richard Milanovich, the chair of the Agua Caliente Band, has worked closely with administrators, faculty, and students of the University of California to plan a major Native American research center. And Theresa Mike, a Lummi from Washington state, was instrumental in furthering the education of Native students at Northwest Indian College by creating and building a scholarship endowment in honor of her daughter, Theresa Andrea Mike. Theresa Mike has also quietly worked with Luiseno leader Gloria Wright to advance the education of Native Americans in Southern California, where both women have led an intertribal effort to establish a permanent community college for Indian students.

Tribal gaming within the Pacific states has emerged through the business acumen of many Native Americans and their friends, but their work to build and maintain casinos repeatedly has been contested by city, county, state, and federal officials. Most non-Native communities enjoy and support tribal casinos, but during the late twentieth century, various law enforcement officials hampered the operation of Indian casinos by raiding them, confiscating equipment, and arresting gaming managers and employees. The San Diego County Sheriff's Department raided the casino on the Barona Reservation several times, challenging Indian gaming in courts until the United States Supreme Court upheld gaming in cases involving the Cabazon and Barona bands. Unsuccessful through many courts, non-Natives opposed to Indian gaming passed the Indian Gaming Regulatory Act of 1988, which forced the tribes to negotiate compacts with state governors so that the states could have a say in Native gaming. In many states, however, governors opposed Indian gaming and refused to enter into a compact with tribes. This was the case in California, where Governor Pete Wilson attempted to destroy Indian gaming.

Indeed, during his two terms as governor in the 1990s, Pete Wilson refused to meet and discuss a compact with Indian tribes. As a result, Indians did not meet the deadline set by the National Gaming Act to operate their gaming facilities legally. An assistant attorney general threatened continually to shut down gaming in California, but at the last minute, granted the tribes a time extension. At this point, the tribes used their political sovereignty to break the deadlock by creating Proposition 5, a referendum placed on the ballot in California to try to legalize Indian gaming. In 1998, Proposition 5 passed in California with the support of about 63 percent of the voters; after years of conflict with the dominant society, Native Californians received the unbridled support of the non-Native population. Still, opponents of Proposition 5 attacked the successful initiative, and a conservative state Supreme Court struck down the proposition as unconstitutional. The tribes had anticipated this move, so they created another initiative, Proposition 1A, to force the gaming issue in California. In 1999, California voters overwhelmingly supported Proposition 1A, but more important, they elected Democratic Governor Gray Davis, a man who was willing to negotiate with the tribes and form gaming compacts that allow the tribes, at present, to operate their casinos legally and unmolested.

Tribes in California, Oregon, Washington, and Idaho successfully used their Native sovereignty to form gaming compacts with the states, and the tribes have successfully managed these businesses for years. But their fight to preserve their sovereign right to create and operate gaming enterprises on their reservations was just another example of their continued use of Native sovereignty. At the beginning of time, when plant, animal, mountain, water, and sky people put the Earth into motion, creative forces infused Native Americans of the Pacific West with their sovereign rights and privileges. This was a gift from the Creator and the holy people who interacted with each other during the "mythic" period of Native American history. American Indians used their Native sovereignty for thousands of years before the arrival of non-Natives, and even during the devastating conflicts between Indians and non-Indians, American Indians held onto their sovereignty, asserting their rights continually throughout the centuries. Sovereignty is by no means a new creation of the tribes living in the Pacific West, and it was not a right given to the tribes through treaties or executives orders. Sovereignty is still alive and healthy among many tribes of the Pacific West, and it will be an important component of Native American history during the centuries to come.

Suggested Reading

The study of Native Americans living within California and the Northwest offers future historians a wealth of research opportunities built on the academic work of several people, including the authors of the publications cited below. For anyone interested in a short, authoritative overview of California Indians, read Edward D. Castillo, "The Impact of Euro-American Exploration and Settlement," *Handbook of North American Indians, California,* 8 (Washington, D.C., 1978). The use of the Maidu story provided here is found in Lee Ann Smith-Trafzer and Clifford Trafzer, *Creation of a California Tribe* (Newcastle, Calif., 1988), while a short version of Chemehuevi creations is in Clifford E. Trafzer, Luke Madrigal, and Anthony Madrigal, *Chemehuevi People of the Coachella Valley* (Coachella, Calif., 1997). A cultural understanding of sovereignty is found in Malcolm Margolin, *The Way We Lived* (Berkeley, Calif., 1981).

Some of the biological consequences of colonialism in the Pacific West are found in Edward D. Castillo and Robert Jackson, *Indians, Franciscans, and Spanish Colonization* (Albuquerque: N. Mex., 1995), Sherburne Cook, *The Conflict between the California Indians and White Civilization* (Berkeley, Calif., 1976), and Clifford E. Trafzer, *Death Stalks the Yakama: Epidemiological Transitions and Mortality on the Yakama Indian Reservation* (East Lansing, Mich., 1997). Issues of population decline resulting from conflicts and Native expressions of tribal rights are found in George H. Phillips, *Chiefs and Challengers* (Berkeley, Calif., 1975) as well as his *The Enduring Struggle: Indians in California History* (San Francisco, 1981). For a recent overview of the Spanish period, see David J. Weber, *The Spanish Frontier in North America* (New Haven, Conn., 1992), but for a detailed study of life within the mission systems, focusing primarily on the Spanish viewpoint, see Edith B. Webb, *Indian Life at the Old Missions* (Lincoln, Nebr., 1952).

One of the best books dealing with California Indians is James J. Rawls, *Indians of California: The Changing Image* (Norman, Okla., 1984). Violence and Native sovereignty is also a part of Clifford E. Trafzer and Joel Hyer, *"Exterminate Them": Written Accounts of Murder, Rape and Enslavement of Native Americans during the California Gold Rush* (East Lansing: Mich., 1999), and the classic work by Robert Heizer and Alan F. Almquist, *The Other Californians* (Berkeley, Calif., 1971). Information regarding the Quechans and other California Indians can be found in Clifford Trafzer, *Yuma: Frontier Crossing of the Far Southwest* (Wichita, Kans., 1980) and Jack D. Forbes, *Warriors of the Colorado* (Norman, Okla., 1965). Treaties in California and the issue of Indians lands are found in Robert Heizer, *Treaty Making and Treaty Rejection by the Federal Government in California, 1850–1852* (Socorro, N. Mex., 1978) and Florence C. Shipek, *Pushed into the Rocks: Southern California Indian Land Tenure* (Lincoln, Nebr., 1987). In recent years, several publications have addressed the Native American takeover of Alcatraz, the best of which is Troy Johnson, *The Occupation of Alcatraz Island* (Urbana, Ill., 1996).

The larger issue of Native American sovereignty in the Northwest is found in Clifford E. Trafzer, ed., *Grandmother, Grandfather, and Old Wolf* (East Lansing, Mich., 1998) and Nashone, *Grandmother Stories of the Northwest* (Newcastle, Calif., 1987). Although the subject is not addressed directly, the stories found in Mourning Dove, *Mourning Dove's Stories,* edited by Clifford E. Trafzer and Richard D. Scheuerman (San Diego, Calif., 1991) addresses the traditional sovereignty of Plateau Indians. This is also the case in the best general histories of the Northwest, including Robert H. Ruby and John A. Brown, *Indians of the Pacific Northwest* (Norman, Okla., 1981) and Donald Meinig, *The Great Columbia Plain* (Seattle, 1968). For those interested in any aspect of the Lewis and Clark expedition, see Gary Moulton's edited journals of the expedition, but for anyone specifically intrigued by the relationship of Native Americans with Lewis and Clark, see James P. Ronda, *Lewis and Clark among the Indians* (Lincoln, Nebr., 1984).

A classic book that deals with many topics relating to Native sovereignty is Eugene Hunn, *Nch'i-Wana "The Big River": Mid-Columbia Indians and Their Land* (Seattle, 1990). The Palouse Indians of the Columbia Plateau are addressed in Clifford E. Trafzer and Richard D. Scheuerman, *Renegade Tribe: The Palouse Indians and the Invasion of the Inland Pacific Northwest* (Pullman, Wash., 1986), while the case for Nez Perce sovereignty is found in Alvin Josephy, *The Nez Perce Indians and the Opening of the Northwest* (New Haven, Conn., 1965). The military consequences of the Plateau Indian War, 1855–1858, is found in Lawrence Kip, *Indian Wars of the Pacific Northwest* (Lincoln, Nebr., 2000). Issues involving land and treaties among the Indian people of the Northwest are found in several of the volumes mentioned above but they can also be found in Kent Richards, *Isaac I. Stevens* (Provo, Utah, 1979), a book that champions the governor.

Young Chief Joseph's own article, "An Indian's View of Indian Affairs," *The North American Review* 128 (1879) provides a window for readers into the thinking of the Nez Perce leadership before, during, and after the Nez Perce War of 1877. Other volumes deal with issues of Native sovereignty, including Steven Evans, *Voice of the Old Wolf* (Pullman, Wash., 1996), L. V. McWhorter, *Yellow Wolf* (Caldwell, Idaho, 1940), and Clifford Trafzer and Richard D. Scheuerman, *Chief Joseph's Allies* (Newcastle, Calif., 1992). Many of the volumes mentioned above deal with Indian identities, but one of the best is Alexandra Harmon, *Indians in the Making* (Berkeley, Calif., 1998).

Chapter 15 ❧
Traditions and Transformations

American Indian Women
in Historical Perspective

Päivi Hoikkala

> Everyone laughed at the impossibility of it,
> but also the truth. Because who would believe
> the fantastic and terrible story of all of our survival
> those who were never meant
>   to survive?
>   From *Anchorage*, by Joy Harjo

Survival and memory are prevalent themes in the work of Creek poet Joy Harjo. Harjo's voice speaks to her experiences as a Native American, as a woman, and as an individual in contemporary times. Her poetry interprets the continuing interaction between the past and the present realities of Native America. This interaction, in turn, lies at the core of the sense of belonging to a community, to a place. As literary critic Laura Coltelli points out, the role of memory in this process is *not* to retrace the past as an inducement to curl inwards, as an escape, but rather to reaffirm ancient heritages on a forward path of constant renewal and transformation. In this way memory makes possible the "story of all of our survival."

Survival, renewal, and transformation characterize the experiences of Native American women from precontact times to the present. While nearly invisible in historical accounts until recently, women have always been active participants in their communities. As mothers, wives, educators, farmers, medicine women, and sometimes warriors, women have placed themselves at the center of tribal life together with men. Matrilineal tribes have afforded women opportunities in the realms of politics, economies, religion, and the family. The presence of female figures in the creation stories of these tribes supports women's pivotal status. Patrilineal societies and their spiritual world have placed more emphasis on males, but they too recognize women's central roles as mothers and sustainers of life, allowing them a degree of autonomy often not afforded their European counterparts until recently.

While change and adaptation form the essence of any living culture, contact with Europeans introduced new elements to Native communities, as well as an accelerated pace of change that often proved devastating. Disease epidemics weakened societal structures and threatened the very survival of tribes. The presence of Europeans created new alliances and contributed to increased warfare, even as the newcomers' weapons made war more destructive. A growing reliance on European trade items undermined relations of production, and traditional social and political mores began to break down as Indian societies became dependent on this trade. Finally, Christian missionaries imposed European social and moral values on Native peoples and introduced their notions of proper gender roles.

To fully recognize the impact of these pressures on Indian communities, the perspective of women is essential. On the frontiers of what is now the United States, Indian women negotiated relationships with an assortment of men—Native, European, and American. Frontier society was predominantly male, placing demands on women's domestic skills, economic assistance, and sexual companionship. Sometimes voluntary, sometimes coerced, these demands put Native women at the center of exchange as cultural mediators. At all times, these exchanges occurred in a context of dependency, transforming gender roles. With the growth of the United States, Indian communities became increasingly marginalized as efforts to assimilate them into the mainstream intensified. Women and men experienced these events as members of their groups, but also as members of their sex. In the process, women's social, political, and economic roles were transformed. Yet, women anchored the center of community life through adaptation, providing a strong basis for resistance, resilience, and renewal of culture. Thus, the women's story *is* the "story of all of our survival."

"In the beginning two female human beings were born," opens the Acoma creation story. These first human beings were sisters, Nautsiti and Iatiku, who were born deep underground at a place called Shipapu. After the two sisters grew, the female deity Tsichtinako taught the sisters their language and gave them two baskets filled with seeds and little images of animals. The sisters planted the seeds of four pine trees, one of which grew into a tall tree that poked a hole through the Earth's surface. Now Tsichtinako told the sisters to give life to an animal figure, the badger, who used his claws to make the hole large enough for the sisters to climb through it. Once above ground, Nautsiti and Iatiku selected their clans and learned to pray. Then they planted more seeds, which became corn, beans, squash, and all other plant life on Earth, and they gave life to the other animal figures in their baskets. "Everything in the baskets is to be created by your word," Tsichtinako instructed, "for you are made in the image of Uchtsiti [the creator] and your word will be as powerful as his word. He has created you to help him complete the world."

This creation story lay at the heart of women's lives in the pueblo of Acoma, giving them a distinct status as givers and sustainers of life and placing them on par with men. The Acoma tale of creation also exemplifies the creation stories of many other North American Indian groups that structured their social order around matrilineal clans. These societies tended to allow women more public visibility and personal independence than their patrilineal counterparts. All Indian communities recognized women's significance as givers of life and sustainers of communities, and all of them sought balance and harmony in the universe. Sexuality symbolized this cosmic balance. In the Acoma creation story, the two sisters inhabit the Earth while Uchtsiti, the male deity, is associated with the sky. Rain, too, represents the masculine, and Nautsiti is impregnated when the rain drops enter her. Human sexuality was thus imbued with sacred meaning, and ritual acts of sexual intercourse concluded the religious ceremonies of several Native cultures.

Women's biology marked their life cycles—menstruation, child birth, and menopause—and specific ceremonies accompanied the passage of each cycle. These ceremonies included exclusively female rituals that enforced women's function as a separate entity within the community. The first menstrual cycle signaled a girl's entry into womanhood and her full integration as a productive member of the group. For Navajos, the Kina'alda marked this rite of passage. Menstrual blood was perceived as a source of power that necessitated the isolation of menstruating women, and a purification ceremony was conducted after menstruation. Accordingly, menopause marked another significant transformation in a woman's life, allowing her entry into roles otherwise denied to women. An example would be the role of shaman, or medicine woman. However, women's greatest source of power came from their ability to bear children. A Tohono O'odham woman named Chona explained this power to anthropologist Ruth Underhill thusly: "Men have to dream to get power. . . . But we *have* power. . . . Don't you see, without us, there would be no men? Why should we envy men? We *made* the men."

The construction of gender, however, was more than a matter of simple biology. Gender was also closely associated with an individual's daily activities as a member of the community. As givers and sustainers of life, women not only cared for the young ones, but nurtured all members of their households as part of their routine chores. Pueblo women ground corn, cut and dried meat, and otherwise prepared foods for family consumption. Pueblo households revolved around senior women, who owned most family property and controlled its use. Pueblo women also built and maintained housing, and, in general, supervised family affairs. Village business, on the other hand, lay in the male domain. Pueblo men tended the cornfields, attended to spiritual matters, conducted trade with outsiders, and, if necessary, defended the village. This clear differentiation between male and female roles was a natural extension of the cosmic balance in everyday life.

But Indian cosmologies allowed for certain flexibility within these strictly defined gender roles. Most historical accounts of cross-gender roles involve men, but women too might choose to assert masculine traits without retribution. The "manly-hearted" women among the Northern Piegan exemplify such a crossing of traditional gender boundaries. These women tended to be older, propertied women who were recognized as manly-hearted because they were outspoken, independent, and assertive in public. The cross-gender role, however, involved more than personality; it indicated that the individual had *chosen* to take on some aspect of the other gender in tasks, rituals, and sometimes dress and hairstyle. Sometimes visions, dreams, and expediency directed this choice. Homosexuality was not necessarily a factor. In any case, these choices were respected by the group and often involved specific duties in tribal ceremonies.

The balance of the Native universe was thrown off kilter when Columbus reached the Western Hemisphere. The Acomas' first contact with the Spaniards came in 1540, with the arrival of Hernando de Alvarado, Don Francisco Vásquez de Coronado's lieutenant. The early chroniclers of the Spanish expeditions into the pueblos commented on the impressive structures on the mesas and the "peaceful nature of the[ir] inhabitants." Yet, the Spaniards lost interest in the region for forty years because it failed to yield the rich stores of gold they had anticipated finding there. Late in the sixteenth century, Spanish Catholic friars took an interest in the region as part of Spain's colonizing efforts, and in 1598, Don Juan de Oñate established the first permanent settlement in present-day New Mexico. Gender figured prominently in the contact between these new settlers and Pueblo Indians.

The Spanish *encomienda* system exacted tribute from the pueblos in the form of property or labor. Because the early Spanish colonial society consisted mostly of men, sexual favors were implied in this tribute, a practice that the pueblos initially saw as part of a gift exchange. When the Spaniards failed to provide any benefits in kind, this view changed. The colonists, however, continued to exact their tribute, introducing rape and prostitution into the Pueblo world. These practices and the resulting pregnancies threatened social harmony, and in many cases, both the pregnant woman and her child became outcasts, forced to join the Spanish social order as *genízaros*, detribalized Indians, at the very bottom of the hierarchy. An intangible result of rape was its trauma, most certainly affecting women's perceptions of their own sexuality.

Not all sexual encounters involved violence. Some Pueblo women married settlers who were looking for female companionship in a predominantly male world; others became concubines. These unions formed a cultural frontier that altered perceptions of gender on both sides of the divide. They also produced a mixed blood, or *mestizo*, population that dominated Hispanic settlements in the Southwest. Furthermore, the mestizos created a new cultural expression on the Spanish colonial frontier, one that combined features of both the colonizer and the colonized.

Another dimension of women's encounters with the settlers involved their work roles, and the Spaniards readily utilized the labor of Pueblo women. Many women worked as maids, some as interpreters. Their blankets and other textiles proved useful to the colonists, and their "earthenware . . . jars of extraordinary labor and workmanship" made their way into the cycle of colonial trade. The

Spaniards even accepted the "strange" labor of women as builders and plasterers, and missionaries employed them to build their churches. In the process, Pueblo women served as agents of change in their own communities as they adopted new materials and methods from the colonists to diversify or improve their artisanship. Women thus played an important mediating role in the meeting of the two worlds.

More devastating to traditional gender roles than these secular encounters were the efforts of the Spanish friars to convert Indians to Christianity. The sexual and gender ideology of Christianity stood in direct opposition to that of the Indians. Spanish friars and Protestant missionaries alike condemned extramarital sex— often stated in terms of the lascivious behavior of women—homosexuality, and polygamy. Divorce was another point of contention, and from the missionaries' perspective, yet another sign of the depravity of the "heathen" Indians. The regulation of sexuality thus figured prominently in the goals of the missionaries.

The experiences of California Indians illuminate the gender-specific effects of the efforts to convert Native Americans to Catholicism. When the Franciscans established their first mission in Alta California in 1769, California was one of the most densely populated regions in Native America, with an estimated 300,000 inhabitants representing over one hundred distinct groups. Into this cultural maze the Franciscans brought their determination to convert the Indians. While sexuality certainly was not the only concern of the priests, the reformation of Indian sexual behavior formed an important part of their efforts. Catholic marriage lay at the core of their idealized vision of empire building in the New World. They strictly enforced monogamy, without the possibility of divorce, in the missions. Another way to control sexuality was the separation of the sexes from puberty to marriage. Especially under the watchful eye of the friars were young women, locked up during the night in *monjerios* and let out during the day to attend mass and to work.

Despite their benign promise of "salvation," the missions became agents of destruction, facilitating the spread of disease by concentrating the previously dispersed Native populations. By the end of the mission era in the 1830s, the original Indian population of California had declined to 150,000. As early as 1787, Governor Pedro Fages noted "the frequent illness and deaths . . . among the neophytes [at Mission San Antonio]." Epidemics of smallpox, dysentery, scarlet fever, tuberculosis, and cholera swept through the missions on a regular basis and with devastating effects. The president of the missions, Father Señan, wrote in 1811: "The births [at Mission San Francisco] scarcely correspond to a third part of the deaths, even in years when there is no epidemic. But in a year like 1806, when there was an epidemic of measles, more than three-hundred died and twenty-three were born." The elderly and the children were most susceptible to these epidemics, but for women, disease had hidden consequences in the form of miscarriages, stillbirths, and infertility.

The high rates of infant and child mortality combined with the declining birth rates alarmed the friars. Father Lasuén of Monterey explained in 1795:

"The failure of the mission Indians to show a greater increase may be attributed to their great incontinence and the inhumanity of the mothers, who in order not to become old and unattractive to their husbands, manage to abort or strangle their newly-born children." This anxiety about possible infanticide and abortions resulted in further restrictions and punishments for women suspected of "these great evils." A sympathetic observer at Mission San Gabriel described the penalty for one woman suspected of infanticide as "shaving the head, flogging for fifteen subsequent days, iron on the feet for three months and having to appear every Sunday in Church on the steps heading up to the altar, with a hideous painted wooden child in her arms!"

Hardships on California Indian women only continued to increase during the American period. Whereas the Spaniards and the Mexicans after them had accepted interracial marriage, the Anglos proved fearful of such unions. Nonetheless, Anglo men took the opportunity to exploit Native women—a trend with disturbing results during the Gold Rush era, when the frontier reached the interior regions of California. Hard work, malnutrition, and the dislocations of the gold rush proved hard on women and men alike. Hunger and privation drove many Indian women to prostitution while sexual attacks on Native women increased in this predominantly young male society. Isolation from the constraints of law and society facilitated this exploitation, even as the dominant society continued to shun peaceful unions of Anglo men and Native women. Based on modern rape research, historian Albert Hurtado postulates on the somatic and emotional results of sexual violence. A more concrete result was the spread of venereal disease, reducing birth rates and lowering women's resistance to illness. The 1860 U.S. census shows that in virtually every Indian age cohort in every county of California there were substantially fewer women than men. This imbalance in sex ratios contributed to the continuing decline in birth rates, and by the 1880s the California Native population reached its nadir at 23,000, the same time during which national efforts at assimilation threatened all Native peoples' cultural survival.

Protestant missionaries shared the goal of Indian conversion with their Catholic brethren. And like Catholic friars, they showed great concern over Indian sexuality and their "improper" behavior. Beginning in the 1640s, the English colonies began establishing "praying towns." The praying towns segregated "good" Indians from the "bad" influence of frontiersmen and paganism while attempting to initiate the former in "civil jurisprudence, evangelical knowledge, and habits of industry." Implied in these goals was the transformation of Indian sexuality and women's roles to conform to Protestant gender ideology. Wifely submission to the male head of household was a cornerstone of this ideology. The favored method of conversion was formal education in schools created to teach Indian youth. In addition to "civilization," the students in these schools learned a trade. For girls, this training meant apprenticeship to local women to learn "the Female part, as House-wives, School-mistresses, [and] Tayloresses."

Despite these efforts at conversion, English claims to dominance and superiority relied on extreme prejudice and notions of Native Americans as barbaric peoples. Historian Kathleen Brown concludes that differences in gender roles between Anglos and Indians provided the English "with cultural grist for the mill of conquest," and gender relations became a metaphor for power relations in colonial New England. Consequently, Indian life and culture experienced rapid change, with particularly devastating effects on women, who now lost much of their independence and influence in tribes. Disease also wreaked havoc among eastern tribes, contributing to the decline of the Native populations and their traditional lifeways. For example, the number of Indian people in Chesapeake Bay and the tidewater was reduced from approximately 14,000 in 1607 to less than 3,000 by the early eighteenth century.

The fur trade added yet another dimension to Indian-European relations in the colonial era. As the fur-bearing animals near the East Coast settlements were depleted, the fur trade began to penetrate into the heart of the continent, "Indian country," eventually reaching the Rocky Mountains and central Canada. Its greatest impact came in the vast wilderness areas surrounding the Great Lakes, home to several Indian tribes including the Ojibways, Chipewayans, and Crees. Fur trade society exemplifies a relationship predicated on a mutual exchange and dependency between Indians and Europeans. Wherever trade centered, there developed what historian Richard White has called a cultural middle ground—a region wherein the two cultures met, clashed, and blended. Women participated in this process as cultural mediators. In some cases, women emerged as diplomats and peacemakers to maintain the profitable trade. More often, Indian women married incoming European traders. Historian Sylvia van Kirk points out that these interracial unions were, indeed, the basis for a fur trade society, and they were sanctioned by an indigenous marriage rite called *à la façon du pays* (according to the custom of the country).

Native groups viewed these unions in an integrated social and economic context. Marital alliances created reciprocal social ties that consolidated the economic relationship with the strangers by drawing them into Indian kinship circles. Traders quickly understood that marriage was an important means of ensuring the good will and cooperation of Indian groups. Apart from these public social benefits, the absence of European women in fur trade society increased the desire for intermarriage. Indian women provided most frontiersmen the only opportunity for the personal benefits of family life. Finally, a Native wife proved an important economic partner, one possessing a range of skills and knowledge necessary for survival in the wilderness. In the middle ground women made moccasins; they gathered and prepared food; they assisted in specific fur trade operations; and they became the mediators and interpreters between cultures.

The Haudenosaunee—or the members of the Iroquois Confederacy—used their power and influence in fur trade transactions to manipulate colonial competition to their own advantage. As a result, they managed to resist the pressures of colonization longer than did most other eastern Indian groups. The Haudenosaunee also afforded their women unusually extensive powers, to the degree that some historians have called them a matriarchate. These claims of high status are generally based on women's economic and political roles. Indeed, the Haudenosaunee were matrilineal and matrilocal, an elder woman heading each extended family. Women controlled land and horticultural production; they owned the tools of production; they nominated the chiefs and exercised some control over their actions; and women were completely responsible for childcare. All these actions occurred in the context of the complementarity of sex roles, as codified in Iroquois cosmology. The Iroquois world, in effect, was divided into two separate worlds: one of sedentary females, the other of nomadic men often absent on hunting, trading, or war expeditions.

Evidence suggests that matrilineage gained importance in the years following contact with Europeans. Fur trade, increasing warfare, and political maneuvering required extended male absences, allowing women to gain more control in village affairs. European trade items also entered Iroquois life with an impact on traditional crafts. Women now preferred metal pots for cooking and calico for their dress. Yet, women's economic roles in the village context changed very little, as they continued to control horticultural production and the fruits of their labor. It is thus probable that contact had a less severe impact on women's roles than it did on men, whose provider role as hunters diminished while their roles as traders, warriors, and diplomats were strengthened.

The Revolutionary War proved a turning point for the Haudenosaunee. The Confederacy split over whom to support in this conflict, with some groups backing the British and other groups allying with the American colonists; but in the end, all its members suffered tremendous losses in human life, land, culture, and power. Historian Anthony Wallace estimates that the war and the concomitant starvation and disease cut the Iroquois population in half in the twenty years following the onset of the conflict. Their acreages were destroyed in the war, and peace brought harsh new conditions in terms of who now claimed their land. By the end of the eighteenth century, the Seneca, for example, retained fewer than 200,000 acres of their original 4,000,000-acre domain. Even more damaging was the loss of confidence and optimism about the future. This decline in morale manifested itself in the great increase of alcoholism and the accompanying family conflict. The remedy to these social ills came in the form of a religious revitalization movement, based on the visions of an Allegheny Seneca named Handsome Lake.

Handsome Lake's visions, in the words of Anthony Wallace, "articulated the dilemmas in which the Iroquois were trapped and prescribed both religious and secular solutions." Based on a combination of Seneca and Anglo values, these solutions clearly reflected the influence of the Quaker missionaries and federal officials who supported the movement. The secular solutions, in particular, had significant consequences for female roles in Seneca society. Handsome Lake's "social gospel" emphasized the nuclear family, wherein the husband-wife relationship took precedence over other kinship ties and the single-family homestead took priority over extended family households. He also recast the sexual division of labor, underscoring the "proper" role of the husband as farmer-provider and that of the wife as the homemaker. Within a generation, this transformation was complete, as families became patrilineal in both name and inheritance. As a result, women's economic power greatly diminished, with an impact on their political influence. The formation of the Seneca Nation in 1848 further eroded women's political roles, for the new constitution disenfranchised Seneca women until 1964. Despite this apparent loss in status, it is important to note that women maintained their focus on the home and children. They continued to collect fruits and berries, plant gardens, weave baskets, and raise and educate the children. Women also held important roles in the new religion. In these functions, they continued to contribute to the survival of their people and culture.

After the colonies gained their independence from Great Britain, the new nation had to figure out how to promote settlement while maintaining peaceful relations with Indian tribes. One solution to this "Indian problem" was the signing of treaties in which groups of Native Americans ceded large tracts of their lands in return for small reserves. But the government's guarantee of these reserves for "as long as the grass shall grow and the waters flow" quickly came under fire in the Southeast, where cotton agriculture and its companion slavery were rapidly expanding. The fertile lands of the Five Civilized tribes—Cherokees, Choctaws, Chickasaws, Creeks, and Seminoles—were increasingly coveted by southern settlers, and these tribes also became the focus of the federal government's new Indian policy: removal.

Like the Haudenosaunee, the Cherokees were matrilineal and afforded their women significant economic and political influence. Colonial trade and warfare upset the balance between the sexes, making men more central to everyday life than women and focusing attention on individual prowess rather than communal productivity. Invasions disrupted village life, over which women presided, and trade made women dependent on men for items they desired but had no means to acquire. On the other hand, women found ways to retain certain traditional rights, preserve communal values, and maintain the structures of Cherokee society on which their status rested. Whenever women tilled the fields and harvested the corn, they reaffirmed their identity and value as women. They continued to subscribe to an ideology of power based on human relationships with the spirit world, not on material possessions. Cherokee society also operated based on matrilineal kinship relations, giving women an extensive support network to rely on at times of crises.

When the Cherokees signed the Treaty of Holston with the United States in 1791, their "civilization" became a major goal. Guided by an idealized view of women and men in American society, the reformers embarked on their mission to turn Cherokee men into industrious, republican farmers, while Cherokee women were to become chaste, orderly housewives. Private property ownership was yet another cornerstone of these efforts. Women responded favorably to these efforts, as they saw the government's civilization program as validation of the work they had always performed: farming, horticulture, and household production. What they failed to see was the threat that the underlying ideology posed to the traditional division of labor in Cherokee society and whatever remained of the autonomy of its women. In the minds of the reformers, animal husbandry and farming were male responsibilities. Furthermore, in a "civilized" society, women became property of men, who headed households and governed the nation.

While Cherokee men proved more deeply suspicious of the civilization program than did women, many of both sexes saw it as the best defense against the increasing pressures for removal. Cherokees learned English, sent their children to school, and converted to Christianity. Private property became a symbol of success as male culture reoriented toward its acquisition. In relatively short order, the "civilized" Cherokees established a republic with written laws, a court system, and a national police force. All these symbols of civilization integrated American notions of gender roles, and women experienced a steady exclusion from the nation's political life. Yet, on another level, women's values and views remained essential to Cherokee national identity and public policy. These values—specifically women's association with the land—figured prominently in the Cherokees' opposition to removal. A women's council petition from 1817 clearly relies on this identification with tradition:

> The Cherokee ladys [sic] now being present at the meeting of the chiefs and warriors in council have thought it their duty as mothers to address their beloved chiefs and warriors now assembled. . . . Your mothers, your sisters ask and beg of you not to part with any more of our land. We say ours. You are our descendants; take pity on our request. But keep it for our growing children, for it was the good will of our creator to place us here. . . .

Such efforts failed to preclude their forced removal from their homelands at the hands of federal officals, and in the winter 1838–39 the main body of the Cherokee nation were "relocated" west to join earlier migrants. At least 4,000 of the estimated 15,000 Cherokees who set out on this "Trail of Tears," stressed and woefully ill-provisioned, died en route. Women gave birth on the trail; they lost children and other family members to malnutrition, disease, and exhaustion; and they suffered abuse by their white guards. Despite the horrors, a distinct women's culture survived removal and contributed to the rebuilding of the Cherokee nation in Indian Territory. Indeed, the amazing endurance of this women's culture has allowed the reemergence of Cherokee women onto a public stage in the late twentieth century. Wilma Mankiller, the first woman to serve as Principal Chief of the Cherokees, reiterated the importance of this transformation: "Women can help turn the world right side up. We bring a more collaborative approach to government. And if we do not participate, then decisions will be made without us."

The U.S. government undertook removal to solve the Indian problem by separating Native peoples from the settlers. However, even at the time of the removal controversy, Americans were already exploring Indian Country west of the Mississippi River. In 1832, George Catlin, a lawyer-turned-artist-and-explorer from Philadelphia, visited the Hidatsas and their neighbors and allies the Mandans along the upper Missouri River. "I found these people raising abundance of corn or maize," Catlin wrote about the Hidatsas, also noting their dependence on buffalo meat. He made reference to women's important role as agriculturalists and described their participation in procuring buffalo meat for the people. Catlin's visit came at a crucial time, shortly before a devastating smallpox epidemic that nearly wiped out the Mandans and cut the Hidatsa population in half. This devastation brought permanent changes in Hidatsa culture, reflective of the experiences of many other tribes in the vast Great Plains region. In 1845, the Hidatsas and Mandans established Like-a-Fishhook village. The Arikaras joined them there in 1862. The three groups negotiated a new existence in this location, not without conflict, and the village remained home until the federal government established Fort Berthold reservation for the Three Affiliated Tribes in 1870.

"We set out for our new home [Like-a-Fishhook] in the spring, when I was four years old," Buffalo Bird Woman recalled when she shared her life with anthropologist Gilbert L. Wilson in the early twentieth century. As a child, Buffalo Bird Woman spent her summer days in the fields with her grandmother, learning to grow corn and vegetables, "as every Hidatsa woman was expected to." With the melting of the snow, the women's Goose Society began the year's agricultural activities with a ceremony to welcome the corn spirits. They then cleared the fields, tended the crops, and at harvest time, picked the corn. Women owned the products of their labor, and those who farmed, dressed skins, built houses, or sewed clothes increased the wealth of their families. Indeed, a man needed an industrious wife because men rarely performed these tasks. Diligence in household duties could also earn a woman great respect, entitling her to wear special ornaments as a sign of her accomplishments.

Women's basic tasks remained unchanged while Buffalo Bird woman was growing up, but she remembered changes, too. Women adopted western tools to help their agricultural pursuits; they began baking wheat bread in Dutch ovens and brewing coffee to supplement the traditional diet of corn, beans, and dried meat. Canned meat and fruits also gained popularity as store-bought foods and government rations became more available—and the great buffalo herds on the Plains disappeared. These influences intensified with the arrival of the first missionary in 1876; the following year, there were two schools in the village: one run by the government, the other by the mission. In 1885, people began leaving Like-a-Fishhook for the reservation.

Now the federal government wished to assimilate Indians further by partitioning communal reservation lands into privately held tracts. This allotment of lands in severalty introduced further changes in Hidatsa life, laden with assumptions about "proper" gender roles. Their communal lifestyle was dismantled by a surveyed gridwork of square plots on which individual families lived isolated from each other. Their round, earthen lodges, in which all activities happened in the same room, were replaced by square houses divided into men's and women's spaces. Furthermore, building a home was no longer sacred nor did women build the homes on the reservation. Men now became the providers, taking over farming and learning to be ranchers, while women had to adjust to new tools and new rules in their remaining domain—the home. Dairy products, eggs, and grains became staples in the diet, and stove cookery introduced new ways of food preparation. Buffalo Bird Woman did not think highly of these innovations: "In old times . . . we did not have to buy food with money, and the new food the white men have brought us, and their diseases, cause our people to die. In old days we did not thus die."

The federal government further intensified its assimilation efforts when it introduced the field matron program in 1891. These American women reformers sought to "improve" Indian lives by focusing on the women, whom the Victorian value system considered the guardians of morality in the home; men, meanwhile, rightfully belonged to the public sphere of politics and economics. The field matrons saw sanitation as a problem too and disapproved of Buffalo Bird Woman's household management. All these changes chipped away at Buffalo Bird Woman's value as a producer and grandmother, her former sources of power. In their stead came an economy that placed power in the hands of those whose work produced money. In her late seventies, Buffalo Bird Woman felt regret about what she had lost: "Often in summer I rise at daybreak and steal out to the cornfields; and as I hoe the corn I sing to it, as we did when I was young. No one cares for our corn songs now."

In assigning land to male heads of household, the allotment process reinforced the nuclear family in which men held economic power. The federal government thus helped create a male–dominated social and economic system in which women's economic independence and property rights became subject to male control. Agents of the Bureau of Indian Affairs further strengthened male domination by restricting their dealings to male representatives of the tribes in their jurisdiction. Victorian gender roles also formed an essential element in the effort to civilize Indian people through formal education in government boarding schools. At the same time, removing the children from their parents further reduced women's responsibilities on the reservations.

To achieve the ideal Victorian woman, boarding school officials attempted to reconstruct the identity and physical appearance of Indian girls. Strict codes of appearance regulated the students' lives in and out of the classroom: girls were drilled in "proper" ways to conduct themselves, and they were closely monitored against improper sexual behavior. A major goal of the boarding school education, however, was "to teach family relationships in a manner that homes become happy places in which all members share the joys and responsibilities that are involved." To achieve this goal, girls learned about menu planning, nutrition, gardening, canning, food preparation, serving, table manners, and entertaining. They spent time sewing, mending and darning, embroidering, and washing clothes. All these activities not only prepared girls for their future roles as wives but also helped keep the institution self-sufficient. Academics and preparation for a working life took a secondary role. A female student at Chilocco Indian School in Oklahoma recalled this of her formal education: "Not anything, I don't think, . . . was expected to really develop into a trade. . . . No, I think at that time it was just, you're a woman, you're going to be a wife, you know. Learn to patch, and sew, and darn."

While most boarding school students returned to their home reservations with an education of little use, some young women made a successful transition to professional lives and became mediators between two seemingly irreconcilable cultures. These women also demonstrate how intertwined the Indian experience had become with the American experience by the turn of the twentieth century, as exemplified in the life of Susan La Flesche Picotte. Born in 1865, a time of great upheaval for the Omaha Nation, La Flesche grew up in a family that mixed Omaha traditions with American cultural practices. This upbringing and her mixed-blood heritage set the stage for her life as a cultural broker. Susan excelled in the mission schools and went on to attend Elizabeth Institute in New Jersey, Hampton Institute in Virginia, and then the Woman's Medical College in Philadelphia. On her graduation in 1889, Susan La Flesche became the first female Indian physician in the United States.

When La Flesche returned to the Omaha Nation, she not only took her medical knowledge to her people but also her belief in the value of education and reform. Through her experiences, she had come to typify the New American Woman: educated, employed, and involved in reform. In her appeal to maternalism and in the battles she chose as a reformer—temperance and improved health care—La Flesche clearly situated herself within the Victorian notions of proper womanhood, notions that other reform-minded women of the Progressive Era used to justify their involvement in the male spheres of political and economic engagement. But these same notions appeared to distance her from the Omahas, as did her years spent in the East. As a broker between two cultures, her life was one of constant negotiation, and renegotiation, of her values and identity. In this, Susan LaFlesche Picotte represents the quintessential American experience.

Those boarding school graduates who chose to make their home in mainstream society experienced a similar process of negotiation, perhaps even more poignantly than did La Flesche. Living among Anglo Americans presented a number of new challenges to the new graduates: finding employment and housing, all the while facing strong prejudices. Anna Moore Shaw, Pima from the Gila River reservation in Central Arizona, and her Pima husband, Ross, chose Phoenix, Arizona, as their home in 1921. Born in 1898, Shaw came from a Presbyterian family and had attended mission school on the reservation before enrolling at Phoenix Indian School in 1909. In her autobiography, she favorably remembers her education and her experiences as a domestic in the outing system, whereby Indian schools sent students to live with white/Anglo families while they took on employment in mostly menial tasks. Anna met Ross Shaw at the school, and the two married in 1920. According to tradition, they moved in with the husband's parents, but boarding school education had distanced the couple from the traditional lifestyle of the Pimas. Shaw poignantly, and with some sadness, illustrates this dissociation when she describes the traditional household of her in-laws: "There was no plumbing, no gas, or electricity. How difficult this simple way of life seemed to Ross and me after our years of enjoying the white man's conveniences!" The Shaws moved back to Phoenix where they lived until their retirement in the 1960s.

While Ross provided for the family, Anna took care of the household and the children—things Pima women had always done. She was at the center of the family, but she also extended her role as mother and nurturer to activities in the Central Presbyterian Church, identified as the Indian church in Phoenix. Women formed a focal point in this support system that encompassed the entire congregation and other Indians who attended the church socials. Anna also decided to get involved in PTA functions with Anglo women, as she wanted "to conquer prejudice by proving that the American Indian is an asset to our nation." This notion reflected the views of many progressive-minded Indian leaders, including Carlos Montezuma who stayed at the Shaw household shortly before his death. In her activism as a parent and church member, Shaw assumed the role of cultural broker in the urban setting. She became increasingly fluent in the language of the mainstream while, at the same time, she developed an interest in recording Pima oral traditions. When the Shaws retired on Ross's home reservation, Salt River, Anna became a leading force in reviving Pima language and traditions. Undoubtedly, proximity to the two Pima reservations allowed both Anna and Ross to maintain a connection to their heritage, something that many of their contemporaries lost in the transition to an urban life far from home. Furthermore, the Shaws' association with Central Presbyterian served as an anchor in what was, at the time, an unaccepting environment.

Unlike the Shaws, most Indian people in the early twentieth century still lived in isolated reservation communities in which families survived at subsistence level. Where men adopted farming, they usually could not produce enough on their small allotments to provide for their families. The Bureau of Indian Affairs (BIA) also failed to create infrastructures supportive of Indian farming. In some communities, men never took to farming, and, instead, leased out their allotments and turned to wage labor. Even then, their seasonal wages were insufficient to support their families. In these poor reservation economies, women's contributions remained essential, thus undermining the mainstream's attempts to turn Indian women into demure housewives. Women supplemented the family diet by gardening and tending poultry, sheep, and goats. They also worked for wages, most often in agriculture or domestic service. The most lucrative business on many reservations, however, came in the form of crafts. Traditionally the producers of many crafts items, women readily took advantage of this new opportunity.

On the Southern Ute Reservation, for instance, women tanned deerskins and fashioned them into articles of clothing and pouches, which they decorated with intricate beadwork and quill embroidery. They also made baskets, which they traded for necessary items or sold for cash. In the Southwest, the completion of the Santa Fe Railroad created a new market for Indian crafts when the company began a promotional campaign that evoked the romance of the American West. Restaurateur Fred Harvey, who had a contract to provision the railroad, filled his hotels and restaurants with Native objects to sell to visitors. Especially desirable was Pueblo pottery. Among the numerous women potters, Maria Martinez of San Ildefonso mastered the ancient craft of Pueblo pottery, and in so doing she found an economic way out of poverty. Martinez's success was not singular for her example and assistance served as incentives for other women to

Nampeyo, a Hopi pottery maker, with examples of her work, 1900. Crafts were often the most lucrative business on the reservations allowing women, the traditional producers of craft items, to better provide for their families. National Archives #NWDNS-79-HPS-6-3277

gain skills as craftsworkers. Gregorita Chavarria of Santa Clara Pueblo spoke to the impact of the trade in crafts items on women's economic roles: "Before the Harvey buses came it was hard for the women. After they started coming it seemed like the women were the ones who were the providers, the moneymakers, and the men did their farming."

Women's participation in this economic activity created a dilemma for the Indian Service. On one hand, the production of arts and crafts fit the idea of housewifery, since this activity did not take women out of the home. On the other hand, these activities appeared to maintain Native tradition, the very thing the Service wanted to discourage. Therefore, while some agents recognized the importance of the tourist trade, supporting and even encouraging crafts work, others remained averse to it. The Bureau did not officially recognize the economic viability of arts and crafts until 1934, when the Indian Reorganization Act (IRA) created the Indian Arts and Crafts Board to promote arts as a means to self-sufficiency. With this sanctioned encouragement came a revival of many traditional crafts: Cheyenne beadwork and moccasins; Navajo weaving and silver work; and Apache baskets, among others.

The Arts and Crafts Board was just one indication of the turnaround in federal policy from a rigid call for assimilation toward an acceptance and appreciation of Native cultures. The IRA also reversed the policy of allotment and began to address the value of preserving Indian cultures and languages. Furthermore, it gave Indian tribes the tools for political and economic self-determination. Under the IRA, tribes could form their own governments and incorporate for economic purposes. However, the models for doing so relied on non-Indian notions of civil rights and democratic government. Tribal constitutions thus included women's enfranchisement but also frequently incorporated articles that reinforced patriarchal property values. Yet, as historian Alison Bernstein has emphasized, the IRA "broke new ground for Indian women from tribes with little or no history of formal public women's political participation." Now, for the first time, women could also impress their significance on non-Indian observers.

World War II contributed greatly to Indian women's new visibility, both on reservations and in the mainstream. By the war's end, some 25,000 Native Americans had served in the military, including 800 women in the military auxiliaries. By 1943, approximately 46,000 Indians had left their reservations—many of them for the first time—to work in the war industries and in agriculture; of them, 12,000 were women. In fact, the Indian schools that trained this workforce preferred female students to males, who might well be drafted during training. On reservations, too, the war opened new opportunities for women; they staffed schools and served as paraprofessionals; they took on jobs as truck drivers and clerks. At the Mescalero Apache agency, women labored in the fields for the first time in history because "few men were left to plow for the women, aged, and children." Another first occurred on the Menominee reservation in Wisconsin, where women took over the second shift in the lumber mills. Several Navajo women even mastered the traditionally male craft of silversmithing and began to display their own jewelry creations alongside those crafted by men. Finally, an increasing number of women realized new opportunities in tribal politics. The significance of the war was thus two-fold: it loosened the definitions of male and female roles in many Indian communities, and it introduced large numbers of Native women to wage employment and the mainstream society.

What the war failed to change were the depressed reservation economies. Industrialization and other wartime improvements never reached the reservations, and new political priorities in the immediate aftermath of the war further stilted their economic growth. Upon returning to the reservation, veterans and war workers found little opportunity for employment, and many decided to move back to the nation's urban areas. Termination and relocation policies fueled this exodus to cities. According to the 1980 census, more than half of the Native American population in the United States lived in urban areas—some of them on reservations; by 1990, this figure had reached 63 percent. "Coming to the city . . . is still a culture shock," said Shoshoni/Paiute Patricia Helton of the experience of moving from the reservation to the city. "It's such a fast pace and [Indian people]

World War II contributed greatly to Indian women's new visibility. Eight hundred Indian women joined the military auxiliaries including (from left) Minnie Spotted Wolf (Blackfoot), Celia Mix (Potawatomi), and Viola Eastman (Chippewa). National Archives #NWDNS-208-NS-4350-2

have such a family-oriented idea about life. Their family comes first, so even if they live [in the city] during the week, every week they're home [on the reservation]."

Helton's comments speak to the devastating effect of relocation on extended families, as it most often took people far away from their reservation communities. Relocation also placed extra pressures on the families that moved. The BIA offered new relocatees initial assistance in finding housing and employment but little in dealing with the strange environment. Because of the Indians' relative lack of skills and, in many instances, inadequate English, their employment opportunities were limited to low-paying, menial jobs. In addition, the cost of living in urban areas including housing, transportation, and medical care, was higher than on reservations. The promise of prosperity and assimilation quickly turned into what Vine Deloria Jr. has called "a one-way ticket to poverty." Urban poverty placed extra demands on women who, in addition to taking care of their children and households, had to find outside employment to help support their families. Women, indeed, were the backbones of Indian urban families.

Women also were at the center of urban support networks. Churches often served as the first point of contact for people of different tribal backgrounds and became centers of social life. The church congregation became the extended urban family, and women took on the role of "community mothers." They prepared food for church socials; they contributed time to charitable causes; they sang in the choir. As elders, they made decisions about the responsibilities of the church in the community. In all these roles, women formed female networks—much as they had done on reservations—discussing their concerns as mothers, as wives, and as women. At Central Presbyterian in Phoenix, women used this network, appealing to their status as mothers, to start a Head Start program to serve the neighborhood. Tohono O'odham Cecelia Miller testifies to the impact of this activism on women: "It gave me a lot more self-confidence in terms of what I could do. . . . I learned that I could do a lot more than I thought I could."

Indeed, the experience launched many women into continued involvement in the community and in the emerging Indian organizations, which took advantage of the increased funding from President Lyndon B. Johnson's Great Society programs. In Phoenix, as in many other major cities around the nation, the Indian Center assumed the role of the custodian of Native American interests by the 1970s. Many of the services offered by these centers—employment and housing assistance, drug and alcohol abuse counseling, educational programs, and programs for the elderly—fell within the traditionally female sphere and thus provided ample opportunity for women's employment. Women also filled the clerical positions. Training and education on the job added to their skills, prompting many women to enroll in college programs or to move on to other employment. Some became political activists, focusing on issues like discrimination and representation in city governments.

Reservations, meanwhile, continued to wage their own battles of survival: poverty, unemployment, lack of services, and poor health care. Women mobilized to fight these ills because "[t]his is home. This is the land here . . . [and not just] a piece of land with a house on it, but the whole connection—the community, the history, the stories." The community action programs of the Great Society addressed the material poverty in reservation communities. And in light of the history of federal paternalism, these programs proved especially significant, helping to "bring about a more structural power base [and] involv[ing] people in the exercise to use the resources and to make decisions." The programs also created new jobs, providing reservation residents viable alternatives to leaving. As in the cities, the programs often dealt with health care, social services, and education, allowing a growing number of women to enter the workforce. As in the cities, this employment and the accompanying training prompted many women to continue their education and to move on to other, often more-demanding jobs. With a newly realized "self-esteem, a sense of accomplishment, and satisfaction— a degree of power through involvement," many women entered tribal politics. By 1980, women headed approximately 12 percent of the nation's federally recognized tribes and Alaskan Native corporations.

The aforementioned Wilma Mankiller became the first female Principal Chief of the Cherokee Nation in 1985 and served in that position until 1995. Her life cycle reflects the many junctures in the lives of twentieth-century Native American women. Mankiller grew up in the rural poverty of Oklahoma, "raised with a sense of community that extended beyond my family." When she was eighteen, her family relocated to the San Francisco Bay area, an experience Mankiller calls her "Private Trail of Tears." She married early and raised her family amidst the turbulence and activism of the 1960s. The occupation of Alcatraz Island mobilized her to participate in Indian causes while she attended college, earning a degree in social work. After divorcing her husband, Mankiller returned to Oklahoma in 1977, completed graduate work in community planning, and spearheaded a community revitalization project. In 1983, she was elected Deputy Chief of the Cherokee Nation and succeeded Principal Chief Ross Swimmer at his resignation in 1985. Mankiller recognized that "I'll have to do extra well because I am the first woman." She focused on unity and economic development, and in 1987 she won the election in her own right. As Principal Chief, Mankiller emphasized indigenous solutions to the problems of the Cherokees, maintaining that "Cherokee values, especially those of helping one another and of our interconnections with the land, can be used to address contemporary issues."

Preserving this connection to the land and its resources for posterity also served as the focus for many activist movements of the 1950s and 1960s. Examples abound: the Senecas challenged the construction of the Kinzua Dam in Pennsylvania; the Mohawks and Tuscaroras resisted the St. Lawrence Seaway project in New York; and, the Puyallup tribe in the Pacific Northwest launched a battle over fishing rights in 1970. But these struggles involved more than dams and fishing rights; they constituted demands for the right of cultural survival. Puyallup Ramona Bennett, active in the fishing rights struggle, explained: "Fishing is part of our art forms and religion and diet, and the entire culture is based around it." Losing this connection to culture and tradition has a profound meaning for Native women. Explained Ojibway Melinda Gopher:

> When the loss of culture happens, the women break down and lose that connection with the traditional value system. When they lose their connection, they begin to lose the sacredness of childbearing. Problems such as fetal alcohol syndrome have become prevalent in recent years. I believe this is one result of the alienation of Native women from their indigenous culture.

A number of Native women's organizations sprang up in the 1970s and 1980s to defend women's connection to tradition in the face of extraordinary assaults, including forced sterilization and removal of Indian children from their families. Principally, these groups formed to maintain the continuity and survival of their people. Thus, their objectives included issues such as the prevention of family violence and substance abuse; the improvement of education and health care; the support of cultural preservation, specifically of tribal languages; and the development of reservation economies. Community issues thus became women's issues. Concluded Shinnecock Margo Thunderbird: "In our struggle, there are not necessarily dividing lines between women's issues and men's issues. We are all struggling to survive as nations, as communities, as societies."

For some Indian women their experience with sexism and their strong sense of themselves as women served as an impetus for organizing. Tulalip/Nisqually Janet McCloud, for instance, had been active in fishing rights and in the American Indian Movement (AIM) but felt that these groups did not address women's concerns. Therefore, in the 1970s she helped organize Women of All Red Nations and the Northwest Indian Women's Circle. McCloud explained her motivation: "We were tired of the sexist macho stuff we got from the men in AIM. We needed to do something for the women. We are the backbone of our communities—men are the jawbone. [Laughs.]" As for feminism as an ideology and catalyst for their activism, Native women remain ambivalent. Cherokee Wilma Mankiller acknowledges being a feminist while Brenda Young, also Cherokee, sees feminism as an elitist movement that sets boundaries on Indian women as members of their communities:

> [Feminist groups have] too narrow a focus. . . . There are certain issues that are difficult. Like some women in the women's movement hate men. Hey, men are victims, too! I mean, they're a victim of this whole rigid system that says women have to act one way and men have to act another. And yes, I think men have the power they pull out of a system, but a lot of the time . . . it's out of ignorance or they don't know any other way. So that [often turns Indian women off]. Feminism is like a subculture, like a club, that feeds itself. They just don't know much about Indian cultures.

In addition to women's organizations, individual Native women have equipped themselves with the tools to affect change. Although the majority of Indian women continue to toil in low-paying jobs, an increasing number are entering the professions. Yankton Dakota anthropologist Ella Deloria paved the way for other Native women in recording their cultures and languages. Sisseton/Wapeton attorney Susan Williams became the first Indian woman to argue a case before the United States Supreme Court in 1988. Mohawk environmental engineer Laura Weber consults on issues such as recycling and waste management. During her career, Lumbee educator Helen Maynor Scheirbeck served a number of human resource agencies and wrote about Indian education. And Cherokee museum administrator and folklorist Rayna Green has written on Native American women and helped plan American Indian programs at several major museums, including the Smithsonian Institution in Washington, D.C.

One of the most important ways for Native women today to exert their influence and to help determine the future of their people is through the arts. Since Kiowa N. Scott Momaday became the first Native person to receive the Pulitzer Prize in 1969, American Indian authors have increasingly penetrated the literary world of the United States. In their writing, male and female authors alike evoke the traditions of their peoples, relying on forms of expression that derive from oral literature: the emphasis on event over process; the significance of language; the concern with place; and the affirmation of tribal values. Women and women's concerns often form the thematic center of these works. Although the protagonist of Leslie Marmon Silko's *Ceremony* is male, the story revolves around the femininity of the Pueblo world and the Earth. Louise Erdrich follows the lives of generations of Chippewa women in her trilogy *Love Medicine, Beet Queen,* and *Tracks.* Poets like Creek Joy Harjo, Navajo Luci Tapahonso and Pueblo Nora Naranjo-Morse address the world through women's eyes. This "reinvention of the enemy's language" is a powerful tool in the hands of Native artists. To quote Joy Harjo:

> We are still dealing with a holocaust of outrageous proportion in these lands . . . But to speak, at whatever cost, is to become empowered rather than victimized by destruction. In our tribal cultures the power of language to heal, to regenerate, and to create is understood. These colonizers' languages, which often usurped our own tribal languages or diminished them, now hand back emblems of our cultures, our own designs: beadwork, quills if you will. We've transformed these enemy languages.

This transformation reflects the story of Native American women. Although a lot has been lost in the face of adversity, Indian communities have survived. They have adjusted to change; they have adopted aspects of the enemy's culture and transformed them to serve their own needs and goals; they have renewed their traditions to work in the present. The women of Native societies have played a central role in leading their people from tradition through renewal to the present. Theirs is "the fantastic and terrible story of all of our survival."

Suggested Reading

Much of the writing on Native American women and their historical roles comes in articles. Useful edited collections include Patricia Albers and Beatrice Medicine's *The Hidden Half: Studies of Plains Indian Women* (Washington, D.C., 1983); Laura F. Klein and Lillian A. Ackennan, *Women and Power in Native America* (Norman, Okla., 1995); and Nancy Shoemaker, *Negotiators of Change: Historical Perspectives on Native American Women* (New York, 1995).

In recent years, book-length studies on American Indian women's historical roles have begun to appear. Examples of these studies include Carol Devens, *Countering Colonization: Native Women and Great Lakes Missons* (Berkeley, Calif., 1992); Devon Mihesuah, *Cultivating the Rosebuds: The Education of Women at the Cherokee Female Seminary, 1851–1909* (Urbana, Ill., 1993); Katherine M. B. Osburn, *Southern Ute Women: Autonomy and Assimilation on the Reservation, 1887–1934* (Albuquerque, N. Mex., 1998); and Theda Perdue, *Cherokee Women: Gender and Cultural Change, 1700–1835* (Lincoln, Nebr., 1998).

Life histories, autobiographies, and biographies provide excellent insights into the lives of Native women throughout history. Gretchen M. Bataille and Kathleen Mullen Sands explore these women' s narratives in *American Indian Women: Telling Their Lives* (Lincoln, Nebr., 1984). Recent autobiographies include Benson Tong, *Susan La Flesche Picotte, M.D.: Omaha Indian Leader and Reformer* (Norman, Okla., 1999); Wilma Mankiller and Michael Wallis, *Mankiller: A Chief and Her People* (New York, 1993); and Mary Crow Dog with Richard Erdoes, *Lakota Woman* (New York, 1990). Other excellent works include Julie Cruikshank, *Life Lived Like A Story: Life Stories of Three Yukon Native Elders* (Lincoln, Nebr., 1992); Marla N. Powers, *Oglala Women: Myth, Ritual, and Reality* (Chicago, 1986); and Jane Holden Kelly, *Yaqui Women Contemporary Life Histories* (Lincoln, Nebr., 1978).

Literature and poetry remain important sources for understanding American Indian women in history and in the present. Edited collections provide an excellent starting point for exploring the diversity of Indian women. See for example, Rayna Green, *That's what She said: Contemporary Poetry and Fiction by Native American Women* (Bloomington, Ind., 1984); Paula Gunn Allen, *Spider Woman's Granddaughters: Traditional Tales and Contemporary Writing by Native American Women* (Boston, 1989); and *Reinventing the Enemy's Language: Contemporary Native Women's Writings of North America* (New York, 1997). Ella Cara Deloria, *Waterlily* (Lincoln, Nebr., 1988); Louise Erdrich, *The Bingo Palace* (New York, 1994); Joy Harjo, *The Woman Who Fell From the Sky* (New York, 1994); and Linda Hogan, *Solar Storms* (New York, 1995) need to suffice as examples of the many literary works by Native American women.

Chapter 16 ❧
Our Dead Are Never Forgotten

American Indian Struggles for Burial Rights and Protections

James Riding In

*S*tanding before a United States treaty delegation in the 1850s in what became known as Washington, Chief Seattle responded to the visitors' demands that the Suquamish and Duwamish peoples cede most of their lands to their country. In doing so, he compared the perspective of his relatives' view of death and the afterlife with those of white Americans, declaring

> To us the ashes of our ancestors are sacred and their resting place is hallowed ground. You [white Americans] wander far from the graves of your ancestors and seemingly without regret. . . . Your dead cease to love you and the land of their nativity as soon as they pass the portals of the tomb and wander way beyond the stars. They are soon forgotten and never return. Our dead never forget the beautiful world that gave them being. They still love its verdant valleys, its murmuring rivers, its magnificent mountains, sequestered vales and verdant lined lakes and bays, and ever yearn in tender, fond affection over the lonely hearted living, and often return from the Happy Hunting Ground to visit, guide, console and comfort them.

Seattle was wrong about one point. White Americans at that time generally cared dearly about the sanctity of the graves of their relatives. Laws in both the United States and Europe were in place that established criminal penalties for those who engaged in the ghastly business of body snatching. However, many white Americans viewed the contents of Indian graves in a diametrically opposite light. The looting of Indian burials for recreation, study, and profit had become a widely accepted practice. Indeed, an industry developed that linked archaeology, museums, law, and individuals in a web that romanticized Indian grave contents.

This chapter presents an aspect of the American Indian experience that most scholars have ignored. History, reified by popular culture, has taught us that it was the Indians who violated the dead with their scalping knife. Our national mythology also presents Indians as having perpetuated uncontrollable acts of violence against unoffending settlers. In actuality, white Americans committed far more atrocities against dead Indians than did Indians against whites, living and dead. Because of the pervasiveness of these practices against the dead Natives, I categorize this phenomenon as a spiritual holocaust. Readers should be aware that abuses committed against dead Natives are innumerable as well as repugnant, irreligious, and offensive. You should be warned that this account includes graphic descriptions that illustrate acts of mistreating human remains. I have purposefully taken this approach so that you may ponder important moral, ethical, and legal issues surrounding my discussion. What are the rights of science? Under what conditions, if any, should the dead be considered the property of science? What is the relationship between law, power, and racism? Do Indians have a sovereign right to rebury all of their dead ancestors? What factors have promoted growing concern for Indian issues?

The incursions of English persons into North America during the seventeenth century brought many oppressive social, economic, and political experiences to those Indians who encountered them. With the founding of the United States in the 1770s, problems facing Indian nations mounted as the new country broadened its borders and spheres of influence. White Americans—viewing Indians as inferior, in the way of progress, and expendable burdens—treated Indians callously in both life and death. While subjecting Native peoples to acts of land losses, removal, genocide, and coercive assimilation, the newcomers disrupted perhaps as many as 2 million Native graves. Out of the carnage grew a network of institutions, organizations, and individuals who profited from the taking, study, displaying, and storing of Indian grave contents.

Common Experiences

Feelings about the dead transcend cultural boundaries. At the onset of contact, American Indians and Euro-Americans possessed vastly different cultures and explanations concerning death and ways to dispose of their dead. Yet, they shared certain common views rooted in their respective religions. Both peoples universally respected the sanctity of the grave, the connection of a spirit with the dead body, and an afterlife. Put another way, Indians and non-Indians alike maintained religious beliefs that recognized the sancity of the grave and an afterlife. As grave looters appeared, members of each group expressed outrage at the sacrilege of having the bodies of their loved ones disinterred and mutilated in the name of science.

In examining cross-cultural attitudes regarding death and the sanctity of the grave, we cannot forget that an astonishing amount of diversity exists within both groups. It is very probably that in the late fifteenth century, at the outset of contact with Europeans, as many as 500 separate and culturally distinct Indian nations lived within what is now the United States. Although five colonial European powers competed for dominance over North America, Great Britain prevailed, meaning that English common law and ethical precepts weighed most heavily in the establishment of ideas concerning the grave. Protestantism, with dozens of distinct sects, comprised the major religion that the earliest and subsequent generations of Englishmen transported across the Atlantic. Catholics, as a rule brought by non-English Europeans, also became a part of the American religious landscape.

American Indian mortuary traditions are deeply rooted in a past that involves millenniums of experiences within the Americas. Creation stories, varying from one Native group to the next, expressed in songs, ceremonial recitals, and family settings indicate that the First Peoples on this hemisphere either came from the heavens or emerged from the underground. As European explorers began arriving in the late fifteenth century, Indian peoples in what is now called the United States may have numbered somewhere between 10 and 15 million. Therefore, since time immemorial in what became the United States, friends and relatives interred the bodies of millions of loved ones. They also placed tens of millions of items in the graves. Because of unexpected circumstances associated with some people's death, including accidents, warfare, and nature, innumerable deceased persons were neither afforded a proper burial nor cremated in accordance with custom.

To Indians of then and now, however, proper disposition of the dead constitutes an important obligation of the living. Mortuary practices and beliefs vary from Indian Nation to Nation. Because space limitations preclude the discussion of all forms of burial within this chapter, I will offer only several examples of the diversity and commonalties in their beliefs and customs. Some communities employed primary interment; others adhered to secondary burial techniques; and still others used cremation. Whatever the funerary practice, members of virtually all Indigenous communities painstakingly prepared their dead for the afterlife. Friends and relatives bathed, clothed, and symbolically fed their loved ones before sending them on a spiritual journey. They customarily placed alongside the body items, or funerary offerings, needed to make the transition to the spiritual world. Furthermore, loved ones considered burial grounds as sacred sites, the sanctity of which lasted indefinitely. Many believed in an attendant spirit to the physical remains, meaning that any injury to the bones harmed the spirit.

Indians went to great pains to ensure that their spirits after death would reach the proper destination. A Shasta's final words, recorded in 1877, explain the religious significance of a proper and lasting burial for many California Indians. After telling his companions not to bury him away from his home village, the dying man gave a passionate "adjuration to them not to let his body molder and his spirit wander homeless, friendless, and alone in a strange country."

Indigenous groups shared many beliefs regarding unauthorized tampering with the dead. They expect a lasting burial in which their remains would deteriorate within Mother Earth. Some believed that disinterment stopped the spiritual journey of the dead, causing the affected spirits to wander aimlessly in limbo. Those affected spirits wreaked havoc among the living, bringing sickness, emotional distress, and even death. Many nations such as the Navajo, Apache, and

Pawnee believed that anyone who disrupted a grave was an evil, profane, and demented person who planned to use the dead as a means of harming the living. Many Indians stressed that disinterment could occur only under the supervision of a priest and only for a compelling reason. For example, Pawnees occasionally opened a grave, but only under strict guidelines requiring the repositioning of holy objects that had been initially placed incorrectly within the burial.

Euro-Americans also respected the rights of their dead. Under English common law, no one owned the deceased. Before the Reformation, burial usually occurred in churchyards with the expectation that the bodies would arise from the grave and ascend to heaven at the Last Judgment. Similar to Indian philosophy, it was believed that a spirit, or soul, remained attached to the body of the deceased and that the corpse must be interred fully intact so it could be resurrected. According to prevailing thought, the body was to be interred fully intact so it could be admitted to heaven. Dissection could separate the spirit from the body. During the Reformation, English attitudes began to change, and most burials took place in a cemetery. Attitudes nonetheless remained intact that the dead deserved respect and protection from desecration.

The Enlightenment followed the Reformation, and along with its focus on secular humanism and the growth of medical science, this new philosophy encouraged a small but influential segment of the English population to view the human body as specimen for study. As medical school curriculums were weighted towards the dissecting of corpses, medical students required a number of cadavers, the supply of which law and religion strictly limited. Court sentences, issued under authority of the Murder Act of 1752, exempted only executed criminals and traitors from a burial without dismemberment. Acts of mutilating the human body by quartering and medical dissection not only served students in medical schools, they also seriously impaired, if not eliminated, the hapless criminals' ascension to heaven. In this sense, medical dissection and autopsy served as a form of spiritual punishment for the wicked and evil.

The demand for cadavers, however, continued to exceed the number circumscribed by the state. In urban areas located near medical schools, body snatching became a serious problem that violated peoples' sensibilities and fundamental understandings of ethics, morality, and religion. Now medical schools, facing a shortage of fresh corpses, turned to criminal elements to secure more dead remains. Resurrectionists, as they were called, frequently entered local graveyards after dark and exhumed recently interred bodies. After digging into the grave and opening the coffin, Resurrectionists placed a rope around the body's neck and pulled it above ground. The body was then transported to the medical school, where the thieves received payment and the body was later surgically mutilated and studied.

The public perceived these acts of the Resurrectionists as sacrilege and inhuman. Given that many citizens viewed the rope-tugging technique to extract the body from the coffin as a spiritual transgression, we can imagine the extent of the anger incited by the physical act of dissection. Public outrage encouraged English lawmakers to enact the Anatomy Act of 1832, which protected the dead from any such practices.

This clash between medicine and respect for the dead was transported across the Atlantic Ocean. When New York City medical students during the late 1780s failed to obtain enough corpses for dissection by legal means, they, too, turned to immoral, unethical, and illegal techniques. A social uprising, known as the Doctors' Riot, erupted in 1788 after a heartless medical student waved a disarticulated arm from the window of the school and told a passing boy that it belonged to his mother. When the boy, who had recently suffered the death of his mother, told his father about the incident, the indigent man rallied support and a two-day riot ensued, damaging much of the New York Hospital. Responding to the violent protest, the New York legislature enacted the first law in the United States that criminalized body snatching. Other states soon followed suit. These laws, however, allowed medical schools to claim bodies of executed criminals, abused and overworked chain-gang prisoners, and unclaimed members of society. By the 1840s, these laws curbed without ending grave looting. In the South, for instance, the Medical College of Georgia employed operatives until the early 1900s to snatch bodies from local cemeteries for study. Careful to avoid arousing public indignation, the thieves targeted the graves of slaves and indigents. Lacking a means to challenge these actions, these powerless populations, generally people with brown skin, served as unwilling "specimens" for the medical profession.

For Indians, the marking of their bodies as objects of postmortem study differed in some important respects. With the dominant culture constructing a view of Indians as falling outside of the bounds of respect, dignity, and protection of the law accorded other people, Indians lived beyond the protection of burial statutes. It is true that until the early twentieth century most Indians were not U.S. citizens, and most had no interest in becoming so, but they had never ceded their rights of ownership over their dead through treaties, agreements, or any other means. Nevertheless, a sinister conspiracy developed that essentially denied them burial rights taken for granted by the vast majority of white citizens.

The Bonding of Colonialism, Scientific Racism, and Imperial Archaeology

European settlement of North America provided the colonizers with access to wealth, land, and opportunity. On the other hand, this dramatic demographic occurrence set a tone of racial intolerance, injustice, and immorality that became imbedded in white intellectual, religious, and popular thought. Those explorers, looters, and settlers (often one and the same) who left Europe during the age of exploration and colonization reached the shores of North America with a number of self-serving ideas and dehumanizing stereotypes about the Natives, the land, and the dead who rested in the soil. Europeans, by virtue of the "Doctrine of Discovery," claimed a right of preeminence to the North American continent. Graves of Indians became fair game. English violations of Indian burials occurred as early as the arrival of the *Mayflower* at Plymouth Bay in 1620 and the practice has spanned the duration of history to the present.

The Revolutionary War Era was a formative one in which white Americans began to assume tacit ownership over dead American Indians. Intellectual figures of the time articulate differing perspectives toward Indians. The newcomers wondered where Indians originally came from and who had built the burial mounds that spread over a vast area of Virginia and other nearby colonies. Some whites viewed them as manifesting the noble characteristics of a people endowed with courage, innocence, chivalry, and generosity. Others took a more negative view, casting Indians as the embodiment of human imperfection, retardation, and evil. Although some white thinkers of this period categorized Indians as members of the human family, the majority seems to have considered them as lacking either intellectual or cultural refinement, or both. Curiosity about the nature of Indian life and death, spawned in part by the growth of scientific inquiry, provided the impetus for the development of archaeology as an honorable profession and thereby encouraged the looting of Indian graves.

Driven by "scientific" inquisitiveness, Thomas Jefferson, along with some of his contemporaries, took a lead in opening Indian graves. Before becoming the third President of the United States, Jefferson had excavated an Indian burial mound located near his Virginia estate of Monticello. Two local legends with conflicting explanations about the content of the mounds seem to have motivated Jefferson's desire to enter the burial site. One version held that the remains within the mound were placed in an upright position, while another implied that only warriors who fell in battle were buried there. In his *Notes on the State of Virginia*, written in 1781 and 1782 and published in 1787, Jefferson rationalized his action: "I wished to satisfy myself whether any, and which of these opinions were just. For this purpose I determined to open and examine it thoroughly." Unearthing the mass grave, Jefferson found the remains of about one thousand bodies of all ages and sexes. From his diggings, he concluded that the mound was "the common sepulchre for the town."

Some scholars assume that Jefferson wrote about Indians with more understanding and sympathy than did most contemporary observers. In fact, he viewed them as a culturally retarded people who need the "blessings of civilization" to elevate them from the degradation and depravity of savagery. Jefferson, who frequently acted in both his private and public life as a political and racial imperialist and hypocrite, lacked empathy for Indians. Jefferson knew that a party of Indians had visited the mound about thirty years earlier. He nevertheless excavated it, declining to locate and seek permission from the next of kin before doing so. Had he respectfully sought permission, he may have solved the mystery of the burial site without disturbing the resting place of all of those people by simply asking the living kin about the nature of the burial. Moreover, as president, Jefferson was the architect of the Indian removal policy, a disastrous program in terms of Native rights that uprooted and relocated tens of thousands of eastern Indians to west of the Mississippi River between the 1810s and 1850s. Removal left many Indian burial sites unprotected. Taking advantage of the situation, white settlers, followed closely by professional and amateur "archaeologists," opened tribal graves, and carried off the contents.

Jefferson considered himself as a force standing against arbitrary justice and tyranny in favor of democracy, equality, and fairness. Reflecting this sentiment, he wrote the following inscription for his tomb: "Here lies buried Thomas Jefferson, Author of the Declaration of American Independence, of the Statute of Virginia for Religious Freedom, and Father of the University of Virginia." Although a degree of truth surrounds Jefferson's self-perception, the monument failed to note the contradictions in his life. He espoused personal liberty, but he owned black slaves and allegedly fathered children with one of them. Equally important, he advocated religious freedom, but his excavation intruded upon the religious practices and beliefs of Indians.

Jefferson was not the first to desecrate an Indian burial site, but he was probably the most famous person to do so. Future generations of students, along with many of his contemporaries, looked upon Jefferson, his writings, and contributions to science with admiration. Because of his political and scientific standing, Jefferson's diggings had lasting ramifications for a society that already viewed Indians as lacking the refinements of "civilized" persons. He essentially gave an illusion of morality to the seizure of contents from Indian graves. Had Jefferson and other Enlightenment figures taken a stance against the looting of Indian graves, the history of Indian burial rights might have developed differently. As it was, however, grave disruptions, along with published reports of such operations, proliferated with the passage of time. By the 1780s, a growing list of individuals and organizations, including the American Philosophical Society and the American Antiquarian Society, had entered the business of acquiring collections of Indian remains. Printed materials such as Caleb Atwater's *Description of the Antiquities Discovered in the State of Ohio* (1820) offered readers explicit drawings of trophies, such as skulls and funerary offerings, found in digs of Midwestern Indian burial sites.

As the United States expanded its borders, the attraction of Indian graves grew simultaneously. Since the early nineteenth century, U.S. soldiers stationed in frontier posts and Indian agents had frequently opened burial mounds and shipped their contents to pseudo-scientists back east. Military expeditions sent to the West also excavated Indian graves. For instance, members of the Stephen H. Long expedition of 1819 and 1820 disrupted some of the burial mounds surrounding St. Louis as they moved westward. Along the way they also collected several Indian crania found lying on the ground in Pawnee country.

During the early 1830s, individuals working under the titles of new pseudo-scientific disciplines called craniometrics and phrenology sought to devise tests to categorize human groups by race and to validate the theory of white supremacy. While seeking to explain the diversity of humanity, they turned the contents of Indian graves into a commodity. Samuel G. Morton, known as the father of physical anthropology, popularized the theory held by phrenologists that brain size was an indication of racial intelligence. Finding few skulls available for study, Morton employed grave looters, including soldiers, settlers, and federal agents, to do his dirty work. Preoccupied with American Natives, he eventually assembled a large collection of Indian crania from North and South America. With economic rewards providing an incentive to enter Indian graves, field collectors often took advantage of the recurring diseases and political forces that periodically depopulated and displaced Indian peoples. One wrote to Morton: "There is an epidemic raging among them which carries them off so fast that the cemeteries will soon lack watchers—I don't rejoice in the prospects of death of the poor creatures certainly, but then you know it will be very convenient for my purposes."

Morton's efforts popularized the theory held by phrenologists that cranial capacity and brain size were indeed indicators of racial intelligence. In writing *Crania Americana* (1839), Morton measured several hundred skulls belonging to members of different races, including American Indian, African, and Australian Aborigine. After pouring mustard seeds into interior of the skulls and weighing the contents, he postulated that the Anglo-Saxon had the largest brain capacity and, therefore, more intelligence than other peoples of Earth did. As the popular paleontologist and historian Stephen Gould points out in *The Mismeasure of Man* (1996), Morton manipulated his methods to obtain the desired results.

Although phrenological inquiry of Morton's era sought to attribute moral traits to Indian skulls based on shapes and indentations, practitioners of this misguided scientific persuasion rarely, if ever, questioned the morality of taking Indian bodies from graves. Actually, society viewed the study of Indian skulls as a worthy intellectual pursuit. For one thing, phrenologists and craniologists engaged in a stratagem that demeaned Indians for allegedly lacking character and ambition to improve their lives. Of course, Western civilization served as the yardstick by which they measured the diversity of humanity. White American apologists, eager to justify the national growth of the United States and slavery, seized the opportunity to incorporate the findings of craniometric research into their own studies. In *Types of Mankind: Or, Ethnological Researches* (1854), Josiah C. Nott summarized Morton's research in order to justify morally the destructive behavior and policies of United States citizens toward Indians and black slaves:

> Intelligence, activity, ambition, progression, high anatomical development, characterize some races; stupidity, indolence, immobility, savagism, low anatomical development characterize others. Lofty civilization, in all cases, has been achieved solely by the "Caucasian" group. Mongolian races, save the Chinese family, in no instance have reached beyond the degree of semi-civilization; while the Black races of Africa and Oceania no less than the *Barba-*

rous tribes of America have remained in utter darkness for thousands of years. . . .

Furthermore, certain savage types can neither be civilized or domesticated. The *Barbarous* races of America (excluding the Toltecs) although nearly as low in intellect as the Negro races, are essentially untameable. Not merely have all attempts to civilize them failed, but also every endeavor to enslave them. Our Indian tribes submit to extermination, rather than wear the yoke under which our Negro slaves fatten and multiply.

Echoing themes of Manifest Destiny, Nott and other writers of this era employed hierarchical rankings to categorize the diversity of humankind. Of course, the lighter the coloration of a group's skin pigmentation, the higher it stood in the linear progression of the races.

Within this milieu, the looting of Indian graves was not defined by class distinction. Although refined men from the upper crust of society often gathered large collections, or libraries, of Indian skulls through purchase, scavenging operations, and trade, others from the lower classes pillaged Indian graves for fun and profit. For example, white Americans entering California during the gold rush mania of the late 1840s and early 1850s ravaged Native burial sites looking for fabled Indian treasure. Describing some 300 skulls taken from a cave and placed on public display in San Francisco, an observer noted: "The cranial developments are very similar to those of the present Indians, though one of the skulls appear[s] to have a very intellectual character." The "owner" later sold the collection of skulls to Harvard University's Peabody Museum.

Executions occasionally provided physicians access to "fresh" Indian bodies. At Mankato, Minnesota, in 1862, the U.S. Army hanged Marpiya Okinajin, or He Who Stands in the Clouds, and thirty-seven other Dakotas for their roles in the Sioux Uprising of that year. On December 24, one of the condemned men, Tazoo, expressed his belief about his death and the fate awaiting his spirit:

> [T]ell our friends that we are being removed from this world over the same path they must shortly travel. We go first, but many of our friends may follow us in a very short time. I expect to go direct to the abode of the Great Spirit, and to be happy when I get there; but we are told that the road is long and the distance great; therefore, as I am slow in my movements, it will probably take me a long time to reach the end of the journey, and I should not be surprised if some of the young, active men we will leave behind us will pass me on the road before I reach the place of my destination.

His words proved to be prophetic. Following the execution, the largest of its kind in United States history, authorities had the bodies interred in a mass grave a short distance outside of town. The following day they allowed medical doctors and representatives from medical schools to exhume the bodies for medical study

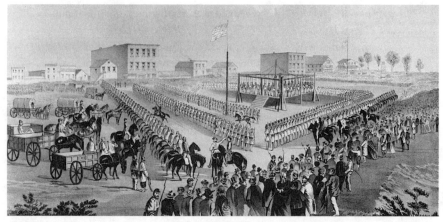

Execution of thirty-eight Sioux at Mankato, Minnesota, December 26, 1862. The day after the bodies were buried authorities allowed medical schools to exhume them for dissection. Courtesy, Minnesota Historical Society AV#1989.44.357

and dissection. According to Indian perceptions, these acts stopped the spiritual journey of Tazoo and the rest of his hanged comrades.

Civilian research popularized the looting of Indian graves, but United States Army officers played an intricate, if not cruel, role in its proliferation for scientific purposes. In an 1856 military excursion up the Missouri River, Lt. G. K. Warren and Frank Hayden looted a Hidatsa cemetery, taking twenty-five sets of remains. In 1862, the Army Medical Museum (AMM) established a program of collecting and studying Indian crania. Some of the first heads shipped to the AMM came from the Sand Creek Massacre of 1864, when Colorado militiamen commanded by Colonel John Chivington, a Methodist minister, slaughtered an encampment of friendly Cheyenne, Kiowa, and Arapaho Indians. In 1867, the U.S. Surgeon General issued a memorandum instructing field surgeons to collect Indian remains for the AMM. Craving more "specimens" to measure, the U.S. Surgeon General's office sent another order the following year, noting that "a craniological collection was commenced last year at the Army Medical Museum, and that it already has 143 specimens of skulls. The chief purpose . . . is to aid the progress of anthropological science by obtaining measurements of a large number of skulls of the aboriginal races of North America." This directive also urged "medical officers stationed in the Indian country or in the vicinity of ancient mounds or cemeteries in the Mississippi Valley or the Atlantic region" to contribute skulls. Finally, it instructed medical personnel to "enhance the value of their contributions by transmitting with the specimens the fullest attainable memoranda, specifying the locality whence the skulls were derived, the presumed age and sex, and, in the case of 'Mound' skulls, or of those from cemeteries, describing the mode of sepulture, and any traces of weapons, implements, utensils found with the specimens, or any other circumstance that may throw light on their ethnic character."

What followed were a series of macabre, gruesome, and remorseless body mutilations and thefts. From the onset of this process, it did not matter whether the skulls came from friends or foes. Various army surgeons mainly stationed in the West followed the Surgeon General's order without questioning the ethical and moral issues surrounding the directive. With the Great Plains witnessing recurring acts of Indian-white violence stemming from U.S. expansion threatening the Indians' ways of life, that area served as a fertile field for the headhunting operations. In an 1869 incident, Major B. E. Fryer, the surgeon at Fort Harker, sponsored an intensive search in Kansas for the bodies of eight unoffending Pawnee who had been gunned down by soldiers and citizens on January 29 near Mulberry Creek. These Native men had been recently discharged from a special U.S. Army detachment known as the Pawnee Scouts and had been fired upon while presenting their discharge papers. Personnel dispatched to Mulberry Creek over the next few weeks found six of the bodies and decapitated them. Noting the conditions of the skulls, Fryer wrote: "four of them [are] excellent specimens, two were injured a good deal by the soldiers who shot into the bodies [and] heads several times after the fight in which these Indians were killed, was ended." That spring, Fryer sent twenty-four severed heads to the AMM. Along with the six Pawnee crania, the shipment included skulls taken from Wichita, Cheyenne, Kaw, and other Indians.

In accordance with the Surgeon General's instructions, not all of the heads accessioned by the AMM came from battlefield casualties. In 1868, a military official at Fort Sumner in New Mexico territory shipped the skull of a Navajo captive to the AMM. In a trade with the Smithsonian Institution the following year, the AMM received Indian remains in exchange for its collection of Native cultural artifacts. About the same time, an army surgeon stationed in the northern Plains raided Ponca, Sioux, and other burials. At a public hanging in northern California in 1873, an army officer directed the surgical decapitation of Captain Jack and three other Modocs who were put to death for their participation in the Modoc War. In a 1892 Montana incident, an army collector described the means he used to obtain fifteen Blackfeet skulls: "On one occasion I was followed by an Indian who did not comprehend my movements, and I made a circuitous route away from the place intended and threw him off his suspicions. On stormy nights—rain, snow or wind & bitter cold, I think I was never observed going or coming, by either Indians or dogs, but on pleasant nights—I was always seen but of course no one knew what I had in my coat . . . the greatest fear I had was that some Indian would miss the heads, see my tracks and ambush me, but they didn't." He had used his coat to hide the crania. When finally ending its policy of collecting Indian remains during the 1890s, the AMM had amassed approximately 4,000 crania representing many different Native groups from North and South America, along with a few from whites, Blacks, Asians, and others.

As might be expected, the AMM's vast collection of Indian remains provided research opportunities for an array of army personnel and scholars. After measuring 734 skulls with the most sophisticated techniques and instruments available, Otis reported in 1870 that Indians ranked lower in intelligence than African Americans and Asians. In 1880, having conducted additional studies, AMM personnel reassessed Otis's findings, moving Indians up a notch on the hierarchical scale. Many others came to the AMM to view, handle, admire, and measure the collection. Whatever means employed to assign intellectual standing to the diversity of humankind, they used flawed scientific methods and racially tinted reasoning. Their research reified popular contentions, with the voice of scientific certainty and authority, the myth of white supremacy.

An important outcome of the grave looting and body snatching was the notion that science had the authority to appropriate the contents of Indian graves. Gaining access to the bodies of deceased Natives had become a privilege acquired through stealth and the use of dispassionate power. At this point, these rights, a reward of conquest, were unassailable. Few, if any, scholars, lawmakers, or leaders showed an inclination to stop the raids on Indian graves. Either forgetting or unconcerned about the reasons for the enactment of state burial protection laws, no one decried the body snatching as a strain on the moral fabric of U.S. society. In fact, an intricate web developed during the last half of the nineteenth century that linked various individuals, institutions, and academic disciplines with the acquisition, warehousing, display, and study of Indian remains. Museums often competed with one another for Indian bodies and cultural artifacts. During the next century, this network elevated white American encroachments into Indian spirituality and burial rights to unprecedented heights. The new academic discipline and profession of archaeology emerged as the leading violator of Indian graves.

Before examining the rise of imperial archaeology and museums as instruments of sacrilege, I will present a composite picture of Indian life during the late nineteenth and early twentieth centuries. This portrait illustrates three interrelated points. First, by this time, Indians had lost their independence and lived under the domination of a coercive federal program of assimilation. Second, their graves and dead had become more vulnerable than ever before to scientific abuse and desecration. Next, despite the first two problems, Indian peoples across the nation refused to abandon their beliefs about death and the sanctity of the grave.

By the 1890s, most Indian nations lived in a deplorable state. Their population had reached a nadir through the ravages of warfare, disease, starvation, and forced removals. Largely living in conditions of abject poverty on reservations scattered across the nation, but mostly in the West, the physical holocaust had left them essentially powerless. Legally relegated to a child-like status as wards of the federal government by treaties, congressional acts, and U.S. Supreme Court decisions, they had virtually lost the ability to chart out their futures without paternalistic oversight from federal policy makers and missionaries.

Essentially, U.S. society not only denied Indians fundamental rights and liberties enjoyed by white America, but it also sought to eradicate customary practices that had existed well before the adoption of Constitution. The philosophy of "Kill the savage, save the man" drove federal Indian policy during this era of coercive assimilation. Professing a sincere interest in the welfare of Indians, numerous individuals and organizations believed that Indians must accept the blessing of "civilization," whether they wanted to or not. This attitude promoted oppression. Infamous Codes of Indian Offenses criminalized customary forms of worship and the Ghost Dance, while scores of missionaries worked energetically to transform Indians into obedient, God-fearing Christians. In 1890, U.S. troops slaughtered several hundred Lakota Ghost Dancers at Wounded Knee on the Pine Ridge reservation in South Dakota. The Dawes Act, passed by Congress in 1887, provided for the allotment of reservation lands and the opening of the so-called surplus lands for non-Indian settlement. Reservation agents simultaneously took thousands of Indian children from the "corrupting" influences of their parents, placing them in distant boarding schools for extended periods. Subjected to a life of military regimentation and harsh discipline, the youth were expected to abandon their spirituality, traditions, and languages in favor of those held by white America.

From 1887 to 1924, the extension of U.S. citizenship to Indians did not dissipate the cloud of oppression hovering over them. Simply stated, Indians, along with other dark-skinned peoples, could not rely on the courts for protection because racial beliefs also influenced the thinking of judges and juries. In *Plessey* v. *Ferguson* (1896), the Supreme Court held that segregation by race was constitutional. In *Lone Wolf* v. *Hitchcock* (1903), it ruled that Congress had plenary power over Indians, meaning those who made the laws had virtually limitless power over Indian lives. This decision empowered Congress, in matters involving Indians, with the authority to break treaties, confiscate lands, and enact oppressive laws.

Indians found ways to resist assimilation, however. Although colonialism by design confines, denigrates, and harms its victims, it often lacks the ability to obliterate fully the cultural consciousness and sensibilities of a subjected people. Facing oppression in a rapidly changing world without a viable means of military resistance, many Indians turned to covert means to pass on revered customs, values, and beliefs to succeeding generations. Others adopted the colonizer's religion and economic pursuits, while clinging to elements of their customary cultures. Those who opted to carry on the religious traditions usually did so beyond the vigilance of watchful federal agents, military officers, and reservation police. Through these means, many Indians maintained the spiritual foundations of their beliefs regarding life and death. To them, acts such as unsanctioned grave disruptions were morally reprehensible, harmful, illegal, and profane.

Meanwhile, the federal policies of removal and reservations had transformed grave looting from an activity often conducted under the cloaks of darkness and secrecy to a more open procedure. For example, shortly after U.S. agents moved the Pawnees from their Nebraska homelands to Indian Territory in the 1870s, thieves descended on the unprotected graves, taking human remains and funerary objects for recreation and profit. It should not come as a surprise that Indians expressed sadness, grief, and sorrow upon discovering that the grave of a loved one had been desecrated. When, in 1896, Harry Coons revisited the Pawnee site in Nebraska where he had lived as a boy, he was heartsick to learn that some unknown individuals had pillaged the contents of his two sisters' graves. With few members of dominant society caring about the feelings of Indians in these matters, plundering the contents of Indian graves had gained the status of a time-honored tradition.

Even as Indians suffered the indignities of poverty and subjugation, new breeds of grave looters, called archaeologists and museum curators, entered the picture, often in competition among themselves and the pothunters, individuals who pillaged Indian burial sites as a profitable hobby. By then, archaeology, a subdivision of anthropology, had established a foothold in many of the most prestigious universities in the United States. It developed both as a profession and academic discipline within the sociopolitical contexts of scientific racism, privilege, power, subordination, and oppression. Its adherents followed the practices of discovery and conquest characterized within the general pattern of Indian-white relations. Advocating the popular misconception of the vanishing Indian to justify their conduct, archaeologists embarked on a campaign to record the histories and preserve the cultural heritage of indigenous populations. Assuming *de facto* ownership over Indian graves, archaeology designated the contents simply as specimens and objects of research. In this environment, terms such as *archaeological sites* and *archaeological resources* became popular fictions, masks to sanctify scientific grave looting. According to this way of thinking, Indians had once lived, created cultures, and died for the benefit of science. Once unearthed, their remains were to be used for teaching collections, research, and display.

As the twentieth century progressed, universities provided teaching and research positions for scholars who specialized in excavating Indian burials. Academic programs not only offered courses for the general student body, but also undergraduate and graduate degrees in archaeology and physical anthropology, which in turn increased the pool of individuals who dug up Indian bodies for the sake of scientific curiosity. Essentially ignoring the fact that archaeology and physical anthropology involved research with human remains that had been taken without the consent and knowledge of the next of kin, instructors communicated the values, morals, and assumptions of an imperial archaeology to scores of impressionable young students, both majors and others. Through the combined effects of educational processes, press coverage of archaeological operations, and public fascination with Indian bodies and belongings, archaeology gained widespread popularity, except in Indian communities.

Directly linked to the imperialistic heritage of Jefferson, Morton, Otis, and others, archaeology and anthropology usually regarded Indians in terms of cultural and racial determinism. Over the years, an outpouring of scholarly work, including theses and dissertations, presented Indians as inferior to Caucasians.

Some archaeologists drew from the cultural deficiency model when discussing the development of Indian and other non-European cultures, while others still relied on craniometrics. Indeed, the latter method continued well into the twentieth century to serve as a scientific technique for ranking races by intelligence levels. As this dubious method of inquiry gradually lost its credibility, the idea that racial intelligence could be ascertained by measuring skulls fell out of vogue. Craniometrics, however, did not disappear completely. Its practitioners of today assert that they can assign racial and cultural affiliation by averaging measurements from sample populations. Meanwhile, many researchers embraced the concept of cultural relativism. Now less concerned with proving racial superiority, their methods concentrated more on discovering information about population characteristics, causes of death, and mortuary traditions. Scholars also applied the concepts of evolution to the study of Indian cultures and early histories. Thus, Indian remains, whether lying in storage boxes or in the ground, remained central to archaeology and related fields. Moreover, non-Indian intellectuals controlled academic discussions about Indian histories, cultures, and identities.

The museum industry shared many of the same assumptions, practices, and policies that characterized imperial archaeology. During the late nineteenth century, the museum became a place in which objects of different cultures were stored, displayed, and studied. Wholeheartedly embracing the prevailing wisdom that scientific privilege outweighed Indian rights, curators from many different museums adopted aggressive collection policies that targeted Indian remains, funerary objects, and cultural items for acquisition. Moving beyond simple collecting, museum personnel also provided interested individuals with archaeology and physical anthropology training.

Museums during this era often competed with one another. By 1900, the Smithsonian Institution had become a leading collector of cultural and physical remains associated with Indian life and death. In 1898 and 1904, its curators accepted most of the AMM's holdings of Native remains. Chicago's Field Museum of Natural History, New York's American Museum of Natural History, Harvard University's Peabody Museum of Archaeology and Ethnology, and the Nebraska State History Society, to name a few, had also adopted policies that called for the stockpiling of Indian cultural items for study and public display. A quest for prestige, distinction, and notoriety encouraged new museums to adopt the aggressive collection practices of their East Coast counterparts. For instance, founded in 1901, the Lowie Museum of the University of California, Berkeley (now called the Phoebe A. Hearst Museum of Anthropology) compiled a collection of Indian grave and cultural objects in an effort to become the first important museum and anthropology department west of the Mississippi River.

The behavior of Franz Boas, considered the father of cultural anthropology, and his network of colleagues offers compelling examples of the duplicity, corruption, and racism involved in the business of collecting Indian remains for museums. Although future generations of anthropologists have lauded Boas for steering anthropology from biological determinism to cultural relativism, he acted ruthlessly on different occasions during his interaction with indigenous peoples. While avowing friendship with and gathering oral traditions from the Kwakiutls of British Columbia, Canada, in 1886, Boas raided their graves at night. Describing his motives, he wrote: "It is most unpleasant work to steal bones from a grave, but what is the use, someone has to do it. I have carefully locked the skeleton into my trunk until I can pack it away. I hope to get a great deal of anthropological material here. Yesterday I wrote to the Museum in Washington asking whether they would consider buying skulls this winter for $600; if they *will*, I shall collect assiduously. Without having such a connection I would not do it." Collecting more than 100 complete skeletons and 200 skulls belonging to the Coastal Salish and Kwakiutl peoples, he sold all of them to the Chicago's Field Museum. He later sold another group of human remains in Berlin, Germany. Grave looting was indeed profitable. During the late nineteenth century, some United States museums paid traffickers $5 per skull and $20 for a complete skeleton.

Boas did not stop there. In 1897, holding the position of the curator of anthropology at American Museum of Natural History, he helped bring six Greenland Inuits, including Qisuk and his five year old son Minik, to the New York museum for scholarly study and public exhibition. After Qisuk and four others died of tuberculois, Boas and his co-conspirators staged a funeral to keep Minik from discovering that doctors had dissected his father's body and prepared it for public display. Ales Hrdlicka, a physical anthropologist who had participated in the burial ruse, subsequently published an illustrated study of Qisuk's brain. A student of Boas, Alfred Kroeber, advanced his career by observing the boy's mourning and writing a paper on it.

When Minik reached the age of fifteen, he learned from a newspaper article about the cruel hoax and that his father's remains sat on public display. Museum administrations rejected the irate boy's demands that his father's body be given to him for a proper burial. In 1915, when a newspaper reporter asked Boas, now an imenent Columbia University professor, why the body was not turned over to relatives, Boas replied callously: "Oh, that was perfectly legitimate. There was no one to bury the body, and the museum had as good a right to it as any other institution authorized to claim bodies." Continuing, he declared that "Mink was just little boy, and he did not ask for the body. If he had, he might have got it."

Then there is the tragic story of Ishi, a Yahi-Yana, and Alfred Kroeber, who had gone on to become the curator of the Lowie Museum. In 1911, Ishi, falsely labeled the last of his people, was found in a state of hunger and despondency in a northern California corral. Placed under the care of Kroeber, Ishi lived at the Lowie until tuberculosis took his life in 1916. Acting against Ishi's wishes and spiritual beliefs, university staff promptly autopsied his body, removing and preserving the brain. The following year, Kroeber donated Ishi's brain to the Smithsonian. Hrdlicka, now a curator at that internationally renowned facility, accepted the gift, which was eventually stored in a Maryland warehouse and all but forgotten.

Dr. Ales Hrdlicka, curator of physical anthropology at the Smithsonian Institution, 1932.
© Bettmann/CORBIS

By the time that Kroeber had transfered Ishi's brain to the Smithsonian, national lawmakers had legalized Indian grave looting conducted in the name of science. Responding to growing pressure from archaeologists and museums to eliminate competition from domestic pothunters and foreign archaeologists, who returned to Europe with disinterred Indian remains, funerary objects, and artifacts acquired from public lands, Congress passed the Antiquities Act of 1906. This law required those seeking to dig on federal lands to obtain a permit and agree to place all of the unearthed artifacts, funerary objects, and human remains in domestic museums and repositories for study in perpetuity. Essentially, the law bestowed federal ownership over the contents of vast numbers of Indian graves and defined Indian remains as archaeological resources. State legislatures in subsequent years enacted laws that classified unearthed Indian grave contents uncovered during construction projects and other disruptions as property of the state.

Although the contents of Indian cemeteries located on private land fell under the ownership of the property holder, professional and amateur archaeologists frowned at the scavenging of pothunters on these sites. Reflecting this view in Nebraska, an amateur archaeologist described an incident of grave pillaging with a sense of self-righteousness: "One farmer told about a party of men who had opened some of the [Pawnee] graves, that, on leaving in an automobile, they had exhibited an Indian skull on a stick at the same time yelling at the top of their voices so that they might be noticed at the places they passed." He asserted that it "must have been a party of 'Smart Alecks,' as no archaeologist would have acted in such a rude and undignified manner."

Nebraska also provides a more sweeping illustration of the fascination of people and institutions within the state for Indian remains. Early in the twentieth century, the University of Nebraska State Museum at the University of Nebraska, Lincoln, obtained several hundred human remains ancestral to the Pawnee, Arikara, and Wichita peoples that R. F. Gilder had dug up in the northeastern part of the state. Over the years the museum collected nearly 2,000 Indian bodies from Nebraska, Alaska, New Mexico, and other states. Founded in the 1870s, the Nebraska State Historical Society (NSHS) acquired Indian remains in a similar fashion. In 1941, NSHS officials paid Asa T. Hill, an amateur archaeologist, the nominal fee of $1 for his collection of 200 Pawnee remains and associated burial goods. During the 1920s and 1930s, Hill had plundered them from a farm he had purchased near McCloud for the express purpose of excavating all of the bodies and burial goods located there. Proud of his efforts, and often attracting large crowds as he worked, Hill boasted that for recreation on Sundays he dug up Indian bodies rather than playing golf. For his efforts, Hill received the honor of being hailed as the father of Nebraska archaeology, as well as a position with the NSHS. By the late 1980s, NSHS had amassed hundreds of human remains belonging to the Pawnee, Sioux, Omaha, Cheyenne, and others, while the Nebraska State Museum held remains belonging to some 1,600 individuals.

Professional archaeologists also sought public involvement with and support of their activities by making excavations open affairs. Seeking to inculcate youthful minds with their values, university archaeologists often took young Girl Scouts and Boy Scouts on digs. Universities sponsored field schools where volunteers and students could learn the craft of digging up Indian bodies and artifacts.

As the twentieth century progressed, professional archaeology, anthropology, and museum organizations surfaced, further solidifying the power of imperial archaeology. Founded in 1934, the Society of American Archaeology (SAA) promoted the excavation and study of Indian burial contents. Over the years, its members sponsored conferences that brought together scholars, students, contract archaeologists, and others who shared the values of imperial archaeology.

With the growth of the scientific body-snatching industry, the assault on Indian graves across the nation reached epidemic proportions. Some digs uncovered relatively few, if any, grave objects, but others produced shocking results. From 1915 to 1929 in New Mexico, Alfred Vincent Kidder of Phillips Academy and his associates unearthed 1,781 human remains and 489 funerary objects from Pecos Pueblo and local mission church. Harvard University's Peabody Museum of Archaeology and Ethnology accessioned these objects. During the 1930s,

Hrdlicka excavated an Alaska Native site at Larsen Bay on Kodiak Island. To the shock of the local people, his diggings netted the National Museum of Natural History, a component of the Smithsonian, roughly 1,000 remains, including some recently buried ones, and associated funerary objects.

The Southwest became an attractive location for many archaeologists. Excavations around the ruins at Chaco Canyon in New Mexico and Mesa Verde in Colorado, which placed hundreds of bodies in National Park Service repositories, contributed to this development. Many archaeologists desired probing Southwest grave and town sites because the region had become "a model for much that has happened in American archeology because of the mystique of so many of its ruins, and the living native Americans whose presence spurs us to finding out about their past." Regarding the impact of the college courses in promoting interest in this region, one recent study noted: "As the young participants received degrees and moved into teaching positions across the United States, they tended, in later years, to look toward the Southwest for archaeological training for *their* students, and this generational mushrooming continues today."

Throughout much of the twentieth century, federal funding sponsored many excavations. During the Great Depression, Works Progress Administration (WPA) programs put numerous archaeologists and unemployed individuals to work in projects involving the desecration of Indian burials. In Nebraska, for example, WPA funding enabled the Nebraska State Museum and NSHS to excavate and acquire hundreds of human remains mostly ancestral to the Pawnees and Arikaras. Following World War II, millions of dollars in federal spending supported Bureau of Reclamation and Corps of Engineers archaeological salvage operations within the drainage systems of the Missouri and other rivers in preparation for the creation of a vast reservoir system throughout the country. The ensuing body-snatching crusades removed thousands of remains and funerary objects associated with the Mandan, Arikara, Hidatsa, Sioux, and others from their resting place to distant storage bins, boxes, and drawers. In addition to the Bureau of Reclamation, Corps of Engineers, and National Park Service, the Forest Service and various branches of the armed forces established collections of disinterred Native remains.

With much of American society enamored by the workings of archaeology, sites with exposed Indian burials became popular tourist attractions. Near Salina, Kansas, a farmer charged the paying public admission to view an unearthed cemetery containing 165 human remains ancestral to the Pawnee, Arikara, and Wichita Indians. To protect the bones from deterioration, he periodically applied shellac to them. Similarly in Illinois during the 1930s, Don Dickson excavated an Indian burial on his lands, leaving the skeletal remains in place, and eventually constructed a building over the site. Crowds of people often flocked there to see skeletal remains. Purchasing Dickson Mounds in 1945, the state legislature turned the burial into a popular state museum.

By the late 1980s, institutions across the nation had amassed extensive collections of Indian remains and funerary objects. The Smithsonian Institution boasted a collection of some 18,500 bodies; the University of California system had over 15,000 remains; and Harvard's Peabody Museum held more than 12,000. The University of Nebraska, Lincoln, listed remains belonging to about 2,000 individuals in its accession records. Tens of thousands more were in the possession of federal and state agencies. The list goes on.

Although archaeologists and museum curators claimed their activities were conducted purely for the sake of study and knowledge, Indian remains and funerary objects in these settings became subjected to a wide range of abuses. Some of the collections were studied repeatedly, but many others sat untouched in boxes or storage cabinets. Eyewitness accounts indicate that crania often served as door-stops, balls to be thrown around, and paperweights, while other skeletal materials provided props for comic relief. With the development of new technologies, researchers destroyed bones using such techniques as carbon 14 dating and isotopic analyses. At the University of Nebraska, Lincoln, during the mid-1960s, the Anthropology Department thoughtlessly discarded a trunk load of human remains deemed as lacking scientific value by cremating them in an incinerator used for the disposal of diseased animals. There and elsewhere, many Indian remains and funerary items were lost and stolen. It was an easy matter for students, faculty, and staff to gain access to the storage rooms and make off with prized objects. Some reports indicate that the sale of burial objects on the international market netted the thieves as much as $40,000. Apparently, those institutions impacted by the thefts made few, if any, discernible efforts to track down and recover the objects or to punish the violators.

Indian Challenges to Imperial Archaeology and Religious Oppression

The fact that archaeology and museums had developed without consideration for Native values, beliefs, and feelings did not go unnoticed. Over the years, Indians had objected strongly to the desecration of the graves of their loved ones. During the 1830s, for instance, a field collector described the risks of looting tribal cemeteries to Samuel Morton: "It is rather a perilous business to procure Indians' skulls in this country. The natives are so jealous of you that they watch you very closely while you are wandering near their mausoleums & instant & sanguinary vengeance would fall upon the luckless . . . who would presume to interfere with the sacred relics . . . ." In an 1868 letter to George Otis of the AMM, B. E. Fryer offered a similar observation from Kansas: "A good deal of caution is required in obtaining anything from the graves of Indians, and it *will* have to be managed very carefully to prevent the Indians from finding out that the graves of their people have been disturbed—as this might be offered as an excuse (of course a trifling one) for taking the "War Path" again, which is always walked each year however, as soon as the grass is high enough for the ponies." Other body snatchers expressed a fear of retribution if caught while carrying out their ghoulish

operations, but the potential rewards apparently outweighed the potential consequences. In short, white society simply ignored the Indians' views until the 1970s,
when the legacy of scientific grave robbing, postmortem headhunting, pothunting,
religious oppression, and unethical research gave rise to the formation of a nationwide repatriation movement. This movement surfaced in an environment
wherein reformers challenged this country's practices of racism, sexism, and discrimination. (In this chapter I use the term *repatriation movement* inclusively to
denote the organized actions taken by Indians since the early 1970s to stop the
desecration, gain burial protection under the law, and rebury their stolen dead.)
By this time, Indians had learned to function within the confines of American
society. In many instances, their reservation governments and elements of their
cultures had survived the onslaught. Many of those individuals who had migrated
to urban areas refused to abandon their identities.

Joining the protests, Indians also spoke out against past and present injustices they had suffered. Along with other brown-skinned peoples, they faced unequal treatment by the criminal justice system, job discrimination, and high levels of poverty. Their demands, however, differed in many respects from those of
other Americans. Their issues revolved around matters of sovereignty, cultural
survival, religious freedom, and burial rights. They fought against the use of offensive logos in sports that cast them as cartoon characters and that made a mock-
ery out of their cultures. They acted to stop the involuntary sterilization of their
women, to assert their water rights, and to preserve hunting and fishing rights as
stipulated in treaties.

The Indian movement made headway in terms of organizing and mobiliz-
ing public support. Indian spiritual leaders, traditionalists, students, professionals, and others offered symbolic support or energetically participated in the various causes. They devised collective measures to articulate their concerns and seek
redress for past wrongs. Founded in 1944 in response to the assimilation and
termination policies of the United States, the National Congress of American
Indians (NCAI) tackled issues of treaty and sovereignty rights facing Indian governments. Headed by Clyde Bellecourt, and his brother Vernon, Dennis Banks
(all Chippewas), and Russell Means (a Lakota), the American Indian Movement
(AIM) gained national media attention as its members protested for Indian treaty
rights, sovereignty, religious freedom, and dignity. An outgrowth of the legal services programs designed to provide legal services to poor and disadvantaged
individuals, the Native American Rights Fund (NARF), based in Boulder, Colorado, formed during the early 1970s as a legal service that addressed matters concerning federal Indian law. Walter Echo-Hawk, a Pawnee attorney at NARF, took
up the dual issues of burial rights and repatriation. He quickly became a significant figure in the repatriation movement.

Several incidents that occurred during the 1960s and early 1970s alerted
Indians to the injustice of matters concerning the mistreatment of their dead.
When in 1972 an Iowa road construction crew uncovered a burial site with the

remains of twenty-six white bodies and an Indian mother and child, the state archaeologist, acting in accordance with state law, reburied the white remains and shipped the Indian bodies to a facility for study in perpetuity. News of the discriminatory treatment of the Indian remains spread rapidly, encouraging Maria Pearson, a Yankton Sioux residing in the state, to organize protests calling for equal treatment under the law. Not long thereafter, in Minnesota, AIM members risked arrest by disrupting an archaeological dig.

In this milieu of social discontent mixed with hope for a brighter future, Indians became painfully aware of how the link between law, imperial archaeology, and museums had deprived them of burial rights. As with other components of their struggles, Indian activists drew from spiritual teachings that gave meaning, substance, and vitality to their critique of scientific grave looting. Because of the diversity of Indian cultures, beliefs about the power and spirit of the dead varied. However, most activists, along with their supporters, shared an opinion that collective action must be taken to stop the evil treatment of Indian dead. Armed with this resolve, many of them came to view archaeologists, physical anthropologists, museum curators, and others who engaged in the commercialization of Indian remains as parasites who fed on the dead. Some saw the construction of the Indian identity by anthropologists as a political act impregnated by paternalistic, racist, and self-serving attitudes. In other words, they emphatically rejected the notion that the bodies of their ancestors constituted this country's archaeological resources and the property of others. They wanted burial rights, protections taken for granted by other Americans, and their spirituality respected.

Through advocacy and protests, the activists gained a few major victories during the 1970s and 1980s. In California and other states, legislatures enacted statues that protected unmarked burials. Iowa passed a burial protection and repatriation act in 1976, but few states were willing to take such a drastic action.

Committed to the cause of reburial, American Indians Against Desecration (AIAD) emerged during the 1980s. Headed by Jan Hammil and Robert Cruz, a Tohono O'odham from southern Arizona, AIAD took its issues directly to professional anthropology meetings, museums, and government agencies, both federal and state. Although AIAD shook the foundations of the archaeology/museum colossus, its opponents maintained their hegemony over Indian remains and staunch resistance to change.

Clashes occurred more frequently as more individuals took up the repatriation cause. With Indian enrollments in colleges increasing, campuses witnessed periodic eruptions over the reburial controversy. When encountering archaeologists, Indian students frequently asked questions such as: "Do we have to be dead and dug up from the ground to be worthy of respect and preservation?" During the late 1980s, University of California, Los Angeles (UCLA) students demanded to know why there were more dead Indians on campus than living ones. At that time, UCLA possessed approximately 4,000 Indian remains, while the student body, staff, and faculty comprised fewer than 200 Indians.

Indian intellectuals doubted whether archaeological research had validity and meaning for their people. In the process, they deconstructed fictive notions found in self-serving scholarly pronouncments endowing archaeology with the label of an objective science. Vine Deloria, Jr., a Dakota, already known for his scathing critique of anthropology as a lecherous profession, points out that the scientific community has never provided Indians with literature showing how experimentation with Indian remains is necessary, proper, or beneficial. He also argues that archaeologists have never given the public a satisfactory explanation for why Indian remains are more valuable than those of other peoples. Deloria suggests that if this brand of study is as important as archaeologists claim, then this same type of inquiry should be launched in cities and towns across the nation to uncover information regarding malnutrition, premature deaths, and other human afflictions. Such a course of action would surely have triggered an immediate public outcry against this science.

The controversy over the beatification of Father Junípero Serra exemplifies the antipathy, aversion, and distrust many Indians held for archaeology. When during the 1980s the Catholic Church advanced Father Serra to beatification, a step below sainthood, for his work in establishing the Spanish missions in California, many California nations angrily protested the Church's action. They declared that the mission settlements under Serra's rule were "little better than concentration camps where brutal slave labor, starvation, and disease killed all but a fraction of the native population." Although research on Indian remains could have blocked Serra's advancement toward sainthood, California Mission Indians denied archaeologists permission to study the remains of individuals who died while in Serra's missions.

Facing growing Indian opposition and public scrutiny, the archaeology/museum community splintered into two factions. Viewing the old way of conducting business as a threat to the future of their profession, a growing number of archaeologists became supportive of some Indian demands for equal burial protection, religious freedom, and repatriation. For example, Larry J. Zimmerman, a former University of South Dakota archaeologist, realized in the late 1970s that the Sioux were truly concerned about the remains of their relatives when he heard the pleas of elders and holy people. Referring to the condescending demeanor of many of his colleagues toward Indians and the burial rights issue, Zimmerman wrote: "I was appalled at the attitudes of my profession. I came very close to leaving archaeology. When one of the SAA [Society for American Archaeology] executive committee members flippantly said at a later meeting, "the only good Indian is an unreburied Indian," I knew I had to do what I could to understand not only Indian attitudes towards reburial, but archaeologists' views of their own profession in regard to the people they studied."

Progressive archaeologists such as Zimmerman recognized the need for limitations on research involving human remains. Reflecting the changing mood, a Princeton University professor of anthropology noticed that "Indians continue to be the victims of a practice that is without scientific or moral justification. . . . Many scientists now agreed that there are no overriding reasons to retain collections of recent Indian remains." Scant research was being done on these collections, and little new has been learned from them. Some progressives even accepted the Indian position that future grave excavations and research should be conducted only after consultation with and approval by the appropriate tribal entity.

The motives of the progressive archaeologists were not purely altruistic, however. Fearing that the customary ways of doing business would endanger all forms of archaeological study involving Indian remains, they sought a middle ground. Acting like missionaries trying to convert lost souls, many of them spouted platitudes about value of the scientific methods employed by archaeologists to uncover the mysteries of history. Indians often refused to accept this "good guy" approach, replying that their oral histories provided them whatever information they need to know about the past. To them, burial rights were far more important than what knowledge might be gleaned from offensive and sacrilegious studies.

While the repatriation movement was busy challenging the imperial archaeology, some Indian governments developed cozy relationships with archaeologists. In the Southwest, for example, the Navajo Nation and Pueblo of Zuni allowed the creation of an archaeology program on their reservations. Zuni policy allowed for disinterment only when unavoidable construction or erosion threatened a burial site. A physical anthropologist then could study the remains near the grave for a short period. After the examination had been completed, the bodies and accompanying burial objects had to be reinterred in a safe location as close as possible to the original burial site.

The old-guard faction of the archaeology/museum network often commended the Zunis and Navajos for their cooperation, but its adherents remained ideologically and politically opposed to change. Museum curators and administrators, university personnel, government employees, as well as contract and amateur archaeologists formed the heart and soul of this group. They expressed an unwavering commitment to preserve at all costs the customary principles, practices, and privileges that had guided their profession. Seeking to stake out the high ground with rhetoric that simply ignored the scandalous, inglorious, and sacrilegious aspects of their work, they concocted moral, ethical, historical, and legal positions as counterarguments. They took a position, dubbed the "Frankenstein defense" by their adversaries, that any endeavor conducted in the name of science was fundamentally more important than human rights. Along with this utilitarian posturing, they equated the reburial of human remains with book burning and the destruction of irreplaceable scientific data. Many even claimed that Indians desperately needed archaeology to teach them their histories and cultures. At times, they defended their work by hiding behind the banner of academic freedom. These hardliners, backed solidly by the SAA and various museums, tenaciously clung to these positions even though the American Anthropological Association had adopted a policy of academic ethics in 1971 declaring that an anthropologists' paramount responsibility is to those they study. The code stated: "When there is conflict of interest, these individuals must come first. The anthropologist must do everything in his power to protect their physical, social and psychological welfare and to honor their dignity and privacy."

Determined to undermine the credibility of their opponents, the old guard lashed out bitterly at the turncoats, moderates, and Indian activists. The American Committee for the Preservation of Archaeological Collections (ACPAC) surfaced during the 1980s as a voice of imperial archaeology. By the end of the decade, ACPAC claimed a membership of some 600 professionals and supporters. It branded Native activists as anti-intellectuals who acted in irrational ways without the ability, or education, to understand the great contributions of archaeology to society in terms of recovering and interpreting the past. Attempting to maintain professional solidarity, ACPAC advocated the blackballing of archaeologists who assisted with repatriation initiatives. It also raised funding to assist the legal defense of members charged with violating burial laws. Using scare tactics to solicit contributions, a 1986 ACPAC newsletter declared:

> Archaeologists, your profession is on the line. Now is the time to dig deep and help ACPAC with its expenses for legal fees. Next year or next month will be too late; we have to act immediately to fight this issue. This one will be resolved in court, not by the press. We will be able to cross-examine Indians on their tribal affinities, religion, and connection to the archaeological remains they seek to destroy. We will be able to challenge anti-science laws based on race and religion. We can make a strong case, but it takes money. Send some!

Despite ACPAC's commitment to the cause of maintaining the status quo, its arguments failed to rally significant public support. However, the old guard controlled, or at least heavily influenced, many of the institutions that held the contested human remains. In 1986, Smithsonian officials rejected a plea from the Larsen Bay Aleuts for the return of the remains taken some fifty years earlier by Hrdlicka. Others institutions held the same line, but some began to break ranks.

With public opinion moving to their side, members of the repatriation movement chipped away steadily at the foundation of scientific grave looting. Virtually every step of the way, however, they faced defiance, verbal abuse, and insults from the old guard cadre who held the keys to the repositories. During the 1980s, the Three Affiliated Tribes of North Dakota, the Arikara, Mandan, and Hidatsa, asked the North Dakota History Society (NDHS) for the return of all the human remains ancestral to them held at that facility. Rather than responding respectfully, NDHS administrators and staff went on the offensive. They challenged the integrity, motivations, and spirituality of Pemina Yellow Bird, an Arikara/Hidatsa, and others who dared to confront them. The activists' resolve outlasted the NDHS's defiance. In a monumental agreement reached in 1986, NDHS officials agreed to repatriate approximately 1,000 remains and funerary objects to the Indigenous nations of the region. At the same time, NDHS also vowed to discontinue its practice of storing human remains and associated grave goods.

As this North Dakota struggle ensued, Robert Cruz, Louisa Javier, and other Tohono O'odhams gained the return of some human remains ancestral to their people from the Museum of Arizona. Elsewhere, other concessions would follow.

In the late 1980s, Nebraska became the scene of another bitterly contested repatriation struggle that pitted the small, impoverished Pawnee Nation of Oklahoma against the powerful Nebraska State Historical Society. When NSHS refused in 1988 to repatriate the Pawnee remains that Hill and others had excavated, the Native American Rights Fund took up the Pawnee cause. Rather than filing suit, NARF engaged NSHS in the political arena. As in other cases, the NSHS position against repatriation lacked a message that most Nebraskans could accept. The following year, with public opinion and the state media siding squarely with the Indians, the Nebraska legislature enacted the Unmarked Human Burial Sites and Skeletal Protection Act (LB340).

The statute provided for the return of Indian remains to the next of kin following a period of study and extended the state's burial protection statute to include Indian graves. Although James Hanson, NSHS's recalcitrant director, employed a series of futile maneuvers to undermine the statue, including a lawsuit, state officials intervened on behalf of the Pawnees, ordering the NSHS to repatriate the remains and burial goods in question for reburial. Through this initiative, the Pawnees conducted their first reburial, solemnly returning some 400 of their relatives to Mother Earth.

Sites featuring Indian burials became targeted for closure. During the late 1980s, protests by students and faculty at Haskell Indian Junior College (now Haskell Indian Nations University) at Lawrence, Kansas, and others publicized the existence of the Salina Burial Pit. With NARF representing the Pawnee, Arikara, and Wichita Nations, the state legislature purchased the offensive tourist attraction and closed it down, allowing the exposed remains to be removed from public gaze and blanketed again with Mother Earth. At Dickson Mounds, Mike Haney, a Seminole/Lakota, Vernon Bellecourt, and other repatriation advocates spearheaded a more acrimonious demonstration over the reburial of the remains exposed there. The State of Illinois finally closed the funeral exhibit in the 1990s over the heartfelt objections of local citizens who claimed the human remains at the site as part of their history.

Several incidents in the late 1980s accelerated the push for protection. In a widely circulated essay that stressed the merits of scientific study with Native remains, Bruce D. Smith, an anthropologist employed by the Smithsonian's National Museum of Natural History, devised the acronym URPies (Universal Repatriation Proponents) to belittle, denigrate, and ridicule the reburial activists.

Because the polemic appeared on Smithsonian letterhead, sharp criticism came from all directions, bringing embarrassment to this world-renowned museum. The backlash from Smith's blunder moved Smithsonian officials a step closer to embracing a position of compromise. By then, Stanford and a few other universities had agreed to repatriate some of the remains in their collections.

Then came the explosive Slack farm incident in Kentucky. In 1989, protests by members of AIM and others encouraged the national media to publicize the flagrant operations of some particularly ruthless grave looters. Using a backhoe to unearth funerary objects on the farm, the thieves had literally ransacked scores of graves. Photos of the grisly scene captured revolting images that resembled a battlefield. They showed a section of farm pitted with deep craters and bones scattered in all directions.

In that same year, a strong contingent of repatriation activists—including Pemina Yellow Bird, Robert Cruz, Jan Hammil, and Roger Bird among others—converged on the annual gathering of the World Archaeology Conference (WAC) in Vermillion, South Dakota. Before going to the conference, Cruz had asked the leaders of his O'odham people what message he should take with him to the meeting. Standing before the assembled conference, he skillfully related the O'odhams' concerns, stating: "You tell them [the archaeologists] that we do not treat our bones with disrespect. Those bones are our ancestors . . . and they are sacred. By disturbing the ancestor's graves and spirits, they have caused many problems and hard times for our people and this makes us very sad. You tell them that the bones of our ancestors must be returned. They are sacred and we do not treat our ancestors with disrespect." Before the meeting concluded, WAC adopted a code of ethics reflective of Indians concerns.

In the wake of the controversies, federal lawmakers took up the issues of Indian burial rights and the disposition of sacred cultural objects. Nevertheless, from 1986 to 1989, Congress rejected several bills along this line. In 1989, the Smithsonian Institution, SAA, and the American Association of Museums energetically opposed a piece of proposed legislation that would have established a national committee to mediate disputes between Indian nations and museums.

Change was imminent, however. At an August 1989 Santa Fe, New Mexico, meeting with Indian representatives, Smithsonian officials capitulated. Still reeling from the backlash brought by the URPies essay and seeking Indian support for the establishment of a national museum of American Indians in Washington, D.C., they agreed to return all "reasonable identifiable" physical remains and burial objects to Indian descendants upon request. Later that year, Congress incorporated the agreement into the National Museum of the American Indian Act (NMAIA). This bipartisan statute required only the Smithsonian to repatriate human remains and funerary objects linked to modern Indians by a preponderance of evidence. In the Senate debate over NMAIA, John McCain, Republican from Arizona, sent a powerful message to the anti-repatriation forces. He declared that the bill "is an important first step . . . [that] sends a clear message to those in the museum community who have dismissed repatriation as a transitory issue that they would be wise to consider the bills [pertaining to museums and federal agencies other than the Smithsonian] currently before the Congress."

In early 1990, a panel composed of Indian representatives, museum personnel, and archaeologists convened in Phoenix, Arizona, at the Heard Museum. Their dialogue focused on matters involving the proper treatment of human remains and cultural artifacts in museums. The resulting document, *Report of the Panel for a National Dialogue on Native/American Indian Relations*, demonstrated the need for a national repatriation law that would balance the interests of Indians and science. Seeking to preserve their profession, elements of the old guard, including SAA representatives, reluctantly accepted a compromise position. Many repatriation activists, however, opposed the notion that they should make concessions in matters concerning the fate of their deceased relatives. To them, changes in law must fully address their position that all Native remains in the nation's institutions and agencies should be reburied.

The following year Congress passed the Native American Graves Protection and Repatriation Act (NAGPRA). Following its passage, Senator Daniel Inouye, Democrat from Hawaii, noted the significance of the new law, declaring, "In light of the important role that death and burial rites play in native American cultures, it is all the more offensive that the civil rights of America's first citizens have been so flagrantly violated for the past century. Even today, when supposedly great strides have been made to recognize the rights to recover the skeletal remains of their ancestors and to repossess items of sacred value or cultural patrimony, the wishes of native Americans are often ignored by the scientific community." This monumental piece of complex legislation provided a legal avenue for Indian nations and Native Hawaiian organizations to recover not only human remains, but also funerary objects, objects of cultural patrimony, and sacred objects linked to them by a preponderance of evidence. Having national effect, the law applied to all museums, universities, and federal agencies that received federal funding, excluding the Smithsonian. Those institutions had a period of five years in which to inventory their collections in consultation with Indian nations and send notifications to the appropriate Indian nations. Those remains determined as culturally unidentifiable, supposedly not connected to present-day Indians and numbering in the tens of thousands, were to stay in the institutions until a NAGPRA committee, to be composed of members of Indian nations and pro-science proponents, could determine their fate. NAGPRA also criminalized disturbances of Native graves on federal and tribal lands and trafficking in Indian remains.

The message carried by the repatriation activists had resonated with the American public and politicians. The matter of burial rights had become an issue that transcended cultural lines. Once learning of the disparities in the law and the legacy of scientific grave looting, many non-Indians saw these activities as repugnant to humanity. In Nebraska during the 1990s, David McCleery reflected this change in consciousness. Penning an apology to members of the Pawnee Tribe, he wrote, "I'm sorry my great-grandfather A. T. Hill was such a bonehead and fouled so much sacred ground. From the stories I've heard he seemed like a decent enough guy—he just couldn't keep out of your graveyard." In various instances, individuals who held skeletal remains by inheritance or by their own looting activities turned them over to museums for repatriation.

Unfortunately, not everyone shared McCleery's concern. Pothunters had no intention of staying out of Indian burial sites. With laws curbing the operations of archaeology, some researchers turned their attention to countries in South America where they could practice their trade without interference. In Texas, the state legislature, perhaps because of lobbying efforts by the powerful oil and gas industry, has refused to enact an unmarked burial protections bill. Thus, looters continue to profit from the contents of Indian graves.

Reburials under NMAIA and NAGPRA

With the new laws in place, American Indian nations began the demanding process of claiming human remains ancestral to them for proper reburial. A problem, however, still confronting them was the presence of the old guard in the museums and universities. For instance, in 1989, when the Pawnee Nation inquired about six crania at the Smithsonian identified as Pawnee, an offical reply declared that there was no credible evidence showing that those remains were Pawnees. In response, the Pawnee Council turned once again to NARF. With NARF sponsoring an investigation, a Pawnee researcher found substantial evidence in the Smithsonian and other archives showing that the remains in question were indeed those of the former Pawnee Scouts who had been gunned down and decapitated at Mulberry Creek in 1869. After the Smithsonian's repatriation office substantiated the NARF/Pawnee report findings, Smithsonian officials agreed to return the remains. Finally, on a breezy spring day in Nebraska in 1995, the Pawnees buried the Scouts in a Genoa cemetery with military honors, not far from the site where the men lived at the time of their violent deaths. At the same time, they, along with their Arikara relatives, put to rest the remains of other people obtained from the Smithsonian. Following the burial ceremony, sympathetic townspeople provided lunch to the delegation in attendance, which included a large number of Pawnees and Arikaras.

Other repatriations occurred at the Smithsonian. In 1991, it finally returned the bodies stolen at Larsen Bay by Hrdlicka to the next of kin. During the ensuing years, the Modoc's claimed the skulls of Captain Jack and the other men who were hanged in 1873. Cheyennes buried the remains of their ancestors killed at Sand Creek and Fort Robinson. Blackfeet, Arapahos, Lakotas, and many other peoples reburied their ancestors. In 1999, Smithsonian officials, facing criticism for stonewalling, returned Ishi's brain to his descendants. Under NMAIA, Native Hawaiian organizations also put to rest human remains belonging to them.

Because of its far-reaching effects, NAGPRA produced more startling results than any other piece of repatriation legislation. Through the inventory letters sent by museums, Indian nations learned of the whereabouts of their ancestors and cultural items. In 1995 and 1996, for example, the Pawnee Nation received several hundred NAGPRA-summary letters from museums: including Harvard's Peabody Museum of Archaeology and Anthropology, Yale's Peabody Museum of Natural History, the Colorado Historical Society, Chicago's Field Museum of Natural History, the University of Nebraska–Lincoln, the Kansas State Historical Society, the University of Iowa, the University of Wyoming, the University of Pennsylvania, the University of Tennessee, and the Carnegie Museum of Natural History in Pittsburgh. These letters indicated that more than 4,000 Pawnee ancestors were still awaiting repatriation.

This step of notification set into motion a process by which Indian peoples across the nation began the spiritual duty of reburying their ancestors. In New Mexico, Jemez Pueblo took from Harvard's Peabody Museum the remains that Kidder had excavated at Pecos. In Nebraska, the Poncas reburied remains held by the University State Museum. In Arizona, the Tohono O'odhams have placed into the ground many of their ancestors held by the University of Arizona. Although many Indian nations have engaged in the repatriation process, others, often for cultural reasons, have not. With NAGPRA restoring ownership rights of the human remains held in museums to the next of kin, their choice is a function of sovereignty.

Despite the laws, the struggle is not over. In 1995, a major controversy erupted over 9,000-year-old bones known as Kennewick Man found along the banks of the Columbia River in Washington state under Army Corps of Engineers land. When a forensic anthropologist, James Chatters, declared that the remains had Caucasoid features, elements of the press and scientific community became extremely interested in the matter. With speculation and imaginations running rampant, some asserted that the find indicated that Europeans had arrived in the Americas before the Indians had. When the Umatillas, Yakama, Nez Perce, Colville, and Wanapan (a federal unrecognized people) and other Indians of the area claimed the remains under NAGPRA, the Corps of Engineers agreed to repatriate Kennewick Man to them. Oral traditions indicate that the Umatillas had originated in the area and that their people once looked different than they do today. Nine archaeologists and anthropologists, joined by a group claiming ancestry to the Vikings, subsequently obtained an injunction, stopping the reburial. A judgment also subjected Kennewick Man to further scientific scrutiny.

The matter ultimately reached Secretary of the Interior Bruce Babbitt. After reviewing the evidence, Babbitt issued a letter on September 21, 2000, stating that the traditions of the Indian claimants met the preponderance of evidence standard set by NAGPRA for determining cultural affiliation. He went on to say that NAGPRA was an Indian law and that any ambiguities in the law must be interpreted in favor of Indian interests. Before the Indians could rebury the "old one," as they called him, a group of nine scientists filed another lawsuit, with the intent to keep the remains for scientific study and to preserve the right of North

American archaeology. At the time of this writing (June 2001), this matter has not been resolved.

As the Kennewick Man flap unfolded, another bitter conflict erupted in Nebraska. This time the University of Nebraska–Lincoln, became the focal point of controversy. With allegations circulating that one of its anthropologists had engaged in professional misconduct, including illegal research on Pawnee, Arikara, Wichita, and Ponca remains, word also spread that during the mid-1960s UNL personnel had incinerated some human remains. Seeking to remedy a public relations nightmare stemming from the charges, UNL convened a meeting on September 1, 1998, with representatives of Indian nations including the Northern Ponca, Southern Ponca, Arikara, Pawnee, Omaha, Northern Cheyenne, Standing Rock Sioux, Cheyenne River Sioux, and others with a historical connection to the area. During the meeting, UNL chancellor James Moeser read a prepared speech admitting that the university had made some serious mistakes in its handling of Indian remains and stating that UNL would work to improve its relations with Indian peoples. When the delegates made a shared group identity claim to the remains in question, he accepted it. Essentially, this meant that UNL would change the designation of the remains listed as culturally unidentifiable to culturally affiliated and repatriate them as soon as possible to the seventeen signatory Indian governments. Moeser also accepted the Indian position that the university had an obligation to pay for the cost of the reburial and to establish a monument near the spot where the incineration had occurred. When the chancellor concurred with the remedies, many of those in attendance cheered, while others sang a Lakota spiritual song. As a gesture of gratitude, the Indian delegation presented Moeser with a blanket and other gifts. But the atmosphere of good feelings emanating from the meeting soured during the ensuing months because of foot dragging by UNL and the National Park Service in terms of processing the repatriation accord and the discovery of Indian remains in unauthorized locations. UNL's reluctance to take disciplinary action against the professor charged with various violations compounded matters.

Many of those human remains located in domestic and foreign collections fall outside of the purvey of NAGPRA. The law does not apply to privately held collections. In the late 1990s, however, the Dakotas managed to recover some of the bones of three of their relatives who were lynched at Mankato in 1862, but the whereabouts of the others remain unknown. Although Native remains have been scattered throughout the world, the laws do not reach beyond the boundaries of the United States. However, the Pawnees recovered parts of White Fox's body, who had died while traveling in Sweden during the 1870s. Rather than receiving a proper burial, his skin was removed, placed on a mannequin, and put on public display. Other Indian nations have also enjoyed some success in retrieving bodies from Europe. Finally, under existing laws, U.S. institutions do not have to return the skeletal remains of Indians from other countries or to treat them respectfully. In fact, during the 1990s, the

Smithsonian's Museum of Natural History had several remains of South American Indians on public display.

Conclusion

Our country's long and inglorious history of violating Indian graves touched off a wave of activism during the 1960s that continues to this day. With the power of racist ideology interwoven with privilege, institutional and professional networks, and the law, the repatriation movement faced an uphill battle. Having been designated as the Other, Indians had experienced a series of abuses stemming from the growth and expansion of the United States, including dispossession, depopulation, religious persecution, assaults on their cultures, economic deprivation, and political marginalization. Many non-Indians simply saw nothing wrong with appropriating the contents of Indian graves and the heads of Indians killed in battle. Imperial archaeology, along with museums, eventually convinced the American public and lawmakers that it had sole authority to take Indian bodies and funerary objects. The federal and state legislation resulting from the repatriation movement extended the burial laws to include Indians.

Despite the repatriation movement's accomplishments, it has failed to resolve some of the problems generated by the archaeological mindset and the quest for profits. The fate of tens of thousands of Indian ancestors labelled as culturally unidentifiable, such as Kennewick Man, remains in question. As long as laws mark out a boundary in which imperial archaeolgy can operate and claim ownership over deceased Indians, conflict will continue. Moreover, the lure of quick profits will encourage pothunters to keep preying on Indian graves. Although Indians have made significant progress in obtaining burial rights, their struggle is not over.

Suggested Reading

Repatriation is a matter that has gained a significant amount of scholarly attention since the early 1990s. This growing body of literature not only discusses matters pertaining to controversy surrounding the mistreatment of ancestral Indian remains, but to cultural objects as well. At least three important journals have been devoted to this hotly debated topic. Articles found in the *Arizona State Law Journal* (Spring, 1992), the *American Indian Culture and Research Journal* (16, No. 2, 1992), and the *American Indian Quarterly* (Spring, 1996) provide readers with a wealth of information about the legal, social, political, cultural, ethical, and historical dimensions of the repatriation conflict. These works offer a detailed discussion of the background, provisions, and results of the Native American Graves Protection and Repatriation Act of 1990. Indian contributors to these volumes include Vine Deloria, Jr., Devon Mihesuah, Edmond J. Ladd, Roger C. Echo-Hawk, Walter R. Echo-Hawk, and James Riding In, while non-Indian writers include Clement W. Meighan, Keith Kintigh, and Robert E. Bieder.

A few books have contributed to our understanding of the conflicts arising from the mistreatment of Indian remains. In *Battlefields and Burial Grounds* (Minneapolis, 1994), brothers Roger C. and Walter R. Echo-Hawk describe the Pawnees' struggle to rebury ancestral human remains and burial items held by museums and the Nebraska State Historical Society. Robert E. Bieder's *Science Encounters the Indian, 1820–1880* (Norman, Okla., 1986) probes the racial and scientific attitudes of early American ethnologists toward Indians. One chapter explores how Samuel G. Morton used flawed methods and reasoning to calculate racial intelligence. The story of Minik can be found in Kenn Harper's *Give Me My Father's Body: The Life of Minik, the New York Eskimo* (South Royalton, Vt., 2000). In *Skull Wars* (New York, 2000), David Hurst Thomas explores the troubled relationship between Indians and archaeologists. Edited by Duane Champagne, *Native America: Portrait of the Peoples* (Detroit, London, and Washington, D. C., 1994) contains a discussion of repatriation. *Repatriation Reader* (Lincoln, Nebr., and London, 2000), edited by Devon Mihesuah, presents the views of Indians and non-Indians on the study of Indian remains and the repatriation of cultural objects.

Various documentaries have examined the hotly debated topic of repatriation. Most notably, *Who Owns the Past?* produced in 2000 by director Jed Riffe, presents a balanced discussion of the perspectives of Indians and non-Indians regarding repatriation. This video is an invaluable educational tool for introducing students to the historical and contemporary complexities of the repatriation conflict. At the time of this printing, it was scheduled to be aired on PBS in the fall of 2001.

Index ❧

Northwest Indian Women's
Circle, 288
Notes on the State of Virginia,
296
Nott, Josiah C., 298

Oakes, Richard, 210, 212
Ohlone Indians, 249, 263
Okinajin, Marpiya (He Who
Stands in the Clouds), 299
Old Looking Glass, 256
Omaha Indians, 149, 151, 281
Omnibus Indian Advancement
Act, 218
Oñate, Juan de, 52, 53, 272
Oneida Indians, 36, 220
*Oneida Nation v. Oneida and
Madison Counties,* 220
Onondaga Indians, 15, 36
Opler, Morris, 185
Opothleyahola, 86–90, 92
Osage Indians, 58–63, 201
Osceola, 80
Otis, George, 302, 304, 310
Otoe-Missouri Treaty, 256
Ouray Indians, 200
Owhi, 256, 257

Paiute Indians, 200
Palma, Salvador, 248, 249
Palmer, Joel, 256
Palouse Indians, 257, 258
Pancoast, Henry S., 150
Parker, Quanah, 134, 136, 142
Parrilla, Diego Ortiz, 59, 60
Passamaquoddy Indians, 220
Patuxet Indians, 21
Pawnee Indians, 58, 61, 110,
152, 294, 319–321
Peach, Arthur, 24
Penn, William, 39
Penobscot Indians, 10, 20, 220
Pequot Indians, 23
Perez, Juan, 246,
Peyote Road, 188
Philip (Metacomet), 24
Picotte, Susan La Flesche, 281
Piegan Indians, 271
Pierce, Franklin, 256
Pike, Albert, 85, 86, 88
Plessy v. Ferguson, 303
Pokanoket Indians, 4, 27
Pomeroy, Samuel, 90

Pontiac, 45
Popé, 140
Pope, John, 96
Portola, Gaspar de, 246
Powell, John Wesley, 152
Powell, Lewis F. Jr., 220
Prairie Traveler, The, 116
Pratt, Richard H., 130, 146, 149,
152, 153, 158–160
Prence, Thomas, 24
Price, Henry, 156
Price, Hiram, 123
Pring, Martin, 20
*Problem of Indian Administra-
tion, The,* (Meriam Report),
173, 175, 179, 180, 232
Pueblo Indians, 50, 52, 53, 56,
63, 64, 176, 177, 179, 183,
212, 215, 271
Pueblo Land Act (1924), 177
Puyallup Indians, 287

Qualchin, 256
Quantrill, William Clarke, 89
Quapaw Indians, 58
Quechan Indians, 248, 249, 250,
253, 254
Quinton, Amelia, 148

Ramsey, Alexander, 95, 96
Rawdon, Marmaduke, 20
Reagan, Ronald, 217
Rector, Henry M., 85
Red Cloud, 130, 134, 137
Red Moon, 138
*Report of the Panel for a Nation-
al Dialogue on Native / Amer-
ican Indian Relations,* 318
Resettlement Administration, 185
Resurrectionists, 294
Rhoads, Charles, 179, 180
Richelieu, Cardinal, 12
Ridge, John, 79, 82, 87
Ridge, Major, 79, 82, 87
Rivera y Moncada, Fernando,
250
Roberval, sieur de (Jean-
François de la Rocque), 9
Rogers, Will, 184
Roosevelt, Franklin D., 180
Roosevelt, Theodore, 215
Ross, John, 79, 85, 87, 88, 90–92
Ryan, W. Carson, 179

Sacajewea, 251
Salisbury, Neal, 21, 22
Salmon People, 262
Samoset, 22
San Manuel Band of Mission
Indians, 265
Sand Creek Massacre, 101, 102,
108, 137, 300
Sand Creek Reservation, 98,
101, 102
Santee Sioux Removal Bill, 97
Sassamon, John, 27, 28
Satanta, 113
Saubel, Katherine, 254
Scheirbeck, Helen Maynor, 289
Seattle, 291
Sekaquaptewa, Emory, 171
Seminole Indians, 68, 73, 74,
80–82, 119, 222, 277
Seneca Indians, 10, 15, 36, 39,
212, 276, 287
Serra, Junípero, 246, 247, 313
Serrano Indians, 253
Seward, William H., 86
Shaw, Anna Moore, 281, 282
Shaw, Ross, 281, 282
Shawnee Indians, 64, 81
Sheridan, Philip, 116, 120
Sherman, William Tecumseh,
11, 258
Shoonaq Tribe of Kodiak, 218
Shoshone Indians, 110, 125
Sibley, Henry Hastings, 96
Silko, Leslie Marmon, 195, 289
Sioux Indians, 93–98,106, 108–
112, 118, 119, 125, 131, 137,
138, 141, 142, 212, 319, 321
Sitting Bull, 138, 141
Smathers, George, 200
Smiley, Albert A., 260
Smiley Commission, 260
Smith, Alva Adams, 198
Smith, Bruce D., 316
Smith, Caleb, 90, 97
Smith, John, 20–22
Smohalla, 140
Soboba Band of Mission
Indians, 265
Society of American Archaeol-
ogy, 308
Soil Conservation Service, 185
Spalding, Eliza, 251
Spalding, Henry, 251

*"They Made Us Many Promises":
The American Indian Experience, 1524 to the Present*
Developmental editor and copy editor: Andrew J. Davidson
Production editor: Lucy Herz
Photo editor and proofreader: Claudia Siler
Cartographer: Jane Domier
Printer: McNaughton & Gunn, Inc.